Alfresco 3 Cookbook

Over 70 recipes for implementing the most important functionalities of Alfresco

Snig Bhaumik

[PACKT] open source*
PUBLISHING   community experience distilled

BIRMINGHAM - MUMBAI

Alfresco 3 Cookbook

First published: July 2011

Production Reference: 1180711

Published by Packt Publishing Ltd.
32 Lincoln Road
Olton
Birmingham, B27 6PA, UK.

ISBN 978-1-849511-08-7

www.packtpub.com

Cover Image by Duraid Fatouhi (duraidfatouhi@yahoo.com)

Credits

Author

Snig Bhaumik

Reviewers

Piergiorgio Lucidi

Adit Patel

Khazret Sapenov

Snehal Shah

Acquisition Editor

Steven Wilding

Development Editor

Alina Lewis

Technical Editor

Gauri Iyer

Copy Editor

Leonard D'Silva

Project Coordinator

Shubhanjan Chatterjee

Proofreader

Mario Cecere

Indexer

Tejal Daruwale

Graphics

Nilesh.R.Mohite

Production Coordinators

Adline Swetha Jesuthas

Arvindkumar Gupta

Cover Work

Adline Swetha Jesuthas

Arvindkumar Gupta

About the Author

Snig Bhaumik is the Technical Director at InfoAxon Technologies Ltd, based in India. He is also the Director of Open Source Innovation and heads the Knowledge Management Practice at InfoAxon – India's first and pioneer Open Source Integration Company.

A computer engineer by education and developer at heart, Snigdhendu has in total ten years of experience in various technologies such as Alfresco, Liferay, Pentaho, and Microsoft .NET. An open source enthusiast and regular community participant, Snigdhendu was the original contributor of Alfresco Calendar component. He specializes in Knowledge Management and Business Intelligence domains, and is responsible for designing and architecting KM and BI solution offerings.

My sweet wife Chaitali was so patient with my late nights, and I want to thank her for her faithful support while writing this book.

I would also like to thank my mother for everything. She has always been the guiding force for me.

Writing of this book could not have been possible but for the ungrudging support from my colleagues at InfoAxon.

Finally, I sincerely thank Packt Publishing for giving me the opportunity to write this book.

About the Reviewers

Piergiorgio Lucidi is an Open Source Product Specialist and a certified Alfresco Trainer at Sourcesense. Sourcesense is a European Open Source systems integrator providing consultancy, support, and services around key open source technologies.

He works as a software engineer and has seven years of experience in the areas of Enterprise Content Management (ECM), system integrations, and web and mobile applications.

He is an expert in integrating ECM solutions in web and portal applications. He regularly contributes to the Alfresco Community Forum supporting newbie and expert users.

He is a project leader and committer of the JBoss Community; he contributes to some of the projects of the JBoss portal platform. He is a speaker at conferences dedicated to Java, Spring Framework, open source products, and technologies.

He is an author and an affiliate partner at Packt Publishing, he has written the technical book Alfresco 3 Web Services in collaboration with Ugo Cei. He also writes and publishes book reviews on his website Open4Dev (http://www.open4dev.com/).

> I would like to thank Packt Publishing for this great opportunity to work again in a very interesting project about Alfresco.

Adit Patel has done his Master's in Computer Applications. He started his career with CIGNEX Technologies in the year 2004. He has successfully handled complex projects for enterprise customers for implementing enterprise content management systems. He has helped many enterprise customers migrate from proprietary content management systems to more efficient and scalable content management systems – like Alfresco. He holds in-depth knowledge and experience of Alfresco architecture and implementations.

> I would like to thank and dedicate my contribution to this book to my guru H.D.H. Pramukh Swami Maharaj.

Khazret Sapenov, a 20-year veteran of ICT, is the founder and chief technology officer of Cloudcor, which serves hundreds of enterprise clients and works closely with a set of managed partners and independent software vendors. In this role, Sapenov is responsible for leading overall strategy and technology direction across the United States and Canada, including employees in IT, partner, marketing, operations, and vertical industry teams.

Sapenov previously served as the corporate director of research and development at Enomaly, where he was responsible for growing the company's virtualization solutions business, including development and service delivery.

Prior to working with Enomaly, Sapenov held positions in technology solutions development in various Fortune 100 companies where he was responsible for global network, data centers, and information security, help desk, core IT services, and enterprise line-of-business applications.

Cloudcor's organizations under Sapenov's leadership have developed into one market and gained wide recognition as thought leader in cloud computing.

Sapenov founded Cloudcor in 2008. Before that, he was in corporate and academic research roles, covering oil and gas resources prospecting and development. Sapenov is a graduate of the University of Karaganda, where he received his Master's degree in Applied Mathematics.

I'd like to thank my parents for giving me life and supporting all my initiatives, my wife Saule and sons Asan and Aidos for being tactful and quiet when working on this book.

Snehal Shah has served as the manager and architect of the engineering teams for seven years in the area of internet applications, system software, and legal applications for customers in the United States, UK, and India.

He is an expert in Content Management Systems (CMS). At CIGNEX, he has successfully delivered various CMS applications using various open source technologies. Snehal earned his Bachelor's degree in Computer Engineering from DDIT, India.

www.PacktPub.com

Support files, eBooks, discount offers and more

You might want to visit www.PacktPub.com for support files and downloads related to your book.

Did you know that Packt offers eBook versions of every book published, with PDF and ePub files available? You can upgrade to the eBook version at www.PacktPub.com and as a print book customer, you are entitled to a discount on the eBook copy. Get in touch with us at service@packtpub.com for more details.

At www.PacktPub.com, you can also read a collection of free technical articles, sign up for a range of free newsletters and receive exclusive discounts and offers on Packt books and eBooks.

PACKTLIB©

http://PacktLib.PacktPub.com

Do you need instant solutions to your IT questions? PacktLib is Packt's online digital book library. Here, you can access, read and search across Packt's entire library of books.

Why Subscribe?

- ▶ Fully searchable across every book published by Packt
- ▶ Copy and paste, print and bookmark content
- ▶ On demand and accessible via web browser

Free Access for Packt account holders

If you have an account with Packt at www.PacktPub.com, you can use this to access PacktLib today and view nine entirely free books. Simply use your login credentials for immediate access.

Table of Contents

Preface

Alfresco is the renowned and multiple award-winning open source Enterprise content management system which allows you to build, design, and implement your very own ECM solutions.

You have read a number of tutorials, blogs, and books on Alfresco. Now you're in the real world, trying to use Alfresco, but you're running into problems with it. This is the book you want, packed full of solutions that can be instantly applied to this cookbook with its practical-based recipes and minimal explanation meets that demand.

This Alfresco 3 Cookbook boasts a comprehensive selection of recipes covering everything from the basics to the advanced. The book has recipes for quickly installing Alfresco in Windows and Linux and helping you use custom content model, rules, and search. There is also a collection of recipes focused on creating Scripts, Freemarker templates, Web Scripts, and new workflow definitions. Steps to integrate Alfresco with other systems like MS-Office are also included. You will be able to use Alfresco's File and e-mail servers. Finally, step-by-step recipes are presented to create an Alfresco build environment and compile the source code. This Alfresco 3 Cookbook is perfect for developers looking to start working on Alfresco quickly, gain complete understanding, write custom implementations, and achieve expertise very easily.

What this book covers

Chapter 1, Getting Started: It introduces Alfresco with brief demonstration of the Alfresco Explorer application. Get Alfresco downloaded and installed on your machine, and finally be acquainted with the default distribution and architecture of Alfresco.

Chapter 2, Creating and Organizing Contents: It explains how to use Alfresco as Content Management System, how to upload or create contents, how to apply tagging or categorization of content, understand content metadata, use the document versioning capability of Alfresco.

Chapter 3, Securing and Searching Contents: It is about another important aspect of the Content Management System – Security. It helps you understand how to secure your contents and folders. How to create users and user groups – and assign permissions for who can do what. You will also know about the search capabilities offered by Alfresco, how to search contents and how search works in Alfresco.

Chapter 4, Rules – the Smart Spaces: It will help you learn how to make your Alfresco repository dynamic, how to implement your business requirements that works automatically in the repository. You will understand how to create and apply rules in the repository; you will also be familiar with different actions that can be performed via a rule.

Chapter 5, Administering Alfresco: It contains recipes for administering Alfresco, demonstrating how to manage users, user groups, create taxonomies, manage content categories. You will also be aware of how to use the Alfresco Node Browser to view and search contents stored in the repository. You will also know how to manage your Alfresco explorer dashboard.

Chapter 6, Customizing Alfresco Web Client: Alfresco offers customization of the Web Client application via a number of XML configuration files. This chapter elaborates various recipes for changing the view and appearance of the web client, customizing the application as per your requirements, and so on.

Chapter 7, Alfresco Content Model: Designing and modeling the content properties and architecture is one of the most important requirements in a content management system. Alfresco offers dynamic capabilities for designing the content models. Using these recipes you will be able to understand the core architecture of Alfresco content models, create your own custom content models, use your custom models in the Alfresco explorer application.

Chapter 8, Alfresco JavaScript API: Alfresco offers the repository functionalities in form of JavaScript APIs. In this chapter, you will understand the API structure and features offered. Several example recipes help you implement various functionalities. You will also learn how to write, execute, and debug scripts written using the APIs.

Chapter 9, Freemarker Templates: Freemarker Template is the presentation layer technology used in Alfresco applications. The recipes of this chapter would help you understand the technologies and model behind the Freemarker templates in Alfresco. Several template examples are included for commonly-used functions such as displaying folder contents, showing workflow tasks, showing contents recursively, displaying content properties and details, and so on.

Chapter 10, Web Scripts : Alfresco Web Scripts provide RESTful APIs of the repository services and functions. The chapter elaborates all related concepts, knowledge and how-to do it recipes that would help you write, deploy and debug web scripts. You will also understand the usage of default web scripts library that come with Alfresco. Several sample web scripts are included, for example sending e-mails using templates, searching and displaying documents, and so on.

Chapter 11, Working with Workflows: Workflow implementation is one of the major requirements in a content management system in a business. This chapter would help you understand the Alfresco business process engine in detail. You will understand how the workflows are implemented in Alfresco repository along with various components of the workflow engine. Several detailed examples and recipes are included to guide you create custom workflows, custom task models, specific resource bundles, customizing the web client to render the custom tasks and workflows properly. You will also be able to use the Alfresco workflow console interface which is useful for debugging the task execution within the BPM engine.

Chapter 12, Integrating with MS Outlook and MS Office : Alfresco can be used from several other applications and interfaces. Being a content management system, it is quite important to have the Alfresco repository accessibility from some popular content authoring applications such as Microsoft Office. This chapter helps you integrate the Alfresco repository with MS Word, Excel, and PowerPoint. Recipes are also included for communicating with repository directly from any standard e-mail client application such as MS Outlook.

Chapter 13, Configuring Alfresco E-mail and File Servers: The Alfresco repository can act has file servers as well and you can expose the repository using several other standard protocols such as FTP, CIFS, WebDAV, and so on. These recipes are a step-by-step guide to configure these protocols and using the content repository from different systems. From this chapter, you will also be able to use Alfresco as e-mail server, and e-mails sent to some specific address will land directly into the repository.

Chapter 14, Building Alfresco: Until now you have used Alfresco as the binary bundle provided and downloaded. Now you can compile and build Alfresco source code also. Recipes in this chapter will guide you to get the source from Alfresco source code repository, compile and build the source code. You can modify Alfresco source code as your will; of course as per Alfresco license, you should contribute your changes back to Alfresco community.

What you need for this book

The software list for this book is as follows:

- Tomcat server
- MySQL server, MySQL Workbench, MYSQL GUI Tools, SQLYog
- JDK
- WinZIP or WinRAR
- OpenOffice
- MS Office, MS Outlook
- ImageMagick
- PDF2SWF

- ▶ Subversion Client – TortoiseSVN
- ▶ Apache Ant
- ▶ Alfresco software

Who this book is for

If you are a software developer interested in content management systems, who wants to work with Alfresco or is already experienced in Alfresco, this cookbook will get you up and running quickly. If you want rapid implementation of Alfresco's most important and effective features then this is the cookbook for you.

Conventions

In this book, you will find a number of styles of text that distinguish between different kinds of information. Here are some examples of these styles, and an explanation of their meaning.

Code words in text are shown as follows: "We choose our InfoAxon folder for this operation."

A block of code is set as follows:

```
<imports>
        <!-- Import Alfresco Dictionary Definitions -->
        <import uri="http://www.alfresco.org/model/dictionary/1.0"
prefix="d"/>
        <!-- Import Alfresco Content Domain Model Definitions -->
        <import uri="http://www.alfresco.org/model/content/1.0"
prefix="cm"/>
    </imports>
```

When we wish to draw your attention to a particular part of a code block, the relevant lines or items are set in bold:

```
<content-types>
    <type name="iabook:Product"/>
</content-types>
```

New terms and **important words** are shown in bold. Words that you see on the screen, in menus or dialog boxes for example, appear in the text like this: "Go to **Company Home** and try to add a new Content.".

> Warnings or important notes appear in a box like this.

Tips and tricks appear like this.

Reader feedback

Feedback from our readers is always welcome. Let us know what you think about this book—what you liked or may have disliked. Reader feedback is important for us to develop titles that you really get the most out of.

To send us general feedback, simply send an e-mail to feedback@packtpub.com, and mention the book title via the subject of your message.

If there is a book that you need and would like to see us publish, please send us a note in the **SUGGEST A TITLE** form on www.packtpub.com or e-mail suggest@packtpub.com.

If there is a topic that you have expertise in and you are interested in either writing or contributing to a book, see our author guide on www.packtpub.com/authors.

Customer support

Now that you are the proud owner of a Packt book, we have a number of things to help you to get the most from your purchase.

Downloading the example code

You can download the example code files for all Packt books you have purchased from your account at http://www.PacktPub.com. If you purchased this book elsewhere, you can visit http://www.PacktPub.com/support and register to have the files e-mailed directly to you.

Errata

Although we have taken every care to ensure the accuracy of our content, mistakes do happen. If you find a mistake in one of our books—maybe a mistake in the text or the code—we would be grateful if you would report this to us. By doing so, you can save other readers from frustration and help us improve subsequent versions of this book. If you find any errata, please report them by visiting http://www.packtpub.com/support, selecting your book, clicking on the **errata submission form** link, and entering the details of your errata. Once your errata are verified, your submission will be accepted and the errata will be uploaded on our website, or added to any list of existing errata, under the Errata section of that title. Any existing errata can be viewed by selecting your title from http://www.packtpub.com/support.

Piracy

Piracy of copyright material on the Internet is an ongoing problem across all media. At Packt, we take the protection of our copyright and licenses very seriously. If you come across any illegal copies of our works, in any form, on the Internet, please provide us with the location address or website name immediately so that we can pursue a remedy.

Please contact us at `copyright@packtpub.com` with a link to the suspected pirated material.

We appreciate your help in protecting our authors, and our ability to bring you valuable content.

Questions

You can contact us at `questions@packtpub.com` if you are having a problem with any aspect of the book, and we will do our best to address it.

1

Getting Started

In this chapter, we will cover the following:

- ▶ Setting up a database for Alfresco
- ▶ Installing Alfresco on Windows
- ▶ Installing Alfresco on Linux
- ▶ Running Alfresco for the first time
- ▶ Using Alfresco explorer
- ▶ Knowing about Alfresco stores
- ▶ Understanding default space hierarchy

Introduction

This chapter will demonstrate how to install Alfresco, introduce Alfresco Explorer – the web client interface for managing the repository, and the applications that are bundled with Alfresco standard distribution.

Towards the end, you will understand how Alfresco stores and organizes the uploaded contents. We will also be acquainted with the default spaces that come with the Alfresco repository.

Today, Alfresco is the leading Open Source alternative to Enterprise Content Management – alternative to **Microsoft SharePoint®**, **Documentum®**, **Open Text®**, and so on. Alfresco is developed using best-of-breed Open Source technologies such as **Spring**, **Hibernate**, **Lucene**, modern standards such as **JSR-168**, **JSR-170**, **Level 2 Web Services**, **Java Server Faces,** and so on. Alfresco manages almost all types of content within an enterprise – documents, records, web pages, images, XML documents, or any other files.

Some of the most important capabilities and features of Alfresco are:

- ▸ Document management
- ▸ Web content management
- ▸ Record management
- ▸ Image management
- ▸ Workflow
- ▸ Search
- ▸ Multilingual support
- ▸ Multiplatform support
- ▸ Clustered and Federated servers
- ▸ Cloud-eady
- ▸ Web 2.0 collaboration
- ▸ Browser-based UI and desktop integration
- ▸ JSR, SOAP, REST interfaces
- ▸ **Content Management Interoperability Services** (**CMIS**)
- ▸ CIFS, SMB, WebDAV, FTP, and IMAP access channels
- ▸ MS Office® Integration using MS SharePoint Protocol®

Alfresco products

Alfresco offers several integrated products and services in the ECM suite.

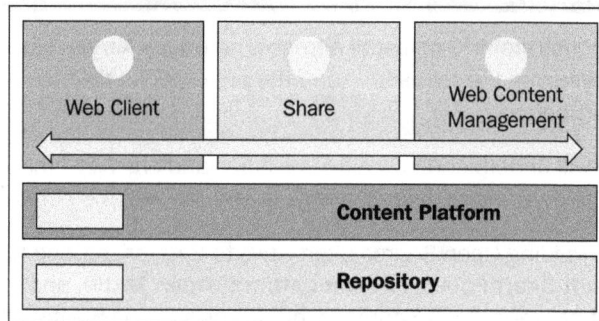

The core component in the architecture of Alfresco is the **Repository**. The Alfresco repository is a collection of services and components. These interact with the Alfresco storage that consists of the contents and indexes stored in binary format, the RDBMS to store the transaction data, tasks and business process information, audit statistics, user and group records, and so on.

On top of the **Repository**, the **Content Platform** serves as the podium of all content management operations. Alfresco Content Platform is one of the most **scalable Java Content Repository (JCR)**. The Content Repository API for Java (JCR) is a specification for Java application APIs to access the repositories in a standard and unified manner. The REST-based lightweight mash up architecture enables Rapid Application Development and other applications to integrate with the content repository easily.

> **REST**, stands for **Representational State Transfer**, it is a software architecture which client programs and server services can interact with on any standard protocol such as HTTP.
>
> A RESTful web service or RESTful web API is a collection of resources with three well-defined aspects.
>
> A base URL of the service.
>
> The Internet media type of the data supported and returned by the service, such as JSON, XML, HTML, and so on.
>
> The set of operations supported by the service using HTTP methods such as GET, POST, PUT, DELETE, and so on.

We will explore how Alfresco APIs can be exposed as RESTful services in later chapters.

Using the flexible Content Platform, several products and services have been exposed such as the **Web Client (Alfresco Explorer)**, **Collaboration (Share)**, **and Web Content Management system**.

Alfresco Explorer

Earlier called Alfresco Web Client, this application is developed using **Java Server Faces (JSF)**. Using Alfresco Explorer, you can explore the full repository of the current installation of Alfresco and perform most of the activities. In future, this application can be phased out in favor of Alfresco Share. However, Explorer has very wide capabilities for managing the repository and can be considered as a system administrator tool.

> Java Server Faces (JSF) is an MVC structured web application framework based on Java. It is created to simplify the development of web-based user interfaces.
>
> For more information on JSF, please see `http://www.oracle.com/technetwork/java/javaee/javaserverfaces-139869.html`.

If you are using Alfresco with Tomcat, you can invoke the web client in your web browser by the URL `http://localhost:8080/alfresco`, or if you are using Alfresco with JBoss, use the URL `http://localhost:8080/portal`.

We are here assuming that the Alfresco server is running in your local machine and the web server is running on port 8080 – this is the default port where the Tomcat or JBoss servers run, unless you manually change the ports.

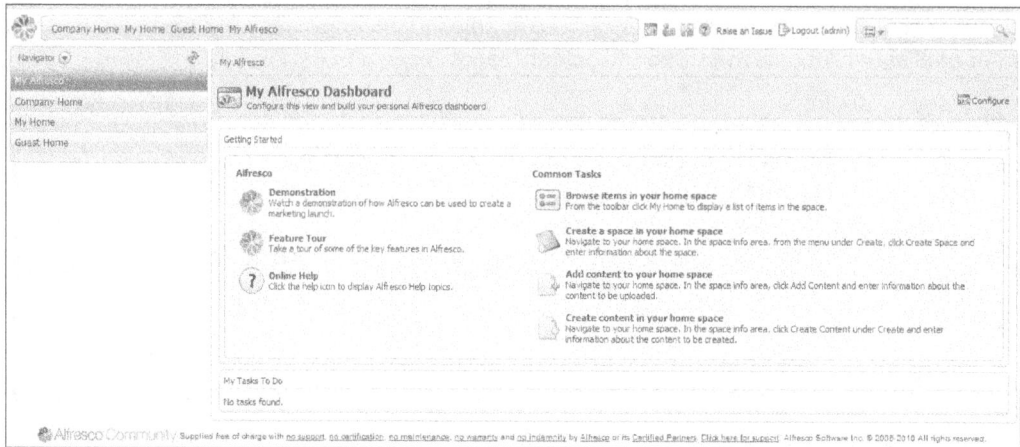

A few operations for which you can use the Alfresco Explorer are:

▸ Browsing the repository

▸ Managing (uploading, creating, updating, deleting) the contents (see *Chapter 2*)

▸ Managing (creating, updating, deleting) the users and groups (see *Chapter 3*)

▸ Managing the users' permissions (see *Chapter 3*)

▸ Setting up rules (see *Chapter 4*)

▸ Running several actions (see *Chapter 4*)

▸ Starting or executing a workflow (see *Chapter 11*)

▸ Performing on a task assigned to you (see *Chapter 11*)

▸ Managing the content categorization (see *Chapter 2*)

▸ Export/Import contents

▸ Managing various scripts and templates in the system

We will be discussing how to install and run Alfresco in the next few sections of this chapter.

Alfresco Share

Share is the Web 2.0 collaboration-based platform providing content management capabilities with simple user interfaces. It provides users with tools for searching and browsing the content, displays thumbnails, and onscreen flash previews of standard documents, enables collaboration between a community of users by various Web 2.0 collaboration tools such as Wikis, Blogs, and Discussion Forums.

Share provides highly-collaborative content management-controlled around sites and activities. End users can easily create collaborative sites for projects, departments, locations, or organization branches. They can invite users to collaborate and participate on contents, approve and publish contents using rich content modeling and lifecycle management of the underlying repository.

The Share application is accessible at `http://localhost:8080/share`.

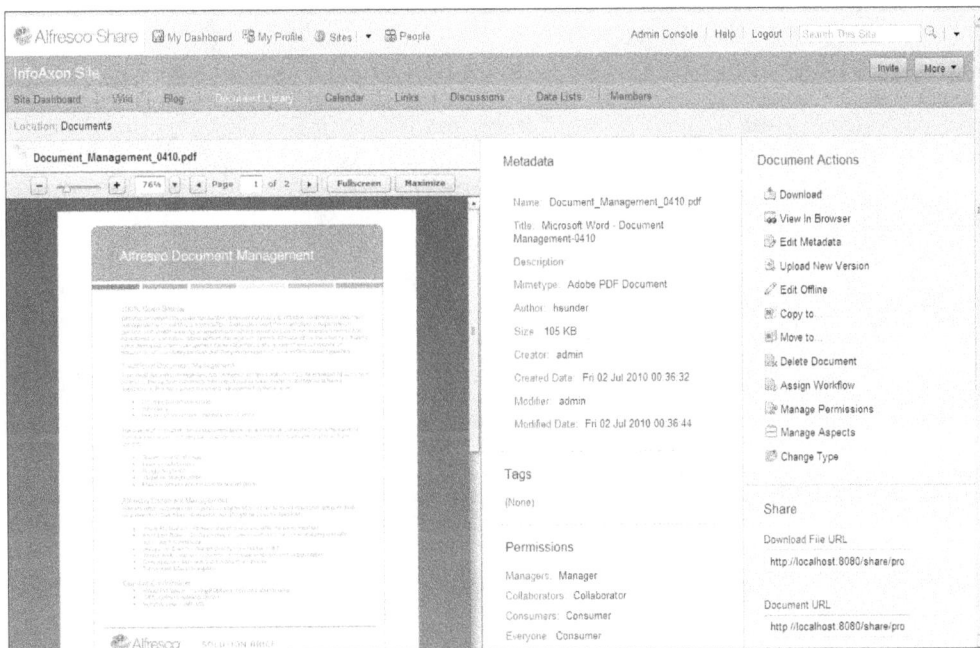

All users have their private dashboard available in the Share platform. A dashboard is a collection of dashlets – a dashlet is a miniature view of an application or of functionality or some information. For example, the Tasks dashlet shows all the pending tasks of the current users with information and controls to manage each of the tasks.

- ▸ User calendar
- ▸ User's tasks
- ▸ User's workspaces, sites, and site activities
- ▸ User's documents
- ▸ RSS feed

Share enables a collaborative environment in an organization where the participation and involvement of the users happens around sites. A site can be viewed as a community or group of users, a department, a branch, or a location of an organization. The most common usage of site can be project, for example, when you start a new project, you start a site, invite the members into the site, collaborate amongst yourselves, and produce knowledge and content.

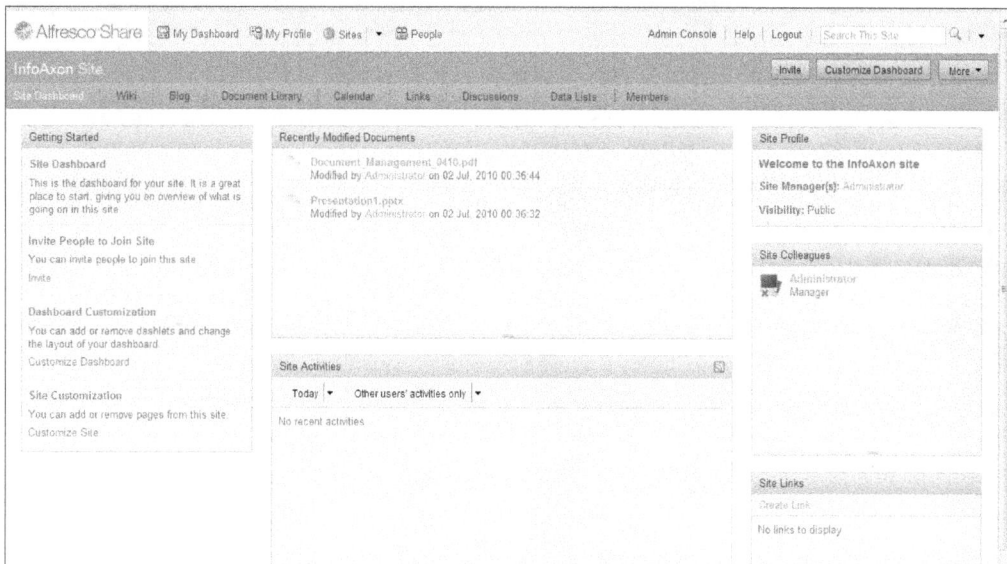

Share normally offers four types of sites - **Collaboration Site**, **Meeting Workspace**, **Document Workspace**, and **Record Management Site**. While Collaborative Site is the default type of site created in Share, Document Workspace is usually created via MS Office®.

Similar to user dashboard, each site also has a dashboard with dashlets such as:

- ▸ Site calendar
- ▸ Site profile and colleagues

- Recently modified documents
- Image preview
- Site wiki
- Site links
- RSS feed

Collaboration Site is preconfigured with a set of default pages. Each page offers different collaboration tools around the site.

- Document library
- Wiki
- Blog
- Calendar
- Links
- Discussion forums
- Members
- Data lists

Setting up a database for Alfresco

Alfresco uses **Hibernate** as the **Object Relational Mapping** (**ORM**) layer. Thus, it is capable of plugging into any of the popular relational databases such as MySQL, PostgreSQL, Oracle, MS SQL Server, and so on.

In this book, we will be demonstrating examples using the MySQL database.

Getting ready

In order to set up your MySQL database for Alfresco, you would need a MySQL database server and an optional MySQL client. A MySQL client could be handy if you are working on Windows.

1. To install the MySQL Server, download the MySQL Server Community Version from `http://dev.mysql.com/downloads/mysql/`.

> The listed setups are available in the form of Microsoft Installers (`.MSI` files). If you do not require Documentations and Development Components (in our case, for running Alfresco in a Developer Machine, we do not need these), you can download the installers without the essentials. Choose the installer that suits you and download.
>
> If you are running a 64-bit Operating System environment, you can download the 64-bit version of the server from `http://dev.mysql.com/downloads/mirror.php?id=390238#mirrors`. Otherwise, go for a 32-bit installation from `http://dev.mysql.com/downloads/mirror.php?id=390237#mirrors`

2. Choose one mirror, download, and save the installer in a suitable location on your computer.

3. Run the installer and choose **Typical** in installation types.

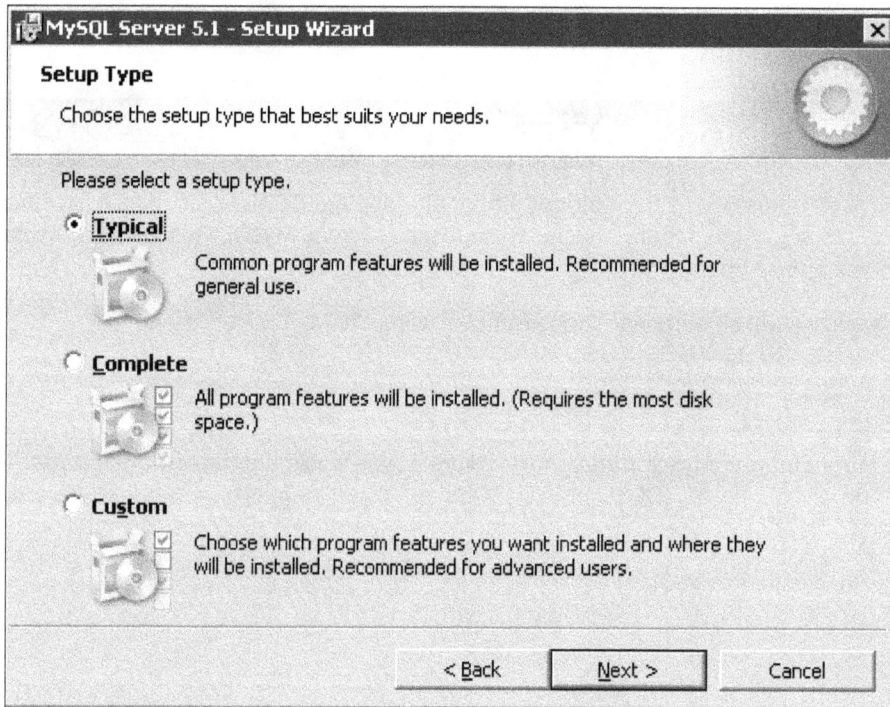

4. After completion of the installation, start configuring the server and choose **Detailed Configuration**.

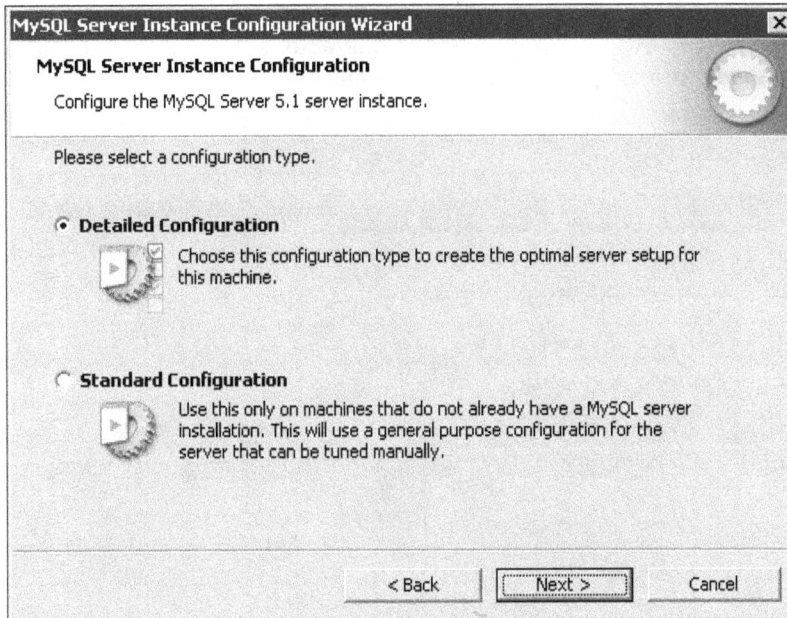

5. Select **Developer Machine** and choose **Multifunctional database**.

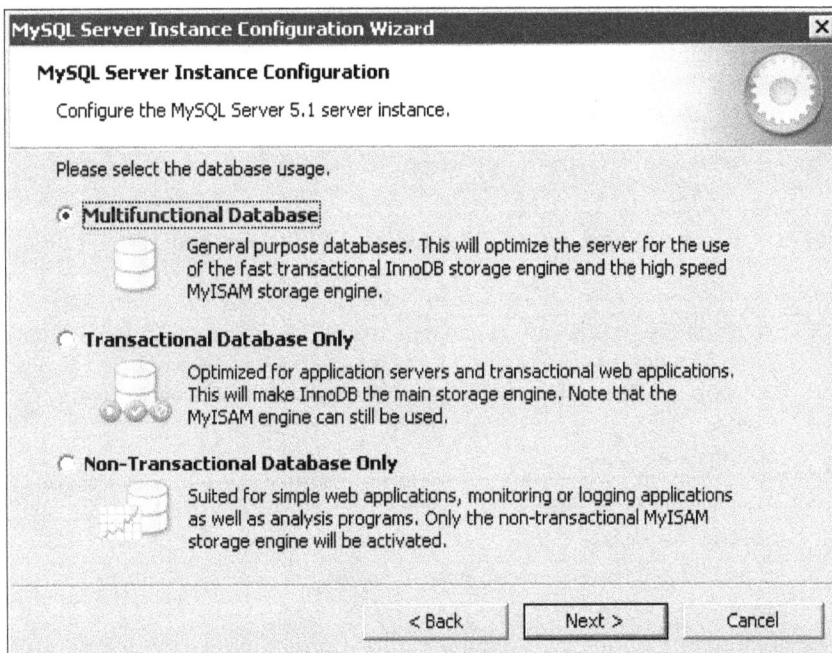

6. For the next steps in **INNODB tablespace settings**, **Concurrent connections settings**, **TCP/IP port settings**, **default character set**, **windows service configuration**, accept the default options and settings provided.

7. Give the **root** password as you like, however, it is advisable not to use a blank password.

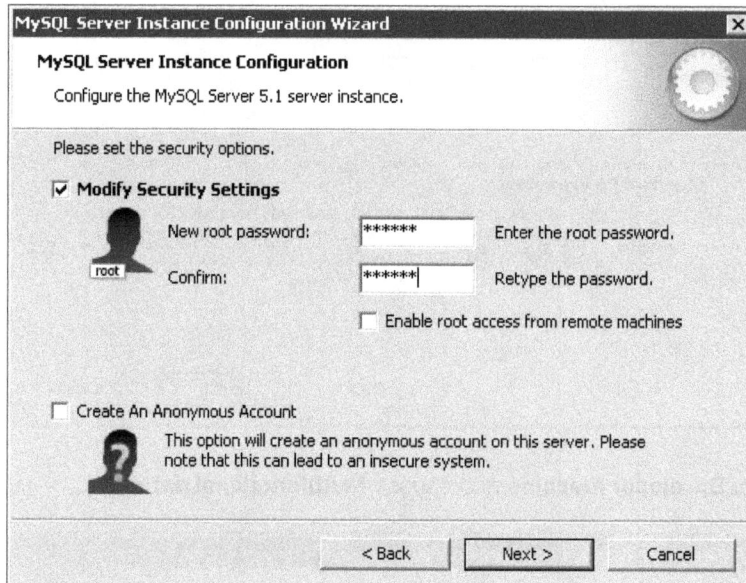

8. Click **Next>**, your MySQL server will be configured.

9. Clicking **Finish** will close the setup wizard and MySQL server is installed.

10. Install MySQL Clients. You can use any of the clients available for MySQL. However, in our example, we will be using the MySQL Workbench.

Note that the MySQL Workbench requires .NET Framework 3.5 to be installed in the machine, in case it is not, there is your machine; you can use MySQL GUI tools or SQLYog. The following are some of the clients available for MySQL:

MySQL Workbench

```
http://dev.mysql.com/downloads/workbench/
```
GUI tools for MySQL 5.0

```
http://dev.mysql.com/downloads/gui-tools/5.0.html
```
SQLYog

```
http://www.webyog.com/en/downloads.php
```

MySQL client applications are not mandatory for Alfresco server setup. However, it is sometimes handy to get a client application of the database server in order to view, create, and configure the database and the database users. In case you do not have any client application installed, you can still use the MySQL server command prompt from your localhost.

How to do it...

After you have installed the server and the client application, let's create a database for Alfresco. By default, Alfresco stack uses the name 'Alfresco' for MySQL database as well as for the username and password. Though you can change these settings, we will go with these default settings for now.

1. Open **MySQL Workbench** and connect to the MySQL Server; we are assuming here that the MySQL server is running on your local machine.

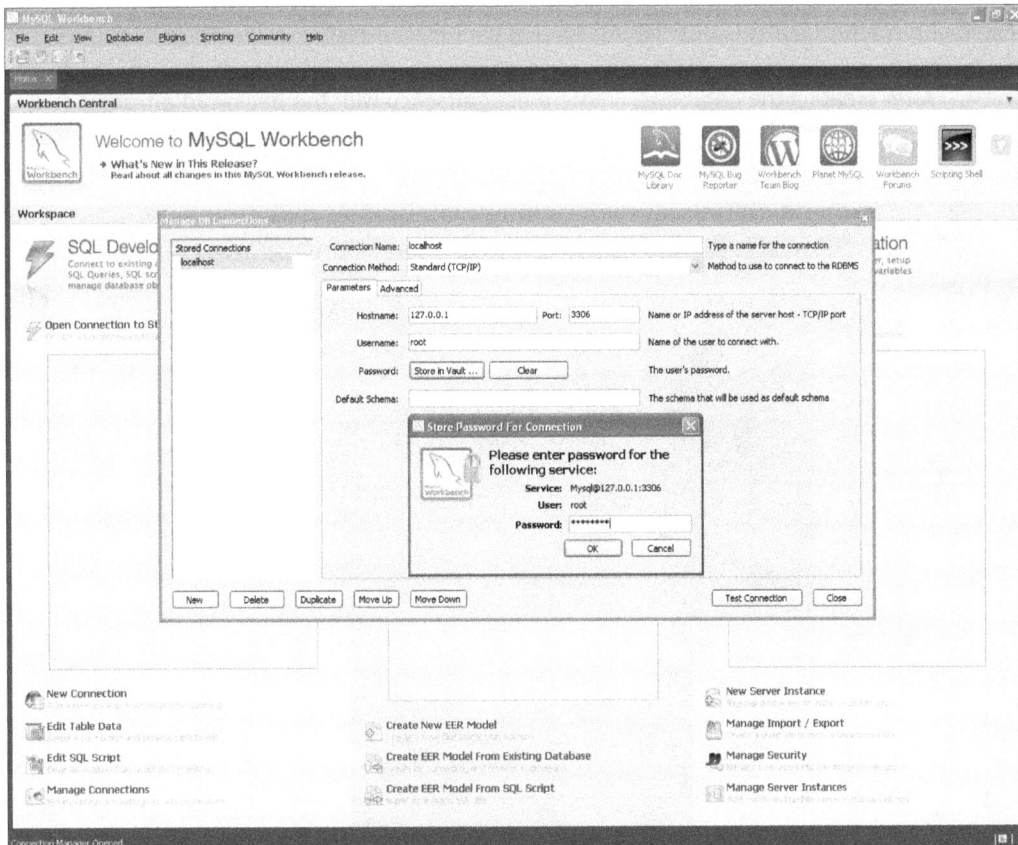

2. We now need to create a database for Alfresco. After establishing the connection, open the connection to invoke the workbench SQL editor.

3. Create a new schema named **alfresco** in the localhost server with UTF-8 encoding and UTF-8-default collation

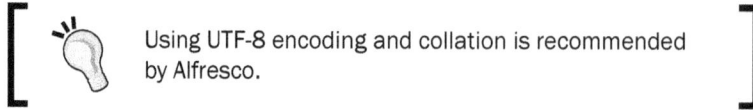

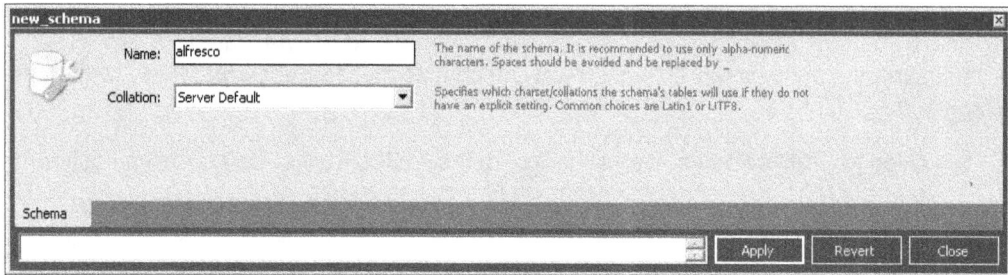

> Using UTF-8 encoding and collation is recommended by Alfresco.

4. After creating the database, create a user **alfresco** with the password **alfresco**. For that, you need to create a **Server Instance** for our localhost MySQL server.

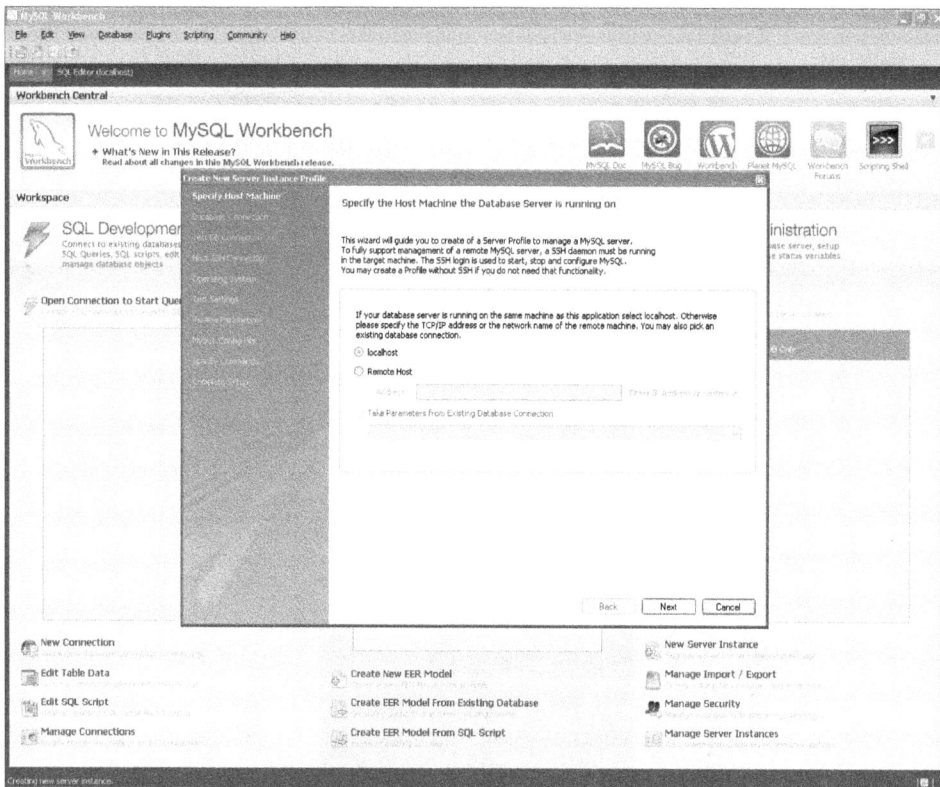

5. In the **server administration** panel, create a new user named **alfresco** and with the password **alfresco**.

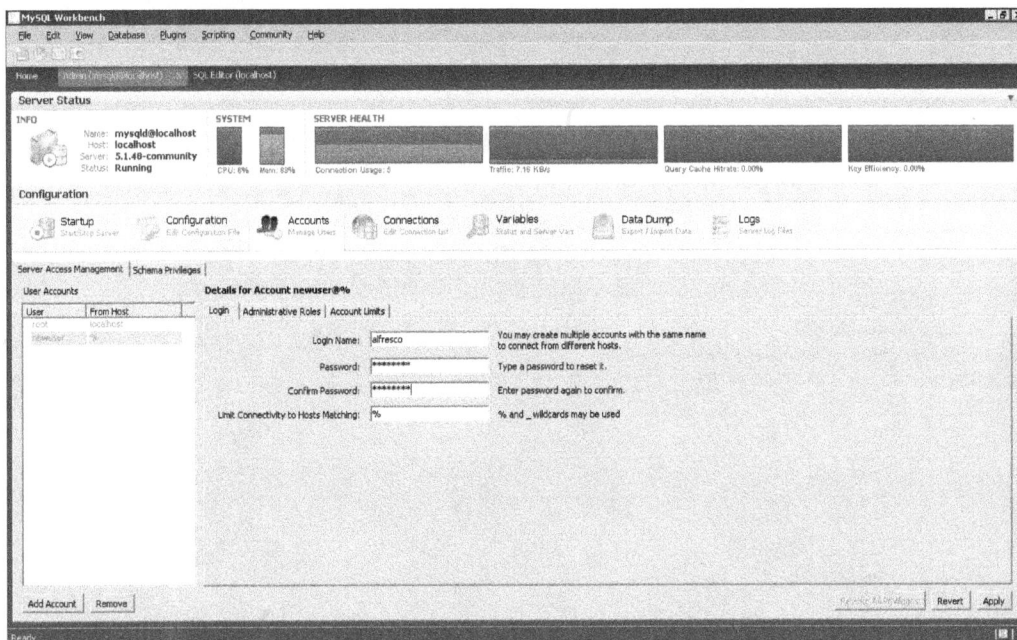

With this, we have set up a blank database for our Alfresco server and created a user. We will now give permissions to this user for using the database schema.

Alfresco's Tomcat bundle contains database creation, user creation script, and grant right script on that database under "`<<ALFRESCO_INSTALLATION_DIR>>\extras\databases\mysql\db_setup.sql`". This allows the creation of a database with a single click only.

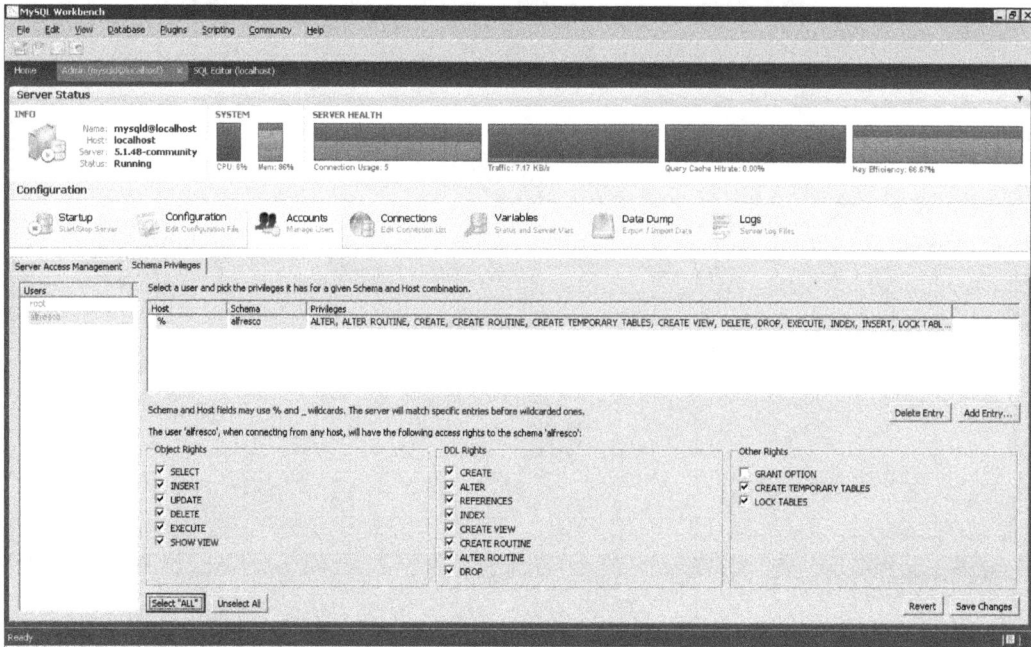

How it works...

In the previous steps, we have created a blank database for Alfresco and created a user and granted it permissions to manage the database. Now when Alfresco Tomcat or JBoss bundle runs for the first time, it will create all the database objects (tables, and so on) automatically.

The Alfresco bundle uses MySQL as the database by default, thus you don't have to perform any changes for that.

We have created a database with the name alfresco. We have also created a user with the name alfresco with the same password. This is because the default setting of Alfresco bundle is configured in this way. Thus, you don't have to change any settings in the default bundle.

Default configurations are mentioned under "`ALF_HOME>>\tomcat\shared\classes\alfresco-global.properties`". If needed, you can change this setting as per the database configuration.

Installing Alfresco on Windows

There are two methods to install Alfresco on a Windows platform.

- ▶ Using the Alfresco packaged installer
- ▶ Deploying the Tomcat or JBoss bundle

The first approach will install Alfresco in Windows along with JDK (optionally), create the Alfresco database automatically, and can configure and start Alfresco as a Windows Service. It will inject the relevant shortcuts in your Start Menu just like any other application installed in your machine. You can start/stop the server using the Start Menu option or a Windows Service. This is a fully-automated and smooth approach to install Alfresco.

The second approach is more manual. You will have the downloaded Tomcat or JBoss bundle of Alfresco. Manually configure a few things, and you are ready to go. However, you cannot have Alfresco as a service in Windows very easily, in this case, and won't have the Start Menu shortcuts ready for you. But in this case, as a developer and explorer of Alfresco, you can have a number of Alfresco bundles deployed and running on your machine.

In this book, we will demonstrate the second option, as the first one is very straightforward and you will find lots of documentation around that. We will also use the Tomcat bundle of Alfresco and not the JBoss one.

Getting ready

1. Download the Alfresco community edition from the Alfresco download site. `http://wiki.alfresco.com/wiki/Community_Edition_file_list_3.3`

2. In **Individual Components and Custom Installs section**, download the `Alfresco-community-tomcat-3.3.zip` file. Or you can directly use the URL `http://process.alfresco.com/ccdl/?file=release/community/build-2765/alfresco-community-tomcat-3.3.zip` and use **standard download**.

3. You will need the following prerequisite programs already installed on your machine –
    - ❑ WinZIP or WinRAR
    - ❑ JDK 1.6.x
    - ❑ MySQL database server

4. Once these programs are installed and after downloading the Alfresco Tomcat bundle, we are ready to go.

How to do it...

Carry out the following steps to install the Alfresco Tomcat bundle on your machine.

1. Download the ZIP archive from the preceding URL.

2. Unzip the archive in a folder in your system. Say the folder you have unzipped the archive into is `c:\Alfresco`. These are the root level files in the unzipped folder.

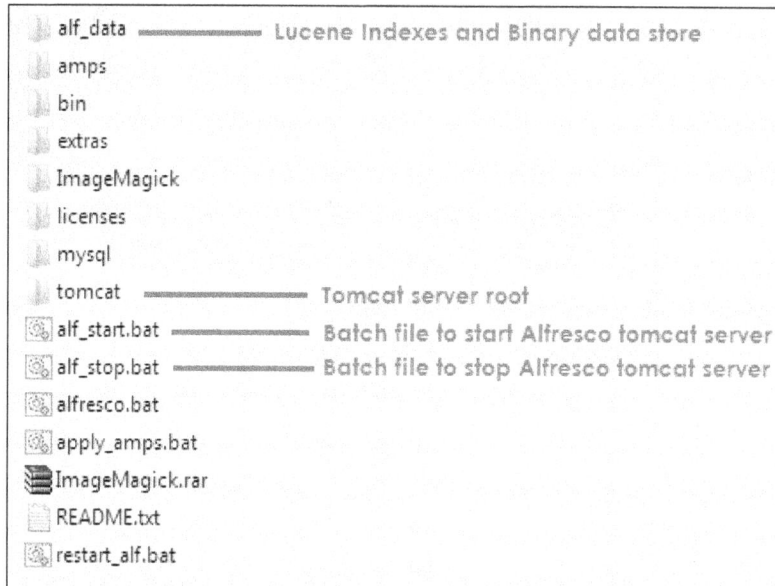

```
alf_data ———————————— Lucene Indexes and Binary data store
amps
bin
extras
ImageMagick
licenses
mysql
tomcat  ———————————————— Tomcat server root
alf_start.bat ——————————— Batch file to start Alfresco tomcat server
alf_stop.bat ———————————— Batch file to stop Alfresco tomcat server
alfresco.bat
apply_amps.bat
ImageMagick.rar
README.txt
restart_alf.bat
```

3. You need to set the `JAVA_HOME` environment variable to make the Tomcat server understand where your JDK or JRE is installed.

    ❑   Open **System Properties** by right-clicking on the `My Computer` icon on your desktop.

    ❑   Open the **Advanced tab**.

    ❑   Click on **Environment Variables**.

    ❑   Check whether the **JAVA_HOME** environment variable is already set or not.

        i.   If not, create a new **System Variable** named `JAVA_HOME` and put the value of the variable to the directory where JDK or JRE is installed.

        ii. For example, if your JDK is installed in the `c:\Program Files\ Java\jdk1.6.0_14` directory, the value of `JAVA_HOME` should be the same.

If the `JAVA_HOME` variable is already defined, validate whether it contains the correct value.

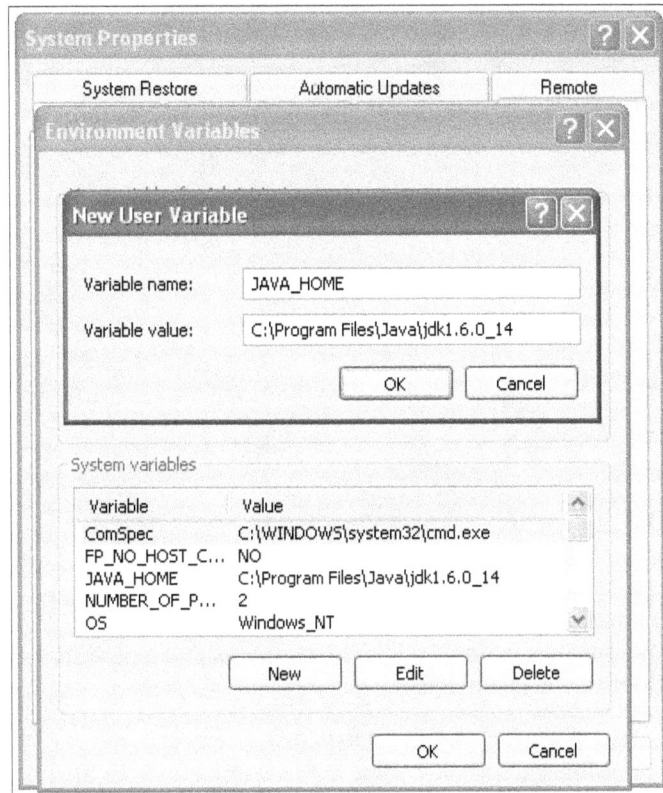

4. You also need to check whether Java runtimes are properly added in your windows `PATH`.

   a. Open **System Properties** by right-clicking on the **My Computer** icon on your desktop.

   b. Open the **Advanced** tab.

   c. Click on **Environment Variables**.

      iii. Open the **PATH** environment variable

      iv. Check whether it is having the JDK binary folder value inserted into it. The value inserted should be `%JAVA_HOME%\bin`

5. Assuming that you have properly created a database named `Alfresco` in your local MySQL server, and created a user with the name `Alfresco` (as in the previous recipe), you can start your Tomcat server now. Run the `alf_start.bat` file and the Tomcat server should have started.

How it works...

The first time the AlfrescoTomcat server starts, the web application files (.WAR files) are exploded in the `tomcat\webapps` folder.

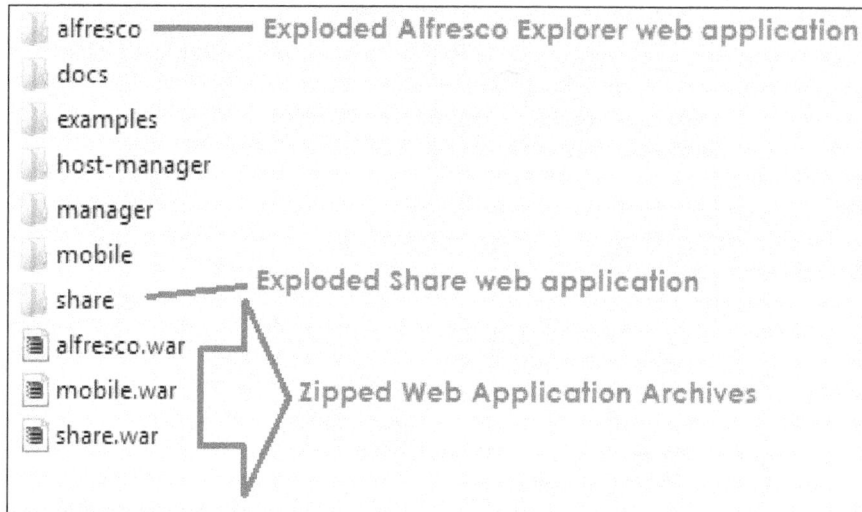

```
alfresco ──────── Exploded Alfresco Explorer web application
docs
examples
host-manager
manager
mobile
share ─────── Exploded Share web application
alfresco.war
mobile.war        Zipped Web Application Archives
share.war
```

Similarly, the deployer also populates the MySQL database, and creates the required database objects (tables, and so on) into it.

Alfresco uses some third-party tools and applications for several purposes. When the Tomcat server starts, Alfresco connects with these applications and performs the necessary actions later on, as required.

- **Open Office** is used by Alfresco in order to convert or transform documents into the portable document format (PDF).

- **ImageMagick** converter is used to generate thumbnail images of documents.

- **PDF2SWF** tool is used to convert PDF documents into flash movies.

ImageMagick and PDF2SWF binaries come with the downloaded Tomcat bundle of Alfresco, thus you do not have to install and configure these separately. However, you may have to install Open Office in your machine separately.

There's more...

Sometimes you may need to configure the `JAVA_OPTS` variable as well, in case you are facing any memory issues while running the application – memory issues like *Java Heap Space, Perm Gen error*, and so on.

For setting up JAVA_OPTS, you have to follow the same procedure as in setting up the JAVA_HOME variable in your environment variable list.

There is no fixed value for JAVA_OPTS, it depends on your application load. However, in a standard developer machine, it should be something like

```
-Xms256m -Xmx1024m -XX:MaxPermSize=512m
```

in a machine having 2 to 4 GB of physical memory.

Installing Alfresco on Linux

You can install Alfresco in the Linux platform with these two methods:

► Using the Alfresco packaged installer

► Deploying the Tomcat or JBoss bundle

The first approach will install Alfresco in Linux along with JDK (optionally). It will create the Alfresco database automatically and is often capable of configuring and starting Alfresco as a Linux init script.

The second approach is more manual. You will have the downloaded Tomcat or JBoss bundle of Alfresco. Manually configure a few things and you are ready to go.

As in the case of windows, in this book, we will demonstrate the second option. And, we will also use the Tomcat bundle of Alfresco, not the JBoss one.

Getting ready

1. Download the Alfresco community edition from the Alfresco download site. http://wiki.alfresco.com/wiki/Community_Edition_file_list_3.3.

2. In **Individual Components and Custom Installs section**, download the Alfresco-community-tomcat-3.3.tar.gz file. Or you can directly use this URL http://process.alfresco.com/ccdl/?file=release/community/build-2765/alfresco-community-tomcat-3.3.tar.gz and use **standard download**.

3. You will need the following prerequisite programs already installed in your machine:

   ❑ JDK 1.6.x

   ❑ MySQL database server

4. Once these programs are installed and after downloading the Alfresco Tomcat bundle, we are ready to go.

How to do it...

Carry out the following steps to install the Alfresco Tomcat bundle on your machine.

1. Download the compressed archive from the above URL.

2. `Untar` the bundle and move it to a suitable location, say `/usr/local/Alfresco`

    ```
    #       tar -zxf Alfresco-xxx.tar.gz
    #       mv Alfresco-xxx /user/local/
    ```

3. You need to give proper permission to the moved folder.

    ```
    #       chmod -R 755 /usr/local/Alfresco-xxx
    ```

4. You need to set the `JAVA_HOME` environment variable to make the Tomcat server understand where your JDK or JRE is installed.

5. Check whether the `JAVA_HOME` environment variable is already set or not.

    ```
    #       echo $JAVA_HOME
    ```

6. If the `JAVA_HOME` variable is already defined, validate whether it is containing the correct value.

7. If not, create a new file named `java.sh` under the `/etc/profile.d` directory and set the `JAVA_HOME` variable with the value to the directory where JDK or JRE is installed.

    ```
    #       touch /etc/profile.d/java.sh
    #       chmod 755 /etc/profile.d/java.sh
    #       echo "JAVA_HOME=/usr/local/jdk1.6.x" >> /etc/profile.d/
              java.sh
    #        source /etc/profile.d/java.sh
    ```

8. You also need to check whether Java runtimes are properly added in your `PATH` variable.

    ```
    #       echo $PATH
    ```

9. If not, set the `PATH` variable to the value of the bin directory of the desired JDK package.

    ```
    #       echo "PATH=$PATH:/usr/local/jdk1.6.x/bin" >> /etc/profile.d/
              java.sh
    #       source /etc/profile.d/java.sh
    ```

10. Assuming that you have properly created a database named `Alfresco` in your local MySQL server, and created a user with the name `Alfresco` (as in previous recipe), you can start your Tomcat server now.
    Run the `startup.sh` file and the Tomcat server should have started.

    ```
    #       cd /usr/local/Alfresco/tomcat-6.0.18/bin
    #       ./startup.sh
    ```

11. You can check out the log file for any unexpected error.

```
#      tail -f /usr/local/Alfresco/tomcat-6.0.18/logs/catalina.out
```

How it works...

The first time the Alfresco Tomcat server starts, the web application files (.WAR files) are exploded in the `tomcat\webapps` folder.

Similarly, the deployer also populates the MySQL database and creates the required database objects (tables, and so on) into it.

Alfresco uses some third-party tools and applications for several purposes. When the Tomcat server starts, Alfresco connects with these applications and performs the necessary actions later on as required.

- ▸ `Open Office` is used by Alfresco in order to convert or transform documents into the portable document format (PDF).
- ▸ `ImageMagick` converter is used to generate thumbnail images of documents.
- ▸ `PDF2SWF` tool is used to convert PDF documents into flash movies.

There's more...

Sometimes you may need to configure the `JAVA_OPTS` variable as well, in case you are facing any memory issues while running the application – memory issues like `Java Heap Space`, `Perm Gen error`, and so on.

For setting up `JAVA_OPTS`, you have to follow the same procedure as in setting up the `JAVA_HOME` variable in your environment variable list.

There is no ideal and fixed value for `JAVA_OPTS`; it depends on your application load. However, in a standard developer machine, it should be something like

```
-Xms256m -Xmx1024m -XX:MaxPermSize=512m
```

in a machine having 2 to 4 GB of physical memory.

Running Alfresco for the first time

Alfresco comes with mainly two pre-packaged products (or applications) – the Web Client (or Alfresco Explorer) and Alfresco Share.

Here we will explore how to invoke these applications in your web browser.

Getting ready

Run the Alfresco Server. Go to `C:\Alfresco` (remember, this is the location we assume our Tomcat stack to be deployed from).

Wait until you see the server start-up confirmation message appears.

How to do it...

1. Open your favorite web browser.

2. To open Alfresco Explorer, type the URL `http://localhost:8080/alfresco`. The login screen will appear. By default, an administrator user comes with the Alfresco bundle with the username **admin** and the password **admin**.

3. After login, clicking on **Company Home** at top-left corner invokes the Alfresco Explorer screen, showing all available spaces in your repository.

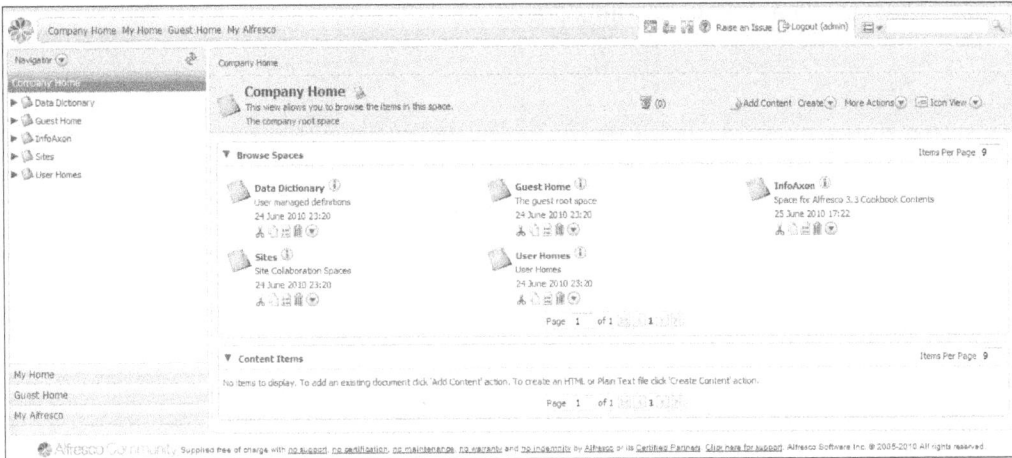

4. To open Alfresco Share, type the URL `http://localhost:8080/share`. The login screen will appear. By default, an administrator user comes with the Alfresco bundle with the username **admin** and the password **admin**.

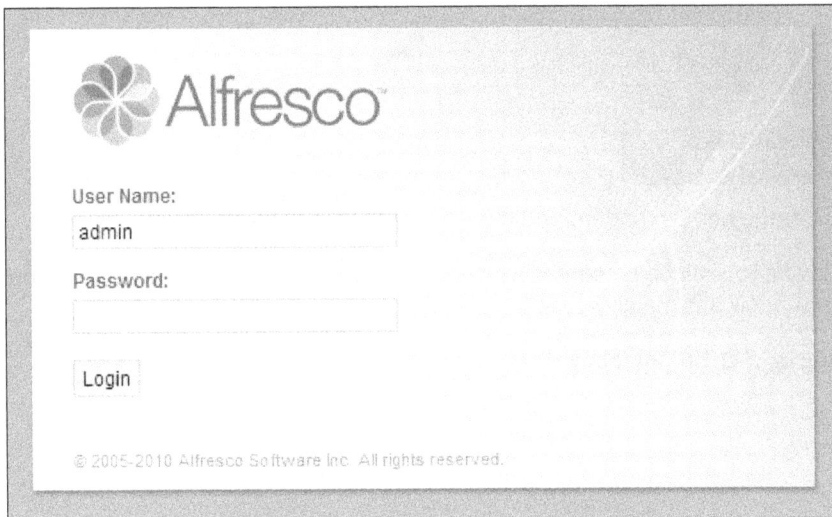

5. After login, the user dashboard will appear.

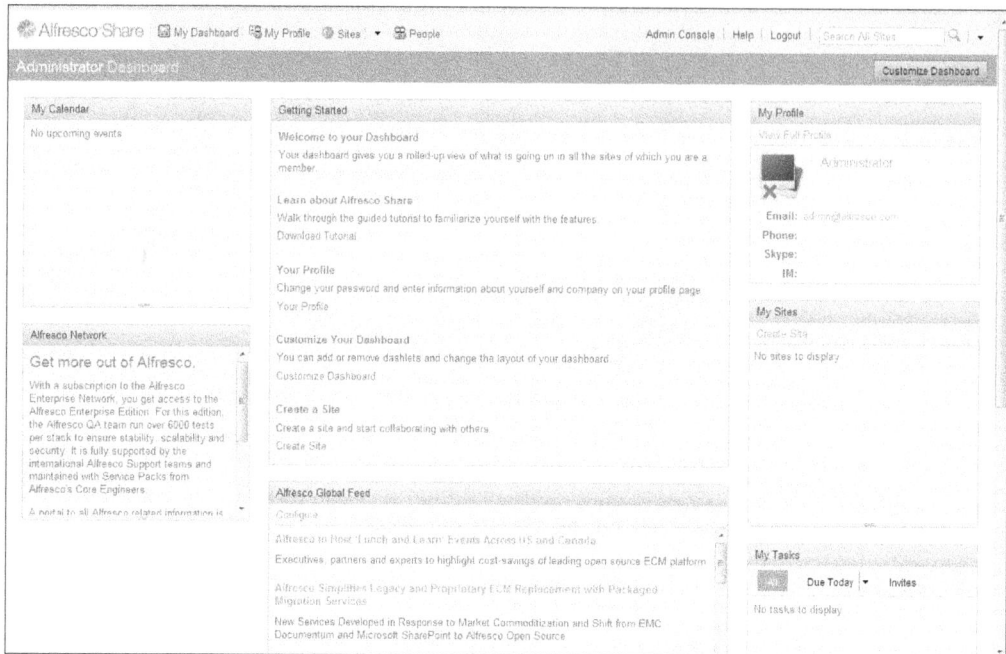

There's more

Let's go under the hood to understand the components of **Alfresco Explorer**.

Once you log in, you will be presented with your Dashboard in the explorer. The explorer web application window has mainly seven sections.

After logging in, click on **Company Home** to navigate to the root folder of the repository.

1. Alfresco accumulates all contents, user information, and process information in several preconfigured stores. Thus, the Alfresco Store is the logical storage space of all contents uploaded in the repository.

2. Some of the important stores in the default configured bundle of Alfresco.

   1. `workspace://SpacesStore`

      This is the main logical storage space where all contents and files are stored. The Alfresco Explorer application enables users to browse through this store only. In a general sense, when we call the Alfresco repository, we mostly refer to this store's contents only. Thus, in the later chapters, when we will talk about contents and spaces, we would refer to the contents of this store.

   2. `user://AlfrescoUserStore`

      Stores information about the users registered in the Alfresco stack.

   3. `workspace://lightWeightVersionStore`

      version2Alfresco, being an ECMS, can handle and manage multiple versions of a document. It enables users to check-in, check-out a document, see different versions of a document, and view the history of versions of a document. The `lightWeightVersionStorev2` contains the archived versions of all versioned documents; that means all documents with the `cm:versionable` aspect. In other words, this store stocks up all versions of the contents of `workspace://SpacesStore`.

   4. `archive://SpacesStore`

      This store is the trash can of `workspace://SpacesStore`. Means the contents that are deleted or removed from any of the repository spaces land up in this store as archive. However, once an item is removed from this store, that one is permanently lost.

   5. `system://system`

      This store is very small and contains software information.

3. All contents and files are stored in folders, in Alfresco language, these folders are called `spaces`. Company Home is itself a space, inside which all other spaces and contents are stored. Under one space, there can be any number of subspaces, subspaces then contain a number of other subspaces and this hierarchy goes on. Each of these spaces can store contents, documents, or other files.

4. By default, Alfresco `workspace://SpacesStore` store comes with **Company Home** and inside Company Home, four spaces are configured.

   ❑ `Data Dictionary`
   ❑ `Guest Home`
   ❑ `Sites`
   ❑ `User Homes`

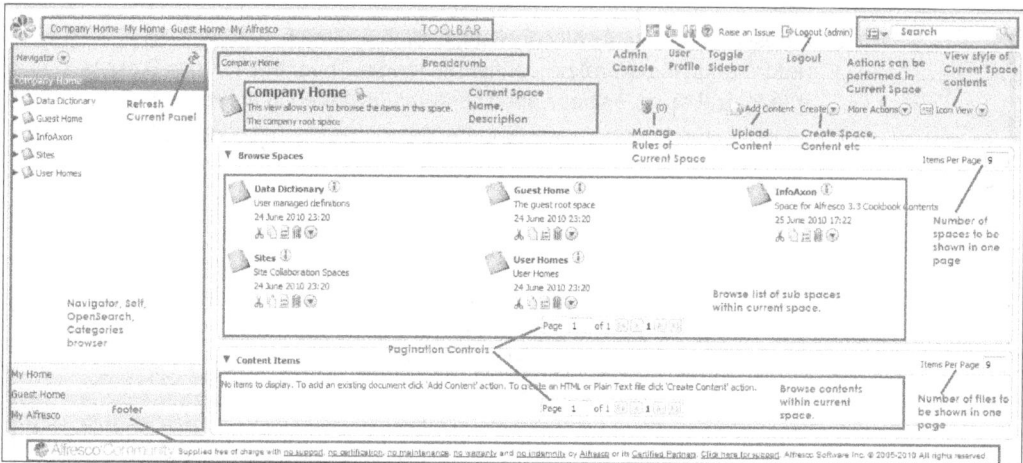

Toolbar

The toolbar at the top section of the explorer window provides links to various spaces and functionalities of Alfresco.

- Company Home: Link to open the repository home space.

- My Home: Link to open your (current logged in user's) home space.

- Guest Home: Link to open the home space of non-logged in users.

- My Alfresco: Link to navigate to your dashboard (current logged in user's dashboard).

- Admin Console: Link to open the Administrative Console of Alfresco. This link is only available to Alfresco Administrators.

- User Profile: Link to open the interface for changing your details, password, preferences.

- Toggle Sidebar: Show / Hide the left navigation sidebar. Hiding the sidebar is often useful when your contents are large in number and you need more space in the screen to view more content at a time.

- Logout: Link to logout from the Alfresco explorer. In parenthesis, it shows the current username.

- Search: Simple and advanced search panel. This is the single and centralized search panel where you can hunt for any content available in the repository.

Sidebar

Sidebar is the left side panel for browsing the repository spaces, managing yourself, performing OpenSearch, or browsing contents by categories.

- ▶ Navigator: This panel helps you to navigate through the repository by the available repository spaces.

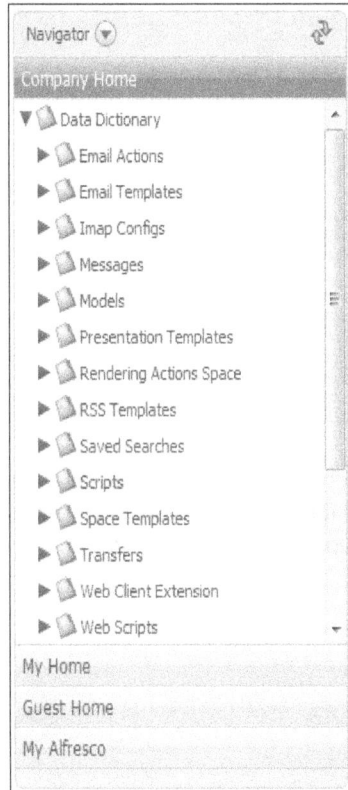

▸ Shelf: Shelf is sort of your mantelpiece where your clipboard is maintained, recent spaces you have navigated are listed, and shortcuts you have created are preserved.

▸ OpenSearch: OpenSearch is a collection of technologies that allow publishing of search results in simple formats suitable for content syndication and aggregation. Alfresco can act as an OpenSearch provider and can expose its search engines via OpenSearch.

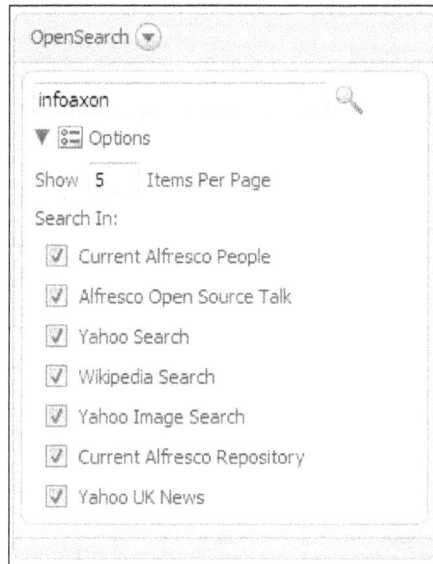

- Category Browser: One of most required and sought after features of an Enterprise Content Management system is the ability to classify or categorize content by custom taxonomy. Alfresco repository has a powerful categorization engine by which you can classify any document or space. This panel enables you to browse the contents by categories.

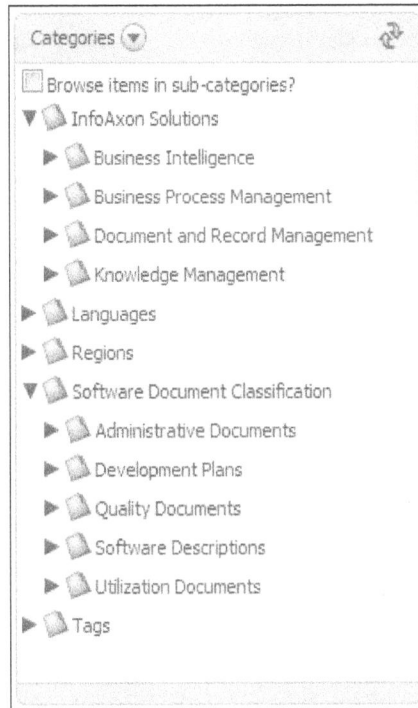

Breadcrumb

Breadcrumb is the routing trail of spaces you have navigated through.

It shows the trace of spaces you have browsed or navigated. Each of these spaces is hyperlinked, enabling you to open any particular space with one click.

Current space information

This panel shows details of the current space you are in or the functionality you are using. For example, if you have opened the `InfoAxon` space, it will display information about the space `InfoAxon`. The right side of this panel shows the number of rules configured in this space.

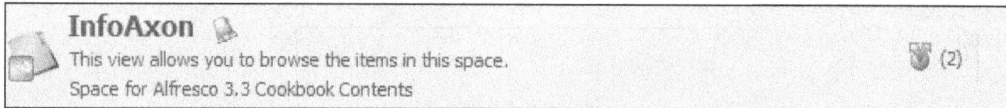

InfoAxon
This view allows you to browse the items in this space.
Space for Alfresco 3.3 Cookbook Contents
(2)

Actions Links

On the right side of the Space information panel, links for actions that can be performed on the current space are provided.

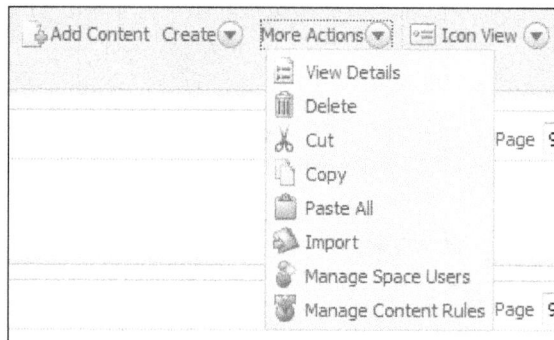

- ▶ **Add Content** enables you to upload a new file in the current space.
- ▶ **Create Options** facilitates you to create new content items and create new spaces.
- ▶ **More Actions** supplies several tasks that can be performed over the current space.
- ▶ **View Options** offers at most four choices to view the contents of the current space
- ▶ **Details View** displays contents along with details of each one – much like windows explorer details view.
- ▶ **Icon View** shows contents with the content icon along with minimal information about the file.
- ▶ **Browse View** renders only the filename, title, and action icons for the content.
- ▶ **Custom View** exhibits the freemarker template you have associated with the space.

Sub-spaces panel

Panel shows all subspaces of the current space. You can set the number of items to show in a page. However, this setting will be applicable for the current session only, meaning if your session is expired or you are logged out, this setting will be reset.

There is a pagination control set also provided by which you can navigate through several pages.

Content items panel

This panel renders the content items (documents, files, and so on) created or uploaded in the current space. As seen previously, you can set the number of items to show in a page. However, this setting will be applicable for the current session only, means as before if your session is expired or you are logged out, this setting will be reset.

There is a pagination control set also provided by which you can navigate through several pages.

Footer

The footer section of the explorer page displays copyrights, license, warranty, and other information about Alfresco. This panel stays read-only unless you fiddle with some of Alfresco explorer's JSP pages and JAVA classes.

2
Creating and Organizing Contents

This chapter will cover:

- ► Creating a space
- ► Creating content
- ► Uploading a document
- ► Viewing content details
- ► Tagging content
- ► Categorizing content
- ► Making a document versionable

Introduction

Alfresco is a Content Management System ready for your Enterprise. You can store and manage your contents in a logical collection named **Spaces**. In your desktop, you store your files and documents in folders. In other words, folders or directories help you organize your files. Similarly, in Alfresco also, you store and systematize your contents in various folders. In addition to storing contents, spaces in Alfresco can execute scripts and actions as well. We will explore this in greater detail in *Chapter 4*.

As your document management system, Alfresco enables you to upload documents, set the details of your documents, tag or classify your documents, and manage the versions of the documents.

In this chapter, you will learn how to use the Alfresco Explorer application to create and organize your contents using spaces, as well as how to upload and manage the details of the documents.

Content metadata

Metadata is "data about data". Content metadata is the details or information about content. If we take an example of a document in your hard disk, the metadata of the document is name, created date, author, date modified, title, and so on.

```
File
Name                   logo.gif
Item type              GIF image
Folder path            C:\Users\snig bhaumik\Desktop\L...
Date created           05-Jul-10 4:50 PM
Date modified          20-Jul-10 4:38 PM
Size                   4.65 KB
Attributes             A
Offline availability
Offline status
Shared with
Owner                  snigbhaumik\snig bhaumik
Computer               SNIGBHAUMIK (this computer)
```

In this example, we are looking at the properties of a file named `logo.gif` in my computer. When we right-click on the file and open the **Properties** dialog, we can view the file property sheet.

Here the properties like **Name**, **Item type**, **Folder path**, **Date created**, **Date modified**, **Size**, and so on are the information or details about this file. This information is the metadata of the file. Windows (or your Operating System), by default, associates some metadata with every file in the disk.

The set of properties being applied to the file depends on the file. For example, in case of an mp3 audio file, the following properties are associated:

```
Description
Title
Subtitle
Rating          ☆ ☆ ☆ ☆ ☆
Comments
  Media
Contributing artists
Album artist
Album
Year
#
Genre
Length          00:03:30
  Audio
Bit rate        320kbps
  Origin
Publisher
```

And in the case of an mpg video file, additional metadata used are shown in the following screenshot:

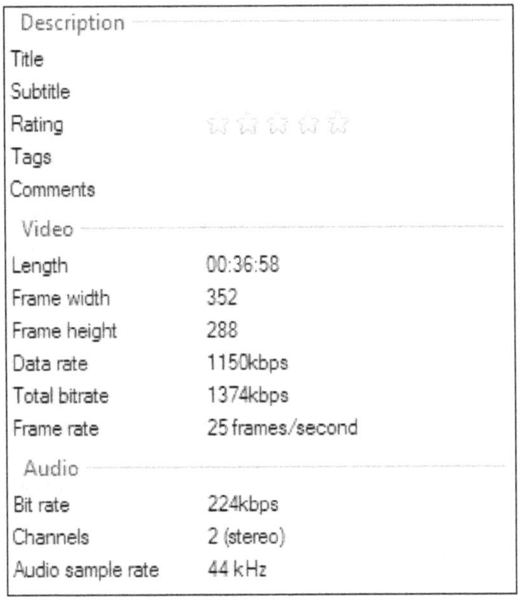

```
Description
Title
Subtitle
Rating          ☆ ☆ ☆ ☆ ☆
Tags
Comments
  Video
Length          00:36:58
Frame width     352
Frame height    288
Data rate       1150kbps
Total bitrate   1374kbps
Frame rate      25 frames/second
  Audio
Bit rate        224kbps
Channels        2 (stereo)
Audio sample rate   44 kHz
```

Thus, as you have seen, a different set of properties or metadata can be applied to content or to a file depending on the type of the file. The first set of properties are the same for all the files in Windows – for example, every file would have a name, a create date, a modify date, an author, and so on.

But in addition to these similar properties, there are some specific properties applied depending on the type of the file – for example, an mp3 audio file would have extra metadata like album, year, genre, length, artist, and so on; and an mpg video would have metadata like frame width, frame height, data rate, and so on.

The type of the file in Windows can be treated as the content types in Alfresco. Alfresco, by default, comes with a base type named `cm:content`. This should be used as the base type for all custom types we create for different content in Alfresco. This consists of standard metadata such as **name**, **creates date**, **modify date**, **created by**, **modified by**, and so on. Similarly, for spaces, there is a type `cm:folder`; for users, the type is `cm:person`.

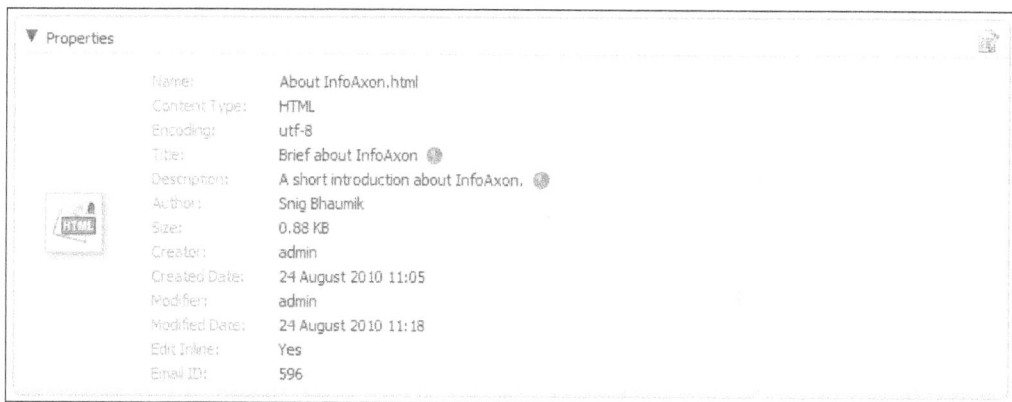

This preceding screenshot shows the default metadata information of the HTML content we had created in the previous recipe. All these metadata structures have been supplied by Alfresco content model; we had entered the values of the metadata. The create date, modify date, and so on are read-only values to you, naturally Alfresco automatically sets these values.

Usually your requirements go beyond the default metadata set supplied by Alfresco. You would like to have your own properties, so that you can identify your content more accurately.

For example, you are uploading your invoice document, and along with this document, you want to enter the invoice number, invoice date, client name, and so on. For this, you will have to create a new content model with this new metadata set. Aspects, in Alfresco, are a modular set of properties and behaviors that can be dynamically associated with contents. For example, `versionable` aspect in Alfresco adds the versioning capability and features with content. Alfresco, thus offers a number of aspects which can be associated with documents in order to add more dynamic behavior of contents. You also create your own aspects and introduce modularity and re-usability of behavior of contents.

Later on, we will learn how to create your custom content model, type, and aspects along with your own properties, metadata, and details.

Creating a space

In Alfresco, spaces are logical collections of files and contents. We will learn how to create a new space in this recipe.

Getting ready

In order to create a space, we need to open the Alfresco Explorer application.

1. Open the URL in your browser `http://localhost:8080/alfresco`.

2. Login using the default administrator user credentials provided by Alfresco. **Username: admin. Password: admin**.

3. Click on **Company Home** or **My Home** in the top left navigation toolbar.

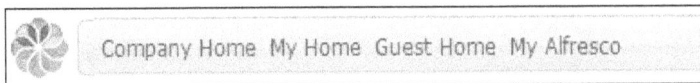

This opens up the root space of Alfresco.

How to do it...

1. Click on **Create Space** from the right links.

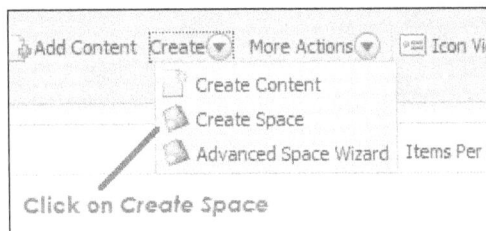

2. The New Space creation form appears. Fill up the **Name**, **Title**, **Description** of the new space you want to create and click on **Create Space**. Choose the icon you want to associate with your space from the available list of icons.

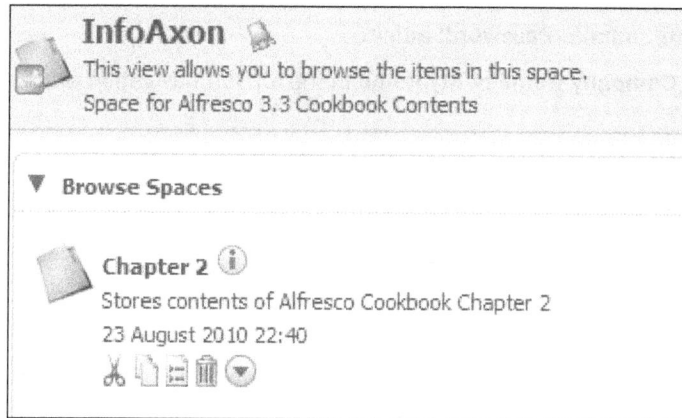

3. Your new space has been created.

How it works...

Quite simply, Alfresco creates the space with the parameters provided by you in the **Create Space** form. The current user has to have the required permission to create contents; otherwise the **Create Space** link will not appear.

Note the new space we have created under a folder named InfoAxon. I have created this space under Company Home for all the illustrations in this book. You can also create the same, or can work directly under Company Home.

You can add your custom icons for associating with the space. See *Including custom Icons* in your Spaces recipe *Chapter 6* for this.

Creating content

After creating space for storing your contents, it is now time to create content. Contents in Alfresco can be created in two ways – create the content using Alfresco Explorer editors or upload an existing content from your computer.

In this recipe, we will see how to create content using the Alfresco Explorer.

How to do it...

1. Click on **Create Content** from the right links.

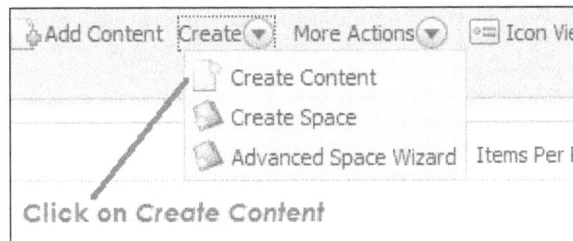

Click on *Create Content*

2. The form to populate the name and type of the content appears.

Step One - Specify name and select type

Specify the name and select the type of content you wish to create.

General Properties

Name:

Type: Content

Content Type: HTML

HTML
Plain Text
XML

Other Properties

Rules applied to this content may require you to enter additional information.

Modify all properties when this wizard closes.

To continue click Next.

3. Provide the name of your new content. The **Type** parameter defines the content and **Content Type** parameter defines the mime-type of the new content.

4. By default, only **Content** is available as the **Type**. However, you can create your custom types easily. Custom types are useful when you want to create and associate new properties, new behaviors with your content.

5. And Alfresco offers simple contents to be created by the Explorer interface – plain text, XML, and HTML. Alfresco Explorer comes with a simple WYSIWYG HTML editor (TinyMCE), which helps you to create HTML contents.

Step Two - Enter Content

Enter your document content into the repository.

| **B** *I* <u>U</u> ᴬᴮᶜ | ≡ ≡ ≡ ≡ | Format ▾ | Font family ▾ | Font size ▾ |

⊟ ⊟ | ⊯ ⊯ | ↺ ↻ | ⊶ ⊷ ⚓ ⚲ ✒ @ ʜᴛᴍʟ | A ▾ ᵃᵇʸ ▾

▱ | ▥ ▥ | ⌐ ⌐ | ⌐ ⌐ | ▦ ▦ | — ∅ ▦ | x₁ x² | Ω

InfoAxon - India's First Open Source Integration Company

offering

- Knowledge Management and Business Intelligence Platforms for IT, Advertising, and Pharma
- fusionKM - Workflow based Social Knowledge Management Platform
- AdUniverse - Worflow enabled Knowledge Management for Advertising Industry
- AxonShare - Collaborative Document Management
- fusionBI - Enterprise 2.0 Business Intelligence Platform

---

6. The editor will be used depending on the content type you have selected for your new content. In case of text and XML, a simple text area will appear where you can put your content; in case of HTML content, the TinyMCE editor will be rendered, offering you to enter the contents in HTML format.

7. Click on **Next** or **Finish**. The last step is to provide proper property values of your new content – properties such as **Name, Encoding, Title, Description, Author**, and so on. If you check the **Edit Inline** option, Alfresco will use its default editor to enable you to edit the contents.

Properties

⊙ Name:	About InfoAxon.html	
Content Type:	HTML	▼
Encoding:	UTF-8	▼
Title:	Brief about InfoAxon	⊙
Description:	A short introduction about InfoAxon.	
		⊙
Author:	Snig Bhaumik	
Edit Inline:	☑	

8. This property sheet will appear only if you have selected the **Modify all properties when this wizard closes** checkbox in step 2.

9. After filling up the property values, click **OK**. Your new content has been created.

There's more...

One important point here is the property sheet having several properties or attributes of the content. These properties are controlled and rendered by the type of the content you are creating.

By default, here you have used the type as **Content**, as this is the one type available for use in Alfresco Explorer in its default distribution. This is the base type for all contents created in Alfresco; and this type has the properties Name, Title, Description, Encoding, Author, and so on. However, there are more properties not displayed in this form which are used in several functionalities on the content. During the course of this book, we will frequently visit the properties and usage of the same.

See also

You can also create your own custom type and properties. See *Chapter 7* for how to create custom types and how to use them.

Uploading a document

You have just learnt how to create content using Alfresco Explorer and populate it. However, this process can only create textual, XML, and HTML documents and contents.

Of course, you have other types of files and documents in your disk such as images, office documents, audio, videos, and so on – which you want to put into the Alfresco repository. The editors of Alfresco Explorer won't help you to create and edit such documents. In addition, you must be able to upload the existing files into the repository for enabling document management, and so on.

This recipe will help you understand how to upload your existing documents from your disk into the repository.

How to do it...

1. Start with opening the space in Alfresco Explorer where you want to upload your document and click on **Add Content**.

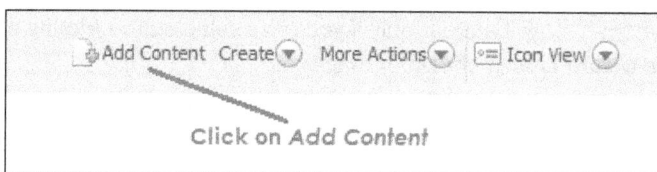

    Add Content Create ▼ More Actions ▼ ☰ Icon View ▼

    Click on Add Content

2. **File upload** control will appear, click on **Browse**, and select the file you want to upload in this space.

3. **Property sheet editor** opens up, where you can set the name and type of the file you are uploading. Suppose, I have selected a file here with the name `logo.gif`. The following screenshot appears:

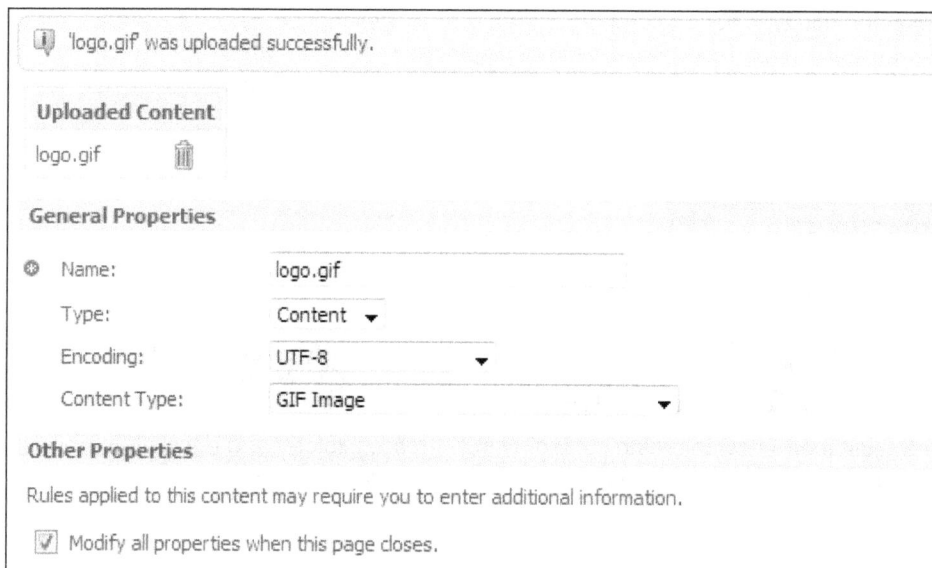

    ⓘ 'logo.gif' was uploaded successfully.

    Uploaded Content

    logo.gif   🗑

    General Properties

⊛ Name:	logo.gif
Type:	Content ▼
Encoding:	UTF-8 ▼
Content Type:	GIF Image ▼

    Other Properties

    Rules applied to this content may require you to enter additional information.

    ☑ Modify all properties when this page closes.

4. Note that, Alfresco has automatically identified the content type (mime type) of the document, in our case, it is a GIF image. If you are uploading any MS Office documents, the Content Type would be Microsoft Word or Microsoft Excel.

5. On clicking **OK**, the file is actually uploaded in the current space, and the property sheet appears offering you to put the name, title, description, author, and so on.

There's more...

Similarly as in the earlier case, here also you can use your custom content types, which enable you to create your own properties, metadata, and details.

Viewing content details

The folders you have created and the documents you have uploaded in Alfresco have several properties and other behaviors associated with it. You can also perform several other operations over content – such as copy, delete, move, download, check-in, check-out, and so on.

In this recipe, we will explore the operations that can be executed over contents and how to do it.

Getting ready...

Open a particular space where the contents are uploaded on which you want to perform certain operations.

In our case, we will navigate to the sample InfoAxon space where we had earlier uploaded the contents and created a space.

How to do it...

1. We choose the **About InfoAxon.html** content here. Click on the **View Details** icon.

2. Screen opens up displaying the details of this content.

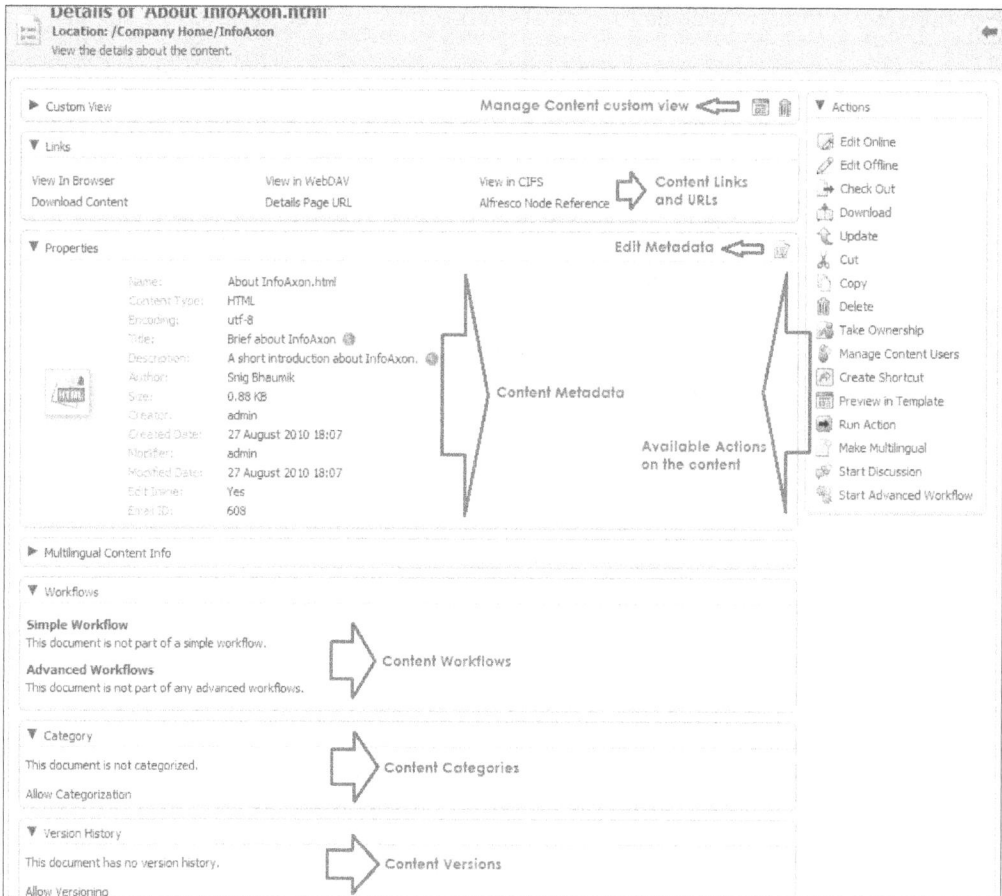

3. All the operations you can perform on this particular content are displayed here along with the properties and metadata of this.

> ❑ **Manage Content Custom View**: You can display formatted custom information associated with content. We will explore this further in *Chapter 9*.
>
> ❑ **Content Links and URLs**: Shows the links and URLs of this content. Alfresco supports HTTP, FTP, WebDAV, and CIFS protocols and you can expose your repository via these protocols. Alfresco Node Reference in particular is interesting here. It returns the `nodeRef` of the particular content of the repository.
>
> ❑ **Content Metadata**: Displays the properties and metadata of the particular content. However, you can configure and control which metadata is displayed and which is not. It is not always required to display all the properties of a document.
>
> ❑ **Edit Metadata**: This link opens up a form that enables you to edit/modify the properties of the content. Similarly, as in the previous case, you can control the properties displayed in the edit form.
>
> ❑ **Actions**: This panel offers the available actions that can be performed on this content. The actions list is filtered depending on the permissions the current user is having and depending on the state of the content. For example, if you have read-only permission on the content, you won't be able to see the edit, cut, delete, and check-out options. Similarly, in case somebody else has already checked-out this content, you won't be able to do the edit operations even if you have the relevant permissions.

Available and possible actions are:

- ▶ **Edit Online**: Opens up the online Alfresco Explorer editor to enable you to edit the content. Note that, clicking this option will automatically check-out the content.

- ▶ **Edit Offline**: This will check-out and download the content for your editing. For example, the online editing option is not available and suitable for editing an MS-Word document; you must use the MS-Office Word application to do that. You click on **Edit Offline**, download the content, and upload again after editing. Then check the document back in.

- ▶ **Check Out**: This option only checks out the content and is ready for editing.

- ▶ **Download**: Downloads the content into your hard drive.

- ▶ **Update**: Enables you to upload the updated document from your hard drive.

- ▶ **Cut**: This is standard windows-like cut operation where the document is put into the Alfresco Explorer clipboard and is ready to be pasted into some other space.

- ▶ **Copy**: Again, standard windows-like copy operation where the document is put into Alfresco Explorer clipboard and is ready to be pasted in some other space. <<How can we paste already copied document? Kindly mention here.>>

- ▶ **Delete**: Deletes the content. The deleted content moves to the trash can of the corresponding user who has deleted the content.

- ▶ **Take ownership**: By default, the user that uploads the content becomes the owner of the content. The owner enjoys the full permissions over the content. By this option, you can take ownership, that is, you can be the owner of the document.

For further understanding of permissions in Alfresco, please see *Chapter 3*.

- ▶ **Manage Content users**: As the owner of the content, you would like to control the access of the content amongst other users. You do not want everybody to do everything with your document. This option enables you to do this.

We will discuss more on this in the next chapter.

- ▶ **Create Shortcut**: You do this quite often in your Windows environment – creating a shortcut of a document or of a folder in your desktop, so that every time you need to open the content, you need not browse through the whole hierarchy of your hard disk folders.

Here also, once you create a shortcut of a particular content or space in Alfresco, the shortcut is created in your shelf. This is the shortcut shelf screen you will get.

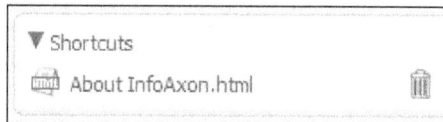

▼ Shortcuts

About InfoAxon.html

- ▶ **Preview in Template**: You can create your custom views also for your content. Alfresco uses Freemarker templates for creating custom views. We will explore this feature later in *Chapter 9*.

- ▶ **Run Action**: Action is a unit of task that can be performed over a particular content. The standard operations like move, copy, delete, check-in, and so on are also examples of Actions. In this way, Alfresco has provided a number of pre-defined actions using these you can perform a wide variety of tasks around a particular content.

Some examples of available actions are:

i. Add or remove aspect on the content

ii. Start workflow for the content

iii. Transform the content, for example, MS-Word to PDF, and so on

iv. Send e-mails to various users

v. Execute a script on the content

- ▶ **Make Multilingual**: Includes the multilingual capabilities of this content. <<Please mention alfresco capabilities for multilingual support>>
- ▶ **Start Discussion**: Enables and starts discussion around this content. <<Please describe this in detail. How discussion can be used? >>
- ▶ **Start Advanced Workflow**: Starts workflow on this content.
- ▶ **Content Workflows**: Alfresco uses JBPM (`http://jboss.org/jbpm`) as the business process management engine. The default distribution of Alfresco comes with a number of simple and complex workflows. You can use these workflows for different purposes of your document life cycle or you can create your own workflows.

This section shows these workflows associated with the content. We will learn more about workflows in *Chapter 11*.

- ▶ **Content Categories**: Categorization of contents is one of the important and necessary requirements of a CMS. Alfresco offers a flexible and customizable framework for creation of your taxonomy and categorization of your content.

We will learn more about this soon in this chapter.

- ▶ **Content Versions**: Alfresco offers document versioning capability where you can check-out and check-in your documents and Alfresco maintains the history of all the versions of the document.

We will also explore this more in this chapter itself.

There's more...

Alfresco is intelligent! It is not that when you delete content it gets removed from the whole repository immediately. Rather, like the Windows recycle bin, the deleted items get accumulated in the store `archive://SpacesStore`; you have learned about this store in *Chapter 1*.

However, if you want one of your pieces of content to be immediately removed from the repository, and not get stored in the trash can, there is an aspect for you, namely, `cm:temporary`. You attach this aspect with your content, and when the content is deleted, it gets completely removed from the whole repository and can never be recovered.

You can perform a different set of tasks and operations using the actions provided by Alfresco. You can bind these actions in rules and execute different business requirements on your content repository. We will explore these features in later chapters.

You can also write your own action, however, that is outside the scope of this book.

Tagging a document

A tag is a non-hierarchical keyword associated with a content or document. Tag is part of the metadata set of a document. A tag helps describe content, and enables keyword-based classification and easy search of information.

In a content management system, it is important to tag content or a document so that finding the actual content becomes easy and accurate.

How to do it...

1. Open a particular space into which the document resides that you want to attach tags to.

2. Here, we will use the same `About InfoAxon.html` content we used in previous recipe. Click on **View Details** and open the details page of the content.

3. Alfresco offers the taggable aspect. Associating this will introduce the capability of attaching tags to a document. By default, this aspect is not associated with the uploaded or created documents, and thus tagging is not enabled for a document uploaded in Alfresco. Hence, we need to associate this aspect first in order to attach tags with this document.

4. Click on the **Run Action** link. In the **Select Action** list, click on **Add an aspect**.

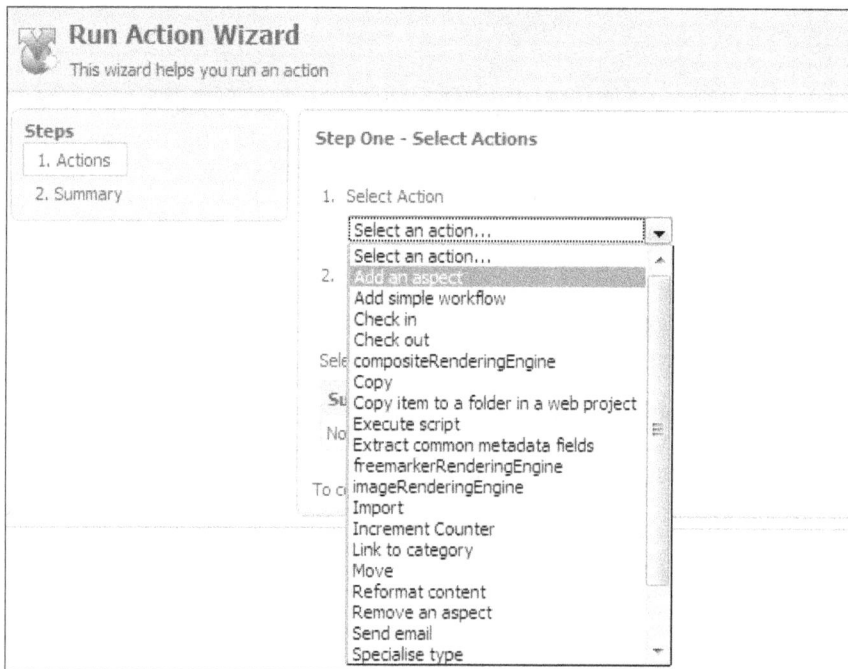

5. Then click on **Set Values** and **Add** beneath the list. A list of the available aspects is displayed. Select the taggable aspect in the list and click **OK**.

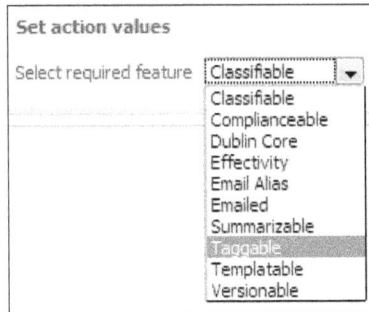

Set action values

Select required feature | Classifiable ▼

Classifiable
Complianceable
Dublin Core
Effectivity
Email Alias
Emailed
Summarizable
Taggable
Templatable
Versionable

6. Click on **Finish** to complete the operation.

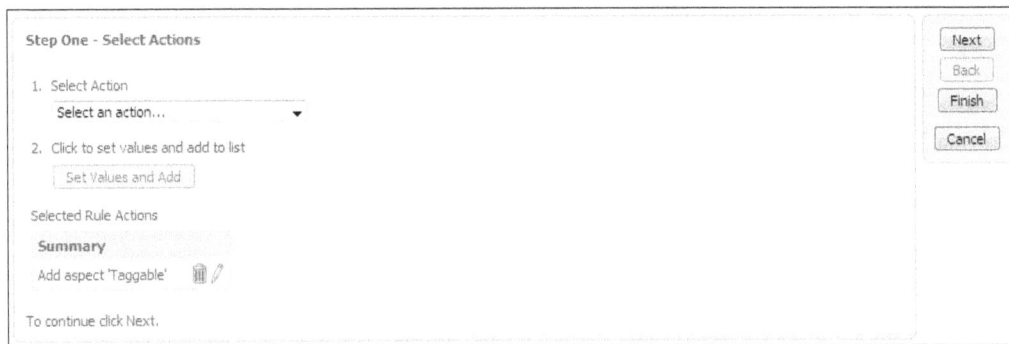

Step One - Select Actions

Next
Back
Finish
Cancel

1. Select Action

   Select an action... ▼

2. Click to set values and add to list

   Set Values and Add

Selected Rule Actions

Summary

Add aspect 'Taggable' 🗑 ✏

To continue click Next.

7. The content details screen re-appears. See the **Properties** section in the screen; you will notice that a new property named **tags** has been added to this content. Now click on the **Modify** link to edit the properties.

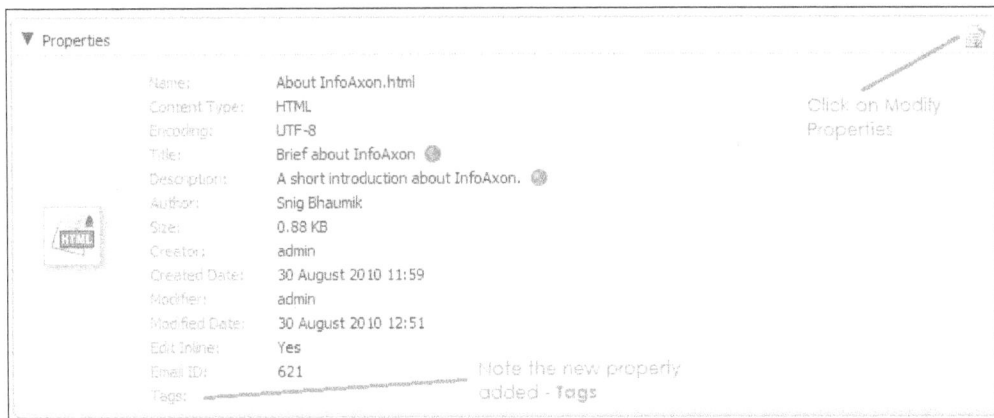

▼ Properties

Name:	About InfoAxon.html
Content Type:	HTML
Encoding:	UTF-8
Title:	Brief about InfoAxon 🌐
Description:	A short introduction about InfoAxon. 🌐
Author:	Snig Bhaumik
Size:	0.88 KB
Creator:	admin
Created Date:	30 August 2010 11:59
Modifier:	admin
Modified Date:	30 August 2010 12:51
Edit Inline:	Yes
Email ID:	621
Tags:	

Click on Modify Properties

Note the new property added - Tags

8. The property editor screen opens up allowing you to edit the metadata. Click on **Click to select tags** to open the tags editor panel.

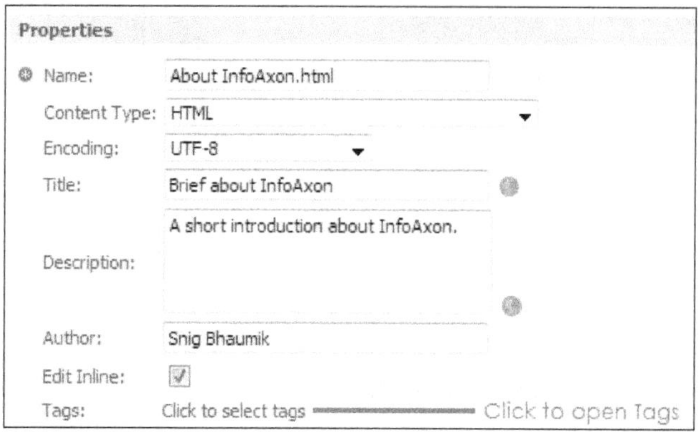

Properties

⊕ Name:	About InfoAxon.html	
Content Type:	HTML	▼
Encoding:	UTF-8	▼
Title:	Brief about InfoAxon	⊙
Description:	A short introduction about InfoAxon.	⊙
Author:	Snig Bhaumik	
Edit Inline:	☑	
Tags:	Click to select tags ———————— Click to open Tags	

9. The tags panel appears. Click on the **Add a tag** link and enter your new tag in the textbox provided. Click on the green tick mark to add the tag.

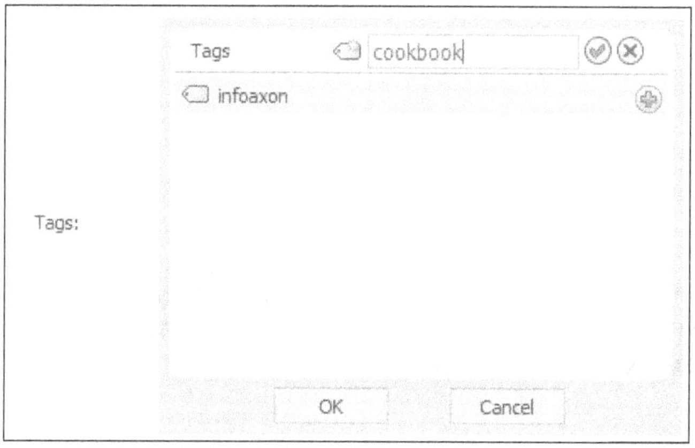

Tags:
- Tags   cookbook   ✓ ✕
- infoaxon   ⊕

OK   Cancel

10. In this way, keep on adding the tags you want. After adding the tags, you need to click on **OK** to save your work. If you click **Cancel**, the tags will be added in the repository space scope, but won't be associated with your content. In that case, you will have to re-open this dialog box and click on the green plus mark of the corresponding tag.

11. Here, we have created two new tags – **infoaxon** and **cookbook**, but only associated tag infoaxon with this content.

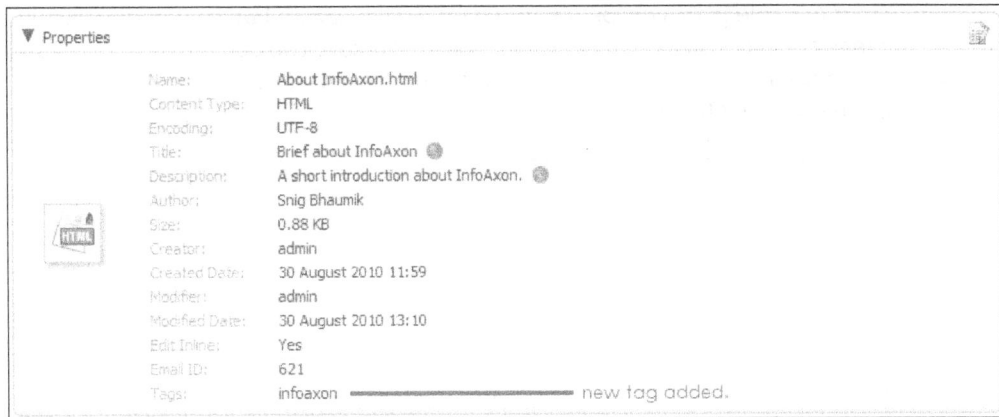

▼ Properties		
Name:	About InfoAxon.html	
Content Type:	HTML	
Encoding:	UTF-8	
Title:	Brief about InfoAxon	
Description:	A short introduction about InfoAxon.	
Author:	Snig Bhaumik	
Size:	0.88 KB	
Creator:	admin	
Created Date:	30 August 2010 11:59	
Modifier:	admin	
Modified Date:	30 August 2010 13:10	
Edit Inline:	Yes	
Email ID:	621	
Tags:	infoaxon	new tag added.

12. Invoking the tag editor again will show this – infoaxon is a tag of this content but cookbook is not.

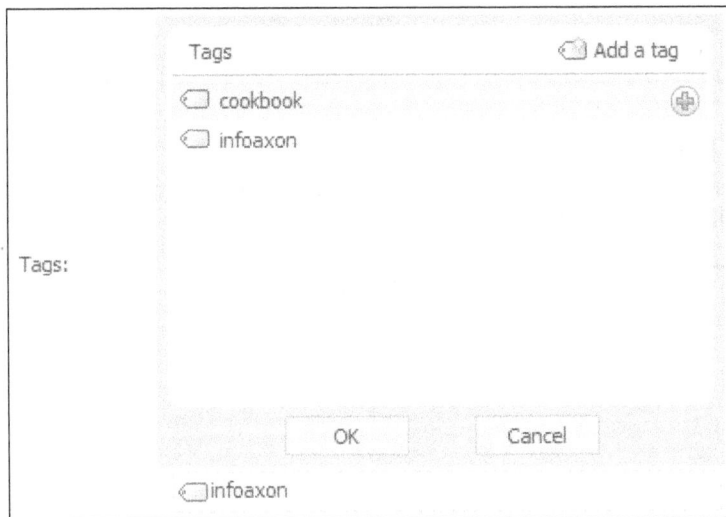

There's more...

One interesting point to be noted here is that Alfresco works with tag scope concept. Every folder or space in Alfresco can be a tag scope. This means if a space is defined as a tag scope, the tags created in the particular space is limited to that space only.

That's why, in our example in this recipe, we have created two tags – **infoaxon** and **cookbook**. So these two tags are in the scope of the current space. We have two documents in this space – **About InfoAxon.html** and `logo.gif`. If you open the tag editor for `logo.gif` file, you can see these tags ready to be attached with the document.

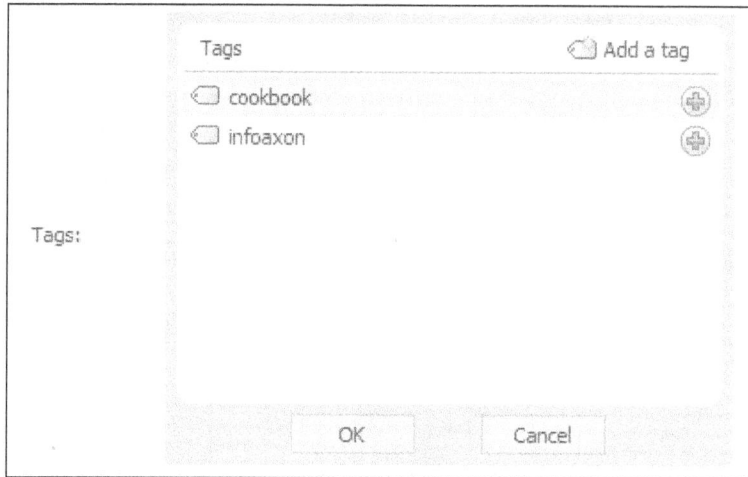

Detaching a tag

For detaching a tag from content, hover over the tag. A red minus icon will appear. Click on this and click **OK**. This will remove the tag from this document.

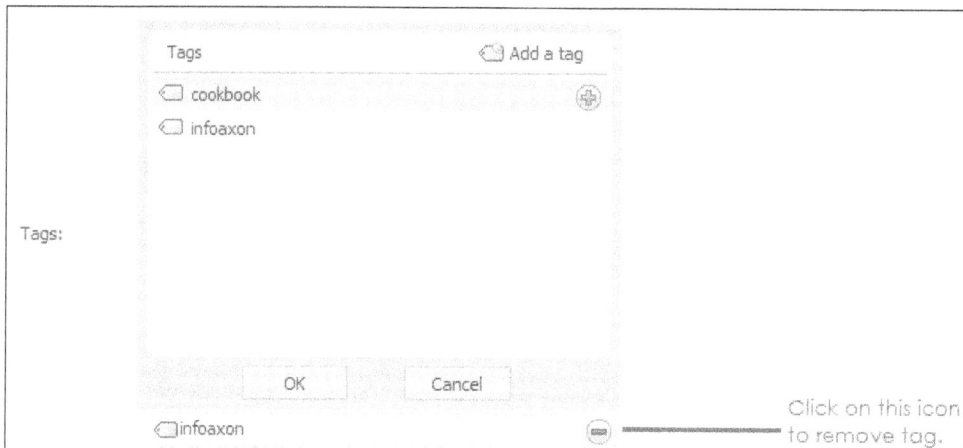

Categorizing content

Categorization enables contents to be grouped and classified. Categories are normally structured as per the organization business taxonomy.

For example, Alfresco comes with a default set of categories which you can use –

1. Regions
2. Software Document Classification
3. Languages

You can create your own categories and classify your documents with those. <<Alfresco administrators can only define new categories other users don't have rights to define new categories in alfresco>>

Getting ready

Let's first have a look at the available categories.

1. Click on the Administration Console link on the top bar.

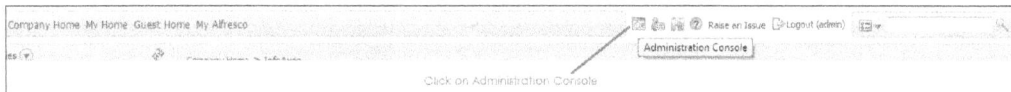

2. Click on **Category Management**. The list of root level categories comes up.

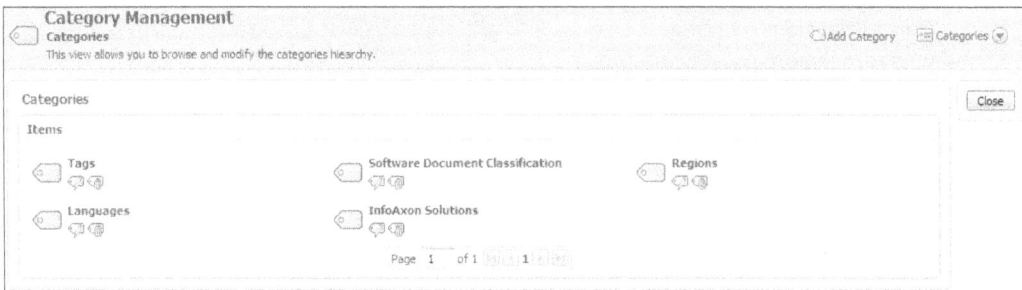

3. Except for the **InfoAxon Solutions**, other categories are supplied by default.

4. This is the **Software Document Classification** category hierarchy.

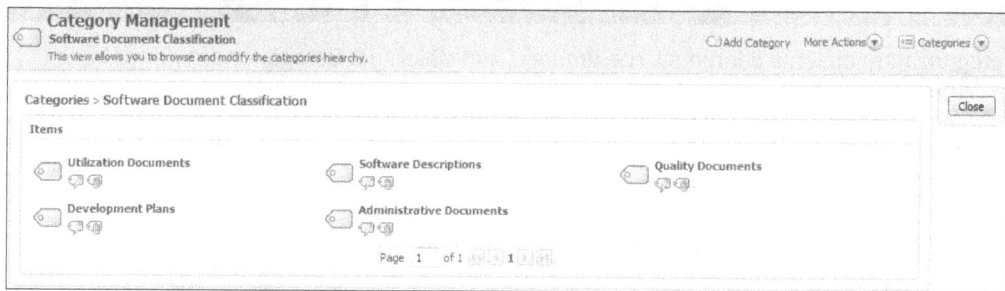

We will use this category further in this recipe.

We again take the `About InfoAxon.html` document to categorize.

How to do it...

1. Open the details screen for this content. Expand the category section. By default, since there is no category associated with this document, it will show the following screenshot:

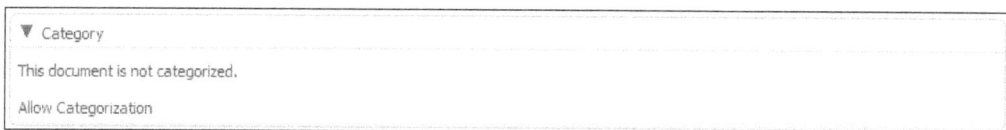

2. First, you will have to allow categorization on this content. For that, click on **Allow Categorization**. A Change Category link will appear, click this to invoke the modify category dialog.

3. Click on **Select** button to open the list of the available categories.

1. Select a category

Software Document Classification ▼ ⊕   ⊕ ———— Clllick here to navigate to
                                                    upper level of this category

⊂⊐ Administrative Documents   ⊕
⊂⊐ Development Plans   ⊕   Click these icons to
⊂⊐ Quality Documents   ⊕ ———— select the category
⊂⊐ Software Descriptions   ⊕
⊂⊐ Utilization Documents   ⊕

Categories:

                        Cancel

2. [Add to List] ————————————————————— Use this button to add the
                                                    selected category in the list

Selected categories

Name

Administrative Documents 🗑 ———————— Click here to remove this
                                                    category from the list

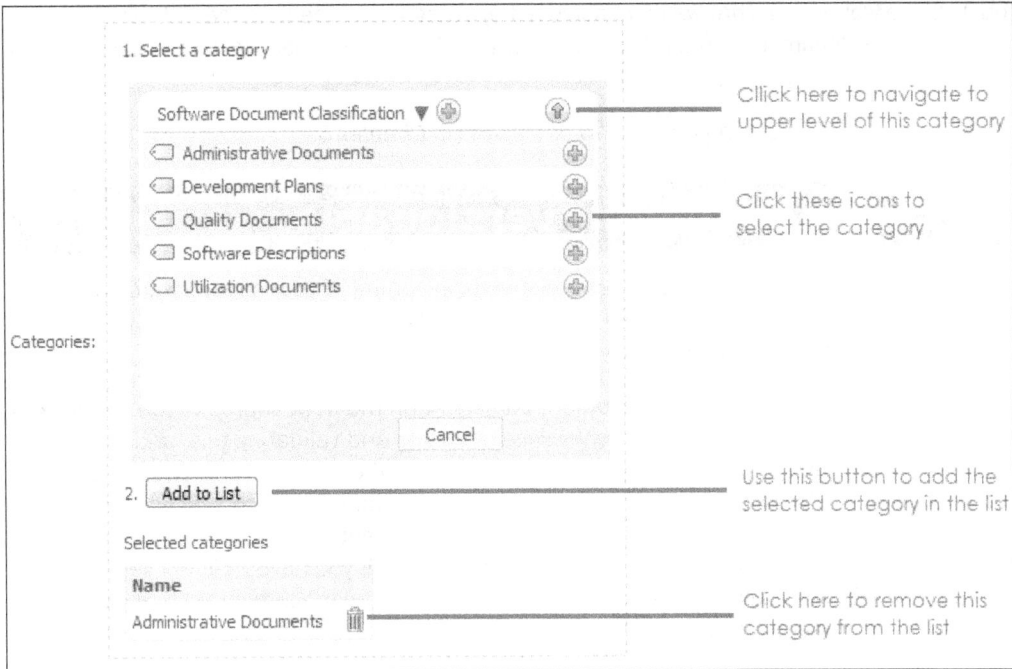

4. Click on the **OK** button to save your categories.

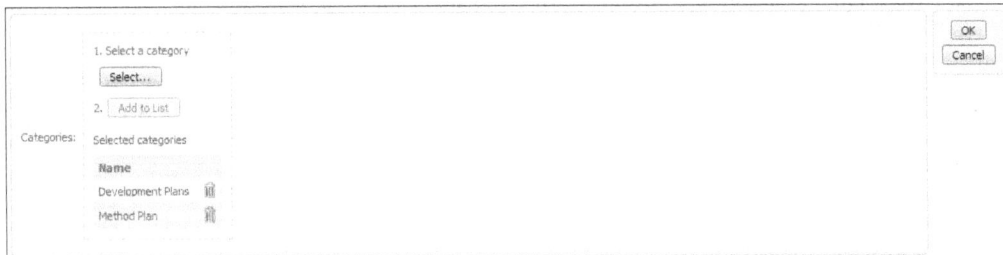

1. Select a category   [OK]
   [Select...]   [Cancel]
2. [Add to List]
Categories: Selected categories
   Name
   Development Plans 🗑
   Method Plan 🗑

5. This brings back the document details page where you can see the associated
    categories in the document.

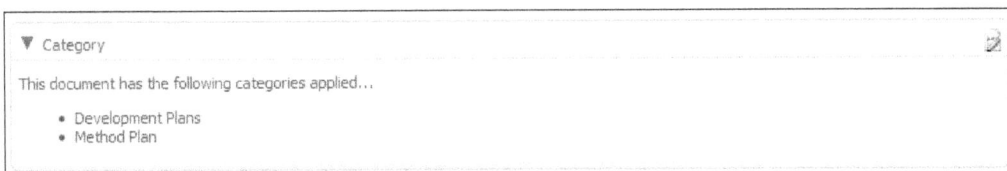

▼ Category   🖉

This document has the following categories applied...

   • Development Plans
   • Method Plan

You must be wondering what we have achieved by categorizing the document. How we can find all the documents under the same category. This we will discuss in our next chapter – *Searching your Content*.

You will also see how you can create new categories in *Chapter 5*.

Making a document versionable

As a software developer, you must be aware of version control of your code. Controlling, managing, and maintaining the history of document versions is equally important in the context of a document management system.

Imagine that you are writing the requirement document on the newest project you are working on. A number of people will probably be involved in writing and validating this; and thus a number of iterations will be taking place for constructing the document and before the document is ultimately finalized. So how will you be able to manage all the versions of the document? Obviously, it is quite difficult to name the document as per the version and change the name every time the version is changed. What happens if you have reached version number 100? You need a version control-enabled document management system. Alfresco provides exactly that and much more beyond that!

How to do it...

1. We once again take the **About InfoAxon.html** document to apply and enable versions.

2. In the details page, the last section is **Version History**. Expanding this will show that the document has no version history. You need to click on **Allow Versioning** for this.

▼ Version History

This document has no version history.

Allow Versioning

3. As soon as you allow the versioning on the document, Alfresco displays its initial version history.

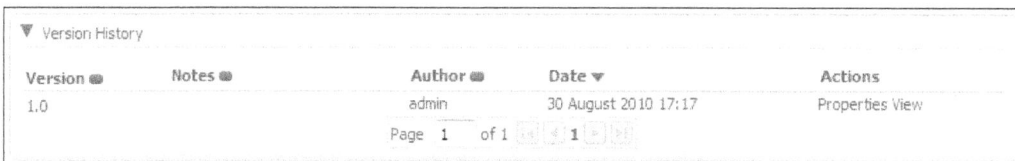

▼ Version History

Version 🔘	Notes 🔘	Author 🔘	Date ▼	Actions
1.0		admin	30 August 2010 17:17	Properties View

Page 1 of 1 ◄◄ ◄ **1** ► ►►

4. Here there is only one version displayed – version **1.0**

How it works...

Now, let's try to work on versioning further on this document.

We click on **Edit Online** from the Action list. Alfresco opens the online HTML editor to enable you to edit the document.

Note the name of the document you are editing. It is **About InfoAxon (Working Copy).html**. This is because Alfresco has automatically checked out the document, and made it ready for you to modify. However, we add a new line in this content and click **Save**.

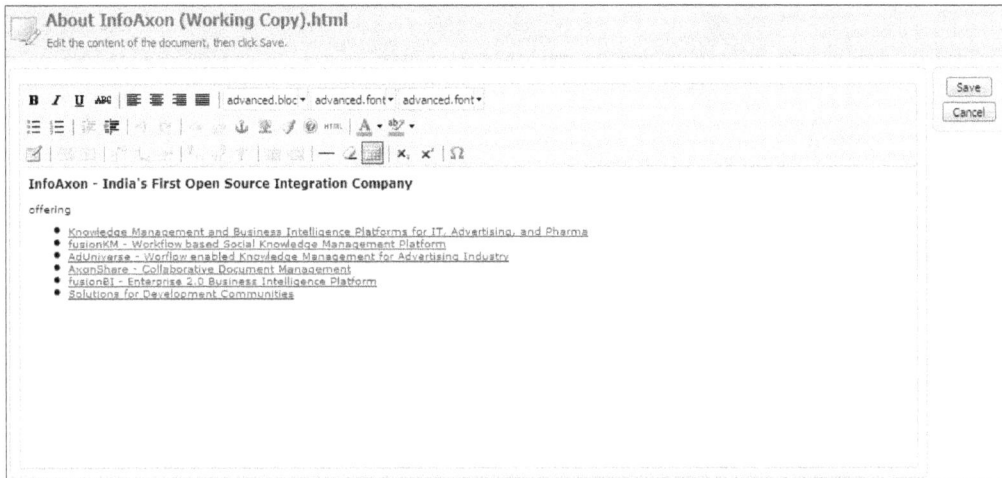

Now notice that you have got a working copy of the document where you can edit the content. Your original document is safe and read-only. Nobody can do anything on the original document until you check-in the working copy.

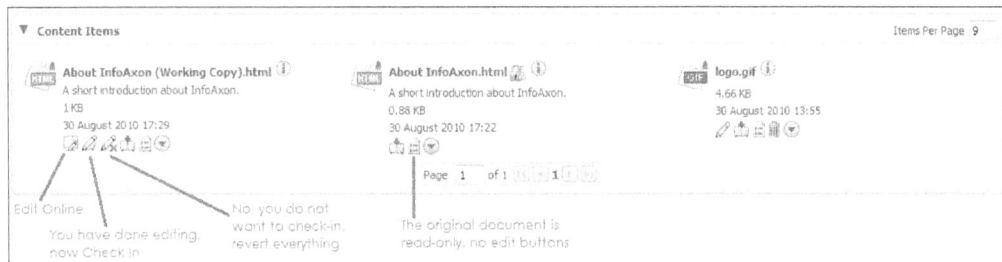

So you click on the **Check In/Done Editing** icon. Alfresco asks about the details of your modification – whether it is a minor change or a major change. You should also put some comments on changes done. Click **OK** after that.

Version Info

This new version has

- ◉ Minor Changes (1.1)
- ○ Major Changes (2.0)

Version Notes

Added another solution offered by InfoAxon.

You can now see the working copy document is gone and the original document has come up with all the operations again activated.

Let's check what happened during this process.

Go to the details page again, and expand the **Version History** section of the document.

▼ Version History

Version ●	Notes ●	Author ●	Date ▼	Actions
1.1	Added another solution offered by InfoAxon.	admin	30 August 2010 17:38	Properties View
1.0		admin	30 August 2010 17:17	Properties View

Page 1 of 1 |◄ ◄ **1** ► ►|

You will see that you have got both the versions of this document. Clicking on the version number will download that version of the document. You can also see the properties values of the document, as per the particular version.

Note that Alfresco also remembers the values of the properties in **Version History**.

3
Securing and Searching Contents

This chapter contains the following recipes:

- ▶ Creating users
- ▶ Creating groups
- ▶ Adding users in groups
- ▶ Securing your folders
- ▶ Securing your files
- ▶ Searching in Alfresco
- ▶ Performing a normal search
- ▶ Performing an advanced search
- ▶ Using the saved search

Introduction

Once you have uploaded your content to a CMS system, the next major challenge is to secure your content from unauthorized usage. Taking the role of the content manager in an organization becomes a thing of paramount importance as there are confidential documents which not everybody should see and access.

Security, in a broader context, can be divided into two parts – Authentication and Authorization.

Authentication means how the user's identity is validated; how to determine whether the person trying to access the system is a valid and registered user or not. You normally do this every time and everywhere by putting your username and password. In Alfresco, however, you can perform authentication in several ways such as, standard Alfresco login, LDAP integration, and so on.

Authorization comes into picture after the user is authenticated, that means the system has recognized that the person is a valid user. Now the system needs to know what this particular user can do and what he cannot do – this mechanism is Authorization.

Some very common authorization aspects which you would like to cover are:

- ▸ Read access
- ▸ Delete access
- ▸ Update access

Alfresco has a flexible security system which you can use to manage the security of your content.

Searching is another imperative necessity in a content management system. Putting lots of documents into the repository won't help if searching for content is not possible or not so powerful.

This chapter helps you explore the authorization implementations using Alfresco Explorer so that you can secure your content from unauthorized access. We will also discover about the search mechanism in the Alfresco repository.

The Alfresco security model

Very simply put, Alfresco security model can be translated as:

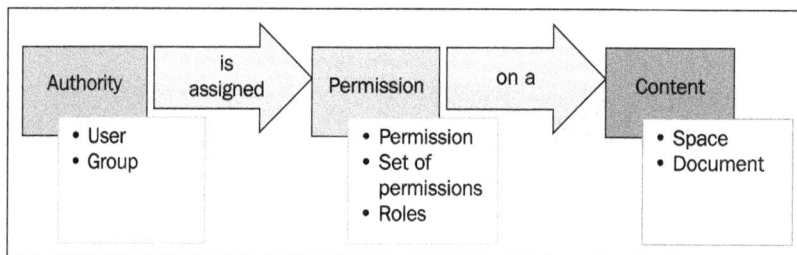

- ▸ **Authority** can be a single user or a group of users.
- ▸ **Permission** can be a single permission or a set of permissions.
- ▸ **Content** can be a space or a document uploaded.

Thus, Alfresco helps you to assign Permission(s) for using Content(s) to a particular Authority group (s).

In addition, some of the functionalities that come under the security umbrella of Alfresco are:

- ▸ Users and user management
- ▸ Provision of personal information about users
- ▸ Groups and group management
- ▸ Ownership of nodes within the repository
- ▸ Repository wide permissions
- ▸ Permissions at the node level
- ▸ Access control, to restrict calls to public services to suitable authenticated users.

Alfresco comes up with five built-in roles which you use in order to give proper access controls to different users.

- ▸ **Consumer**: This role has only `Read` permission. Users having this role can only read content and cannot change anything.
- ▸ **Editor**:This includes `Write` and `Checkout` permissions in addition to Consumer permissions. These users, however, cannot create new content and cannot upload documents.
- ▸ **Contributor**: In addition to editor permissions, this adds the `AddChildren` permission. Means users having this role will be able to upload new documents and will be able to create content.
- ▸ **Collaborator**: Collaborators are a combination of editor and contributor roles.
- ▸ **Coordinator**: Users of this role will have all permissions of a particular content.

Thus, whenever you want to allocate permissions to a user on one of your spaces or a document, you normally assign one or many of these roles to the users on a particular content.

We will explore how to do this later in this chapter

Creating users

This recipe helps you understand how to create users in Alfresco.

How to do it...

1. In the Alfresco explorer application, log in as the administrator. Click on the **Administration Console** icon from the top toolbar.

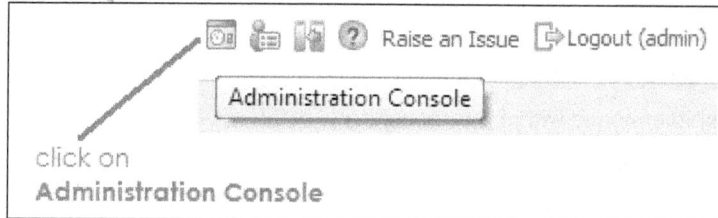

2. Click on **Manage System Users**.

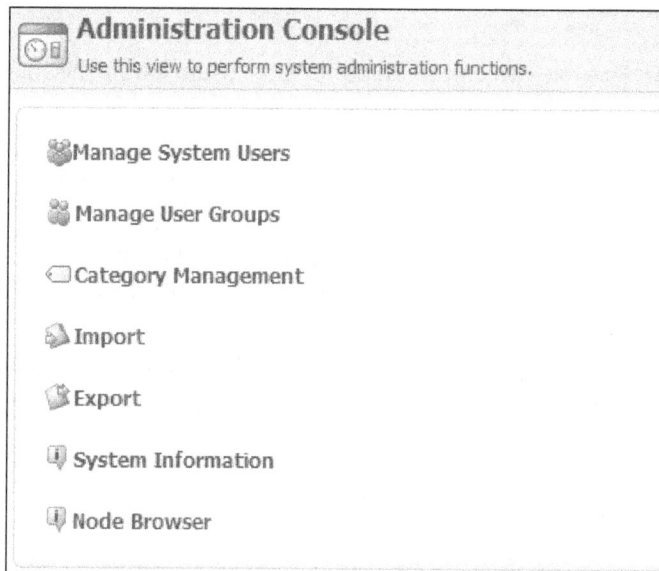

3. In the next screen, click on **Create User**.

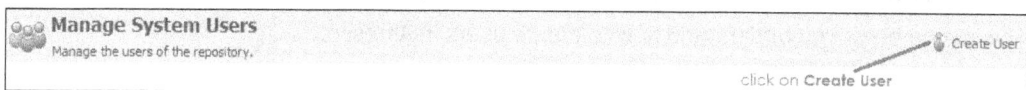

4. In the next screens, Alfresco asks you the details of the new user. The new user details form is divided into two main screens.

5. **Person Properties** screen expects you to enter the individual's details – name, e-mail address, company name, organization, IM name, storage quota, and so on. Feed the proper details and click **Next**.

> There are some extra properties for the user provided by Alfresco such as **Organization**, **Job Title**, **Location**, **Skype Id**, and so on. These properties can be used for populating full user details in an organization.
>
> The user's **Quota** also can be set up; this is useful to restrict how much space the user can consume by uploading contents in the repository.

New User Wizard
This wizard helps you to add a user to the repository.

Steps	Step One - Person Properties	
1. Person Properties	Enter information about this person.	Next
2. User Properties		Back
3. Summary	**Person Properties**	Finish
	First Name: Snig	Cancel
	Last Name: Bhaumik	
	Email snig.bhaumik@gmail.com	

6. Next screen asks you to enter the user details of this person in Alfresco – username, password, user's home space, and so on. This **Username** is the login name of the user; this must to be unique across this installation of Alfresco.

7. The **Home Space Location** is normally **User Homes**. Though you can change it, but in our example, we will keep it the same. In this case, we must write the **Home Space Name**. This will be the home space of this particular user. Upon completing all information, click **Next**.

New User Wizard
This wizard helps you to add a user to the repository.

Steps	Step Two - User Properties	
1. Person Properties	Enter information about this user.	Next
2. User Properties		Back
3. Summary	**User Properties**	Finish
	User Name: snig.bhaumik	Cancel
	Password: ••••	
	Confirm: ••••	
	Home Space	
	Home Space Location: User Homes	
	Home Space Name: snig.bhaumik	
	To continue click Next.	

8. The next screen is just to confirm all information you have entered is correct. Click on **Finish** to complete the operation.

9. The application goes back to the manage users screen. Click on the **Show All** button to see the registered users in your system.

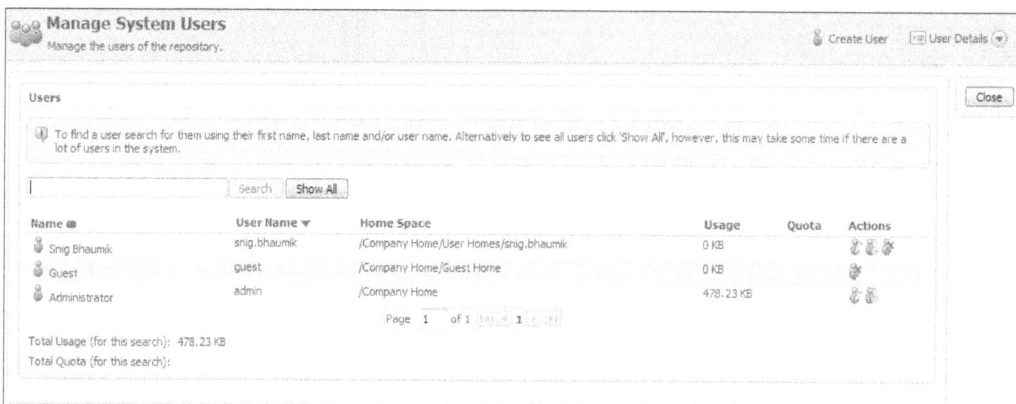

There's more...

Guest and **Administrator** are built-in users that come with the Alfresco installation. And now the new user we have added is coming into the list. Clicking **Close** will bring you back to the **Administration Console**.

Creating groups

As you have understood, users are assigned to different roles for a particular content. For example, a particular user can have the Collaborator role for a space and the same user can have the Consumer role for another space.

However, in an enterprise-wide installation, you, of course, will have to maintain many users. Assigning the roles for each user for different content will be a troublesome and lengthy exercise. You cannot manage this easily either.

For that, you create a group of users and assign roles to the group, instead of each individual user.

How to do it...

1. In the Alfresco explorer application, log in as the administrator user. Click on the **Administration Console** icon from the top toolbar. Then click on **Manage user Groups**.

2. The next screen displays all available groups in Alfresco, click on **Create Group**.

3. Creating a group is rather easy, it requires only one parameter – the name (identifier) of the group. Let's name it **Alfresco Cookbook Authors**.

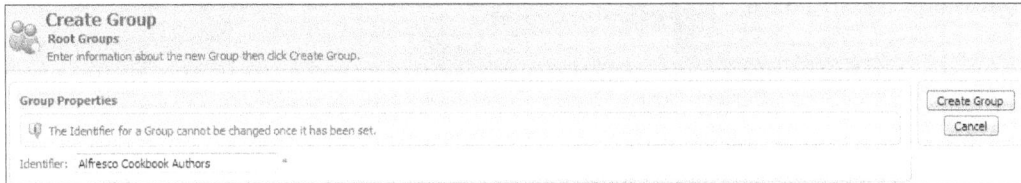

4. Clicking on the **Create Group** button will create the group in Alfresco.

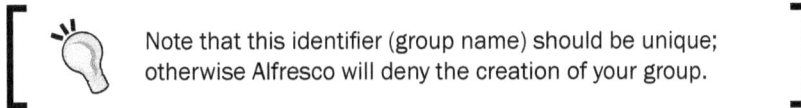

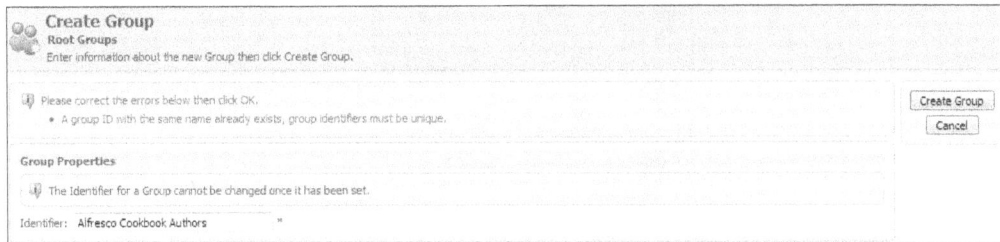

> Note that this identifier (group name) should be unique; otherwise Alfresco will deny the creation of your group.

5. You are now brought back to the Group Management screen. Click on the **Show All** button to see all the available groups in the system.

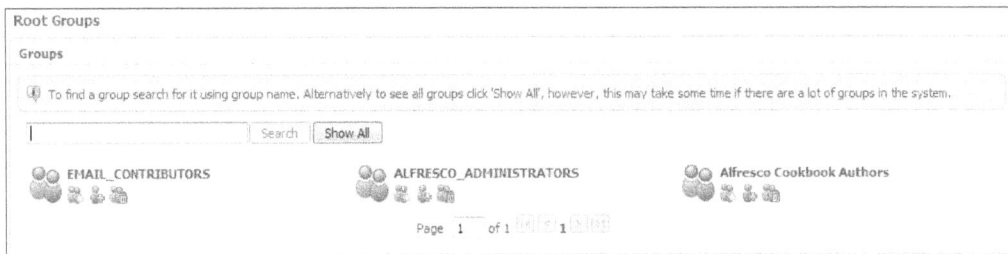

6. Alfresco comes with two default groups created – **EMAIL_CONTRIBUTORS** and **ALFRESCO_ADMINISTRATORS**. You will see our newly created group here.

Adding users into groups

Now, as you know about how to create users and new groups, let's explore the process to add users into the user groups.

How to do it...

1. In the Alfresco explorer application, log in as the administrator user. Click on the **Administration Console** icon from the top toolbar. Then click on **Manage user Groups**.

2. Click on the **Show All** button. Alfresco displays all the available root level groups. The new group we have created **Alfresco Cookbook Authors** is also listed.

3. Click on the **Add User** icon corresponding to the **Alfresco Cookbook Authors** group.

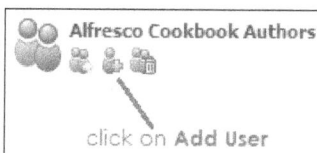

4. That invokes the interface for associating new users to this group.

5. First you need to search for the user you want to associate with the group. For that, you write the name of the user in the search box. However, in case you are not very sure about the name of the user, Alfresco helps.

6. You need to write any character of the username you want to add. For example, I have entered only **m** in the search box, clicked **search** – and Alfresco came up with all the users who have **m** in the name somewhere.

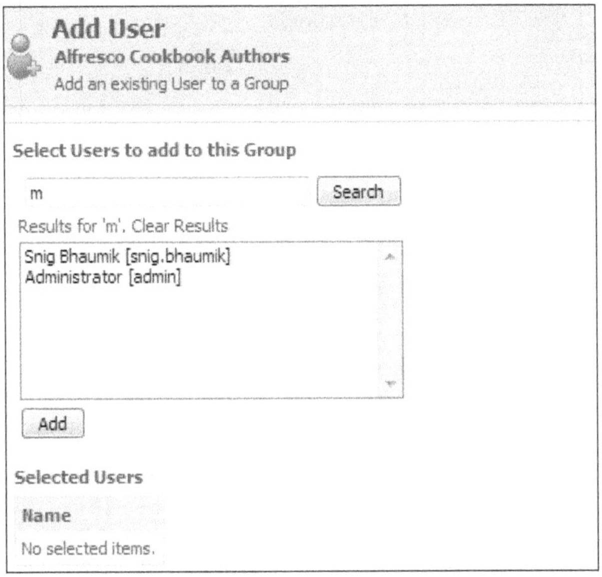

Add User

Alfresco Cookbook Authors

Add an existing User to a Group

Select Users to add to this Group

m   [Search]

Results for 'm'. Clear Results

Snig Bhaumik [snig.bhaumik]
Administrator [admin]

[Add]

Selected Users

Name

No selected items.

7. Select the particular user you want to associate and click **Add**. In the following **Selected Users** list, all chosen users will be accumulated.

Add User
Alfresco Cookbook Authors
Add an existing User to a Group

Select Users to add to this Group

m   Search

Results for 'm'. Clear Results

Snig Bhaumik [snig.bhaumik]
Administrator [admin]

Add

Selected Users

Name

Snig Bhaumik 🗑

8. In this way, keep on searching and adding users you want to associate with this group. Finally, click on **OK**. The main **Root Groups** screen re-appears.

9. Click again on **Show All**. And click on the **Alfresco Cookbook Authors** group name. Details of this group are rendered. You can see the new user(s) associated with this group.

Root Groups > **Alfresco Cookbook Authors**

Groups

Users

Snig Bhaumik
snig.bhaumik

There's more...

There are more functionalities that can be done for group management. For example, adding subgroups. We will cover these in the recipe *Managing user groups* in *Chapter 5*.

Securing your folders

Now that you can create new users, new user groups, and can add new users into groups, it's time to use these. We will now see how we can apply permissions on your folders or spaces and secure them.

How to do it...

1. Let's create a new folder to learn how to secure your folders. Go to the **InfoAxon** folder we created earlier, and create a new space named **Chapter 3**.

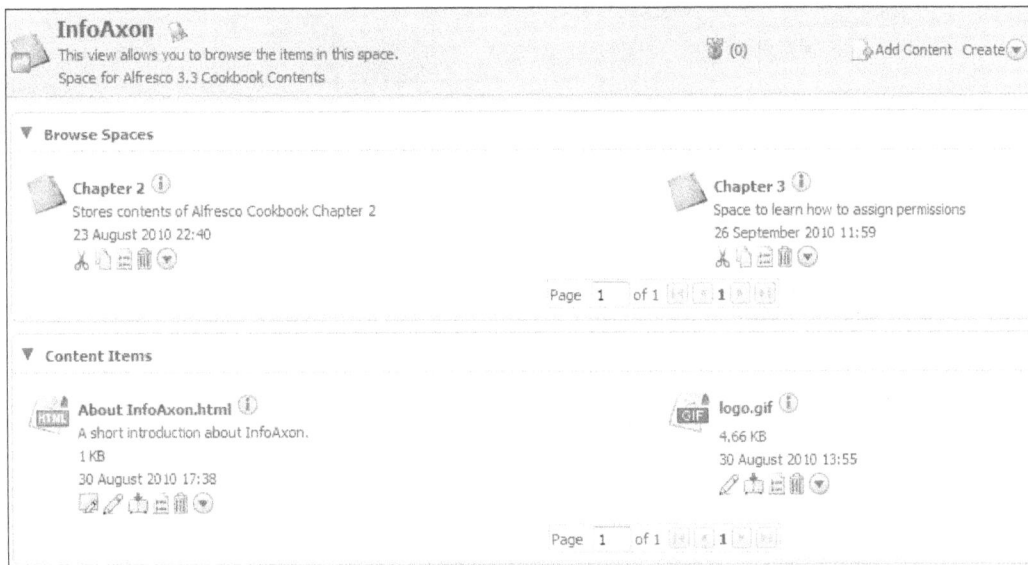

InfoAxon
This view allows you to browse the items in this space.
Space for Alfresco 3.3 Cookbook Contents

(0)   Add Content Create

▼ Browse Spaces

Chapter 2 ⓘ
Stores contents of Alfresco Cookbook Chapter 2
23 August 2010 22:40

Chapter 3 ⓘ
Space to learn how to assign permissions
26 September 2010 11:59

Page 1   of 1   1

▼ Content Items

About InfoAxon.html ⓘ
A short introduction about InfoAxon.
1 KB
30 August 2010 17:38

logo.gif ⓘ
4.66 KB
30 August 2010 13:55

Page 1   of 1   1

2. Click on the **View Details** icon of **Chapter 3**.

3. In the details interface, click on the **Manage Space Users** link.

4. **Manage Space Users** screen comes up. You will use this interface to manage the users and groups that have permissions in this space.

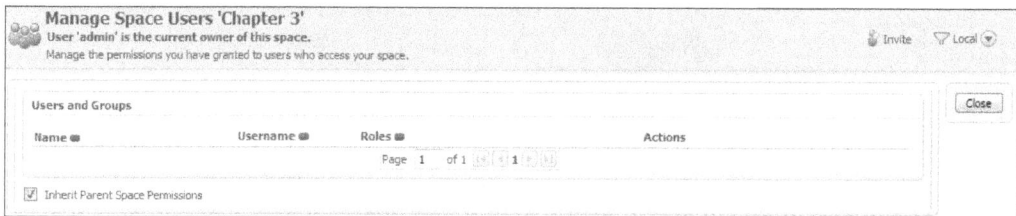

5. At this point of time, the list of users is blank. By default, Alfresco only *inherits permissions* from the parent space.

6. *Inheriting Permission* means just duplicating whatever permission settings are there in the parent folder. This is just like inheritance works in typical Object-Oriented designs. You can, however, stop inheriting permissions by de-selecting the **Inherit Parent Space Permissions** checkbox.

7. Now, we will assign permission to a user for this folder. Before we do that, let's see what the user `snig.bhaumik` can do in this folder – meaning what permission he has in this folder.

8. In order to check this, let's log in through this user and navigate to the folder `InfoAxon`.

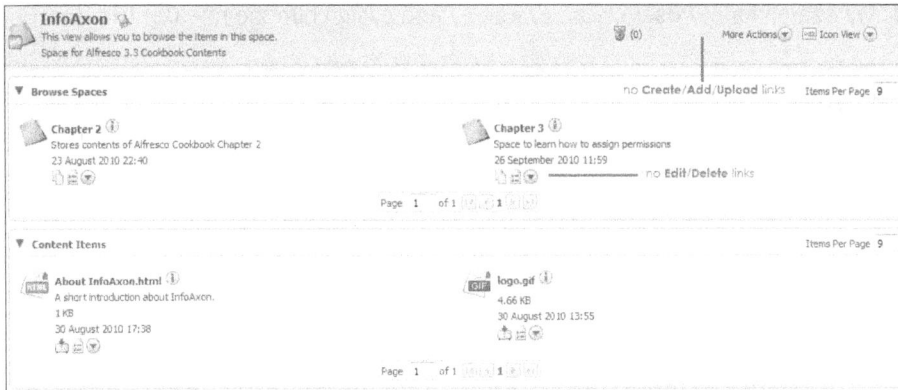

9. Here, we can see there is no add, edit, delete, create, or upload links and operations available to this user. If you open the folder `Chapter 3`, you won't find any of these functionalities available for this user there.

10. This is because, by default, the `snig.bhaumik` user only has _consumer_ access to this folder, which means _read-only_ access.

11. Now, let's assign some permission to this user. For that, you log in using the `admin` user. And again navigate to the **Manage Space Users** of **Chapter 3** (just like step no 4 in this recipe). Click on the **Invite** link in this screen.

12. The process of giving certain permissions to users is done by _inviting_ users to that particular space.
Search for your user (or group) by writing in the name in the search box. After that, choose the role that you want to give to the user. Click on **Add to List** after selecting the suitable role.

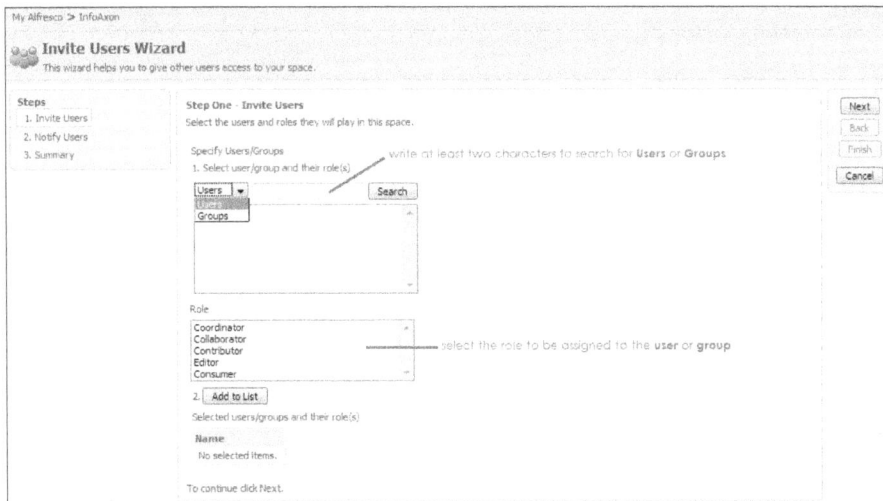

13. We search for our user `snig.bhaumik` and assign him the role **Contributor**.

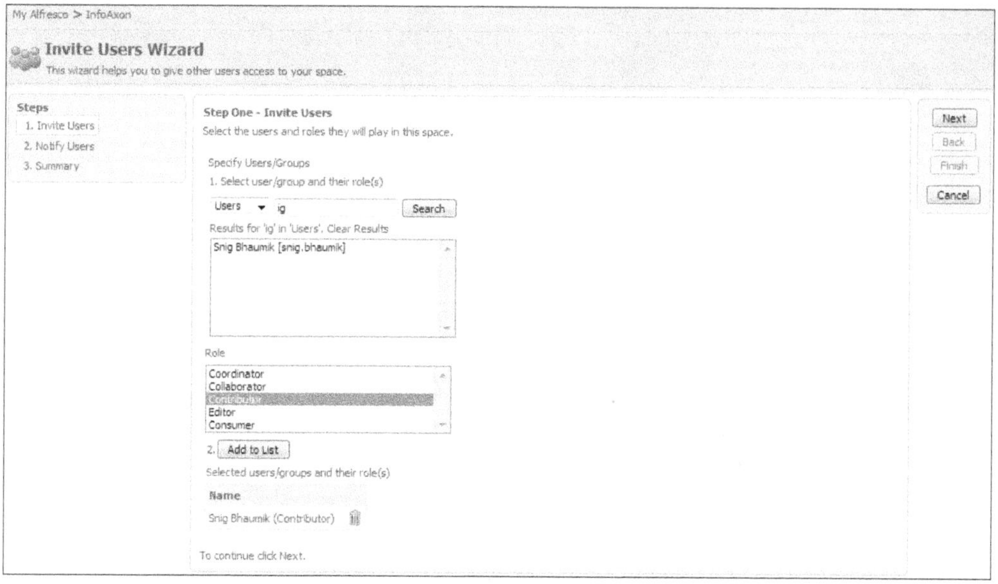

14. As you know, the contributor role comes with **read**, **write**, **check-in, check-out**, and **addchildren** permissions. So by giving this role to this user, you have actually given him all these permissions to this particular folder. Click **Next**.

15. The next screen offers you to send an e-mail to the concerned user(s) that they have been assigned roles in this folder.

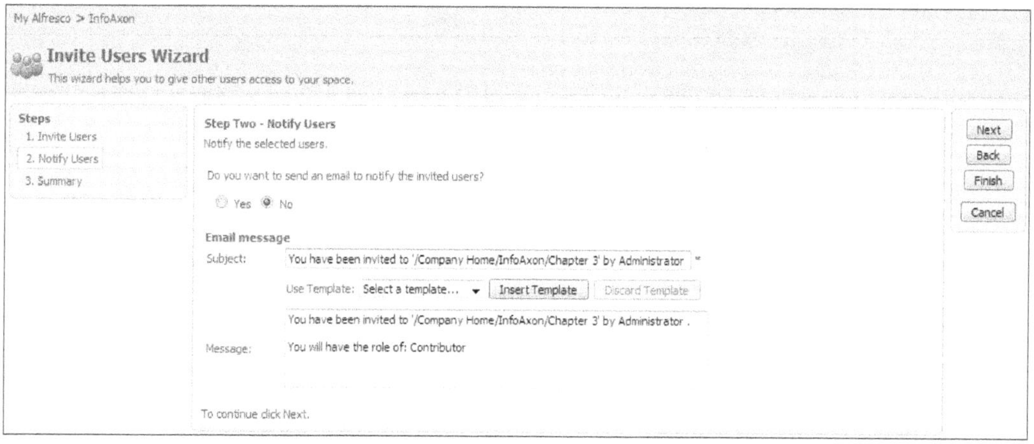

16. However, for now, we choose not to send any emails. So just click **Finish**.

17. The next screen shows that the **Snig Bhaumik** has been added as a user for this space.

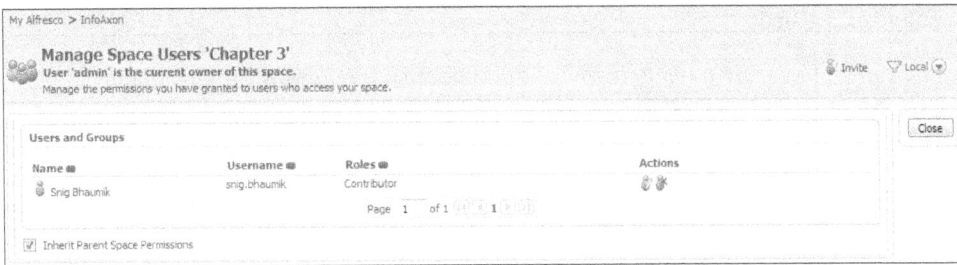

18. Well, now let's check whether and how the permission has been assigned. For that, again log in as **Snig Bhaumik** and navigate to the space Chapter 3.

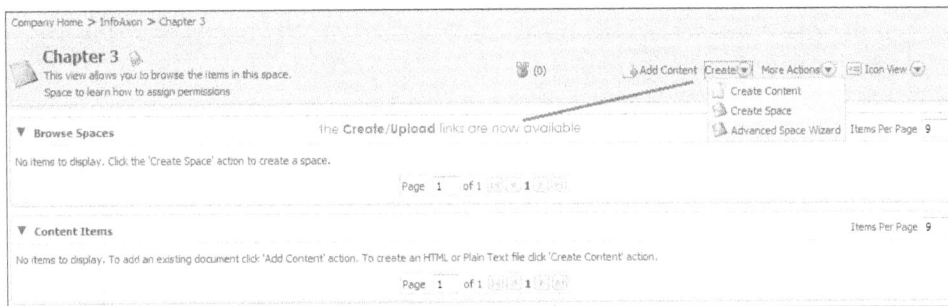

19. Now you can see the **Create Content** and **Add Content** links are available to this user. Try uploading a document here.

How it works...

You have just seen that, by default, the user **Snig Bhaumik** didn't have any permission on folder Chapter 3. However, after assigning the role **Contributor** to this user on this space, he could upload new contents. He also has edit permissions to all the contents uploaded in this space.

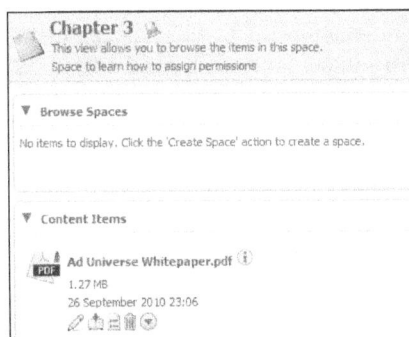

Thus, if a user is given permissions to a particular space, he will have similar permissions to all the contents of that space – if the **Inherit Parent Space Permissions** option is selected for the content to the user.

Similarly, he will have same rights to all the sub-folders if the **Inherit Parent Space Permissions** option is selected for the same.

In this way, you can manage the permissions of the spaces of your repository – you can control who can do what. As you have assigned only the **Contributor** role to this user, many operations will not be available to this user.

Securing your files

Assigning roles and permissions to a particular content is not very much different from assigning the same to a particular space. The difference is that once you assign some rights to a user for a space, the rights are automatically inherited to all the contents and sub-folders of that space; whereas, in case of content, this applies to and affects only that particular content.

How to do it...

Let's now explore how to assign permissions to a group. Create a new user named, say, william.jones. Also for this example, we will consider the AdUniverse Whitepaper.pdf document we have uploaded earlier. As in the previous case, this user won't have any rights to the space Chapter 3 and to this document – only **read-only** access would be there.

We will now try to assign permissions to the group **Alfresco Cookbook Authors** to this space. As you know, assigning permissions to groups actually translates to assigning the same permissions to all users under that particular group.

1. First add the user **william.jones** to this group.

2. Then assign the **Editor** role to this group.

Company Home > InfoAxon > Chapter 3

Invite Content Users Wizard
This wizard helps you to give other users access to your content.

Steps	Step One - Invite Users	
1. Invite Users	Select the users and roles they will play for this content.	Next
2. Notify Users		Back
3. Summary	Specify Users/Groups	Finish
	1. Select user/group and their role(s)	Cancel

Groups ▼ alf   [Search]

Results for 'alf' in 'Groups'. Clear Results

```
Alfresco Cookbook Authors
ALFRESCO_ADMINISTRATORS
EVERYONE
```

Role
```
Coordinator
Collaborator
Contributor
Editor
Consumer
```

2. [Add to List]

Selected users/groups and their role(s)

Name

Alfresco Cookbook Authors (Editor)

To continue click Next.

3. Finish the process without sending an e-mail notification. You can see that this group has been included in the users' list of this content.

Company Home > InfoAxon > Chapter 3

Manage Content Users 'Ad Universe Whitepaper.pdf'
User 'snig.bhaumik' is the current owner of this content.
Manage the permissions you have granted to users who access your content.

Invite   Local ▼

Users and Groups   [Close]

Name ●	Username ●	Roles ●	Actions
Alfresco Cookbook Authors	Alfresco Cookbook Authors	Editor	

Page 1   of 1

☑ Inherit Parent Space Permissions

4. Now, let's log in as `william.jones` and open the details interface of this document.

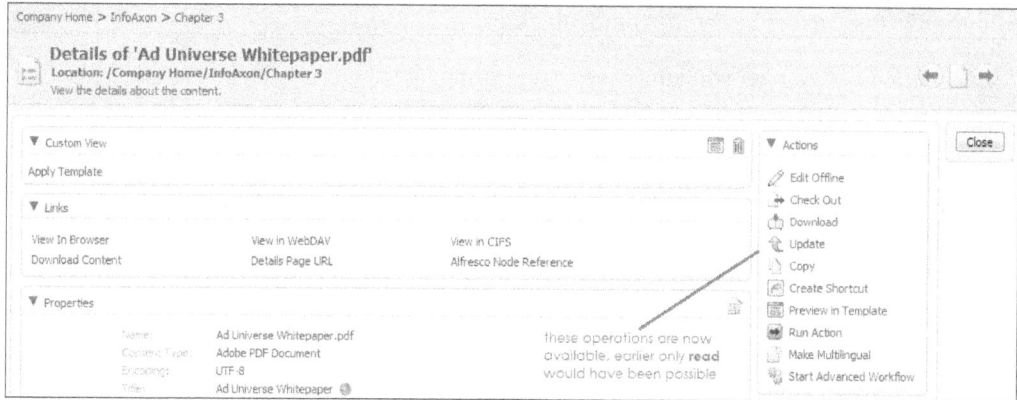

5. Now this user (william.jones) has rights to update the document, check-in or check-out the document etc.

How it works...

As you have seen, by default, users have only read permissions to spaces and documents (except of their own home spaces). And you can use the built-in roles to assign various rights and permissions to different users – using an individual user or using groups.

The limitation is that, in this process, you can only use the default available roles and you do not have much scope to make any permutation and combination of different rights and create custom roles. In an advanced scenario, this situation is not rare. Creating new roles and customizing the permission settings of Alfresco is not a part of the scope of this book, however, using **JavaScipt APIs**, you can still perform some of these tasks. We will explore more on this in *Chapter 8*.

Searching in Alfresco

Once you have uploaded your content and documents in the repository and your team is also continuously uploading documents, it is now required to have a potent search functionality that can help you to find your document correctly and easily.

The Search functionality is one of the important aspects when choosing a CMS, and as you may know, Alfresco uses the **Apache Lucene search engine**; a high-performance, full-featured text search engine.

Along with the Lucene search engine, Alfresco's search capability is powered by Open Office, which is able to extract text from many file formats and make them available to the Lucene search engine. Thus, Alfresco, as a Content Management System, provides a powerful search mechanism by which users can easily search and find documents they are looking for.

Searching for content is normally done by users by *keywords* and *metadata*. Metadata means a property of files such as name, title, author, description, date, and so on. For example, you may want to find all files that are written by Patrick; or you may be looking for a document which is named "something like cookbook". These cases are examples of searching files by metadata. In addition to these, also you want to perform *full-text search* very often. For example, you may want to find the documents which have Alfresco mentioned somewhere. Alfresco provides both these functionalities very flexibly.

All of this is possible because Alfresco makes Lucene index all metadata of the documents uploaded in the repository, Lucene also performs full-text indexing of the documents uploaded.

Alfresco provides two types of searches by the Explorer application – simple search and advanced search. We will explore more on these searches in the next couple of recipes.

Performing normal search

Simple normal search means you do not have much control over on which parameters the search will be performed. This search you normally execute very frequently because you usually look for documents by name and also probably by contents.

Hence, the normal search is available in the application interface very easily in the top-right corner.

How to do it...

1. Open Alfresco Explorer and log in with a valid user.
2. On the top-right corner the search box is available. Write the keyword you want to search and press *Enter* or the go icon on the right-hand side.

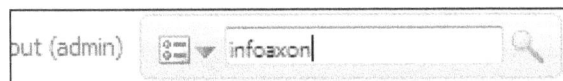

3. Alfresco comes up with the content items and spaces by this keyword.

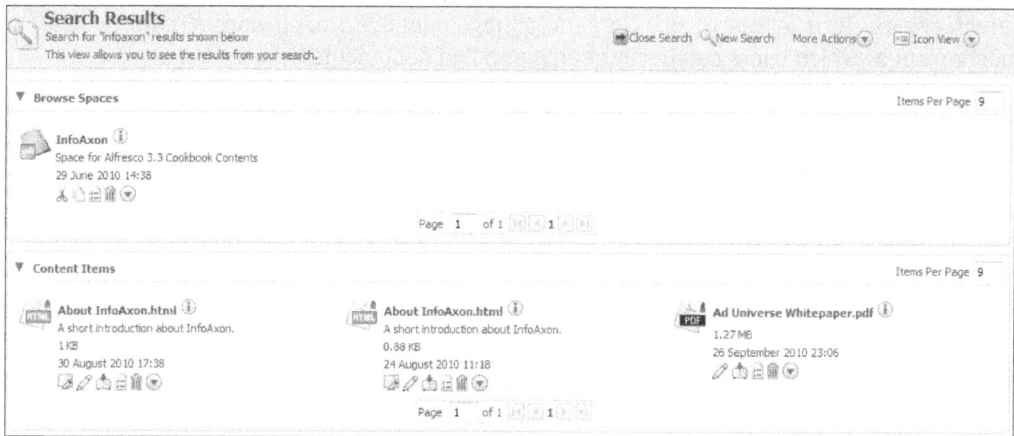

4. One space and a couple of content items have been found. This is because Alfresco has searched by the name of documents, the name of the spaces, and also inside the content of the documents.

5. It is interesting to see the `About InfoAxon.html` document has been displayed twice here – each of these corresponds to one version of the document. As you can remember we had uploaded a new version of this document in *Chapter 2*'s recipe, *Making a document versionable*. So, Alfresco search engine found this twice and displayed twice. And, the `Ad Universe Whitepaper.pdf` document has the `infoaxon` keyword in the content.

6. However, you can control what to search and what not in normal search. Click on the down arrow link left of the search box. The following options will be presented. By default, Alfresco searched for **All Items** – and the name of spaces, documents, and contents were searched.

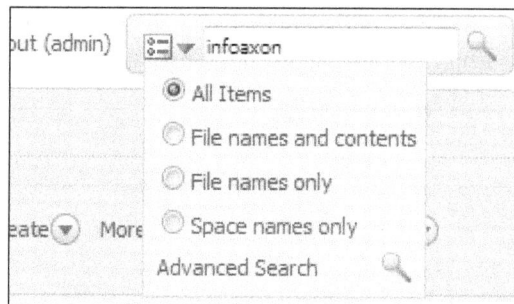

7. Now, let's explore the search operation by selecting each of these options, with the same keyword – `infoaxon`.

8. Select **File names and contents** and perform the same search operation. This is the output, as you can see, no space is found in this case.

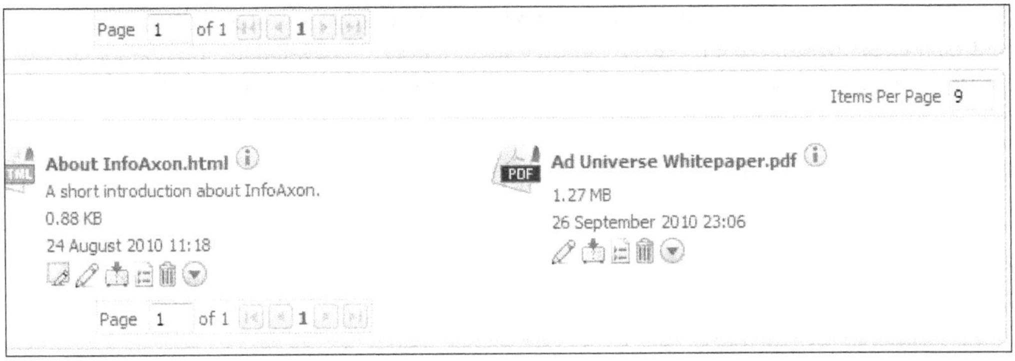

Page 1 of 1 |◄ ◄ **1** ► ►|

Items Per Page 9

About InfoAxon.html ⓘ
A short introduction about InfoAxon.
0.88 KB
24 August 2010 11:18

Ad Universe Whitepaper.pdf ⓘ
1.27 MB
26 September 2010 23:06

Page 1 of 1 |◄ ◄ **1** ► ►|

9. Select the **File names only** option. In this case, the `Ad Universe Whitepaper.pdf` document is not listed as now the search operation has not been held in the contents of documents.

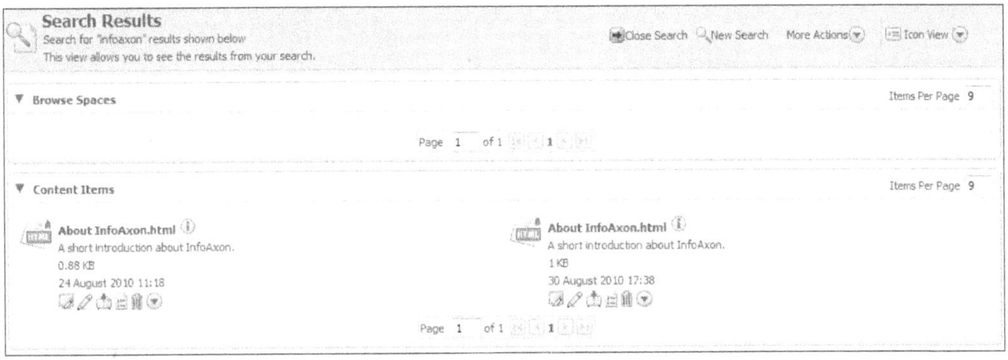

Search Results
Search for "infoaxon" results shown below
This view allows you to see the results from your search.

⊕Close Search 🔍New Search   More Actions▼   ⊞ Icon View▼

▼ Browse Spaces

Items Per Page 9

Page 1 of 1 |◄ ◄ 1 ► ►|

▼ Content Items

Items Per Page 9

About InfoAxon.html ⓘ
A short introduction about InfoAxon.
0.88 KB
24 August 2010 11:18

About InfoAxon.html ⓘ
A short introduction about InfoAxon.
1 KB
30 August 2010 17:38

Page 1 of 1 |◄ ◄ 1 ► ►|

10. Select **Space names only**. Here only one space has been found out, no documents and files.

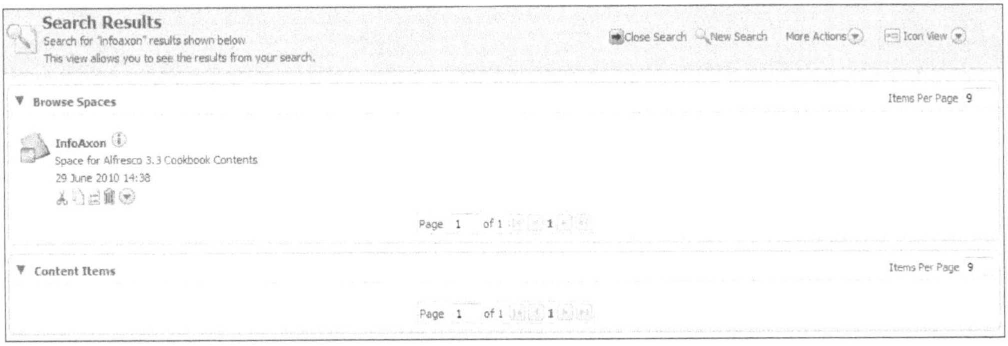

Search Results
Search for "infoaxon" results shown below
This view allows you to see the results from your search.

⊕Close Search 🔍New Search   More Actions▼   ⊞ Icon View▼

▼ Browse Spaces

Items Per Page 9

InfoAxon ⓘ
Space for Alfresco 3.3 Cookbook Contents
29 June 2010 14:38

Page 1 of 1 |◄ ◄ 1 ► ►|

▼ Content Items

Items Per Page 9

Page 1 of 1 |◄ ◄ 1 ► ►|

Performing advanced search

Though the normal search does provide a little bit of flexibility over searching of contents and controlling what to search, it is still limited to these four options available. You cannot control the metadata search scope. Normal search will try to find documents from the full repository, you cannot control where to search and where not.

In order to perform a more powerful and controlled search operation, you must exercise advanced search.

How to do it...

1. Open Alfresco Explorer and log in with a valid user.

2. On the top-right corner, the search box is available. Open the down arrow and click on **Advanced Search**.

3. In this screen, you can control a number of parameters and scope on which the search should be performed.

   ▸ **Show me results for** section enables you to control what to search – this is much like the normal search parameters which we explored in the previous recipe.

▸ You can control where to search using the **Look in location** section. Clicking on **Click here to select a Space** shows all the spaces in the repository (depending on your rights); you can choose any space from there. **Include child spaces** toggles whether you want to search into all the child spaces or you want to limit your search only to the selected space.

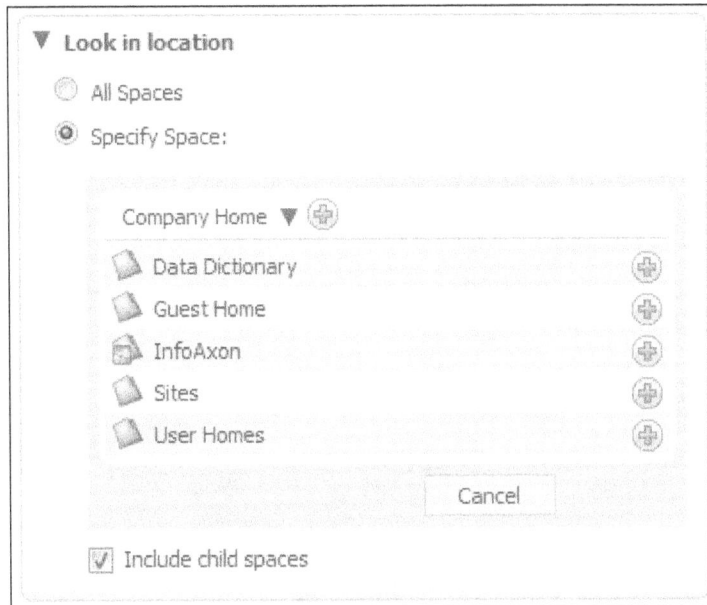

▸ **Show me results in the categories** section helps you to limit your search to only those content items which have the selected categorization. We will explore more on this in later chapters.

▸ **More search options** enable you to restrict on what basis the search should be performed.

    ❑ You can filter search by **Folder Type** – normal space or forum space.

    ❑ Using **Content Type**, you can filter what type of content to be searched. We will study more on content types in *Chapter 6*.

    ❑ **Content Format** enables you to search for any specific type of document such as MS Word, Adobe PDF, JPEG Image, and so on.

    ❑ You can use the **Title**, **Description**, and **Author** parameters if you want to search by these attributes.

    ❑ **Modified Date** and **Created Date** helps you to find documents by date ranges. For example, you are trying to find a document which has been created between a certain period.

□ **Additional options** section, by default, is blank. However, this is used to add your custom properties in the search criteria. We will learn how to do this in *Chapter 7*.

4. Let's see a scenario showing how these search options can be used. For example, you want to find a document(s) which has the word **Alfresco** in the title, the word **cookbook** in the description, **snig** as the author, the create date should be between 20th April 2011 and 30th April 2011, and the document should be PDF. These are the criteria you would like to put.

▼ More search options

Folder Type: Folder   ▾

Content Type: Content   ▾

Content Format: Adobe PDF Document   ▾

Title: alfresco

Description: cookbook

Author: snig

☐ Modified Date:

From: 28 ▾ September ▾ 2010 ▾   Today

To: 28 ▾ September ▾ 2010 ▾   Today

☑ Created Date:

From: 20 ▾ April   ▾ 2011 ▾   Today

To: 30 ▾ April   ▾ 2011 ▾   Today

▶ Additional options

5. After putting all the required search criteria, enter the keyword you want to search in the **Look for** box and click **Search**. The search results will be rendered.

<<Search result also keeps security intact and represents only that content/folder as per the logged in user's roles and permission. This is a major part and needs to be clearly mentioned here>>

Using saved search

Saved search is an interesting feature. As you have seen in the previous recipe, you need to feed a number of parameters in the advanced search interface to find the exact and most relevant document(s). However, doing so every time is definitely a time-consuming and repetitive process – you don't want to do that.

Thus the saved search comes into the picture where you can save the search operation or criteria set. Once you have saved your search, you can retrieve that anytime, and in one click, you can perform the search operation again; without repeating the same entry of search criteria.

What's more, you can save the search for your own use or for all other users also. In Alfresco terms, it is called *Private Search* and *Public Search*.

How to do it...

1. Open Alfresco Explorer and log in with a valid user.

2. Perform a simple search, say the keyword in **infoaxon**. Alfresco will come up with the search results, as you have seen in the previous recipes. Click on the **More Actions – Save New Search** link in this screen.

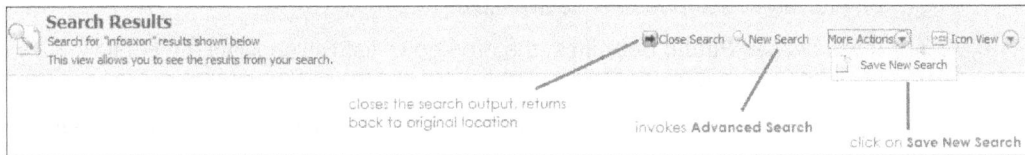

3. In the next screen, Alfresco asks for the **Name** of the saved search and an optional **Description**. Click on **Save** to complete your work.

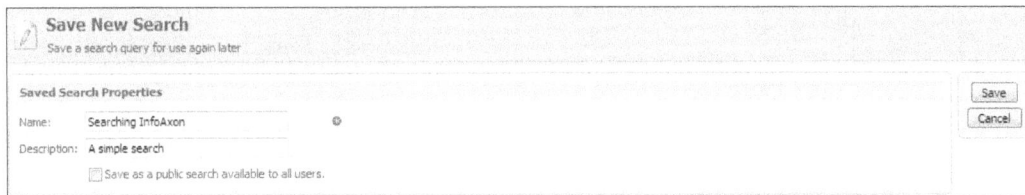

4. If you select the **Save as a public search available to all users** checkbox, this search will be available to all the other users.

5. Now let's check how to use the saved search which we just have created. Click on the **Advanced Search** link (as you have seen in the previous recipe). Open the **Select a Saved Search** drop-down list – **Searching InfoAxon** item is available there.

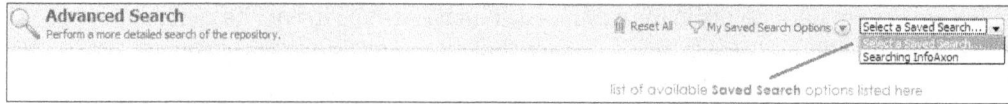

6. Clicking on this item will populate all the search criteria we had entered at the time of saving the search. In our case, we had fed only the keyword, so **infoaxon** is populated in the **Look for** box.

7. Thus you have retrieved all the search parameters you had saved – now you can execute your search using the same criteria.

8. Using the **My Saved Search Options**, you can see all the public saved searches and your own private searches.

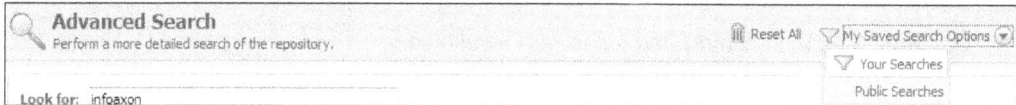

   ▸ If you select **Your Searches**, in the right-hand side drop-down list only your private saved searches will be available.

   ▸ If you choose **Public Searches**, the drop-down list will show all the publicly available saved searches.

9. You can also modify an existing saved search. Use the **More Actions** – **Save Modified Search** option for that.

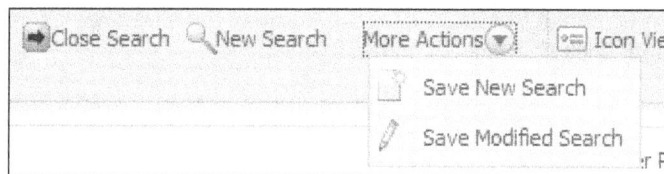

See also

   ▸ *Searching in Alfresco*
   ▸ *Performing a normal search*
   ▸ *Performing an advanced search*

4

Rules—the Smart Spaces

In this chapter, we will cover:

- ► Understanding components of a rule—condition, action, details
- ► Creating and applying rules
- ► Understanding conditions of a rule
- ► Understanding actions that can be performed by rules
- ► Other aspects of rules

Introduction

Rules can be defined as *some actions automatically executed on certain pre-defined events and conditions*.

Rules are instantly triggered whenever the configured event takes place. The rules engine checks the validity of the associated condition. If the condition is satisfied, the defined actions are carried out.

Just as an example, in case you are a database professional, you might be aware of database triggers. A trigger gets automatically fired whenever a certain event happens and it performs certain jobs. Rules are very similar to this. In daily life, you also probably use rules in a number of places – such as Outlook Rules. Alfresco rules are also analogous to this.

Understanding the components of a rule

In today's business, a content management system is not only supposed to manage files, provide document management capabilities, and so on. An enterprise content management system should also manage all the business processes around the enterprise's content.

Rules can be used to implement such Business Requirements, Business Rules, and Scenarios in the whole content management endeavor of your enterprise.

You can leverage Alfresco's powerful and flexible rules engine for performing several business operations automatically every time an event transpires.

How to do it...

For example, your organization may want to send notification mails to a group of people whenever somebody uploads a new document or somebody updates an existing document on a particular space; or you may want to assign a review and approve task someone when a document is uploaded in a space. You may also want to send the notification mail only for PDF documents, but not for MS Word documents.

In many cases, the folder hierarchy of the system for a large organization becomes quite complex and lengthy. Users face a real tough task for uploading a file navigating to the appropriate folder – a rule can be used to automatically organize the documents.

There is no need to write any complex business rule implementation in order to achieve any of these. You can implement these just by configuring rules over spaces.

Rules bring in special characteristics to a space; for example, a rule can be added to a space which will automatically transform any uploaded MS Office documents into Adobe PDF documents – the PDF documents are then watermarked and mailed to certain people. Imagine all these tasks are automatically done for you – without any human interaction and manual processing. Thus, rules can bring extraordinary behavior to spaces – making Smart Spaces.

How it works...

As you have understood, rules are a set of *actions* executed on occurrence of certain *events* depending on some particular *conditions* being satisfied.

Thus, there are three main components that construct a rule.

1. **Condition**: This defines on which content items this particular rule will be executed. This works like filter conditions of the content items. You can define more than one condition for a rule. In that case, all the conditions need to be fulfilled to run the rule. For example, you may want to send a due approval mail to someone only for PDF documents, not for MS Word documents. Thus, in this case, you would set the condition of the rule as – the content item should be an Adobe PDF document, not an MS Word document. Alfresco offers a number of predefined conditions which you can use to establish the actual content condition you are looking for.

2. **Action**: This determines exactly what is to be done as the rule's execution. Similarly, you can define more than one action as well. In our earlier example, sending the due approval e-mail is the action for this rule.

3. **Event**: As the name suggests, this defines on what situation the rule needs to be invoked and fired. Often, the type of the rule is determined by the event on which the rule will be fired. In our example, the event could be whenever a new document is uploaded or created in the particular space.

Thus the flow of execution of a rule is:

1. Whenever the event takes place, the engine triggers the rule execution.
2. Rule's condition is then evaluated. If the condition is satisfied, the rule is executed.
3. The execution of the rule means that the configured action is performed.

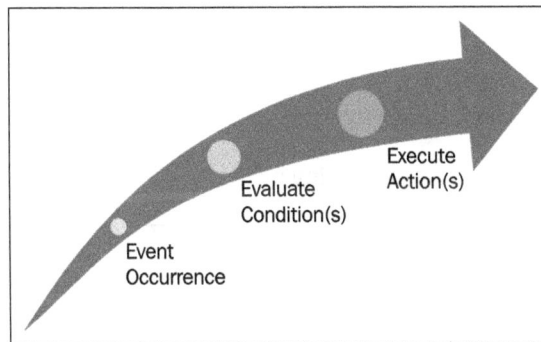

A rule can be configured and applied with space only, it cannot be associated with a content item. However, rules do operate on individual content items and sub-spaces of that particular space.

Creating and applying rules

Now as we understand the basic structure and purpose of rules, we will see how to create and apply a rule on a specific space.

Let's take a specific scenario; let's say, you want to automatically convert your MS Word documents into an Adobe PDF document. We will see how to do these using rules.

How to do it...

1. Open Alfresco Explorer and log in with a suitable user.

2. Create a new space (say **Chapter 4**) in our **InfoAxon** space.

3. Open the **Chapter 4** space by clicking on it.

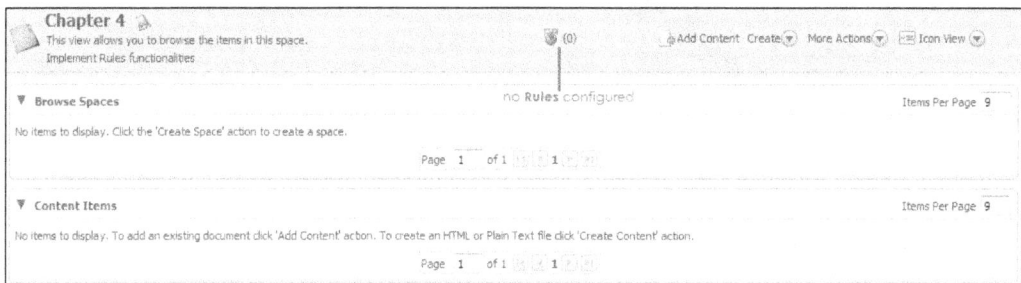

4. You can see there are no content items; no rules are configured in this space.

5. Now let's create a new rule. Click on **More Actions** and **Manage Content Rules**.

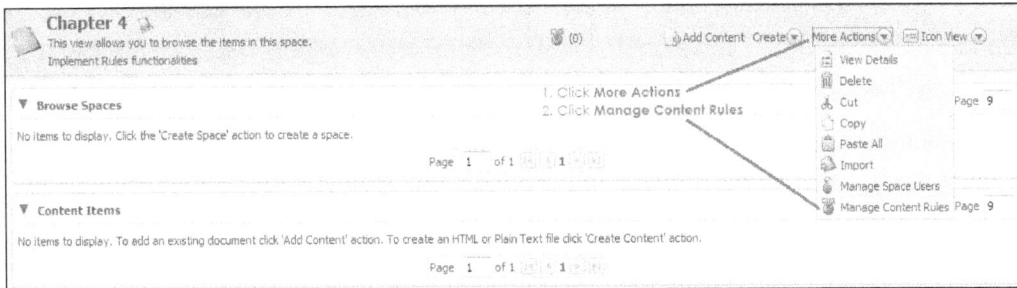

6. No rules are there, click on **Create Rule**.

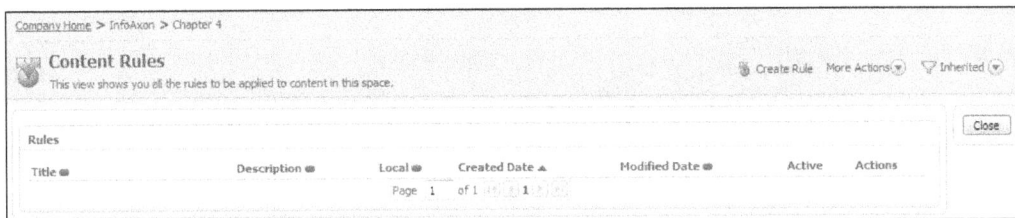

7. **Create Rule Wizard** opens up. The wizard will provide step-by-step guides on how to create a rule. The first step is to define the **Conditions** of the rule.

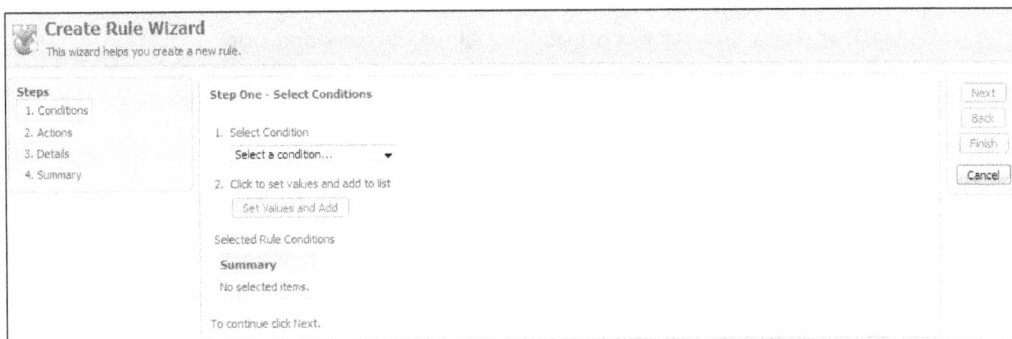

8. From the **Select Condition** drop-down list, select **Content of mimetype** and then click **Set Values and Add**. Alfresco asks for **condition value** in the next screen. Since we have selected condition for a fixed mimetype, in this screen, Alfresco has listed all the available mimetypes. Select **Microsoft Word** from the drop-down list, and click **OK**.

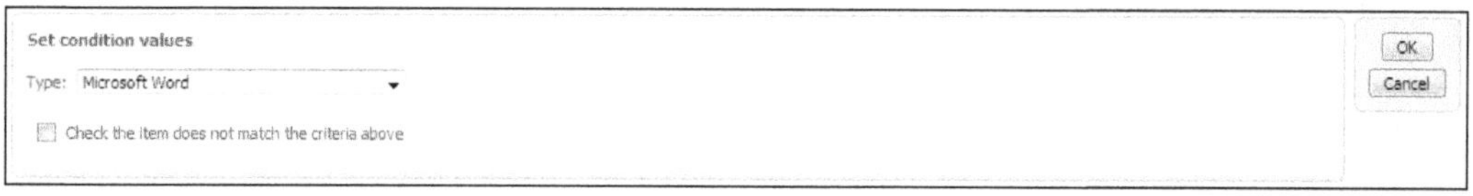

Set condition values   OK   Cancel
Type: Microsoft Word   ▼
☐ Check the item does not match the criteria above

9. The **Conditions** screen comes back. You can add more of such conditions if you want. However, we have only condition to use in our case. So click **Next**.

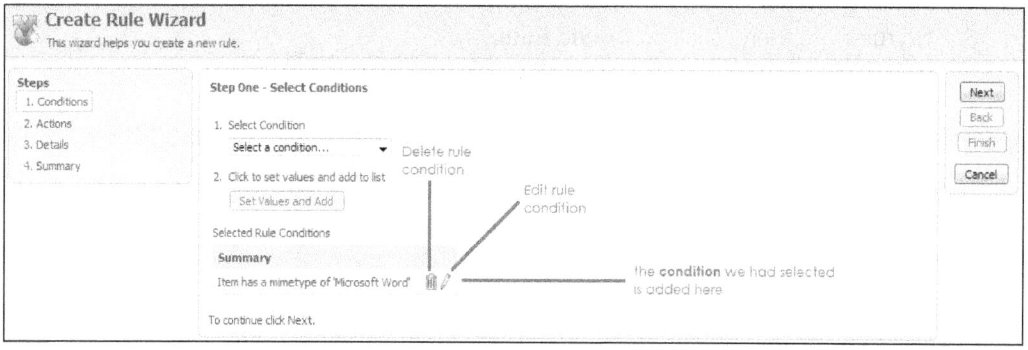

Create Rule Wizard
This wizard helps you create a new rule.

Steps	Step One - Select Conditions		Next
1. Conditions			Back
2. Actions	1. Select Condition		Finish
3. Details	Select a condition... ▼ Delete rule		Cancel
4. Summary	2. Click to set values and add to list condition		

Set Values and Add

Selected Rule Conditions

Summary
Item has a mimetype of 'Microsoft Word' 🗑 ✏   the **condition** we had selected is added here

Edit rule condition

To continue click Next.

10. In the next screen, Alfresco asks for **Actions** to be performed in this rule. As you recollect, we want to transform the document into the Adobe PDF format. Hence we select **Transform and copy content**. Click on **Set Values and Add**.

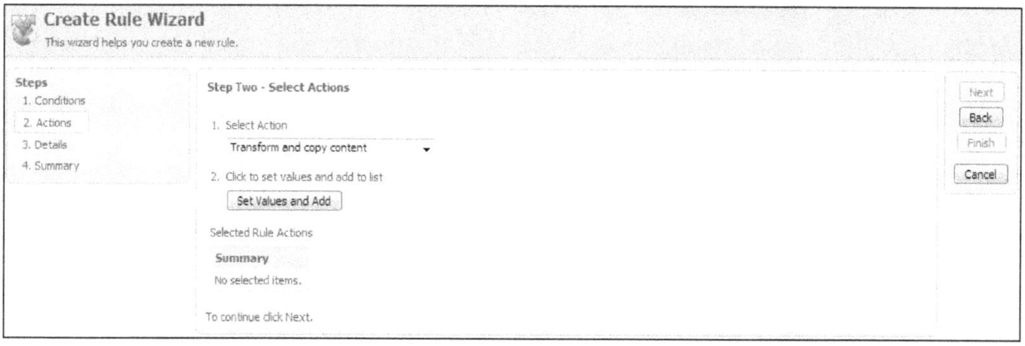

Create Rule Wizard
This wizard helps you create a new rule.

Steps	Step Two - Select Actions		Next
1. Conditions			Back
2. Actions	1. Select Action		Finish
3. Details	Transform and copy content ▼		Cancel
4. Summary	2. Click to set values and add to list		

Set Values and Add

Selected Rule Actions

Summary
No selected items.

To continue click Next.

11. In the next screen, you need to set what format you want your document to be transformed to. Select **Adobe PDF Document** as the required format. Click on the **Click here to select destination link**. And choose **Chapter 4** space by clicking on the **Add** icon. Click **OK**.

12. The **Actions** screen appears. You can add more of such actions if you require. However, in our case, we don't need any more actions to be performed here. So we click **Next**.

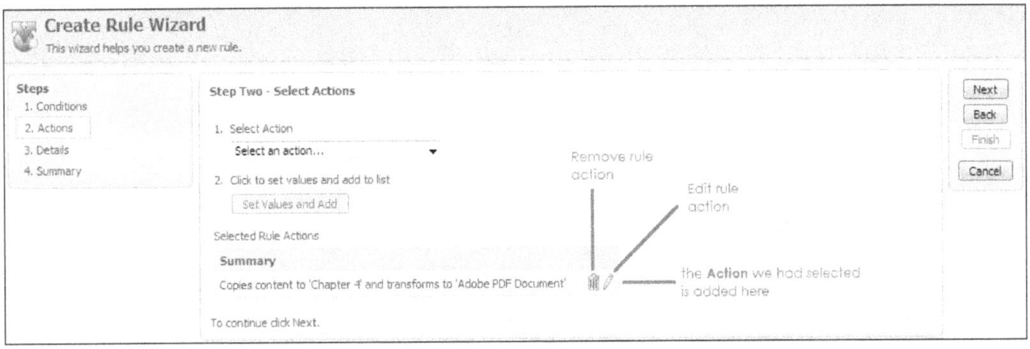

13. In the next step, Alfresco asks you the **Type** of the rule – this governs the event on which the rule will be triggered. We select **Items are created or enter this folder**. This ensures the rule will be executed whenever any new content item is uploaded or copied into this folder (that is, **Chapter 4**).

14. You need to provide the name of the rule, let's put it as **Convert to PDF**. Your rule setup is ready. Click on **Finish** to complete the process.

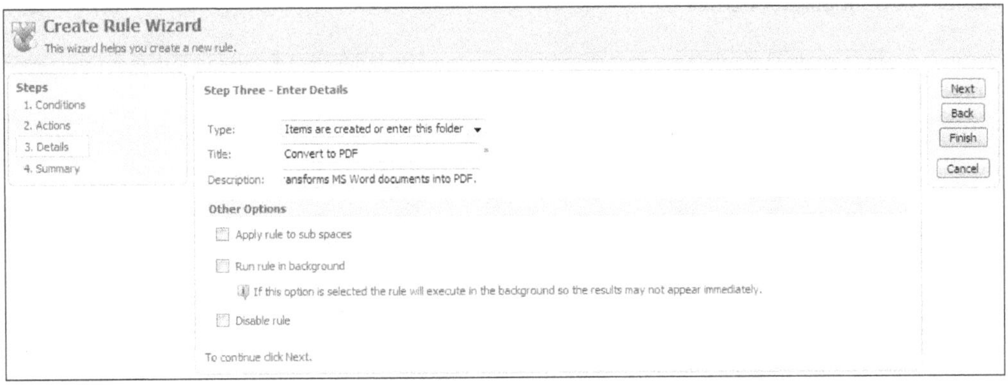

15. The main **Content Rules** interface opens up. You can see that the rule we have created is listed here. Click **Close** to go back to **Chapter 4**.

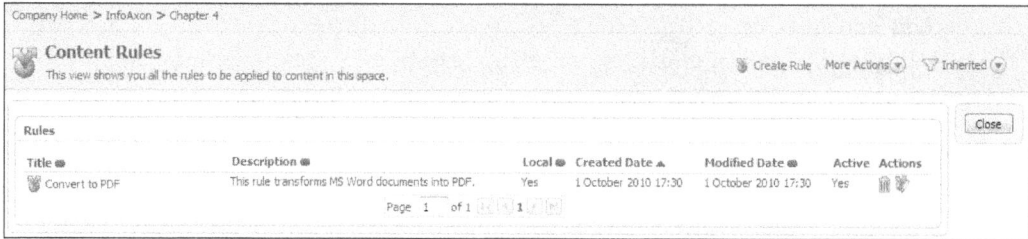

Company Home > InfoAxon > Chapter 4

Content Rules
This view shows you all the rules to be applied to content in this space.

Create Rule   More Actions ▼   Inherited ▼

Rules							Close
Title	Description	Local	Created Date ▲	Modified Date	Active	Actions	
Convert to PDF	This rule transforms MS Word documents into PDF.	Yes	1 October 2010 17:30	1 October 2010 17:30	Yes		

Page 1 of 1

16. You will notice Alfresco is showing that there is a rule applied to this space.

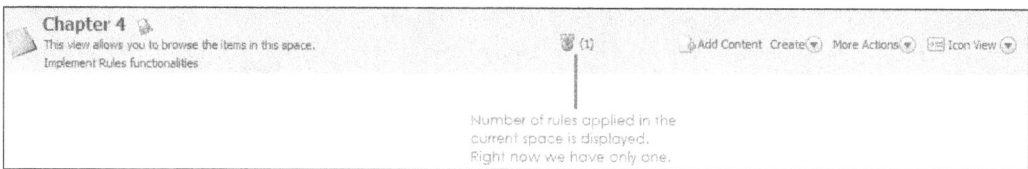

Chapter 4
This view allows you to browse the items in this space.
Implement Rules functionalities

(1)   Add Content   Create ▼   More Actions ▼   Icon View ▼

Number of rules applied in the current space is displayed. Right now we have only one.

How it works...

Now as you have successfully created a rule, let's test how it works.

For that, upload a new MS-Word document in this space. You can see Alfresco has automatically created a PDF version of the same document in the same space. You can see the name of the document remains the same; Alfresco has, however, managed to set the extension PDF instead of DOC.

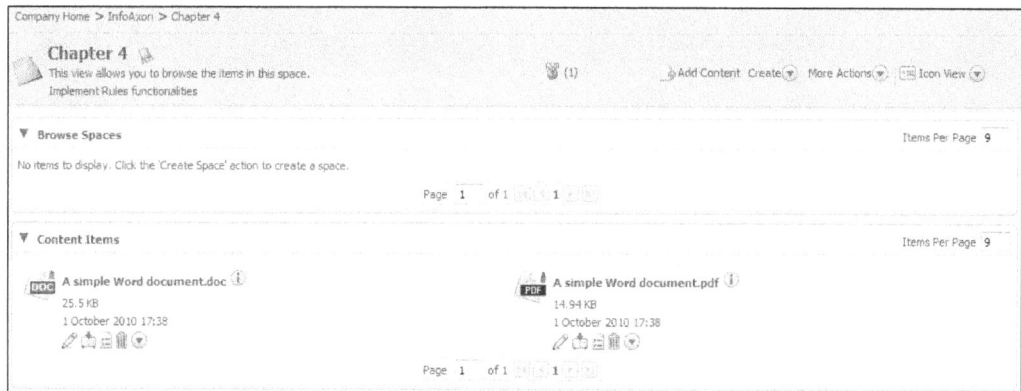

Company Home > InfoAxon > Chapter 4

Chapter 4
This view allows you to browse the items in this space.
Implement Rules functionalities

(1)   Add Content   Create ▼   More Actions ▼   Icon View ▼

▼ Browse Spaces   Items Per Page 9

No items to display. Click the 'Create Space' action to create a space.

Page 1 of 1

▼ Content Items   Items Per Page 9

DOC A simple Word document.doc
25.5 KB
1 October 2010 17:38

PDF A simple Word document.pdf
14.94 KB
1 October 2010 17:38

Page 1 of 1

And if you upload a document other than MS-Word, you can see the transformation is not executed.

Alfresco uses **Open Office services** for the transformation of documents from MS-Office to Adobe PDF format.

Understanding conditions of a rule

It is important to understand the possible options of conditions you can put as rules in Alfresco. In the previous recipe, we have witnessed only the **mimetype** condition. Alfresco, however, offers a number of other conditions you can use in your rules to implement a wide variety of business requirements.

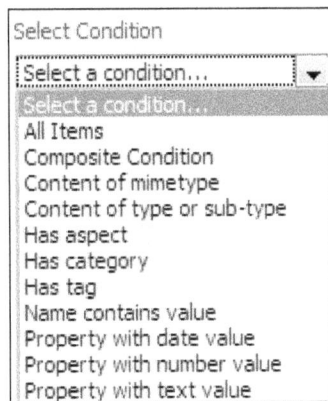

▶ **All Items:** This is practically no condition applied at all. All the content items and sub-spaces in the space will be affected by the rule.

▸ **Content of mimetype**: We have seen how this condition works. This is useful when you want to apply your actions only on those documents which have certain specific mimetypes. When a document is uploaded, Alfresco automatically identifies its mimetype, and then uses this mimetype to select on which document the rule should be executed.

▸ **Content of type or sub-type**: Sometimes you want to apply your rules on specific types of content. This can be content items or sub-folders or custom content types.

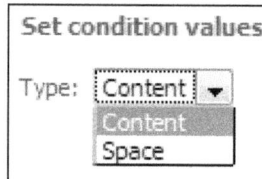

```
Set condition values

Type:  [Content ▼]
       ┌─────────┐
       │Content  │
       │Space    │
       └─────────┘
```

▸ **Has aspect**: We will learn about **Aspects** in later chapters. However, in brief, logically an aspect is a collection of properties and associations. An aspect can be dynamically associated with any content item – thus enhancing the behavior of the content.

Using this condition, you can check which content items are associated with certain specified aspects, and then the rule will be executed on those items only.

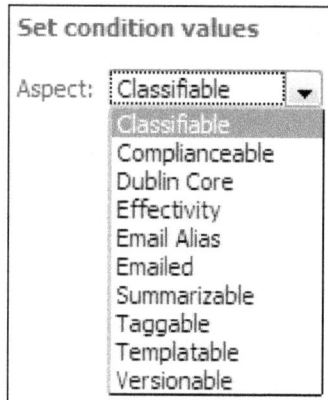

```
Set condition values

Aspect:  [Classifiable      ▼]
         ┌──────────────────┐
         │Classifiable      │
         │Complianceable    │
         │Dublin Core       │
         │Effectivity       │
         │Email Alias       │
         │Emailed           │
         │Summarizable      │
         │Taggable          │
         │Templatable       │
         │Versionable       │
         └──────────────────┘
```

Here, the default available aspects are displayed; however, you can add your own custom aspects as well – we will learn how to do this in later chapters.

▸ **Has category**: You have seen how to categorize contents in *Chapter 2*, recipe *Categorizing a Content*. For selecting on which contents you want to run your rules, you can use this option.

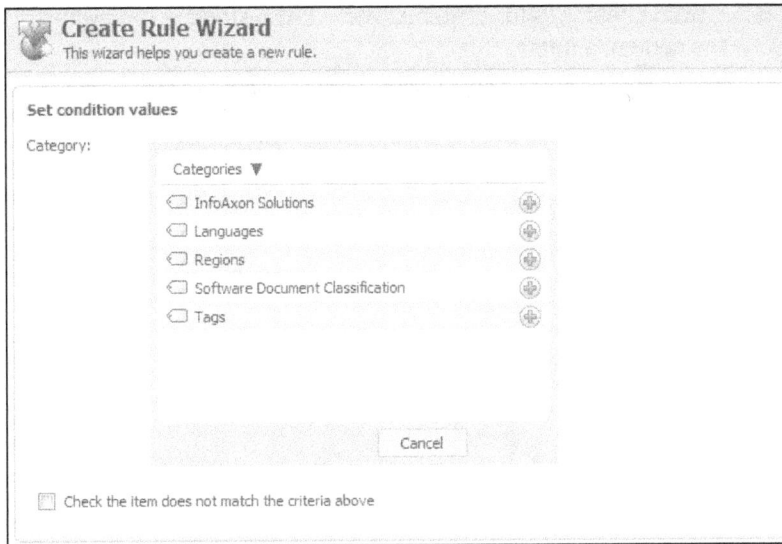

Has tag: You have also seen how to apply tags on your contents. Tags can also be used as filter conditions to choose which content items should be executed on the rule. This condition will select all the content items which have tags associated with them.

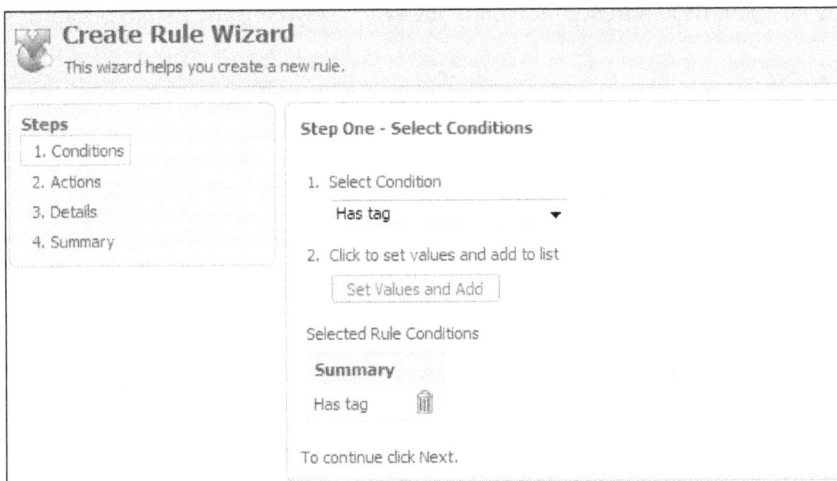

▶ **Name contains value**: You can use this filter condition to search for contents with a particular name or name pattern. For finding out particular content items which use supported regular expressions such as:

  ❑ `info*` would find contents whose **name** starts with `info`.

> ❑ *info* searches for contents where info string is somewhere in the content's **name**.
>
> ❑ Similarly, *info finds contents whose name ends with info.

Create Rule Wizard
This wizard helps you create a new rule.

Set condition values

Enter the text pattern required, including any wildcards. The file name includes the file type extension when matching.

File name pattern: info*

☐ Check the item does not match the criteria above

Hints:

Use zz* to match any name that begins with zz; use *.txt to match any text file; use *zz* to match any file name that contains z

---

▶ **Property with date value**: Similarly to the name condition, this option helps you filter content items which have any particular date value in any of the content properties. You need to provide the property name on which you are expecting the date value should be matched.

In this screenshot, we have used the cm:modified property – this property is, by default, available to all contents in Alfresco. You can, however, use your own custom properties as well.

> For more information on content properties (such as cm:modified we have used here), please see recipes from *Chapter 7*.

Create Rule Wizard
This wizard helps you create a new rule.

Set condition values

Enter condition parameters for a date-valued property

Property name (e.g. created or cm:created):   cm:modified

Operation: Equals To ▼

Value of the property: 4 ▼ October ▼ 2010 ▼ 12 : 26   Today

☐ Check the item does not match the criteria above

- **Property with number value:** This option is used to filter contents by date property value. This option should be used to filter contents by integer property value.

Create Rule Wizard
This wizard helps you create a new rule.

Set condition values

Enter condition parameters for an integer-valued property

Property name (e.g. count or my:count):	cm:size
Operation:	Greater Than Or Equals ▾
Value of the property:	10

☐ Check the item does not match the criteria above

- **Property with text value:** Similarly, you may employ this option to find contents with any text property value. This option also provides you with Operation type – **Equals To**, **Contains**, **Begins With**, **End With**.

Create Rule Wizard
This wizard helps you create a new rule.

Set condition values

Enter condition parameters for a text property

Property name (e.g. description or cm:description):	cm:author
Operation:	Begins With ▾
Value of the property:	snig

☐ Check the item does not match the criteria above

- **Composite Condition:** Until now you have seen a number of conditions that can be used separately to match the required documents.

Most of the conditions described can be used here compositely. You can either apply **OR** operation or **AND** operation between each of the individual conditions.

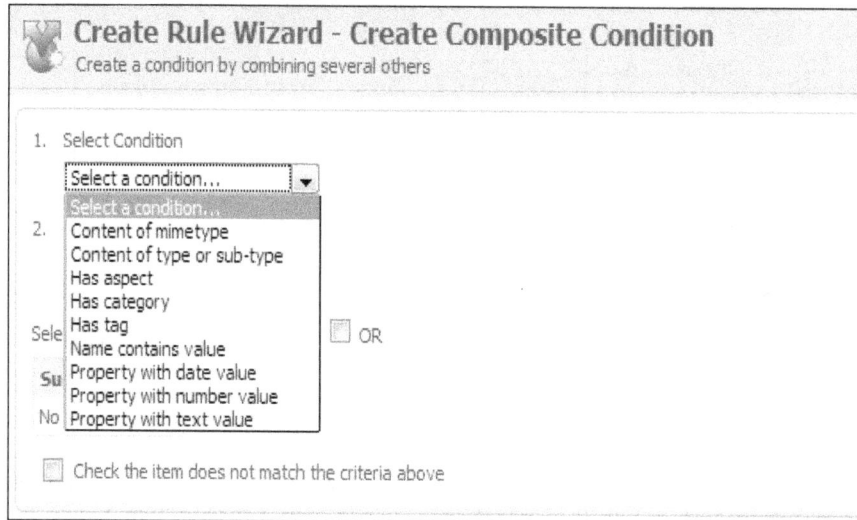

Create Rule Wizard - Create Composite Condition
Create a condition by combining several others

1. Select Condition

   Select a condition...

   | Select a condition... |
   | Content of mimetype |
   | Content of type or sub-type |
   | Has aspect |
   | Has category |
   | Has tag |
   | Name contains value |
   | Property with date value |
   | Property with number value |
   | Property with text value |

2.

   Sele   OR

   Su

   No

   ☐ Check the item does not match the criteria above

Thus, there are a number of options available which you can use to find contents on which you want to run your rules in order to implement any business requirement of your content management life cycle.

> In every condition interface, you can see a checkbox **Check the item does not match the criteria above**. This can be used to filter out those content items which do not match the mentioned criteria.

Understanding possible actions of a rule

So now you have seen that Alfresco has provided a wide variety of options you can utilize as conditions of your rule. Similarly, many action options have also been offered – using these, you can implement most of your content management business scenarios and requirements.

In this recipe, we will understand some of the important actions offered by Alfresco Explorer.

How it works...

The following are the list of possible actions that can be performed while the rule execution. You can perform one or more of these actions in a rule.

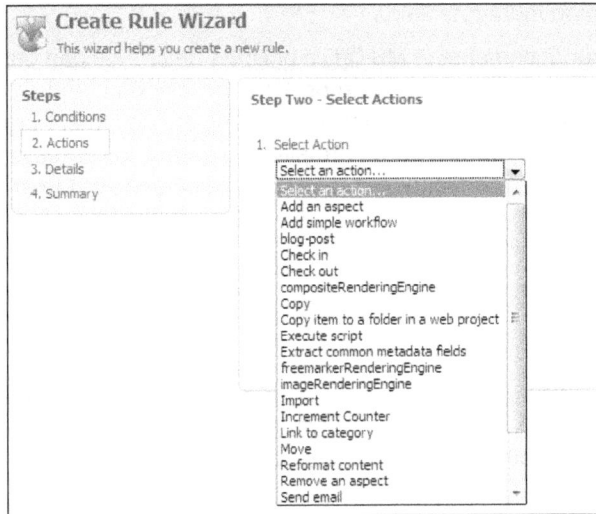

▶ **Add an aspect**: Use this action to add an existing aspect to the selected content items.

▶ **Add simple workflow**: You can initiate a simple **Approval/Rejection** workflow on your content items using this. We will learn more about workflows in *Chapter 11* in the recipe *Invoking and using a Workflow*.

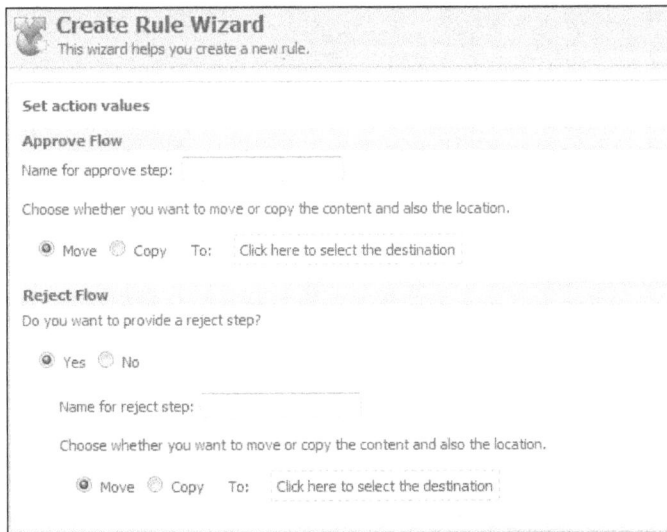

- Check in: This action **checks in** the corresponding document.

- Check out: Used to automatically **check out** the document.

- Copy: Copies a document to a specified folder. This can be used to create a backup copy of certain important documents.

- Extract common metadata fields

When you prepare your documents in MS Office or Open Office, you can put certain basic properties in your documents – such as **Author**, **Title**, **Description**, and so on (the following screenshot shows the **MS Word 2007** window for editing the document properties). When you upload your documents into Alfresco, you normally would want to set these properties into the content metadata in the repository – and this should be done automatically.

You can exercise this action to do this.

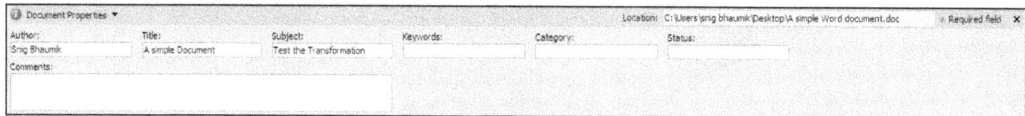

- Move: Moves a document to a specified folder.

- Remove an aspect: This option removes a particular aspect from the document(s).

- Send e-mail: This is another useful action. You can send e-mails to different users on certain events using this option. The e-mail content is also configurable via the Freemarker templates stored in the **Email Templates** space in **Data Dictionary**.

You can use these templates by using the **Insert Template** button, as shown in the following screenshot:

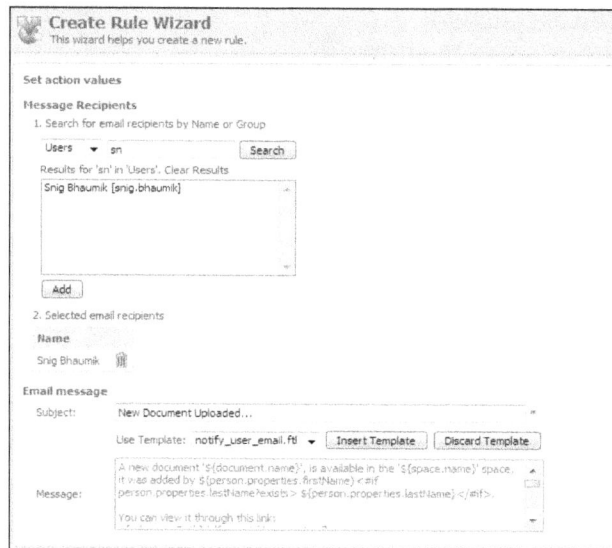

- ▸ Specialize type: We can create new custom content types to reflect your own properties and other behaviors (see *Chapter 7*). You need to create your documents in the repository using these custom types. However, this action can be used to make your documents of that type – by default, the documents are created using Alfresco's default cm:content type. If you want certain documents to be created by your own type, you need to use this action.

- ▸ Transform and copy content: We have briefly used this action in our earlier example to convert the format of MS Word documents into Adobe PDF. This way, you can transform your documents into various supported formats and put the transformed document into the desired folder.

> For some of these transformations, Alfresco uses the **Open Office** (http://www.openoffice.org/) transformation engine.
>
> You need to configure Open Office in the alfresco-global.properties files (this has been introduced in *How to Integrate alfresco with MS Outlook* recipe in *Chapter 12*).

- ▸ Transform and copy image: Similarly as the previous action, this action transforms image files into different types of images – for example, PNG images into GIF, GIF images into JPEG, and so on.

> For these transformations, Alfresco uses the **ImageMagick** (http://www.imagemagick.org/script/index.php) converter engine.
>
> You need to configure Open Office in the alfresco-global.properties files (this has been introduced in *How to Integrate Alfresco with MS Outlook recipe* in chapter 12).

- ▸ Execute script: Often, all these actions are entirely not sufficient to implement your business requirements. Alfresco provides custom requirements to be implemented using **JavaScript API** (see *Chapter 8*). Using this action, you can invoke your scripts and implement various requirements.

There's more...

There are some other important behaviors of rules worth exploring.

Steps	Step Three - Enter Details
1. Conditions	
2. Actions	Type: Items are created or enter this folder
3. Details	Title: Convert to PDF
4. Summary	Description: This rule transforms MS Word documents

Other Options

☐ Apply rule to sub spaces

☐ Run rule in background

   ⓘ If this option is selected the rule will execute in the background so the results may not appear immediately.

☐ Disable rule

To continue click Next.

Rule inheritance

While creating a rule, if you select the **Apply rule to sub spaces** checkbox, all the sub folders of the current folder will inherit the rule. In other words, the rule will be applied to all the sub folders of the current folder. Alfresco calls the rules as **Local** for the current folder. And for all the sub folders the inherited rules are not local.

You can use this behavior to create the rule only once, and apply the rule in all the sub folders. Thus there is no need to create the rule multiple times for each of the sub folders.

Asynchronous rule

You have an option to run the rule asynchronously – you can do this by selecting the **Run rule in background** checkbox.

Normally, the rule gets executed whenever the event takes place. For example, an inbound rule is executed when a new item is uploaded in the folder; and the process of uploading the file is not complete until the rule is fully executed. In case any error occurs while executing the rule, the upload operation is also terminated abruptly. On the other hand, if you choose the rule to be run in the background, the main upload operation is not affected by the execution of the rule. In this case, however, you may not see the output of the rule immediately.

> Users must take care about the use of asynchronous rules because for each request, a new thread will be created in the application server. Typically, this method must be used only when it is strictly necessary.

Disabled rule

Sometimes, you may not want a rule to run; but at the same time, you may not want to delete the rule entirely.

For this situation, you select the **Disable rule** checkbox here, means you put the rule out of action. Later on, when required, you again enable the rule by de-selecting the checkbox.

Editing rule

You can edit an existing rule using the **Changes Details** (Edit Rule) icon provided.

However, editing or deleting rules are not possible for inherited rules.

Permissions

Permission for creating new rules and modifying existing rules on a space lies only with space owners and users having the **Coordinator** role on the space.

5
Alfresco Administration Console

In this chapter we will cover:

- ▶ Managing System users
- ▶ Managing System groups
- ▶ Managing Content categories
- ▶ Using Alfresco content package
- ▶ Using Alfresco node browser
- ▶ Configuring the Alfresco dashboard

Introduction

Administration Console comes with Alfresco Explorer application—you use this module to perform all management operations of your content management system.

The administrative functionalities this offers are:

- ▶ You can create/manage system users
- ▶ You can create/manage system groups
- ▶ Managing available system categories
- ▶ Import and Export Alfresco content packages

▶ Browse the Alfresco content repository

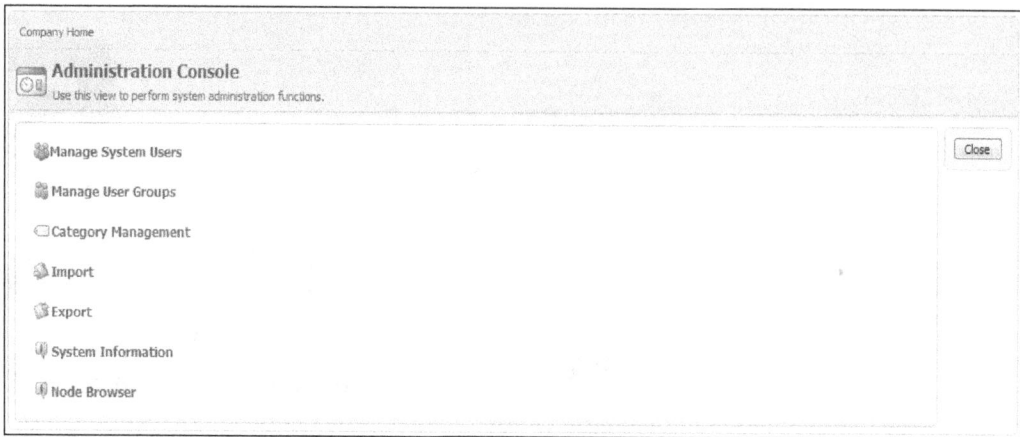

Company Home

Administration Console
Use this view to perform system administration functions.

Manage System Users   Close

Manage User Groups

Category Management

Import

Export

System Information

Node Browser

In this chapter we will explore all these functionalities of Alfresco Administration Console—how to administer Alfresco using this console.

Managing system users

You have mostly covered this functionality in *Chapter 3*. We have seen how we can create new user in the system. In next recipe, we will explore how to perform other actions over system users.

Getting ready

Open the list of available users in the system. The following screen will appear:

Users

To find a user search for them using their first name, last name and/or user name. Alternatively to see all users click 'Show All', however, this may take some time if there are a lot of users in the system.

Search   Show All

Name	User Name ▼	Home Space	Usage	Quota	Actions
William Jones	william.jones	/Company Home/User Homes/william.jones	0 KB		
Snig Bhaumik	snig.bhaumik	/Company Home/User Homes/snig.bhaumik	1.27 MB		
Guest	guest	/Company Home/Guest Home	0 KB		
Administrator	admin	/Company Home	296.11 KB		

Page 1 of 1   1

Total Usage (for this search): 1.56 MB
Total Quota (for this search):

▶ **Name**: This column shows the full name of the user.

- **User Name**: This column is the unique user identification – this is used to log in in to the system.

- **Home Space**: The home folder path of the user.

- **Usage**: Total size of the contents uploaded/created by the user.

- **Quota**: The space quota allocated for the user. This is useful when you want to restrict how much space the particular user can have for his/her contents.

- **Actions**: These options would be used to perform several operations on the user. You can edit the user details, change the user's password or can delete the user from the system.

How to do it...

Follow these steps to edit user details:

1. Click on the **Modify** icon for the user you want to edit. In our case, we will take user `snig.bhaumik` to explore how to update user details.

2. System comes up with **Edit User Wizard**. The first step is to modify the **Person Properties** of the user. You can set/change user's name, e-mail id and other details of the user. After feeding relevant details, click **Next**.

3. In the next screen, step 2, you can change user's home space location.

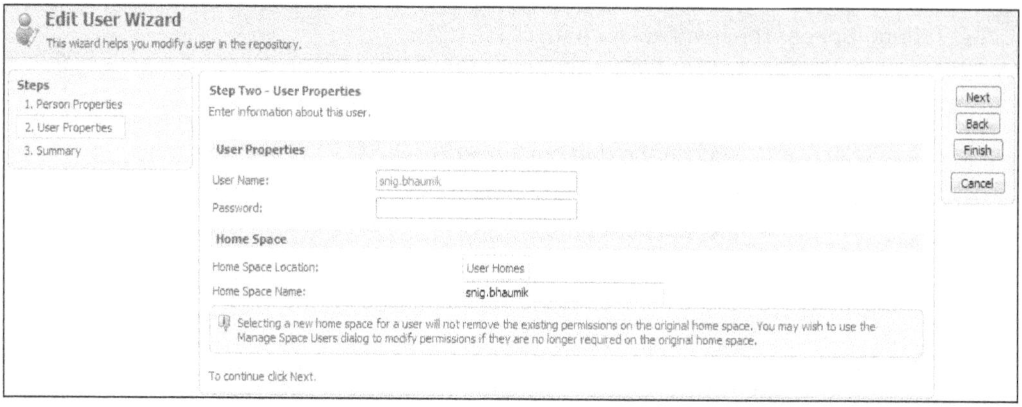

Note that, you cannot change **User Name** – once a user is created in Alfresco, you cannot change user name ever. However, in this screen the changing of **Password** also is disabled. Should you wish to change user's password, you must click on **Change Password** icon in manage user screen.

4. The next screen just displays the summary information of the user – this is your chance to review the entries and validate whether everything is correct. In case you find any issues in any of the entries you can click **Back** button and re-correct enter the values.

5. Clicking on **Finish** completes your operation. Your values are saved here. If you hit on **Cancel**, all your data will be lost and none of the user details will be updated.

There's more...

Follow the steps to change a user's password.

Changing the user password

1. Click on the **Change Password** icon for the user you want to edit. In our case, we will take user `snig.bhaumik` to change the password.

2. System opens the password changing interface where you can set the new password of that user.

Change Password

Use this view to change an existing user password.

Enter the new password for this user.

User Name:	snig.bhaumik
Password:	✕
Confirm:	✕

3. Enter the new password and click **Finish**. System comes back to the list of users screen.

See also

▸ *Managing user groups*

Managing user groups

We have seen how to create a new user group and add users into groups in *Chapter 3*. In this recipe we will learn how create a subgroup and associate users with it.

Getting ready

Open the available groups in the system, this would be the interface.

Root Groups

Groups

To find a group search for it using group name. Alternatively to see all groups click 'Show All', however, this may take some time if there are a lot of groups in the system.

Search   Show All

EMAIL CONTRIBUTORS   ALFRESCO_ADMINISTRATORS   Alfresco Cookbook Authors

Page 1   of 1   1

You can see this listing is for **Root Groups** – this means the root level groups available in the system.

How to do it...

Let's create a subgroup in `Alfresco Cookbook Authors` group (remember, we created this group in recipe Creating Groups in *Chapter 3*).

1. Click on **Alfresco Cookbook Authors** group name. The group details information will appear. We had earlier added two users in this group.

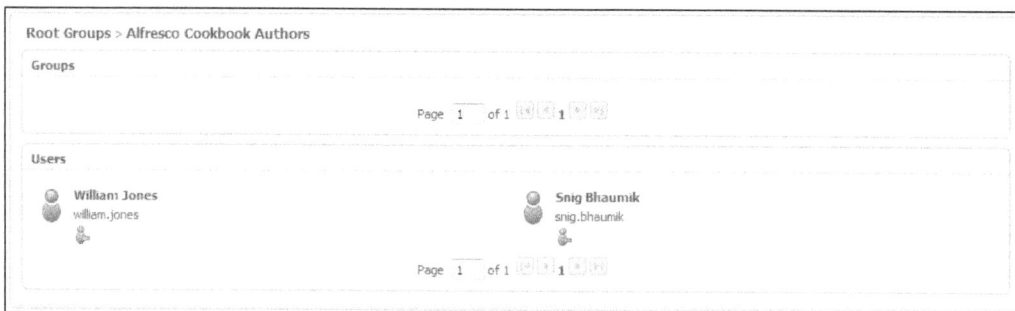

Root Groups > Alfresco Cookbook Authors

Groups

Page 1 of 1

Users

William Jones
william.jones

Snig Bhaumik
snig.bhaumik

Page 1 of 1

> Note that, there is a breadcrumb trail displayed in this screen – **Root Groups > Alfresco Cookbook Authors**. This shows the hierarchy of the currently opened group.

2. Click on **Create Group** to create a subgroup under **Alfresco Cookbook Authors**. Let's call our new group as `Chapter-5 Authors`. Click on **Create Group** button.

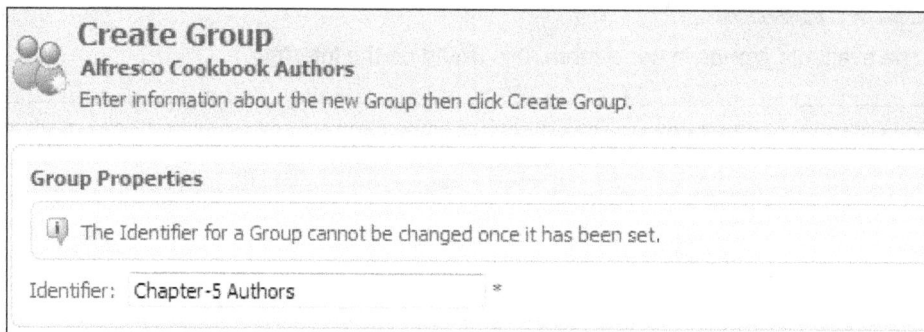

Create Group
Alfresco Cookbook Authors
Enter information about the new Group then click Create Group.

Group Properties

The Identifier for a Group cannot be changed once it has been set.

Identifier: Chapter-5 Authors   *

3. As you can see, a new sub-group has been added in this group.

Chapter 5

Root Groups > Alfresco Cookbook Authors

Groups

Chapter-5 Authors

Page 1 of 1

Users

William Jones
william.jones

Snig Bhaumik
snig.bhaumik

Page 1 of 1

4. You can now add more sub-groups and users in this new group in similar fashion by opening the **Chapter-5 Authors** group.

Groups Management
Chapter-5 Authors
Manage the members of a group, create new groups or remove existing groups.

Create Group   More Actions   Children   Groups

Delete Group

Add User

Root Groups > Alfresco Cookbook Authors > Chapter-5 Authors

Close

Groups

Page 1 of 1

Users

Page 1 of 1

> Sub-group (groups within groups) is a useful concept you can use when you want to create hierarchical security groups and policies in your system.
>
> For example, if you assign some permission on a content item to group **Alfresco Cookbook Authors**, users of all the sub-groups under it will inherit the same permission. However, if you assign permission only to group **Chapter-5 Authors**, the rights will be limited to those users and corresponding sub-groups only.

You can mentioned here sub-group in details like one sub-group can't be part of two groups. You can add users at group level, sub-group level etc. Also how the user rights will be managed if user is added in sub-group but not in group, and so on.

Managing categories

You have seen how to categorize a content item in *Chapter 2* in *Categorizing content*. However, you might be wondering how to create those categories in your system. You can use Alfresco Administration Console to create, and manage the available categories for your enterprise content management. We will explore this in this recipe.

There are some default categories created in alfresco standard distribution. Categories, in Alfresco, are hierarchical – much similar to the real life categories. Let's consider taking an example of an existing category – **Regions**.

Note that not all the hierarchies are displayed in this diagram.

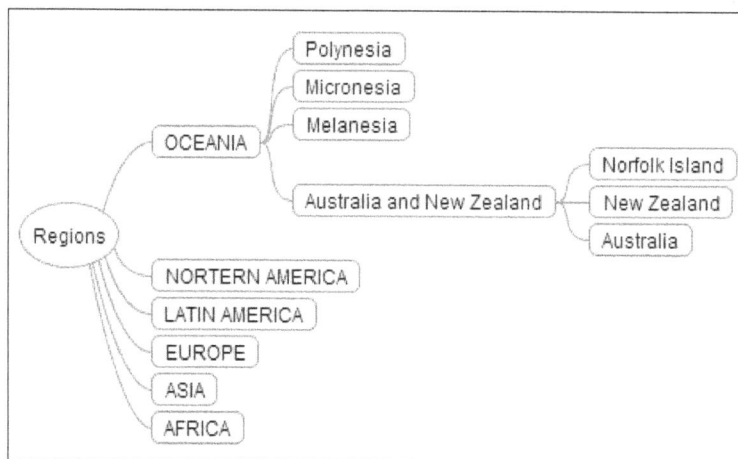

Six sample regions are created, and under each of these sub-regions are created. The next level contains countries within that region. This hierarchy can go on up to any level depicting the business scenario you are looking for.

Now, let's see how to create and edit these categories.

How to do it...

1. In the **Administration Console**, click on **Category Management**. A List of available categories will be displayed. Click on **Add Category** to create a new category.

Category Management

Categories

This view allows you to browse and modify the categories hierarchy.

Add Category   Categories

Categories   Close

Items

Tags

Software Document Classification

Regions

Click to add
New Category

Languages

Page 1   of 1 [|<] [<] [1] [>] [>|]

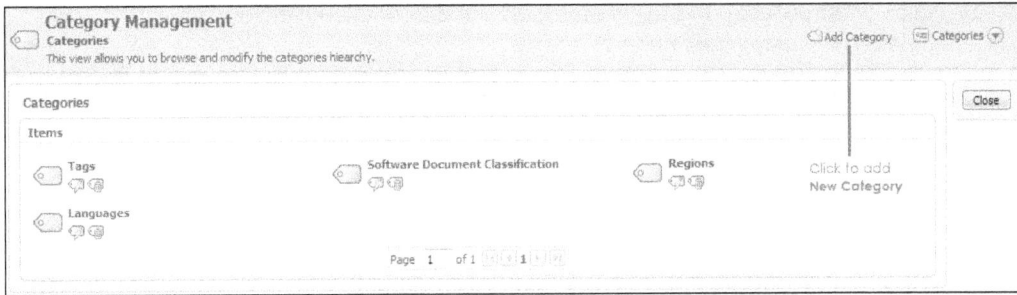

2. In the next screen, enter the name of your new category – suppose we name it
    InfoAxon Solutions. Click on **New Category** button to create it.

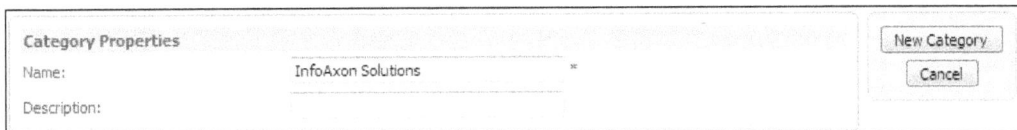

Category Properties   New Category

Name: InfoAxon Solutions   ✱   Cancel

Description:

3. The application comes back to the list of root level categories with the new category
    InfoAxon Solutions listed into it. There are two icons associated with each of
    the categories enabling you to edit and delete the particular category.

4. We now will create a sub category in **InfoAxon Solutions**. For that click on the
    category name. Alfresco will display all the sub-categories under this one. Again, click
    on **Add Category**. We create the new category named **Knowledge Management**.
    Similarly, we create another category named **Business Intelligence**.

> Note that, the breadcrumb path is displayed depicting the currently
> open category.

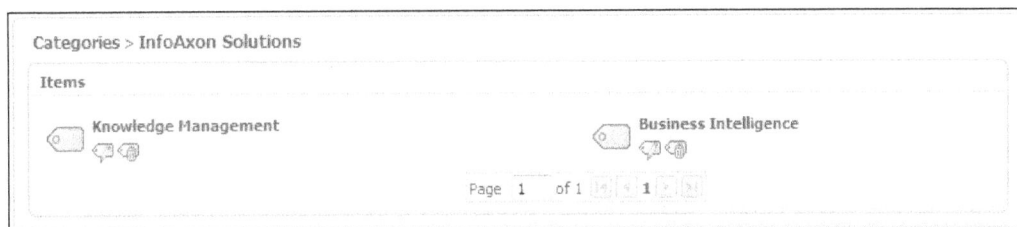

Categories > InfoAxon Solutions

Items

Knowledge Management   Business Intelligence

Page 1   of 1 [|<] [<] [1] [>] [>|]

5. Click on **Knowledge Management** to create another sub-category beneath it. We create three categories here.

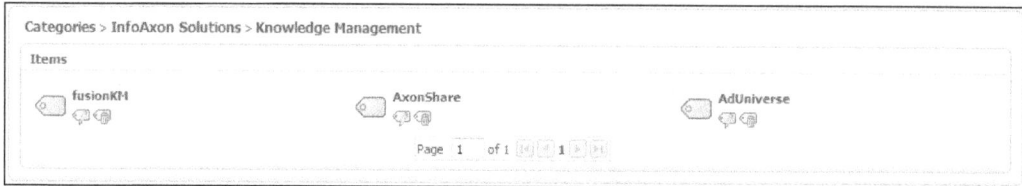

Categories > InfoAxon Solutions > Knowledge Management

Items

fusionKM   AxonShare   AdUniverse

Page 1   of 1 |◄ ◄ 1 ► ►|

6. Similarly, create a couple of new categories under **Business Intelligence**.

7. Finally, the full category tree we have created would look like this:

Categories ▼

☐ Browse items in sub-categories?

▼ InfoAxon Solutions

   ▼ Business Intelligence

      ► embeddableBI

      ► fusionBI

   ▼ Knowledge Management

      ► AdUniverse

      ► AxonShare

      ► fusionKM

► Languages

► Regions

► Software Document Classification

► Tags

These categories are now available to be applied in any content item of your repository. In this way, you can create category hierarchy to represent your content taxonomy in your organization; and apply the taxonomy to the content items.

> You can delete any existing categories as well. However, deleting categories won't affect the contents associated with these. Only the mapping between the categories and the contents will be removed, the content items would stay as they are.

See also

- *How to categorize a content, Chapter 2.*

Exporting Alfresco content packages

At this point, you will know how to upload files in your Alfresco repository, and also how to download your content items from the repository.

However, consider a few business scenarios and requirements; you might face these frequently in your organization environment:

- Export all the items of a particular folder in an archive, and create a backup.
- Export all items of a folder into an archive, and import the same into another alfresco repository – in other words, you want to transfer content items from one alfresco installation into another, provided the two systems are compatible.
- Upload a large number of files in a particular folder in alfresco.
- Upload an existing ZIP archive in a folder and automatically extract all the items in that folder.

Though there are several solutions for these scenarios, we can implement these using Alfresco's Import/Export features easily.

How to do it...

The **Export** option in Administrative Console helps you to create a file archive of type **Alfresco Content Package** (file extension – `.acp`).

1. Open the folder with content items you want to export. We choose our `InfoAxon` folder for this operation.

2. Open Alfresco Administration Console and click on **Export**. The following screen will be displayed. You can see Alfresco is ready to export the contents of folder InfoAxon.

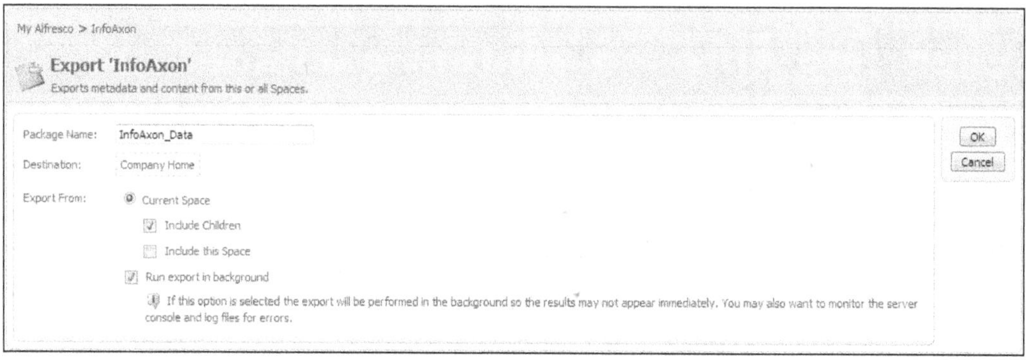

3. In the **Package Name**, put the name of the content package archive file you want to create. We call it here InfoAxon_Data.

4. **Destination** is the folder name where you want to save your archive file. We select **Company Home** here.

5. **Export From** parameters enable you to control contents from all folders you want to export. If you select **Include Children**, contents from all the subfolders of InfoAxon folder will be exported; content items of the current folder will be exported too. If you select **Include this Space**, the current space also will be exported in the archive file. If you choose to **Run export in background**, the application won't be blocked until the full export operation is completed.

> Users must take care about running tasks in background because for each request a new thread will be created and queued in the application server. Typically this method must be used only when it is necessary.

6. We perform the export operation by these given settings. Click **OK**. When you go back to Company Home space, you can notice a new content item is created namely InfoAxon_Data.acp.

▼ **Content Items**

InfoAxon_Data.acp ⓘ
Alfresco content package for Space 'InfoAxon'.
1.2 MB
27 October 2010 16:18

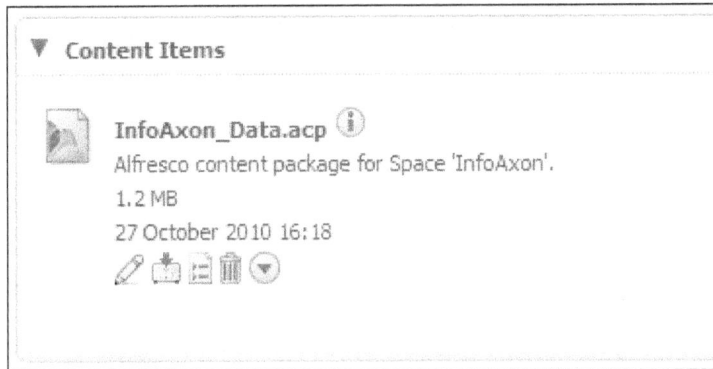

7. This file now contains all the subfolders and content items from `InfoAxon` space. You can download this file and keep it for further use.

There's more...

Now that we have exported one folder into an archive file, let us explore how to import the file into the repository.

Importing content items

This operation should create an exact replica of all the files and folders stored in `InfoAxon` space.

> You need permission on a particular space to import items into it. Minimum required permissions are Collaborator or Coordinator. Of course, Administrators and space owners have full permissions on the space, thus they can import items.

Import operation can be performed in two ways:

▸ Using Administration Console
▸ Using Import action in space

Using Administration Console

1. Let's create a space under **Company Home**, namely `InfoAxon_New`.
2. Open this new space.
3. Open Administration Console, and click **Import**.

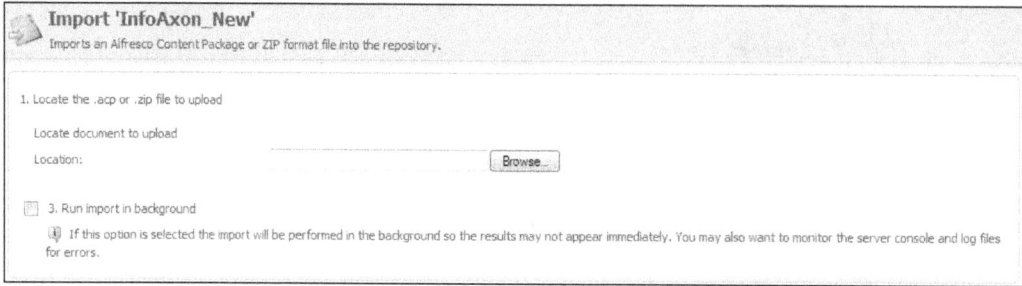

4. Select the downloaded ACP file (`InfoAxon_Data.acp`) and click **OK**. Uncheck the **Run import in background** box as we do not want the import process to run in the background.

5. Then navigate the space `InfoAxon_New`. You can see all the folders and content items are imported into this new space.

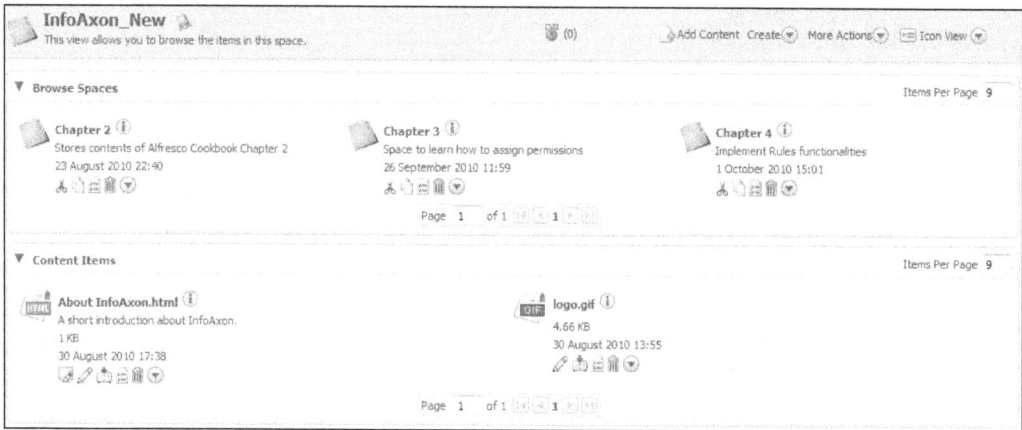

Using Import Action

An alternative way to import the content archive is to use the Import action in space. This is useful since a non-administrator user cannot use the Administration Console – thus they won't be able to use the **Import** operation there.

1. Let's create the `InfoAxon_New` space once again (you can delete the space we earlier created earlier along with all the content inside).

2. Open the new space. Click on **More Actions | Import** option.

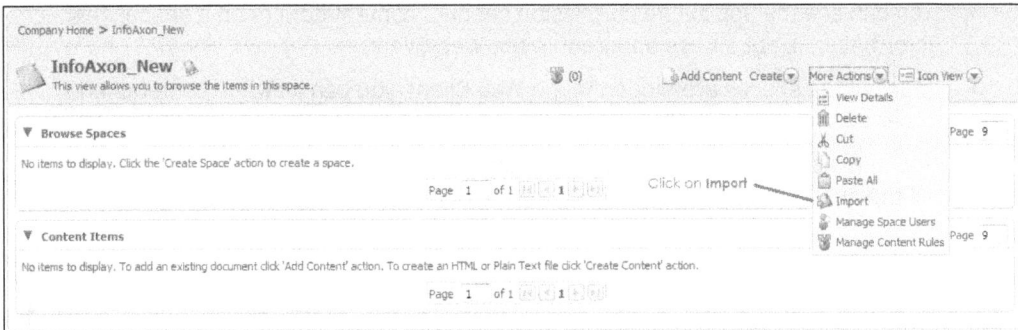

3. Select the downloaded ACP file (`InfoAxon_Data.acp`) and click **OK**. Uncheck the **Run import in background** box as we do not want the import process to run in the background.

4. Then navigate the space `InfoAxon_New`. You can see all the folders and content items are imported into this new space – just like in the previous instance.

Using the Alfresco Node Browser

Alfresco Node Browser is one important and useful feature provided in the Web Client application.

Some of the valuable usages of this browser interface are:

▶ Not all the properties and attributes are visible in the Alfresco Web Client interfaces. Should you need to see all the properties of a content item or of a space, you can use this interface.

▶ You can perform custom search operations using this interface which is sometimes quite handy to investigate and debug the search queries.

- You can see the applicable permission set on a content item or on a space. This information is not always apparent in the Web Client.

- Many of the spaces are hidden in the Web Client; you can view the contents and other information from this interface.

- You can also see the hidden aspects applied to a content item and can view all the associations available.

> In Alfresco, all the content items and spaces are logically stored and architected as XML Nodes, in hierarchical structure. In this way, all the content items, spaces, users, groups, category entries, and task entries are individual **Nodes** in Alfresco repository.
>
> This interface is used to browse through all these nodes of the repository.
>
> It is important to note that the **Node Browser** is a read-only interface; you cannot perform any add/update/delete operation using this.

Getting ready

Clicking on the **Node Browser** link in Administration Console you can open this interface.

Alfresco Node Browser

Refresh view

Stores

Reference
user://alfrescoUserStore
system://system
workspace://lightWeightVersionStore
workspace://version2Store
archive://SpacesStore
workspace://SpacesStore
avm://sitestore

As we have discussed in *Chapter 1*, the preceding list represents several stores available in the repository. As we know, the main store is **workspace://SpacesStore** where all the contents and spaces are stocked up.

Click on **workspace://SpacesStore** to open this particular store content.

Stores ————— Click to go back
to the **Store list**

Search

noderef ▼   Search

Node Identifier

Primary Path: /

Reference: workspace://SpacesStore/71597174-f3af-4795-b9d1-3bb30b314fd3

Type: {http://www.alfresco.org/model/system/1.0}store_root

Parent:

Properties

Name	Value	Property Type	Value Type	Residual
{http://www.alfresco.org/model/content/1.0}name	71597174-f3af-4795-b9d1-3bb30b314fd3	{http://www.alfresco.org/model/dictionary/1.0}text		false
{http://www.alfresco.org/model/system/1.0}node-dbid	12	{http://www.alfresco.org/model/dictionary/1.0}long		false
{http://www.alfresco.org/model/system/1.0}store-identifier	SpacesStore	{http://www.alfresco.org/model/dictionary/1.0}text		false
{http://www.alfresco.org/model/system/1.0}node-uuid	71597174-f3af-4795-b9d1-3bb30b314fd3	{http://www.alfresco.org/model/dictionary/1.0}text		false
{http://www.alfresco.org/model/system/1.0}store-protocol	workspace	{http://www.alfresco.org/model/dictionary/1.0}text		false

Aspects

{http://www.alfresco.org/model/system/1.0}referenceable
{http://www.alfresco.org/model/system/1.0}aspect_root

Permissions

Inherit: true

Assigned Permission	To Authority	Access
Read	guest	ALLOWED
Read	GROUP_EVERYONE	ALLOWED

Store Permission	To Authority	Access
All <No Mask>	All	Allowed

Children

Child Name	Child Node	Primary	Association Type	Index
company_home	workspace://SpacesStore/522c71f9-93c3-4e3d-8e12-33aabfc60fbf	true	children	0
system	workspace://SpacesStore/157d5f2d-579b-46dc-b1be-0242509367a7	true	children	1
categoryRoot	workspace://SpacesStore/ef7ae72d-9af0-45cd-82e6-52ad6880a3ca	true	children	2
multilingualRoot	workspace://SpacesStore/a968146d-32ae-4c14-80dd-b6fb4af7e302	true	children	3

Associations

To Node	Association Type

Parents

Child Name	Parent Node	Primary	Association Type

There are several sections in this interface.

- ▶ **Search**: You can perform different search operations using this. The available search modes are – **noderef, xpath, lucene, fts-Alfresco, cmis, selectnodes.**

- ▶ **Node Identifier**: Displays the basic identification information of the current node.

- ▶ The **Reference** value is one of the important information here – it shows the **noderef** of the node item. **noderef** means **Node Reference** – this is the unique Id of the node across the entire Alfresco repository.

- ▶ Similarly, the **Type** value depicts the **content type** of the particular node. We have touched the content types briefly in chapter 2 and 3. We will further explore this in *Chapter 7*.

- ▶ **Properties**: Lists all the properties and attributes of the node.

- ▶ **Aspects**: Presents all the associated aspects in the node.

- ▶ **Permissions**: You can see who has which permission on the current node.

- ▶ **Children**: Lists the child nodes of the current node. For example, all the content items of a space are the children of the space node. You can click on the **Child Node** column values to navigate to that particular item – this column shows the *noderef* of that particular item.

- ▶ **Associations**: Shows the list of nodes that are associated with this particular node.

- ▶ **Parents**: Displays the parent node item of the current one.

As an example on how to use the Node Browser, let's navigate to the InfoAxon space and contents we had created earlier.

How to do it...

1. Open the **workspace://SpacesStore** store from the Node Browser store list. This opens up the *store root* of this store.

2. Scroll down to the **Children** section – this is because we need to start with **Company Home** – the home space of all content items; and the **Company Home** is a child node of store root.

3. Click on the **Child Node** value corresponding to the **company_home** entry – this is the noderef of the Company Home space.

Children

Child Name	Child Node	Primary	Association Type	Index
company_home	workspace://SpacesStore/522c71f9-93c3-4e3d-8e12-33aabfc60fbf	true	children	0
system	workspace://SpacesStore/157d5f2d-579b-46dc-b1be-0242509367a7	true	children	1
categoryRoot	workspace://SpacesStore/ef7ae72d-9af0-45cd-82e6-52ad6880a3ca	true	children	2
multilingualRoot	workspace://SpacesStore/a968146d-32ae-4c14-80dd-b6fb4af7e302	true	children	3

4. In the next screen, again go to the **Children** section – you will find the **InfoAxon** node entry present there.

Children

Child Name	Child Node	Primary	Association Type	Index
dictionary	workspace://SpacesStore/dbabf37e-a9f0-48ca-b946-e07ce3420f26	true	contains	0
guest_home	workspace://SpacesStore/5cb70bf5-e603-4d3b-b212-6ea5bd70496f	true	contains	1
user_homes	workspace://SpacesStore/6b82a1e6-da5c-461a-b9e9-674f427a9253	true	contains	2
sites	workspace://SpacesStore/077f3303-7009-4992-8a2b-34b5146f478b	true	contains	3
InfoAxon	workspace://SpacesStore/50672cf8-75b5-430e-8f8b-4600cfd9f447	true	contains	4
InfoAxon_Data.acp	workspace://SpacesStore/a41f410a-3296-4ac8-a442-174882c88abf	true	contains	5

5. Click on the `noderef` of `InfoAxon`. You have now reached the node details of `InfoAxon` space. If you see again the **Children** list to, you can see all the spaces and content items we had created in this space.

Children

Child Name	Child Node	Primary	Association Type	Index
ruleFolder	workspace://SpacesStore/28298827-40e9-408f-9648-b354ab51b006	true	ruleFolder	0
Chapter 2	workspace://SpacesStore/7e5d1b55-9735-4804-9850-207da95d8546	true	contains	1
logo.gif	workspace://SpacesStore/72028e23-99e8-46a1-8a32-7b3529ec46dc	true	contains	2
About InfoAxon.html	workspace://SpacesStore/7571eb04-0532-43ca-bd70-df15777dfbd7	true	contains	3
Chapter 3	workspace://SpacesStore/a4f8966e-9cc7-446d-a07f-10ffb539353d	true	contains	4
Chapter 4	workspace://SpacesStore/04993940-2d98-4b65-acfc-93fa643ed423	true	contains	5

6. Click on the `noderef` of `About InfoAxon.html` content. Details of this node appear. Notice the Properties section of the content node.

7. You can see there are a number of properties listed which are not visible in the web client application property page of a content item. These properties are responsible for controlling the behavior of a content; for example,

8. **autoversion** is `true` means version of the content increases automatically each time you check-out and check-in the content.

9. **autoVersionOnUpdateProps** is `true` means version will also be changed if you update the content properties. If this value is false, update property value won't change the version of the content.

10. You cannot change and control these properties using the web client application; however, you can change these by writing codes using Alfresco JavaScript API or Java API. We will explore these in later chapters.

There's more

Let us now see a simple example of how search happens in this **Node Browser**.

1. Copy the `noderef` value of `About InfoAxon.html` content item into your clipboard.

2. Close the **Node Browser** and re-open it.

3. Open the **workspace://SpacesStore** store. By default, it will open the store root location.

4. In the **Search** panel, select **noderef** as search mode and paste the `noderef` value in the search box. Click **Search**.

Search		
noderef ▾	workspace://SpacesStore/7571eb04-0532-43ca-bd70-df15777dfbd7	Search

5. As you can see, the `About InfoAxon.html` content item is searched and displayed in the screen. Thus if you know the noderef value of a content item, you can search it in the repository and view its attributes.

6. We will explore later how to search using other modes, such as Lucene, `xpath` and so on.

> The architecture of Alfresco Stores and Nodes are designed following the JCR specifications. JCR is the content repository structure implementation standard as per JSR-170 specification.
>
> Alfresco repository is architected following this specification, which consists of multiple workspaces, content stored as nodes etc. Thus you can see alfresco repository is structured by multiple spaces (for example, **workspace://SpacesStore**, and so on); and each item in the repository is stored as Nodes. Each node has a unique identifier – **Noderef.**
>
> To know more about JCR API and specification, please see `http://www.jcp.org/en/jsr/detail?id=170`.

Configuring the Alfresco Dashboard

When you log in into the web client application, by default you land up in your Alfresco dashboard – named **My Alfresco**.

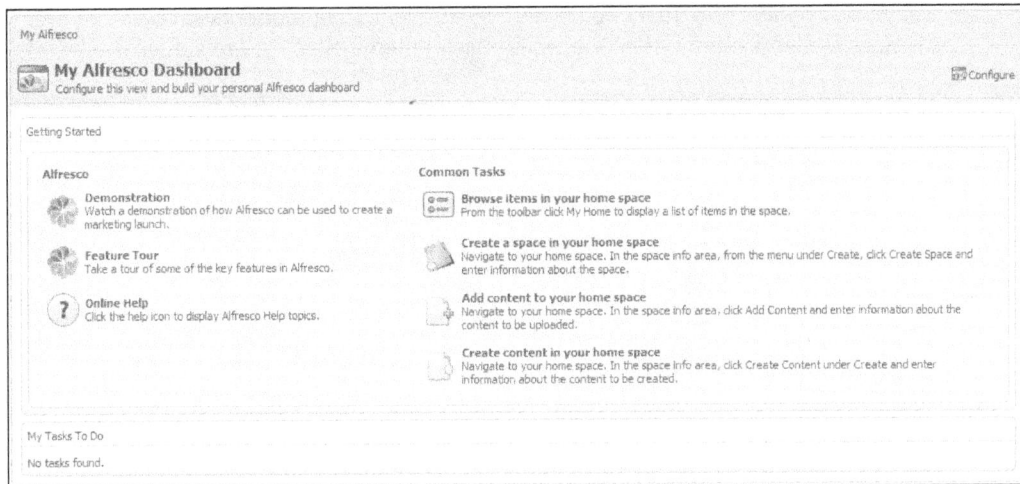

How to do it...

You can configure this landing page using the **Configure** link on top right corner.

1. The first step in the configuration wizard is to set up your screen **layout** – four options are offered here.

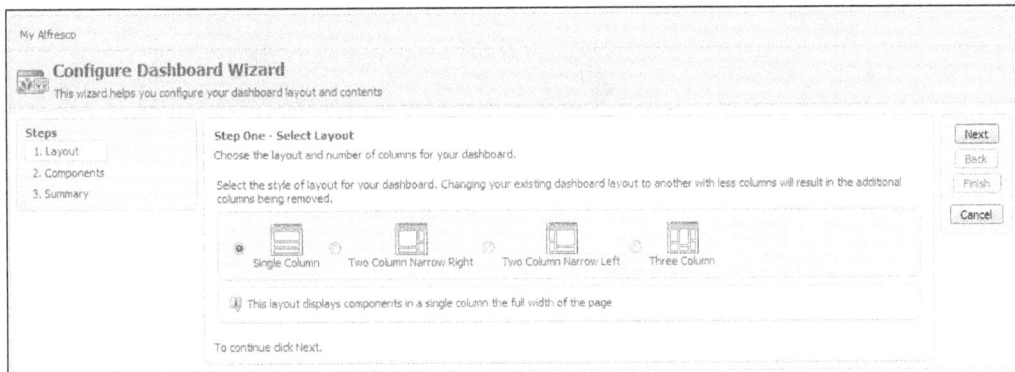

2. Choose the layout you like, and click **Next**. Suppose we select **Two Column Narrow Right** layout.

3. The next screen enables you to put the **components** in each of the available columns of your layout. There are a number of components available, which you can use and configure your dashboard to configure.

4. Suppose, we select My Tasks To Do and `OpenSearch` components in column-1 and My Spaces List component in **Column-2**. Click **Finish** when you are satisfied.

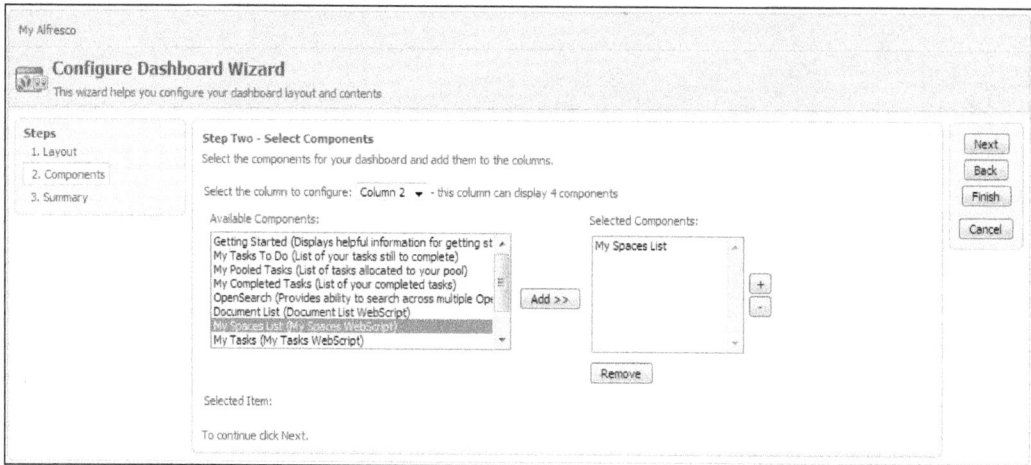

5. You now have a new set of components and layout in your dashboard.

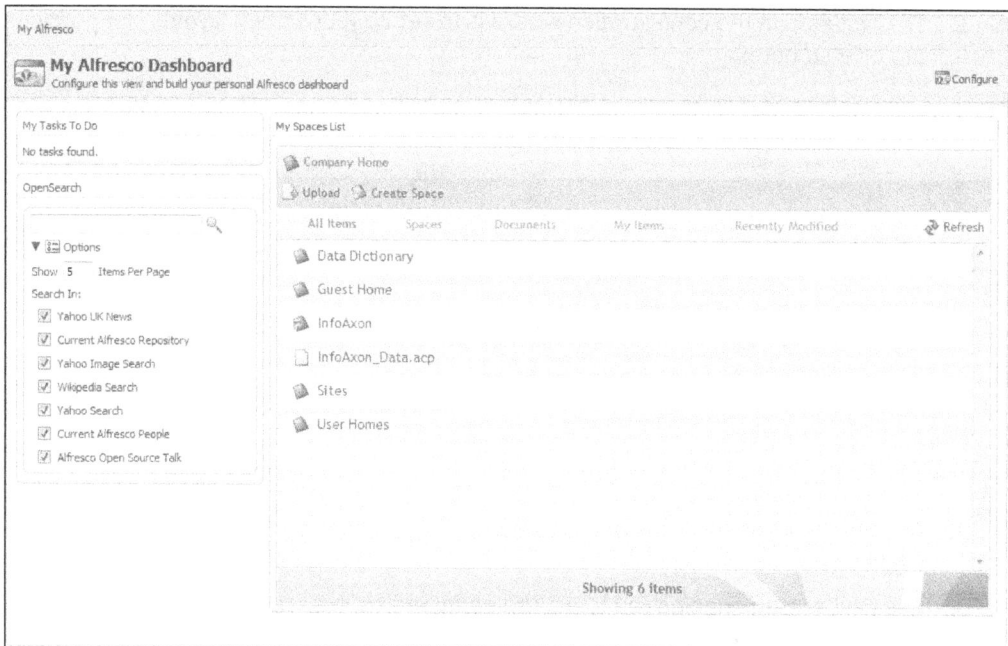

6. The **My Spaces List** is a particularly a useful component. You can perform a wide variety of document management functionalities using the interface shown in the screenshot.

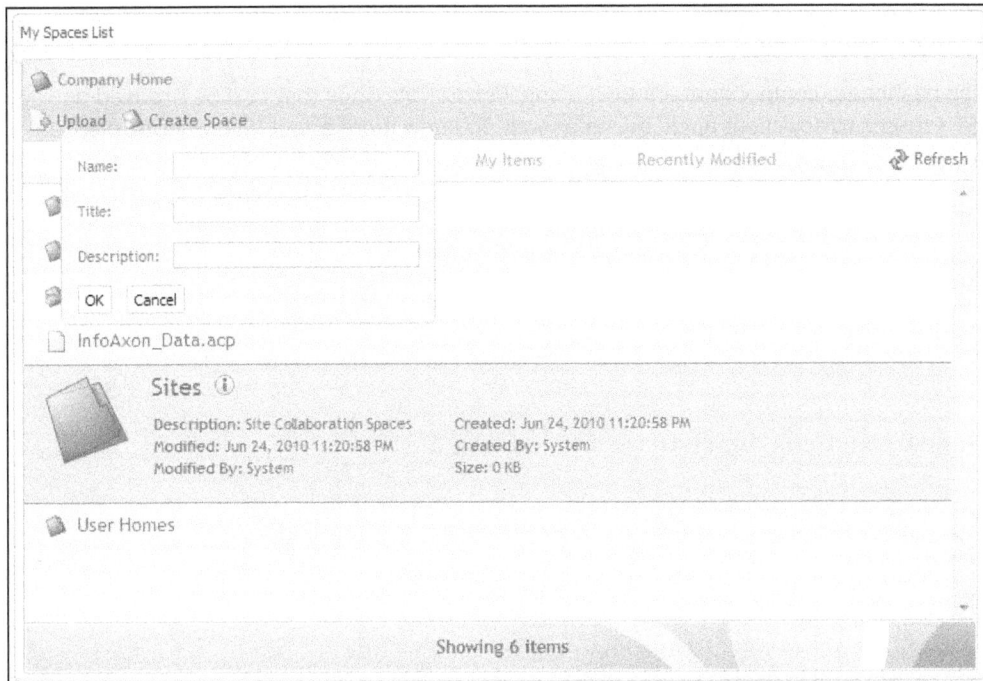

7. Other important components offered by the web client application are:

   ❑ **My Tasks To Do**: Displays your pending tasks.?? What do you mean by pending tasks here? Please give reference to future workflow section here.

   ❑ **My Pooled Tasks**: Displays pooled tasks assigned to you?? What do you mean by pooled tasks here? Please give reference to future workflow section here.

   ❑ **My Completed Tasks**: Displays the tasks completed by you.?? What do you mean by completed tasks here? Please give reference to future workflow section here.

   ❑ **OpenSearch**: Shows the `opensearch` interface. Please describe `OpenSearch` here

   ❑ **Document List**: List of documents uploaded or updated by you.

   ❑ **My Spaces List**: List of spaces which you have created.

   ❑ **My Tasks**: Your task list, in a different view.

   ❑ You can use these components to configure your dashboard.

There's more...

These dashboard components are built using Web Scripts, thus they can be exposed as REST services to any client applications as well. To know more about Web Scripts, please see *Chapter 10*.

6
Customizing Alfresco
Web Client

In this chapter, we will cover:

- ▶ Changing the default view of items in Space Contents
- ▶ Changing languages in the Login Page
- ▶ Changing textbox length and text area size
- ▶ Controlling Alfresco Date Picker
- ▶ Controlling the Sidebar display
- ▶ Adding your custom icons in Alfresco Spaces
- ▶ Changing Alfresco default fonts and color

Introduction

The web client application offers a lot of customizability options in order to suit your purpose. More interestingly, there are no code changes and technical language knowledge required to do this.

All you need to do is to change or add something in a couple of XML configuration files.

Getting ready...

The configuration file which is mostly responsible for setting up all required values is `web-client-config.xml`. You can find this file in the `\tomcat\webapps\alfresco\WEB-INF\classes\alfresco` folder where you have installed your Alfresco server.

If you change some values properly in this XML, and restart your server – you will be able to see that your changes have taken effect in the web client application interface. However, since it is the main file that controls the UI, it is strongly suggested you don't change the file directly.

Instead, Alfresco has provided a mechanism to create and use custom files on top of all configuration files. All these custom files are located in the extension folder in `\tomcat\ shared\classes\alfresco\extension` location. The file you will use to customize the web client UI is `web-client-config-custom.xml`.

Note that the `-custom` keyword is suffixed after the name `web-client-config.xml`. This is a standard convention followed in most of such cases where standard Alfresco configuration XML files are overwritten by some custom XML files.

Open the `web-client-config-custom.xml` file in a text editor like *Notepad, Editplus*, or something similar. You can see except for the root level node `<alfresco-config>`, everything else is commented – there is some sample code provided by Alfresco that you could use as per your requirements. However, for clarity, we will first remove all the commented items and append our own.

Changing the default view of Items in Space contents

By default, all the spaces and content items under a folder are displayed in the **icon** view. Let's assume we want our default view to be **details**. This is much like your windows explorer view options and patterns.

How to do it...

1. Open the `web-client-config-custom.xml` file in your favorite editor and put this code segment inside the root node – `<alfresco-config>`.

```xml
<config evaluator="string-compare" condition="Views">
  <views>
    <view-defaults>
      <browse>
        <!-- allowable values: list|details|icons -->
        <view>details</view>
        <page-size>
          <list>20</list>
          <details>20</details>
          <icons>20</icons>
        </page-size>
      </browse>
    </view-defaults>
```

```
        </views>
      </config>
```

2. Assuming the file was blank, after adding this code, the full file will look like:

```
<alfresco-config>

   <config evaluator="string-compare" condition="Views">
      <views>
         <view-defaults>
            <browse>
               <!-- allowable values: list|details|icons -->
               <view>details</view>
               <page-size>
                  <list>20</list>
                  <details>20</details>
                  <icons>20</icons>
               </page-size>
            </browse>
         </view-defaults>
      </views>
   </config>

</alfresco-config>
```

3. Save the file and restart your tomcat server. Open the **Company Home** folder in the web client. You can see that the default view of the items has been changed to **details** view.

▼ Browse Spaces				Items Per Page 20
Name ▲	Description	Created	Modified	Actions
Data Dictionary	User managed definitions	24 June 2010 23:20	24 June 2010 23:20	
Guest Home	The guest root space	24 June 2010 23:20	24 June 2010 23:20	
InfoAxon	Space for Alfresco 3.3 Cookbook Contents	25 June 2010 17:22	29 June 2010 14:38	
Sites	Site Collaboration Spaces	24 June 2010 23:20	24 June 2010 23:20	
User Homes	User Homes	24 June 2010 23:20	24 June 2010 23:20	

Page 1 of 1

▼ Content Items					Items Per Page 20
Name ▲	Description	Size	Created	Modified	Actions
InfoAxon_Data.acp	Alfresco content package for Space 'InfoAxon'.	1.2 MB	27 October 2010 16:18	27 October 2010 16:18	

Page 1 of 1

4. You can also control the number of items displayed in space contents – by default, it is 20. The code segment in the preceding example defines the number of content items and sub-spaces that would be displayed. You can also control the number of items displayed for each of the view options available.

```
<page-size>
  <list>20</list>
  <details>20</details>
  <icons>20</icons>
</page-size>
```

Changing languages in the Login page

By default, only **English** is activated in the login page of Alfresco.

Sometimes, you do want to show other supported languages in this list.

> Alfresco supports internationalization; this means the framework supports
> a number of languages, locales, and regional settings, using i18n strings
> and resources. For more information on internationalization, please see
> `http://en.wikipedia.org/wiki/Internationalization_and_`
> `localization`
>
> In this recipe, we will see how to enable other languages in Alfresco, apart
> from standard English.

How to do it...

1. Open the `web-client-config-custom.xml` file in your text editor, and put this
   code segment inside the root node - `<alfresco-config>`.

   ```
   <config evaluator="string-compare" condition="Languages">
     <languages>
       <language locale="de_DE">German</language>
   ```

```
        <language locale="es_ES">Spanish</language>
        <language locale="fr_FR">French</language>
        <language locale="it_IT">Italian</language>
    </languages>
  </config>
```

2. Once you invoke the login screen again, you can see that the other added languages have appeared.

3. Thus, you can use other supported and installed languages as well. Similarly, if you delete any language line items from the list, that particular language would be removed.

How it works...

Alfresco uses `LanguagesElementReader` and `LanguagesConfigElement` classes to read the languages defined in the configuration file and populate it into the language list.

These classes are defined in the `org.alfresco.web.config` package definition in the `alfresco-web-client-3.3.jar` file.

There's more...

You can also add new languages in your Alfresco installation. Addition of new languages is done by installing the Language Packs in Alfresco. These language packs are essentially standard Java Resource Bundles (for i18n) along with Alfresco configurations.

For a list of available language packs, please see `http://wiki.alfresco.com/wiki/Language_Packs`.

You can follow the steps mentioned here to install new language packs in your Alfresco installation.

`http://wiki.alfresco.com/wiki/Language_Pack_Installation`

Changing textbox length and text area size

Alfresco web client application uses Java Server Faces (JSF) as the presentation layer. Thus for changing any UI components and controls, you need to set the JSF-related configuration settings.

How to do it...

The following settings should be configured in the JSF configuration file, `faces-config-custom.xml` file in the `\tomcat\webapps\alfresco\WEB-INF` folder.

1. Open the `faces-config-custom.xml` file in your text editor and put this code segment inside the root node – `<faces-config>`.

```
<managed-bean>
    <managed-bean-name>TextFieldGenerator</managed-bean-name>
    <managed-bean-class>org.alfresco.web.bean.generator.
TextFieldGenerator</managed-bean-class>
    <managed-bean-scope>request</managed-bean-scope>
    <managed-property>
        <property-name>size</property-name>
        <value>150</value>
    </managed-property>
</managed-bean>

<managed-bean>
    <managed-bean-name>TextAreaGenerator</managed-bean-name>
    <managed-bean-class>org.alfresco.web.bean.generator.
TextAreaGenerator</managed-bean-class>
    <managed-bean-scope>request</managed-bean-scope>
    <managed-property>
```

```
        <property-name>rows</property-name>
        <value>25</value>
    </managed-property>
    <managed-property>
        <property-name>columns</property-name>
        <value>100</value>
    </managed-property>
</managed-bean>
```

2. The first setting will make the text box size as 150 and the second setting will set the height/width of text areas as 25/100.

3. Restart the server and you can see the effect.

How it works...

As a standard mechanism of JSF components, Alfresco uses managed beans for constructing HTML UI components. The managed bean responsible for creating and rendering text boxes in Alfresco Explorer UI interface is `TextFieldGenerator` and the `TextAreaGenerator` bean is responsible for creating the text areas in various screens.

These classes are defined in the `org.alfresco.web.bean.generator` package definition in the `alfresco-web-client-3.3.jar` file. This package constitutes all the UI generator classes used in Alfresco Web Client. Some other generators are `LabelGenerator`, `LinkGenerator`, `CheckBoxGenerator`, `LanguageSelectorGenerator`, and so on. The `LanguageSelectorGenerator` class is used to create the language drop-down box we had discussed in the previous recipe.

You can also create your own generators for your custom HTML components.

Controlling the Date Picker

The web client application accepts date values using **Date Picker** control. The Year values of this control are rendered as drop down – thus you cannot select any year which is not listed in the drop down. Hence, you sometimes would want to change the year listing as per your requirements.

Following is a snapshot of the date picker control in Alfresco explorer.

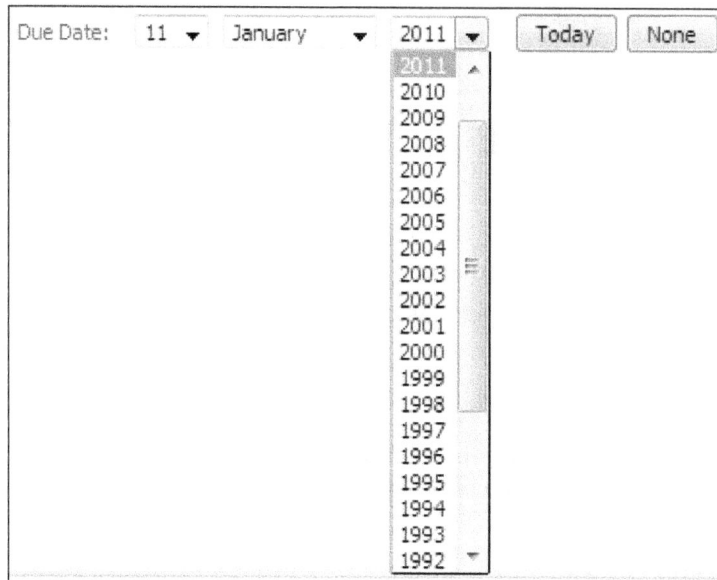

Getting ready

Again, like the previous recipe, change any behavior of the date picker control used in the application, we need to add the settings in the `faces-config-custom.xml` file in the `\tomcat\webapps\alfresco\WEB-INF` location.

How to do it ...

1. Open the `faces-config-custom.xml` file in your text editor and put this code segment inside the root node – `<faces-config>`.

```
<managed-bean>
    <managed-bean-name>DatePickerGenerator</managed-bean-name>
    <managed-bean-class>org.alfresco.web.bean.generator.
DatePickerGenerator</managed-bean-class>
    <managed-bean-scope>request</managed-bean-scope>
    <managed-property>
        <property-name>startYear</property-name>
        <value>2080</value>
    </managed-property>
    <managed-property>
        <property-name>yearCount</property-name>
        <value>100</value>
```

```
        </managed-property>
    </managed-bean>
```

2. This setting will create the available year listing from 1980 to 2080. Means the `startYear` parameter is the maximum value offered in the year drop down of the date picker and `yearCount` defines how many years the picker control should render.

3. Restart your server, navigate to any form with a date parameter, and you can see the changes in effect.

How it works...

Similarly as in the previous recipe, the `DatePickerGenerator` component in the `org.alfresco.web.bean.generator` package is responsible for creating and rendering the Date Picker UI component.

Controlling the sidebar display

The sidebar is the left panel on your screen, that displays a host of useful information such as space navigation, categories, OpenSearch, clipboards, shortcuts, and so on.

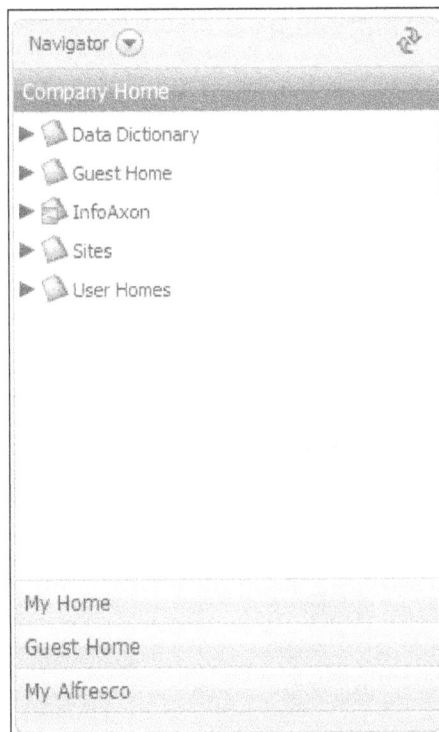

By default, this sidebar is rendered. You can, however, control its visibility using the toggle sidebar icon on the top toolbar.

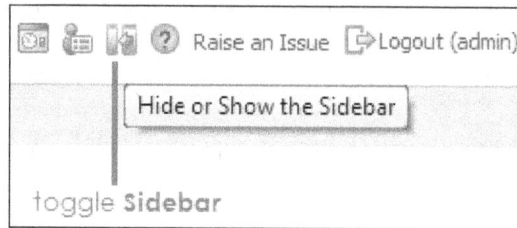

However, if you want the sidebar to not show up by default, you can use this code segment.

How to do it...

1. Open the `web-client-config-custom.xml` file in your text editor and put this code segment inside the root node – `<alfresco-config>`.

   ```
   <config>
     <client>
       <shelf-visible>false</shelf-visible>
     </client>
   </config>
   ```

2. Restart your server, and you will see the sidebar is by default not visible. You can, however, reopen the sidebar using the toggle control illustrated earlier.

3. There can also be requirements where you may want to see the Shelf panel in the sidebar instead of the default navigator panel. For that, use this code segment in the file `web-client-config-custom.xml`.

   ```
   <config evaluator="string-compare" condition="Sidebar">
     <sidebar>
       <default-plugin>shelf</default-plugin>
     </sidebar>
   </config>
   ```

Including custom Icons in your Spaces

You have seen that Alfresco has provided some six icons that you can use as your folder icons in the explorer.

However, you might need more icon options to be available while creating new spaces. For this, you need to have the icon in at least two sizes – 32X32 and 16X16. Optionally, you could have 64X64 size icon as well. You can have your icon images in GIF format.

How to do it...

1. First create your GIF-formatted icons in two sizes, as mentioned previously.

> The names of your icons' files are important. Suppose the name of the image file of 32X32 size is `ia-logo.gif`. In this case, the name of 16X16 size image file should be `ia-logo-16.gif`. Alfresco web client uses the 32X32 size icon while creating the space. However, the miniature version of the same icon would be used in other places where the smaller display is required.

2. Copy your icons to the `\tomcat\webapps\alfresco\images\icons` folder. This is the folder from where the Alfresco web client, by default, displays images and icons.

3. Open the `web-client-config-custom.xml` file in your text editor, and put this code segment inside the root node – `<alfresco-config>`.

```
<config evaluator="string-compare" condition="cm:folder icons">
    <icons>
        <icon name="space-icon-custom" path="/images/icons/ia-logo.
gif" />
    </icons>
</config>
```

4. Restart your server, and try to create a new space. You can see that a new icon option for your space is available.

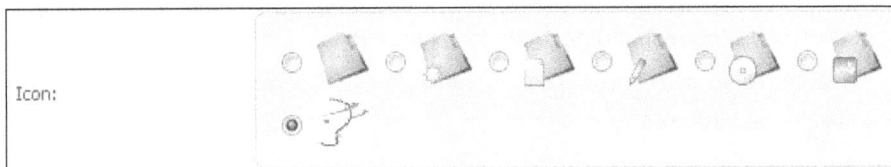

Changing the default font and color

Alfresco uses Cascading Style Sheets (CSS) for managing the font style and colors of the web client application interface.

Amongst other files, the main CSS file used is `main.css`, located in the folder `\tomcat\webapps\alfresco\css`. In this recipe, we will briefly explore how to change the default font style and color of the explorer interface.

How to do it...

1. Open the `main.css` file in your text editor and go to line #23. The CSS code written should be:

```
td,tr,p,div
{
    color: #004488;
    font-family: Tahoma, Arial, Helvetica, sans-serif;
    font-size: 11px;
}
```

2. Let's say, we want our font to be `Verdana`, instead of the default `Tahoma` family. For this, change the `font-family` parameter as follows:

```
td,tr,p,div
{
    color: #004488;
    font-family: Verdana, Tahoma, Arial, Helvetica, sans-serif;
    font-size: 11px;
}
```

3. No need to restart the server; just refresh your web client browser window. You will be able to see the changed font style.

4. However, this change won't update all the sections of the screen. For example, the hyperlinks are still rendered as `Tahoma`. As you know, there should be another entry in the CSS file corresponding to the hyperlinks style.

5. In the same file, `main.css`, go to line #47. The CSS code written should be

```
a:link, a:visited
{
    font-size: 11px;
    color: #004488;
    text-decoration: none;
    font-family: Tahoma, Arial, Helvetica, sans-serif;
    font-weight: normal;
}
```

6. Again, we would add `Verdana` in the `font-family`.

```
a:link, a:visited
{
    font-size: 11px;
    color: #004488;
    text-decoration: none;
    font-family: Verdana, Tahoma, Arial, Helvetica, sans-serif;
    font-weight: normal;
}
```

7. As earlier, refresh the web client browser window, and you will be able to see the changed font style for hyperlinks as well.

8. For changing the color of texts, we update the same classes in the same CSS file. Here is the new code snippet:

```
td,tr,p,div
{
    color: #0000FF;
  font-family: Verdana, Tahoma, Arial, Helvetica, sans-serif;
    font-size: 11px;
}
```

9. You may notice we have changed the color parameter from #004488 to #0000FF. Similarly for the hyperlinks color:

```
a:link, a:visited
{
    font-size: 11px;
    color: #0000FF;
    text-decoration: none;
  font-family: Verdana, Tahoma, Arial, Helvetica, sans-serif;
    font-weight: normal;
}
```

10. This change won't affect the hover color of the hyperlinks. Should you want to do that, you must change the `a:hover` entry details. We have changed the color from #4272B4 to #00FF00.

```
a:hover
{
    color: #00FF00;
    text-decoration: underline;
    font-weight: normal;
}
```

11. Again, refresh your application browser and you can witness the changes in effect.

How it works...

`main.css` is the main cascading stylesheet file used by the Alfresco explorer web application. Thus, you can change the look and feel of the web client application by changing styles in this file.

> Before changing the CSS files, it is advisable to keep a backup copy of the original files.

There are a few CSS files used by the application. A couple of these are `picker.css` and `calendarMain.css`. For changing the styles of the relevant items, you may need to change these files.

7
Alfresco Content Model

In this chapter, we will cover:

- ▶ Creating a new custom content type
- ▶ Displaying custom content type while uploading content
- ▶ Showing custom properties
- ▶ Creating custom aspects and associations
- ▶ Showing custom aspects and associations
- ▶ Displaying custom type in type specialization
- ▶ Customizing advanced search to include custom content types

Introduction

Contents in Alfresco can be defined as any document, file, or folder created in the repository and content models are the structure of these contents. Alfresco content models are defined in the Data Dictionary as meta-model. The meta-model consists of two main structures – **Content Type** and **Content Aspect**.

The following diagram depicts a logical design of the content model architecture:

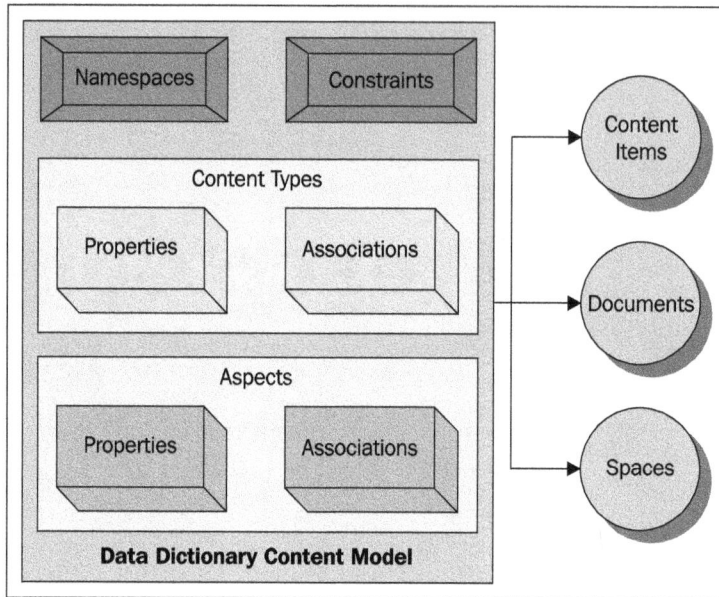

Content Type

Content Type is the fundamental structure of a content item. It defines the composition of properties and behaviors of a content item. Much like in the object-oriented programming model where an object always has to be of a defined class type, in Alfresco an item has to be of a defined type also. The content types in Alfresco abide by the inheritance construct of a object-oriented programming model.

There is a root content type defined in Alfresco, all other content types are created inheriting this root type – `cm:content` or `http://www.alfresco.org/model/content/1.0} content`.

Thus, whenever you want to create your custom content type, you must inherit your type from the `cm:content` base type.

It is important to note the semantics of the name of the content type –
`{http://www.alfresco.org/model/content/1.0}content`.
There are two parts in defining the name – the _namespace_ of the content
type and the _name_ of the content type. In this example, the namespace is
`{http://www.alfresco.org/model/content/1.0}` and the name
is `content`.

The namespace is used to differentiate the content type, much like your Java
class packages. Thus `{http://www.infoaxon.com/models/1.0}`
`invoice` and `{http://www.packtpub.com/models/1.0} invoice`
are different. So you can use the same name _invoice_ multiple times for
different purposes.

Often you can use a shortened form of the namespace instead of using the
full name or fully qualified name. This works as an alias of the full name.

In our example, `cm:content` and `{http://www.alfresco.org/`
`model/content/1.0}content` are both the same. You define this alias
in your content model XML file as the **prefix** of your namespace.

Normally, while creating your own custom content model, you use your own
namespace – this will differentiate your types with Alfresco's default models.
Further, in case you plan to handle different models in a single repository, it
is suggested you use different namespace in order to uniquely identify the
different model definitions.

Content Aspect

Content Aspect is a reusable encapsulation of properties and behaviors. An aspect can be
applied or associated with any content both at design time as well as at runtime. This feature
follows the Aspect-Oriented Programming model. It allows an increase of modularity in content
modeling by separation of common concerns and behaviors.

For example, a popular and common out of the box aspect is **Dublin Core aspect**. It includes
properties like Publisher, Contributor, Subject, Rights, and so on. Thus, whenever this aspect
is associated with any content item, all these properties are available to this content. You can
programmatically associate such an aspect to any content item, thus enhancing the content
type with their properties dynamically.

Thus you should create an aspect encapsulating all the common and cross-cutting properties,
instead of creating a content type with those properties. You can add that aspect with any
content items either at design time or at runtime. This would give you more flexibility and
modularity in your content model design and maintenance.

Important content models

The default content models are also defined in the XML file – in the `\tomcat\webapps\alfresco\WEB-INF\classes\alfresco\model` folder in your Alfresco setup. Some important models worth noting are:

- `dictionaryModel.xml`: The core and base model of Alfresco data. This defines all the basic data types that will be used for defining other content models. It defines the namespaces `http://www.alfresco.org/model/dictionary/1.0` that, in most cases, are used as an alias d, such as `d:text`, `d:int`, `d:date`, `d:Boolean`, and so on.

- `systemModel.xml`: System model, as the name suggests, defines the models used by Alfresco system and the most abstract models in Alfresco. It defines the namespace `http://www.alfresco.org/model/system/1.0` that is most commonly used as `sys`. It defines the `sys:base` model which is the base of everything in Alfresco.

- `contentModel.xml`: This is the definition of all base objects and content types in the Alfresco repository. It defines the namespace `http://www.alfresco.org/model/content/1.0` which is usually utilized as `cm`. It defines base content type as `cm:content`, space type as `cm:folder`, user as `cm:person`, category as `cm:category`, and so on. It also defines commonly used aspects such as `cm:dublincore`, `cm:author`, `cm:versionable`, `cm:taggable`, `cm:emailed`, and so on.

- `bpmModel.xml`: This stores all the business process models in Alfresco. Till now, Alfresco uses **JBPM** as the workflow engine. Alfresco allows custom tasks to be created as part of your business process implementation. This `bpmModel` defines all base task types that you would use to define your custom tasks, task owners, and workflows. It defines the namespace `http://www.alfresco.org/model/bpm/1.0`, commonly used as `bpm`. Some important types and aspects to be noted here are `bpm:task`, `bpm:workflowTask`, `bpm:startTask`, `bpm:assignee`, `bpm:workflowPackage`, and so on. There are a few more useful and important concepts we should know before we start creating our custom model.

- **Constraints**: While creating your model, you definitely would want to put some restrictions on the possible values of the properties.

  - For example, if you create a property for date-of-birth, you might not want the value to be something like 10th January, 1750 – for this you might want to put some valid and allowed date ranges.

  - The constraint mechanism in the content model is used for such cases. Alfresco has a strong constraint evaluation and enforcement engine that you can use for implementing your business requirements.

  - A constraint definition is also reusable, this means you can use a single defined constraint several times, in several places and across namespaces.

▶ **Associations**: Consider a scenario. You want to define and store related items to a particular content item. In order to make it easier, suppose the related items can be any other content items, not spaces. That means the related items can be of type `cm:content`.

  ❑ To implement such scenarios we would use *associations*. Association, as the name suggests, can be defined as a relationship between two items. Even the content items stored in a particular space in Alfresco are **associated** to that space.

  ❑ Using these base types, aspects, constraints, and associations you can create your own custom content model.

There are two ways of creating a custom model in Alfresco.

1. Create and deploy content model XML file in classpath – content models are not stored in the Alfresco repository, thus you can use the model in different repositories.

2. Create and upload content model XML file in Data Dictionary in Explorer – content models are stored in Alfresco repository. Not stored in your file system.

In this book, we will explore the first method of creating our own content models. The folder location where you should deploy your own content model files is the `extension` folder where we put the `web-client-config-custom.xml` file – in the `\tomcat\shared\ classes\alfresco\extension` folder. If you scan the default file list in this folder, you will discover a file named `customModel.xml`. Alfresco has provided this sample model file which is ready to be consumed for creating custom models.

```
<!-- Custom Model -->
<!-- Note: This model is pre-configured to load at startup of the
Repository.  So, all custom -->
<!--       types and aspects added here will automatically be
registered -->
<model name="custom:customModel" xmlns="http://www.alfresco.org/model/
dictionary/1.0">
    <!-- Optional meta-data about the model -->
    <description>Custom Model</description>
    <author></author>
    <version>1.0</version>
    <imports>
        <!-- Import Alfresco Dictionary Definitions -->
        <import uri="http://www.alfresco.org/model/dictionary/1.0"
prefix="d"/>
        <!-- Import Alfresco Content Domain Model Definitions -->
        <import uri="http://www.alfresco.org/model/content/1.0"
prefix="cm"/>
    </imports>
    <!-- Introduction of new namespaces defined by this model -->
```

```
<!-- NOTE: The following namespace custom.model should be changed
to reflect your own namespace -->
<namespaces>
    <namespace uri="custom.model" prefix="custom"/>
</namespaces>

</model>
```

This gives a good platform and starting point for creating our model.

However, for better understanding, we will create our own model file and use that.

Creating new custom content type

We will create a new file for our custom content model. As you know, the file ideally should be created in the `\tomcat\shared\classes\alfresco\extension` folder. Although you can create your file in any other folder as well, it is a standard convention to put all custom configuration files in this folder only. This folder is usually referred to as the **extension** folder of Alfresco.

When you create your own custom content model file, you must let Alfresco know about your content model file – that is, you need to register your model in the Alfresco repository. This is done by the `custom-model-context.xml` file located in the `\tomcat\shared\classes\alfresco\extension` folder.

> By default, this file is named `custom-model-context.xml.sample`, you need to rename it `custom-model-context.xml`.

This file is used to bootstrap all the custom models you create in the Alfresco repository.

Getting ready

First we will create the file where our custom model will be defined.

1. Create a new XML file named `catalogueModel.xml` in the `extension` folder.

2. Open the `custom-model-context.xml` file in a text editor. This is the default code of this file.

   ```xml
   <?xml version='1.0' encoding='UTF-8'?>
   <!DOCTYPE beans PUBLIC '-//SPRING//DTD BEAN//EN' 'http://www.springframework.org/dtd/spring-beans.dtd'>

   <beans>

       <!-- Registration of new models -->
   ```

```
    <bean id="extension.dictionaryBootstrap" parent="dictionaryMod
elBootstrap" depends-on="dictionaryBootstrap">
        <property name="models">
            <list>
                <value>alfresco/extension/customModel.xml</value>
            </list>
        </property>
    </bean>

</beans>
```

3. Remove the previously highlighted line and insert the following. This is because the custom content model file we will write is named `catalogueModel.xml`.

```
<value>alfresco/extension/catalogueModel.xml</value>
```

The `custom-model-context.xml` file would look like:

```
<?xml version='1.0' encoding='UTF-8'?>
<!DOCTYPE beans PUBLIC '-//SPRING//DTD BEAN//EN' 'http://www.
springframework.org/dtd/spring-beans.dtd'>

<beans>
    <!-- Registration of new models -->
    <bean id="extension.dictionaryBootstrap" parent="dictionaryMod
elBootstrap" depends-on="dictionaryBootstrap">
        <property name="models">
            <list>
                <value>alfresco/extension/catalogueModel.xml</
value>
            </list>
        </property>
    </bean>

</beans>
```

How to do it...

1. Now open the `catalogueModel.xml` file in a text editor; and put in the following code segment:

```
<?xml version="1.0" encoding="UTF-8"?>

<model name="iabook:catalogue" xmlns="http://www.alfresco.org/
model/dictionary/1.0">

  <description>Retailer Product Catalogue</description>
  <author>Snig Bhaumik</author>
  <version>1.0</version>
```

```
    <imports>
        <import uri="http://www.alfresco.org/model/dictionary/1.0"
prefix="d"/>
        <import uri="http://www.alfresco.org/model/content/1.0"
prefix="cm"/>
    </imports>

    <namespaces>
        <namespace uri="http://www.infoaxon.com/book/models/
catalogue/1.0" prefix="iabook"/>
    </namespaces>

    <types>
    </types>

</model>
```

2. A few points worth noting here:

   - We have created a new model named {`http://www.infoaxon.com/book/models/catalogue/1.0`} `catalogue` or `iabook:catalogue`.

   - We have defined the alias `iabook` of the namespace `http://www.infoaxon.com/book/models/catalogue/1.0`.

   - We have imported the minimum required namespaces `http://www.alfresco.org/model/dictionary/1.0` and `http://www.alfresco.org/model/content/1.0` with regular aliases `d` and `cm`.

3. You can see a blank tag `types` in this code. We will now define our custom content types in this node.

   Let's say we want to define a type named `Product` having properties like Name, Manufacturer, Brand, SKU, Price, and so on. Paste the following code in the `types` node in the `catalogueModel.xml` file.

```
<type name="iabook:Product">
  <title>Retailer Product</title>
  <parent>cm:content</parent>
  <properties>
    <property name="iabook:sku">
      <title>Product SKU</title>
      <type>d:text</type>
      <mandatory>true</mandatory>
    </property>
    <property name="iabook:manufacturer">
      <title>Manufacturer</title>
      <type>d:text</type>
      <mandatory>true</mandatory>
    </property>
    <property name="iabook:color">
```

```
        <title>Product Color</title>
        <type>d:text</type>
        <mandatory>false</mandatory>
      </property>
      <property name="iabook:brand">
        <title>Manufacturer Brand</title>
        <type>d:text</type>
        <mandatory>false</mandatory>
      </property>
      <property name="iabook:unitPrice">
        <title>Product Unit Price</title>
        <type>d:double</type>
        <mandatory>true</mandatory>
      </property>
      <property name="iabook:displayUntil">
        <title>Date until Product should be displayed</title>
        <type>d:datetime</type>
        <mandatory>true</mandatory>
      </property>
      <property name="iabook:competitorProducts">
        <title>Competitor Products List</title>
        <type>d:text</type>
        <mandatory>false</mandatory>
        <multiple>true</multiple>
      </property>
      <property name="iabook:competitorDetails">
        <title>Details of Competitor Products</title>
        <type>d:text</type>
        <mandatory>false</mandatory>
      </property>
    </properties>
  </type>
```

4. Thus we have defined a new content model here named `iabook:Product` or `{http://www.infoaxon.com/book/models/catalogue/1.0}Product`.

5. Now let's say we have products only of three colors – Red, Green, and Blue. So you definitely want to restrict your content model to put this control. As you know, you can do this using the constraint mechanism in the content model.

6. To do this, add this code snippet between namespaces and types nodes in your model file.

```
<constraints>
  <constraint name="iabook:productColors" type="LIST">
    <parameter name="allowedValues">
      <list>
```

```
        <value>Red</value>
        <value>Green</value>
        <value>Blue</value>
      </list>
    </parameter>
    <parameter name="caseSensitive">
      <value>false</value>
    </parameter>
  </constraint>
</constraints>
```

> Note that the location of this constraints tag is not important. However, it is good to have your content model file properly organized.

7. Add the following in the `color` property declaration in your content type:

```
<constraints>
<constraint ref="iabook:productColors" />
</constraints>
```

8. Finally the model file should look like this:

```
<?xml version="1.0" encoding="UTF-8"?>

<model name="iabook:catalogue" xmlns="http://www.alfresco.org/
model/dictionary/1.0">

  <description>Retailer Product Catalogue</description>
  <author>Snig Bhaumik</author>
  <version>1.0</version>

  <imports>
     <import uri="http://www.alfresco.org/model/dictionary/1.0"
prefix="d"/>
     <import uri="http://www.alfresco.org/model/content/1.0"
prefix="cm"/>
  </imports>

  <namespaces>
     <namespace uri="http://www.infoaxon.com/book/models/
catalogue/1.0" prefix="iabook"/>
  </namespaces>

  <constraints>
    <constraint name="iabook:productColors" type="LIST">
      <parameter name="allowedValues">
        <list>
           <value>Red</value>
           <value>Green</value>
```

```xml
              <value>Blue</value>
            </list>
         </parameter>
         <parameter name="caseSensitive">
           <value>false</value>
         </parameter>
      </constraint>
  </constraints>
<types>
   <type name="iabook:Product">
      <title>Retailer Product</title>
      <parent>cm:content</parent>
      <properties>
         <property name="iabook:sku">
            <title>Product SKU</title>
            <type>d:text</type>
            <mandatory>true</mandatory>
         </property>
         <property name="iabook:manufacturer">
            <title>Manufacturer</title>
            <type>d:text</type>
            <mandatory>true</mandatory>
         </property>
         <property name="iabook:color">
            <title>Product Color</title>
            <type>d:text</type>
            <mandatory>false</mandatory>
            <constraints>
               <constraint ref="iabook:productColors" />
            </constraints>
         </property>
         <property name="iabook:brand">
            <title>Manufacturer Brand</title>
            <type>d:text</type>
            <mandatory>false</mandatory>
         </property>
         <property name="iabook:unitPrice">
            <title>Product Unit Price</title>
            <type>d:double</type>
            <mandatory>true</mandatory>
         </property>
         <property name="iabook:displayUntil">
            <title>Date until Product should be displayed</title>
            <type>d:datetime</type>
```

```
                    <mandatory>true</mandatory>
                </property>
                <property name="iabook:competitorProducts">
                    <title>Competitor Products List</title>
                    <type>d:text</type>
                    <mandatory>false</mandatory>
                    <multiple>true</multiple>
                </property>
                <property name="iabook:competitorDetails">
                    <title>Details of Competitor Products</title>
                    <type>d:text</type>
                    <mandatory>false</mandatory>
                </property>
            </properties>
        </type>
    </types>
</model>
```

How it works...

It is important to understand the XML tags used to define the properties. Some of the important tags are:

▶ Title: The caption of the property, when to be displayed in the Explorer application.

▶ Type: The data type of the property. Some of the important data types are:

Type Name	Description	Type
text	Textual value	d:text
int	Integer value	d:int
long	Long Integer value	d:long
float	Float value	d:float
double	Double numeric value	d:double
date	Date value (without time entry)	d:date
datetime	Datetime value	d:datetime
boolean	Boolean value (true/false)	d:boolean
noderef	Noderef value	d:noredef
any	Any value	d:any

> You can see these data types defined and listed in the `dictionaryModel.xml` file in the `\tomcat\webapps\alfresco\WEB-INF\classes\alfresco\model` folder.

- ▶ `mandatory`: Defines whether the property is mandatory or not – this value should be true or false. If you do not add this tag, the default value is false.

- ▶ You can add an attribute `enforced='true'` with the `mandatory` tag. This would ensure that no content item would be possible to exist in the repository with the null value of this property. By default, without the `enforced` attribute, the `mandatory` element allows us to control only the contents created and modified using the Alfresco Explorer interface. Adding the `enforced` attribute allows setting this constraint for all the other application interfaces exposed by Alfresco such as Foundation API, JCR, CMIS, Web Services, Webdav, and FTP. `<mandatory>` is only for changes done using the Alfresco Explorer. `<mandatory enforced="true">` is for changes using all the other application interfaces.

- ▶ The full tag would be:

  ```
  <mandatory enforced='true'>true</mandatory>
  ```

- ▶ `multiple`: Defines whether more than one value is possible for this property. This value should be `true` or `false`. If you do not add this tag, the default value will be `false`.

- ▶ `default`: If you want to put any default value for a property, use this:

  ```
  <default>some default value</default>
  ```

Until now, we have developed a new custom content type named Product. However, if you restart your Tomcat server now, you won't be able to see your new content type anywhere in the Alfresco Explorer application.

This is because your content model has been registered, but the Alfresco Explorer application is not aware of how and where to display your content type.

See also

Displaying custom Content Type while content uploading.

Displaying custom Content Type while content uploading

As you know, all the customization settings for the Alfresco explorer application should be done using the `web-client-config-custom.xml` file in the `extension` folder. So for displaying your custom content types in the explorer application, you need to put all required settings in this file.

How to do it...

1. Open the `web-client-config-custom.xml` file in a text editor.

2. At the end of this file, add this code snippet:

```xml
<config evaluator="string-compare" condition="Content Wizards">
  <content-types>
    <type name="iabook:Product"/>
  </content-types>
</config>
```

3. The file now should now look like this:

```xml
<alfresco-config>

  <config evaluator="string-compare" condition="Views">
    <views>
      <view-defaults>
        <browse>
          <!-- allowable values: list|details|icons -->
          <view>details</view>
          <page-size>
            <list>20</list>
            <details>20</details>
            <icons>20</icons>
          </page-size>
        </browse>
      </view-defaults>
    </views>
  </config>

  <config evaluator="string-compare" condition="Languages">
    <languages>
      <language locale="de_DE">German</language>
      <language locale="es_ES">Spanish</language>
      <language locale="fr_FR">French</language>
      <language locale="it_IT">Italian</language>
    </languages>
  </config>

  <config>
    <client>
      <shelf-visible>false</shelf-visible>
    </client>
  </config>

  <config evaluator="string-compare" condition="Sidebar">
    <sidebar>
```

```
        <default-plugin>shelf</default-plugin>
      </sidebar>
    </config>
    <config evaluator="string-compare" condition="cm:folder icons">
      <icons>
        <icon name="space-icon-custom" path="/images/icons/ia-logo.
gif" />
      </icons>
    </config>

    <!-- Custom Content Type Settings -->
    <config evaluator="string-compare" condition="Content Wizards">
      <content-types>
        <type name="iabook:Product"/>
      </content-types>
    </config>

  </alfresco-config>
```

4. Restart your Tomcat server.

5. Go to **Company Home** and try to add a new Content. In the list of content types available, you will now see that the `Retailer Product` type is presented.

ℹ 'Noname1.txt' was uploaded successfully.

Uploaded Content

Noname1.txt   🗑

General Properties

⊙ Name: Noname1.txt

    Type: | Content ▾ |

    Encoding: | Content   ▾ | new type *Retailer Product* is
                      | Retailer Product | listed in the available types.

    Content Type: | Plain Text   ▾ |

Other Properties

Rules applied to this content may require you to enter additional information.

☑ Modify all properties when this page closes.

---

6. Use your new content type and upload a document.

How it works...

In the previous recipe, we created and registered our custom content types. In this recipe, we have learnt how to include the custom type in the list of available content types while creating new contents in Alfresco explorer.

> The `title` value of the custom type is displayed in the drop-down list. Thus, whatever the name of the type is, the title value would be automatically used for displaying the type in the various explorer screens.
>
> You can also add the model `Resource Bundle` for setting up the title, description values of your custom types, and aspects.

If you try to **Create Content**, you would also have the **Content Type Retailer Product** available in the list.

Step One - Specify name and select type
Specify the name and select the type of content you wish to create.

General Properties

Name:

Type: Content

Content Type: | Content | new type **Retailer Product** is
| Retailer Product | listed in the available types.

Other Properties

Rules applied to this content may require you to enter additional information.

☑ Modify all properties when this wizard closes.

To continue click Next.

This is done by inserting the type name `iabook:product` in the `web-client-config-custom.xml` file.

```
<config evaluator="string-compare" condition="Content Wizards">
  <content-types>
    <type name="iabook:Product"/>
  </content-types>
</config>
```

Note the condition attribute settings in this code – `Content Wizards`. This indicates that the values will be applicable in all the content creation wizard screens.

In the `content-types` node, you need to include all the custom types you want to display in the content creation screens.

Showing custom properties

Now if you view the details of the new content uploaded, you won't be able to see any of the properties you have added in your custom type. Only the default content properties are displayed.

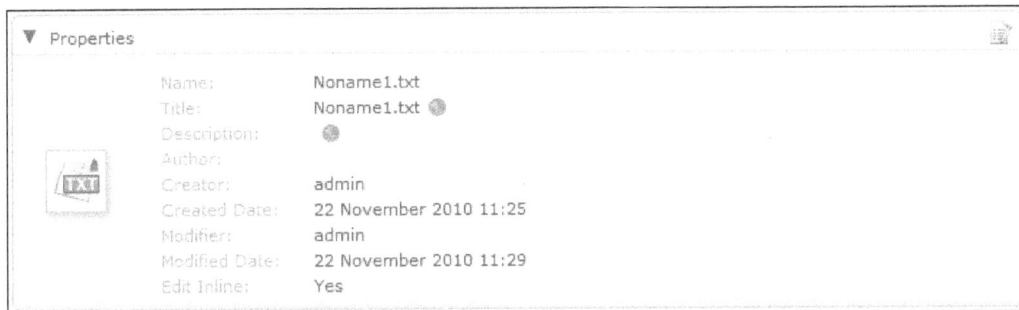

▼ Properties

	Name:	Noname1.txt
	Title:	Noname1.txt
	Description:	
	Author:	
	Creator:	admin
	Created Date:	22 November 2010 11:25
	Modifier:	admin
	Modified Date:	22 November 2010 11:29
	Edit Inline:	Yes

Similarly, in the properties editor dialog, the new properties are not displayed.

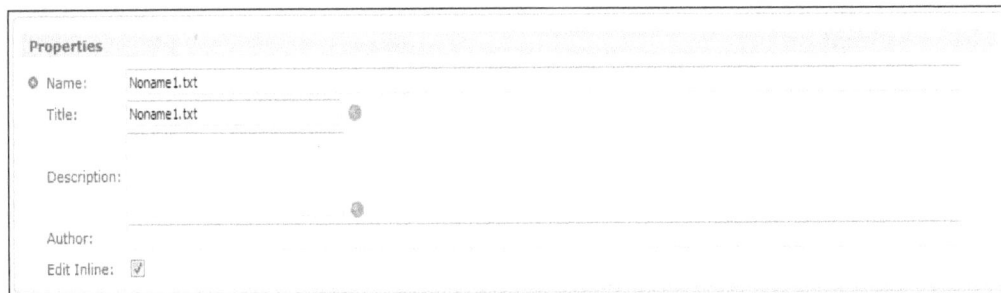

Properties

Name: Noname1.txt

Title: Noname1.txt

Description:

Author:

Edit Inline: ✓

For this, you need to include the property sheet display settings in the `web-client-config-custom.xml` file.

How to do it...

1. Open the `web-client-config-custom.xml` file in your text editor.

2. Add the following code snippet at the end of the file.

```
<config evaluator="node-type" condition="iabook:Product">
  <property-sheet>
    <show-property name="name" />
    <show-property name="mimetype" display-label-id="content_
type" component-generator="MimeTypeSelectorGenerator" />
```

```
        <show-property name="encoding" display-label-id="encoding"
ignore-if-missing="false" component-generator="CharsetSelectorGene
rator" />
        <show-property name="size" display-label-id="size"
converter="org.alfresco.faces.ByteSizeConverter" show-in-edit-
mode="false" />
        <show-property name="title" display-label-id="title" ignore-
if-missing="false" />
        <show-property name="description" display-label-
id="description" ignore-if-missing="false" component-generator="Mu
ltilingualTextAreaGenerator" />
        <show-property name="iabook:sku" />
        <show-property name="iabook:manufacturer" />
        <show-property name="iabook:color" />
        <show-property name="iabook:brand" />
        <show-property name="iabook:unitPrice" />
        <show-property name="iabook:displayUntil" />
        <show-property name="iabook:competitorProducts" />
        <show-property name="iabook:competitorDetails" component-
generator="TextAreaGenerator" />
      </property-sheet>
    </config>
```

3. Thus the `web-client-config-custom.xml` file would look like this:

```
<alfresco-config>

  <config evaluator="string-compare" condition="Views">
    <views>
      <view-defaults>
        <browse>
          <!-- allowable values: list|details|icons -->
          <view>details</view>
          <page-size>
            <list>20</list>
            <details>20</details>
            <icons>20</icons>
          </page-size>
        </browse>
      </view-defaults>
    </views>
  </config>

  <config evaluator="string-compare" condition="Languages">
    <languages>
      <language locale="de_DE">German</language>
      <language locale="es_ES">Spanish</language>
```

```
            <language locale="fr_FR">French</language>
            <language locale="it_IT">Italian</language>
         </languages>
      </config>

      <config>
         <client>
            <shelf-visible>false</shelf-visible>
         </client>
      </config>

      <config evaluator="string-compare" condition="Sidebar">
         <sidebar>
            <default-plugin>shelf</default-plugin>
         </sidebar>
      </config>

      <config evaluator="string-compare" condition="cm:folder icons">
         <icons>
            <icon name="space-icon-custom" path="/images/icons/ia-logo.
gif" />
         </icons>
      </config>

      <!-- Custom Content Type Settings -->
      <config evaluator="string-compare" condition="Content Wizards">
         <content-types>
            <type name="iabook:Product"/>
         </content-types>
      </config>

      <config evaluator="node-type" condition="iabook:Product">
         <property-sheet>
            <show-property name="name" />
            <show-property name="mimetype" display-label-id="content_
type" component-generator="MimeTypeSelectorGenerator" />
            <show-property name="encoding" display-label-id="encoding"
ignore-if-missing="false" component-generator="CharsetSelectorGene
rator" />
            <show-property name="size" display-label-id="size"
converter="org.alfresco.faces.ByteSizeConverter" show-in-edit-
mode="false" />
            <show-property name="title" display-label-id="title" ignore-
if-missing="false" />
            <show-property name="description" display-label-
id="description" ignore-if-missing="false" component-generator="Mu
ltilingualTextAreaGenerator" />
            <show-property name="iabook:sku" />
```

```
        <show-property name="iabook:manufacturer" />
        <show-property name="iabook:color" />
        <show-property name="iabook:brand" />
        <show-property name="iabook:unitPrice" />
        <show-property name="iabook:displayUntil" />
        <show-property name="iabook:competitorProducts" />
        <show-property name="iabook:competitorDetails" component-
generator="TextAreaGenerator" />
    </property-sheet>
  </config>
</alfresco-config>
```

4. Restart Tomcat and open the details of the new content we have just uploaded. If you see the **Properties** section, new properties are rendered.

5. Of course, there are no values of the properties, as we haven't fed any values till now, and also there are no default values set.

> Note that the `title` value of each property, as defined in the content model, is displayed as the label or caption in the screen. You can also have a model resource bundle in the title and description of each of the properties and have multi-lingual capabilities in the explorer.

6. Let's now see how it displays while we edit the properties. Open the property editor dialog.

Properties

Name: Noname1.txt
Title: Noname1.txt
Description:
Author:
Edit Inline: ☑
Content Type: Plain Text
Encoding: UTF-8
Product SKU:
Manufacturer:
Product Color: Red
Manufacturer Brand:
Product Unit Price:
Date until Product should be displayed: 22 November 2010 16 : 51 [Today] [None]
[Add to List]

Competitor Products List: Selected Items
Name
No selected items.

Details of Competitor Products:

[OK] [Cancel]
Ok button remains disabled until all mandatory properties are set

default properties

mandatory values indicator

color property rendered as drop-down to ensure fixed list of values

date property automatically rendered using *datePickerGenerator*

custom properties

multiple values

7. You can enter the values of your properties and save.

▼ Properties

Name:	Noname1.txt
Title:	Noname1.txt
Description:	
Author:	
Creator:	admin
Created Date:	22 November 2010 16:44
Modifier:	admin
Modified Date:	22 November 2010 17:07
Edit Inline:	Yes
Content Type:	Plain Text
Encoding:	UTF-8
Size:	3.06 KB
Product SKU:	102890
Manufacturer:	Canon
Product Color:	Blue
Manufacturer Brand:	Powershot
Product Unit Price:	345.6
Date until Product should be displayed:	22 November 2010 16:51
Competitor Products List:	Sony Cybershot, Nikon Coolpix, Panasonic Lumix, Fujifim Finepix
Details of Competitor Products:	Zoom is lesser. Price is competitive.

How it works...

The code responsible for rendering the custom properties in explorer is highlighted in the earlier code snapshot.

- The condition we have entered in this code is `iabook:Product`. Thus, this section of settings would be applicable for all the content items which are of type `Product`.

- `property-sheet` denotes that the following setting would be applicable to the content property sheet.

- `show-property` node defines how the particular property should be rendered in different screens of the explorer.

- `name` defines the property.

- `display-label-id` refers to the resource from the resource bundle.

- `show-in-edit-mode` instructs whether this property should be displayed in the property editor dialog. It is a boolean value.

- `component-generator` setting defines which JSF component generator the explorer should use in order to render the component in the property editor dialog.

In many cases, the explorer is intelligent enough to identify which is the best component to be used to displaying the property. For example, in our case, `displayUntil` property has been automatically rendered using `datePickerGenerator`; multiple values are also enabled in case of `competitorProducts`.

Creating custom aspects and associations

Until now, we have seen how to create custom content types and how to display the types and properties in the explorer. Now, we will explore how to create custom aspects and associations.

Getting ready

As you know, we have created the `catalogueModel.xml` custom model file for developing our custom content types. We will be adding our custom aspects using this file only, although you can create new model files and bootstrap those in the `custom-model-context.xml` file.

How to do it...

1. Let's say we want to create an aspect for Related Products. We would use this aspect for storing related products into any existing product. Add the following code snippet in the `catalogueModel.xml` file under the `types` node:

   ```
   <aspects>
   ```

```
<aspect name="iabook:relatedProducts">
  <title>Related Products</title>
  <associations>
    <association name="iabook:relatedProductList">
      <title>List of Related Products</title>
      <source>
        <mandatory>false</mandatory>
        <many>true</many>
      </source>
      <target>
        <class>iabook:Product</class>
        <mandatory>false</mandatory>
        <many>true</many>
      </target>
    </association>
  </associations>
</aspect>
</aspects>
```

2. Finally, at this point in time, the `catalogueModel.xml` file would look like this:

```xml
<?xml version="1.0" encoding="UTF-8"?>

<model name="iabook:catalogue" xmlns="http://www.alfresco.org/
model/dictionary/1.0">

  <description>Retailer Product Catalogue</description>
  <author>Snig Bhaumik</author>
  <version>1.0</version>

  <imports>
    <import uri="http://www.alfresco.org/model/dictionary/1.0"
prefix="d"/>
    <import uri="http://www.alfresco.org/model/content/1.0"
prefix="cm"/>
  </imports>

  <namespaces>
    <namespace uri="http://www.infoaxon.com/book/models/
catalogue/1.0" prefix="iabook"/>
  </namespaces>

  <constraints>
    <constraint name="iabook:productColors" type="LIST">
      <parameter name="allowedValues">
        <list>
          <value>Red</value>
          <value>Green</value>
          <value>Blue</value>
```

```
          </list>
        </parameter>
        <parameter name="caseSensitive">
          <value>false</value>
        </parameter>
      </constraint>
    </constraints>

  <types>
    <type name="iabook:Product">
      <title>Retailer Product</title>
      <parent>cm:content</parent>
      <properties>
        <property name="iabook:sku">
          <title>Product SKU</title>
          <type>d:text</type>
          <mandatory>true</mandatory>
        </property>
        <property name="iabook:manufacturer">
          <title>Manufacturer</title>
          <type>d:text</type>
          <mandatory>true</mandatory>
        </property>
        <property name="iabook:color">
          <title>Product Color</title>
          <type>d:text</type>
          <mandatory>false</mandatory>
          <constraints>
            <constraint ref="iabook:productColors" />
          </constraints>
        </property>
        <property name="iabook:brand">
          <title>Manufacturer Brand</title>
          <type>d:text</type>
          <mandatory>false</mandatory>
        </property>
        <property name="iabook:unitPrice">
          <title>Product Unit Price</title>
          <type>d:double</type>
          <mandatory>true</mandatory>
        </property>
        <property name="iabook:displayUntil">
          <title>Date until Product should be displayed</title>
          <type>d:datetime</type>
          <mandatory>true</mandatory>
```

```
        </property>
        <property name="iabook:competitorProducts">
          <title>Competitor Products List</title>
          <type>d:text</type>
          <mandatory>false</mandatory>
          <multiple>true</multiple>
        </property>
        <property name="iabook:competitorDetails">
          <title>Details of Competitor Products</title>
          <type>d:text</type>
          <mandatory>false</mandatory>
        </property>
      </properties>
    </type>
  </types>
<aspects>
  <aspect name="iabook:relatedProducts">
    <title>Related Products</title>
    <associations>
      <association name="iabook:relatedProductList">
        <title>List of Related Products</title>
        <source>
          <mandatory>false</mandatory>
          <many>true</many>
        </source>
        <target>
          <class>iabook:Product</class>
          <mandatory>false</mandatory>
          <many>true</many>
        </target>
      </association>
    </associations>
  </aspect>
</aspects>
</model>
```

3. After restarting your Tomcat server, the new aspect will be registered.

How it works...

Similarly, as the types are defined, aspects can also be defined in the custom content model. An aspect can have properties and associations – similar to the content types. In our example, we have, however, added only one association `iabook:relatedProductList` in our aspect `iabook:relatedProducts`.

As this aspect contains one association, applying the aspect into any existing content item would mean the `iabook:relatedProductList` association is enabled to the item. The association, as the name suggests, associates some destination (or `target`) content items with the item where the aspect is applied (or `source`).

In our example, we want to store all the products which are somewhat related to any existing product, probably because they belong to the same family. For example, *Canon Powershot A3000 IS* camera is related to *Powershot A3100 IS*. In this case, we can apply the `iabook:relatedProducts` aspect to the content item for *Powershot A3000 IS* – this is the `source`. Once the aspect is applied, you can add many related products with this. All these related products would be as `target` – in our case, *Powershot A3100 IS*.

You can define which content items can be the possible targets of associations – this is done by the `class` entry under the `target` node in the above XML code. We have put the target class as `iabook:Product`; this means only content items of type `iabook:Product` can be the related product of this. If we had put the class as `cm:content`, any type of content items would have been the possible related product.

You can also control where single or multiple associations are possible. This is done by the `many` entry under the `target` node. We have put this as `true`, thus more than one product can be associated with one product. Putting it as `false` would allow only one product to be associated – this is more used in the case of one-to-one mapping.

There's more...

Even if after restarting your server, and if the new aspect has been registered, in the Explorer application, the aspect won't be visible anywhere. Similar to the custom types, you need to put the aspect display settings in the `web-client-config-custom.xml` file in order to make it visible. We will explore how to do this in the next recipe.

> Even though the custom types and aspects are not visible in the explorer application until you make changes in the `web-client-config-custom.xml` file, you can still use these in our code – either JavaScript API or Java API in Alfresco. We will explore the JavaScript API in depth in *Chapter 8*.

Showing custom Aspects and Associations

Let's first see where and how the aspects potentially will be displayed in the Explorer application. Then we will customize the `web-client-config-custom.xml` file to display our custom aspects.

Getting ready

1. Log in to the Explorer application; open the **details** page of any existing content item. In the **Actions** menu, click on **Run Action**.

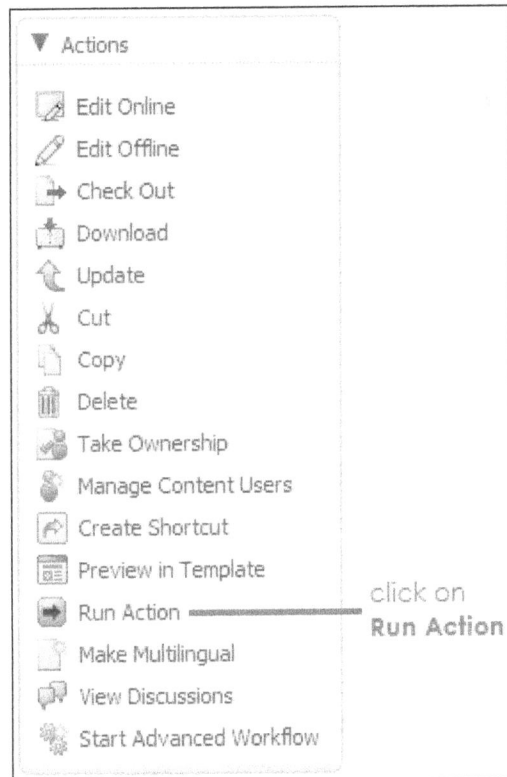

▼ Actions

🖉 Edit Online
✏ Edit Offline
➡ Check Out
⬇ Download
⬆ Update
✂ Cut
📋 Copy
🗑 Delete
🔧 Take Ownership
👤 Manage Content Users
🔗 Create Shortcut
📑 Preview in Template
➡ Run Action ━━━━━━━━━━ click on
                          Run Action
📄 Make Multilingual
💬 View Discussions
⚙ Start Advanced Workflow

2. In the **Run Action Wizard**, select the action **Add an aspect**; and click on **Set Values and Add**.

3. In the next screen, the available aspects are listed in **Set action values**. You can see that our new aspect **Related Products** is not included in the list.

4. You can use this screen to apply an aspect into an existing content item. However, by default, our custom aspect is not available here. Thus, we will see how we can add our aspect to this list so that we can apply this aspect into a content item.

How to do it...

1. Open the `web-client-config-custom.xml` file for editing and append the following code at the end:

```
<config evaluator="string-compare" condition="Action Wizards">
  <aspects>
    <aspect name="iabook:relatedProducts" />
  </aspects>
</config>
```

2. Also add the following code to this file:

```
<config evaluator="aspect-name" condition="iabook:relatedProducts">
  <property-sheet>
    <show-association name="iabook:relatedProductList" />
  </property-sheet>
</config>
```

3. The final `config` file would look like this:

```
<alfresco-config>
  <config evaluator="string-compare" condition="Views">
    <views>
      <view-defaults>
        <browse>
          <!-- allowable values: list|details|icons -->
          <view>details</view>
          <page-size>
            <list>20</list>
            <details>20</details>
            <icons>20</icons>
          </page-size>
        </browse>
      </view-defaults>
    </views>
  </config>
  <config evaluator="string-compare" condition="Languages">
    <languages>
      <language locale="de_DE">German</language>
      <language locale="es_ES">Spanish</language>
      <language locale="fr_FR">French</language>
      <language locale="it_IT">Italian</language>
    </languages>
  </config>
  <config>
    <client>
      <shelf-visible>false</shelf-visible>
    </client>
  </config>
  <config evaluator="string-compare" condition="Sidebar">
    <sidebar>
      <default-plugin>shelf</default-plugin>
    </sidebar>
  </config>
  <config evaluator="string-compare" condition="cm:folder icons">
    <icons>
      <icon name="space-icon-custom" path="/images/icons/ia-logo.
gif" />
    </icons>
  </config>
  <!-- Custom Content Type Settings -->
  <config evaluator="string-compare" condition="Content Wizards">
    <content-types>
      <type name="iabook:Product"/>
```

```
          </content-types>
        </config>

        <config evaluator="node-type" condition="iabook:Product">
          <property-sheet>
            <show-property name="name" />
            <show-property name="mimetype" display-label-id="content_
type" component-generator="MimeTypeSelectorGenerator" />
            <show-property name="encoding" display-label-id="encoding"
ignore-if-missing="false" component-generator="CharsetSelectorGene
rator" />
            <show-property name="size" display-label-id="size"
converter="org.alfresco.faces.ByteSizeConverter" show-in-edit-
mode="false" />
            <show-property name="title" display-label-id="title" ignore-
if-missing="false" />
            <show-property name="description" display-label-
id="description" ignore-if-missing="false" component-generator="Mu
ltilingualTextAreaGenerator" />
            <show-property name="iabook:sku" />
            <show-property name="iabook:manufacturer" />
            <show-property name="iabook:color" />
            <show-property name="iabook:brand" />
            <show-property name="iabook:unitPrice" />
            <show-property name="iabook:displayUntil" />
            <show-property name="iabook:competitorProducts" />
            <show-property name="iabook:competitorDetails" component-
generator="TextAreaGenerator" />
          </property-sheet>
        </config>

        <config evaluator="aspect-name" condition="iabook:relatedProduc
ts">
          <property-sheet>
            <show-association name="iabook:relatedProductList" />
          </property-sheet>
        </config>

        <config evaluator="string-compare" condition="Action Wizards">
          <aspects>
            <aspect name="iabook:relatedProducts" />
          </aspects>
        </config>
      </alfresco-config>
```

4. Restart the server, again open the **Run Action Wizard**, and try to **Add an aspect**. You will now be able to see that the **Related Products** aspect is available in the list.

5. Clicking **OK** and then **Finish** will apply the aspect in the particular content item.

How it works...

By following the preceding steps, create a couple of new content items of type **Retailer Product**. In my example, I have uploaded two documents `PSASeriesBrochure3000.pdf` and `PSASeriesBrochure3100.pdf`.

Apply the **Related Products** aspect to one of these items, let's say, with `PSASeriesBrochure3000.pdf` content.

Open the **Property Editor** of the content item.

You can see the List of **Related Products** in the **Property Editor** interface. This is achieved by the following code segment that we added in the `web-client-config-custom.xml` file:

```
<config evaluator="aspect-name" condition="iabook:relatedProducts">
  <property-sheet>
    <show-association name="iabook:relatedProductList" />
```

```
    </property-sheet>
  </config>
```

> Thus, you need to include all properties and associations you want to display for an aspect.
>
> For another aspect, you need to have another block of this code.

In the property editor screen, click **Search**. One item should be searched out – **PSASeriesBrochure3100.pdf**.

List of Related Products:	1. Search for and select items.
	[ ] [Search]
	/company_home/InfoAxon/Chapter 7/PSASeriesBrochure3100.pdf
	2. [Add to List]
	Selected Items
	Name
	No selected items.

This is because in our association target, we had added the class `iabook:Product`. We have only one such content item in the repository with this type (apart from the **PSASeriesBrochure3000.pdf**).

Add this item into the list. Click on **OK** to save the property changes. You can see the **Related Products** list in the property sheet of the item.

There's more...

You have seen how to apply an aspect into an existing content item using the Explorer screen. You can also do this in your scripts. This gives the required dynamic and modular behavior in your repository and content management system.

However, what if you want one of your custom content types to have an aspect compulsorily applied? For that, you can add this code segment in your content model type definition.

```
<mandatory-aspects>
    <aspect>iabook:relatedProducts</aspect>
</mandatory-aspects>
```

Thus, your content type definition would look like:

```
<type name="iabook:Product">
  <title>Retailer Product</title>
  <parent>cm:content</parent>
  <properties>
    <property name="iabook:sku">
      <title>Product SKU</title>
      <type>d:text</type>
      <mandatory>true</mandatory>
    </property>
    <property name="iabook:manufacturer">
      <title>Manufacturer</title>
```

```
        <type>d:text</type>
        <mandatory>true</mandatory>
      </property>
      <property name="iabook:color">
        <title>Product Color</title>
        <type>d:text</type>
        <mandatory>false</mandatory>
        <constraints>
          <constraint ref="iabook:productColors" />
        </constraints>
      </property>
      <property name="iabook:brand">
        <title>Manufacturer Brand</title>
        <type>d:text</type>
        <mandatory>false</mandatory>
      </property>
      <property name="iabook:unitPrice">
        <title>Product Unit Price</title>
        <type>d:double</type>
        <mandatory>true</mandatory>
      </property>
      <property name="iabook:displayUntil">
        <title>Date until Product should be displayed</title>
        <type>d:datetime</type>
        <mandatory>true</mandatory>
      </property>
      <property name="iabook:competitorProducts">
        <title>Competitor Products List</title>
        <type>d:text</type>
        <mandatory>false</mandatory>
        <multiple>true</multiple>
      </property>
      <property name="iabook:competitorDetails">
        <title>Details of Competitor Products</title>
        <type>d:text</type>
        <mandatory>false</mandatory>
      </property>
    </properties>

    <mandatory-aspects>
        <aspect>iabook:relatedProducts</aspect>
    </mandatory-aspects>
  </type>
```

Displaying custom type in Type Specialization

Until now, we have been creating content items and specifying the content type at the time of creation or uploading of the content item.

However, what happens if we want to change or specialize the content type of an existing item? Let's say we have an existing content of type `cm:content`. We want to change the type to `iabook:Product`. We will explore how to do this in the following recipe.

Getting ready

First let's see how and in which screen of the Explorer we can change the type.

1. Upload a new content item. Let's upload with the type **Content**, not **Retailer Product**.

2. Open the **Run Action Wizard** and select the action **Specialise Type**.

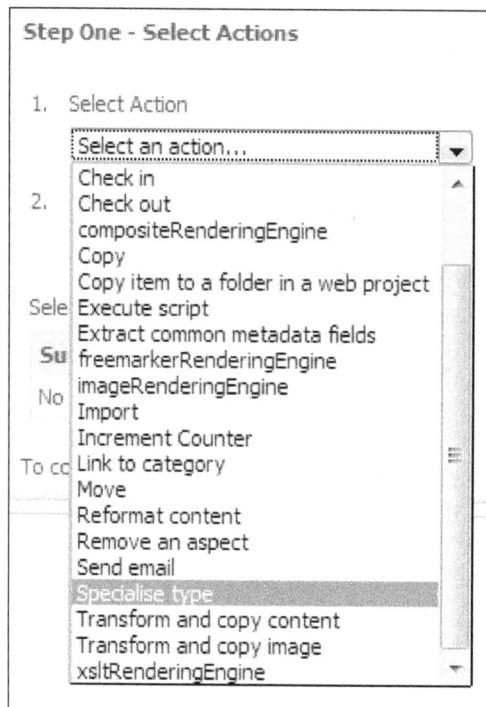

```
Step One - Select Actions

1.  Select Action

    Select an action...                    ▼
        Check in                           ▲
2.  Check out
        compositeRenderingEngine
        Copy
        Copy item to a folder in a web project
Sele Execute script
        Extract common metadata fields
Su  freemarkerRenderingEngine
        imageRenderingEngine
No  Import
        Increment Counter
        Link to category                   ▬
To cc Move
        Reformat content
        Remove an aspect
        Send email
        Specialise type
        Transform and copy content
        Transform and copy image
        xsltRenderingEngine                ▼
```

3. When you click on **Set Values and Add**, in the next dialog, no type values are offered in the drop-down list.

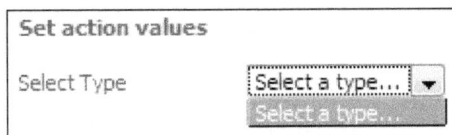

4. We need our **Retailer Product** type listed here in order to change the type of the item.

How to do it...

1. Open the `web-client-config-custom.xml` file and append the following code segment in the `<config evaluator="string-compare" condition="Action Wizards">` node:

```
<specialise-types>
  <type name="iabook:Product"/>
</specialise-types>
```

2. The final file would look like this:

```
<alfresco-config>

  <config evaluator="string-compare" condition="Views">
    <views>
      <view-defaults>
        <browse>
          <!-- allowable values: list|details|icons -->
          <view>details</view>
          <page-size>
            <list>20</list>
            <details>20</details>
            <icons>20</icons>
          </page-size>
        </browse>
      </view-defaults>
    </views>
  </config>

  <config evaluator="string-compare" condition="Languages">
    <languages>
      <language locale="de_DE">German</language>
      <language locale="es_ES">Spanish</language>
      <language locale="fr_FR">French</language>
      <language locale="it_IT">Italian</language>
    </languages>
```

```
      </config>

      <config>
        <client>
          <shelf-visible>false</shelf-visible>
        </client>
      </config>

      <config evaluator="string-compare" condition="Sidebar">
        <sidebar>
          <default-plugin>shelf</default-plugin>
        </sidebar>
      </config>

      <config evaluator="string-compare" condition="cm:folder icons">
        <icons>
          <icon name="space-icon-custom" path="/images/icons/ia-logo.
gif" />
        </icons>
      </config>


      <!-- Custom Content Type Settings -->
      <config evaluator="string-compare" condition="Content Wizards">
        <content-types>
          <type name="iabook:Product"/>
        </content-types>
      </config>

      <config evaluator="node-type" condition="iabook:Product">
        <property-sheet>
          <show-property name="name" />
          <show-property name="mimetype" display-label-id="content_
type" component-generator="MimeTypeSelectorGenerator" />
          <show-property name="encoding" display-label-id="encoding"
ignore-if-missing="false" component-generator="CharsetSelectorGene
rator" />
          <show-property name="size" display-label-id="size"
converter="org.alfresco.faces.ByteSizeConverter" show-in-edit-
mode="false" />
          <show-property name="title" display-label-id="title" ignore-
if-missing="false" />
          <show-property name="description" display-label-
id="description" ignore-if-missing="false" component-generator="Mu
ltilingualTextAreaGenerator" />
          <show-property name="iabook:sku" />
          <show-property name="iabook:manufacturer" />
          <show-property name="iabook:color" />
          <show-property name="iabook:brand" />
```

```
        <show-property name="iabook:unitPrice" />
        <show-property name="iabook:displayUntil" />
        <show-property name="iabook:competitorProducts" />
        <show-property name="iabook:competitorDetails" component-
generator="TextAreaGenerator" />
      </property-sheet>
    </config>

    <config evaluator="aspect-name" condition="iabook:relatedProduc
ts">
      <property-sheet>
        <show-association name="iabook:relatedProductList" />
      </property-sheet>
    </config>

    <config evaluator="string-compare" condition="Action Wizards">
      <aspects>
        <aspect name="iabook:relatedProducts" />
      </aspects>

      <specialise-types>
        <type name="iabook:Product"/>
      </specialise-types>

    </config>
  </alfresco-config>
```

3. Restart your Tomcat server and retry the **Specialize Type** action. You can see that the **Retailer Product** type is now available.

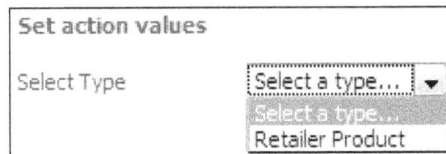

Set action values	
Select Type	Select a type... ▼
	Select a type...
	Retailer Product

4. Select **Retailer Product** from the drop-down list and click **OK**. After **Finish**, the type of the content item will be changed.

How it works...

All the type names that are listed in the `specialize-types` tag in the `web-client-config-custom.xml` file are picked up and listed in the available types of the **Action Wizard** dialog.

Thus, you need to include all your custom types that you want to be listed in the **Specialize Type** drop-down list.

Customizing Advanced Search to include custom content types

In *Chapter 3*, you saw how to use the Alfresco Explore **Advanced Search** interface for performing complex content searches. There you can search contents by content type as well. In this recipe, we will see how it is possible to search contents by custom content type – say, `iabook:Product`.

Getting started

Let's revisit the default interface of the **Advanced Search**. In the **More search options – Content Type** list, you can see that our custom type `iabook:Product` is not available.

We will again use the `web-client-config-custom.xml` file in order to include the custom type in the Advanced Search list.

How to do it...

1. Open the `web-client-config-custom.xml` file and add the following code segment at the end:

    ```xml
    <config evaluator="string-compare" condition="Advanced Search">
      <advanced-search>
        <content-types>
          <type name="iabook:Product" />
        </content-types>
        <custom-properties>
          <meta-data type="iabook:Product" property="iabook:sku" />
        </custom-properties>
      </advanced-search>
    </config>
    ```

2. The final file should look like this:

```xml
<alfresco-config>

  <config evaluator="string-compare" condition="Views">
    <views>
      <view-defaults>
        <browse>
          <!-- allowable values: list|details|icons -->
          <view>details</view>
          <page-size>
            <list>20</list>
            <details>20</details>
            <icons>20</icons>
          </page-size>
        </browse>
      </view-defaults>
    </views>
  </config>

  <config evaluator="string-compare" condition="Languages">
    <languages>
      <language locale="de_DE">German</language>
      <language locale="es_ES">Spanish</language>
      <language locale="fr_FR">French</language>
      <language locale="it_IT">Italian</language>
    </languages>
  </config>

  <config>
    <client>
      <shelf-visible>false</shelf-visible>
    </client>
  </config>

  <config evaluator="string-compare" condition="Sidebar">
    <sidebar>
      <default-plugin>shelf</default-plugin>
    </sidebar>
  </config>

  <config evaluator="string-compare" condition="cm:folder icons">
    <icons>
      <icon name="space-icon-custom" path="/images/icons/ia-logo.
gif" />
    </icons>
  </config>
```

```xml
<!-- Custom Content Type Settings -->
<config evaluator="string-compare" condition="Content Wizards">
  <content-types>
    <type name="iabook:Product"/>
  </content-types>
</config>

<config evaluator="node-type" condition="iabook:Product">
  <property-sheet>
    <show-property name="name" />
    <show-property name="mimetype" display-label-id="content_
type" component-generator="MimeTypeSelectorGenerator" />
    <show-property name="encoding" display-label-id="encoding"
ignore-if-missing="false" component-generator="CharsetSelectorGene
rator" />
    <show-property name="size" display-label-id="size"
converter="org.alfresco.faces.ByteSizeConverter" show-in-edit-
mode="false" />
    <show-property name="title" display-label-id="title" ignore-
if-missing="false" />
    <show-property name="description" display-label-
id="description" ignore-if-missing="false" component-generator="Mu
ltilingualTextAreaGenerator" />
    <show-property name="iabook:sku" />
    <show-property name="iabook:manufacturer" />
    <show-property name="iabook:color" />
    <show-property name="iabook:brand" />
    <show-property name="iabook:unitPrice" />
    <show-property name="iabook:displayUntil" />
    <show-property name="iabook:competitorProducts" />
    <show-property name="iabook:competitorDetails" component-
generator="TextAreaGenerator" />
  </property-sheet>
</config>

<config evaluator="aspect-name" condition="iabook:relatedProduc
ts">
  <property-sheet>
    <show-association name="iabook:relatedProductList" />
  </property-sheet>
</config>

<config evaluator="string-compare" condition="Action Wizards">
  <aspects>
    <aspect name="iabook:relatedProducts" />
  </aspects>
  <specialise-types>
```

```
      <type name="iabook:Product"/>
    </specialise-types>
  </config>

  <config evaluator="string-compare" condition="Advanced Search">
    <advanced-search>
      <content-types>
        <type name="iabook:Product" />
      </content-types>

      <custom-properties>
        <meta-data type="iabook:Product" property="iabook:sku" />
      </custom-properties>
    </advanced-search>
  </config>

</alfresco-config>
```

3. Open the **Advanced Search** interface and you can see that the **Retailer Product** type is available in the list.

4. Now once you search by these, you can get the appropriate search results.

How it works...

In the `content-types` node under `advanced-search`, you need to list all the custom types you want to add in the **Advanced Search** interface.

Similarly, you can include your custom properties in the search criteria set as well. This is done by the `meta-data` node under `custom-properties`.

> For more information, visit the Advanced Search form at
> `http://wiki.alfresco.com/wiki/Advanced_Search_Custom_`
> `Attributes`

8
Alfresco JavaScript API

In this chapter, we will cover:

- ▶ Writing and executing scripts
- ▶ Adding/Changing the contents of a document
- ▶ Creating a backup copy of a document
- ▶ Adding a tag to a document
- ▶ Assigning Permissions to a User
- ▶ Debugging Alfresco JavaScript

Introduction

An **API** (**Application Programming Interface**) is an interface implemented and offered by a software program that enables other applications to interact with it, or enables developers to write other applications on top of it. An API can be exposed in several different forms, such as internal class model and implementation–using which you can write your program, or as different services, for example, web services. As a solution developer of an Enterprise framework, you need to be proficient on the APIs provided and exposed by the framework.

Alfresco, like any other enterprise open source framework, exposes a number of APIs including Alfresco SDK (Software Development Kit) a set of development tools that allows the creation of an application for a certain software package or framework and JavaScript API.

The JavaScript API is a unique model for writing programs and services using JavaScript (ECMA Script) 1.6 compatible files. The API enables developers to write scripts that can access, modify, or create various Alfresco Repository objects such as users, nodes, groups, tags, categories, and so on.

Available JavaScript APIs

Alfresco JavaScript API exposes all important repository objects as JavaScript objects that can be used in a script file. The API follows the object-oriented programming model for well known Alfresco concepts such as Nodes, Properties, Associations, and Aspects.

The JavaScript API is capable of performing several essential functions for the script developer, such as:

- Create Node, Update Node: You can create, upload, or update files using these.
- Check In/Check Out: You can programmatically check-out and check-in your content.
- Access Rights Management Permissioning: You can manage your content's security aspects.
- Transformation: You can transform your content using this. For example, you want to generate a PDF version of your MS-Office document.
- Tagging: Tagging APIs will help you tag your contents.
- Classifying: You can categorize or classify your contents using this.
- People: Using these APIs, you can handle all user-and group-related operations in your script; such as creating a new user, changing the password of a user, and so on.
- Searching: One of most important and powerful APIs exposed. You can search your contents using these APIs. You can perform Lucene-based search or XPath-based search operations using these APIs.
- Workflow: You can manage the tasks and workflows in your system using these APIs and services.
- Thumbnail: Exposes APIs to manage the thumbnail operations of various content items.
- Node operations: You use these APIs to perform several node-related functions such as Manage Properties, Manage Aspects, copying, deleting, moving, and so on

Thus, as you can see, pretty much most of the things can be done in a JavaScript file using these APIs.

> However, one thing is important, that you should not mix the usual JavaScript code you write for your HTML or JSP web pages. Those scripts are executed by your browser (this means, at the client side). The scripts you write using Alfresco JavaScript API are not client-side JavaScript file – this means these do not get executed by your browser. Instead, they get executed in your server and the browser has nothing to do in these scripts.
>
> It is called JavaScript API since the APIs are exposed using the ECMA script model and syntaxes. The programs you develop using these APIs are written in JavaScript language.

The JavaScript API model

Alfresco has provided a number of objects in the JavaScript API – these are more usually named as *Root Scope Objects*. These objects are your entry point into the repository. Each of the root level objects refers to a particular entity or functional point in the repository. For example, `userhome` object refers to the home space node of the current user. Each of these objects presents a number of properties and functionalities, thus enabling the script writer to implement several different requirements. For example, the `userhome.name` statement will return the name of the root folder of the current user.

Some important and most frequently used root scope objects are:

- `Companyhome`: Returns the company home script node object
- `Userhome`: Returns the home folder node of the current user
- `Person`: Represents the current user person object
- `Space`: Stands for the current space object
- `Document`: Returns the currently selected document
- `Search`: Offers fully functional search APIs
- `People`: Encapsulates all functionalities related to user, groups, roles, permissions, and so on.
- `Sites`: Exposes the site service functionalities
- `Actions`: Provides invocation methods for registered actions
- `Workflow`: Handles all functionalities related to workflow implementation within the repository

Among these, `companyhome`, `userhome`, `person`, `space`, and `document` objects represent Alfresco Node objects and allow access to the properties and aspects of the corresponding node object. Each of the node objects provides a number of APIs which are termed *ScriptNode API*.

The others – `search`, `people`, `sites`, `workflow`, and `actions` – expose several methods that would help you implement specific business requirements. For example, if you want to write a script that searches some documents and contents, you would use the search API. If you want to create a new user – the people API will help you.

In our next few sections, we will discuss these APIs. However, let's first see how we can execute our script files written in Alfresco JavaScript.

Writing and executing scripts

There are a few options and implementation models by which you can write your JavaScript files and execute them in Alfresco. A couple of the most usual models are:

- ▸ Writing and storing scripts in the Data Dictionary
- ▸ Using Web Scripts

We will explore Web Scripts later in *Chapter 10*. However, in this recipe, we will see how to write and execute simple scripts from the **Data Dictionary**.

Getting ready

1. Open the Alfresco explorer and navigate to the **Company Home | Data Dictionary | Scripts** folder.

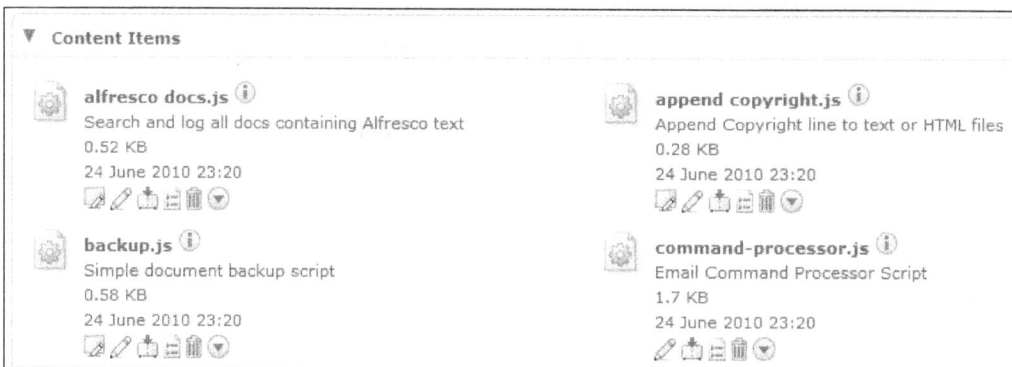

▼ **Content Items**

alfresco docs.js ⓘ	**append copyright.js** ⓘ
Search and log all docs containing Alfresco text	Append Copyright line to text or HTML files
0.52 KB	0.28 KB
24 June 2010 23:20	24 June 2010 23:20
backup.js ⓘ	**command-processor.js** ⓘ
Simple document backup script	Email Command Processor Script
0.58 KB	1.7 KB
24 June 2010 23:20	24 June 2010 23:20

2. This is the space where all the JavaScript files should be stored. Alfresco explorer looks for JS files by default from this location. Alfresco has provided some sample scripts to make the scripting methodology more understandable.

3. We will try executing the `backup.js` script provided in this space. One way you can execute the script files is with the `Run Action` method.

4. Let's assume in a particular space we have a document. We will run the `backup.` `js` script against this document. Suppose these are the contents of a space we are working on. It has only one content item – **My Movie.wmv**.

Company Home > InfoAxon > Chapter 8

Chapter 8

This view allows you to browse the items in this space.
JavaScript API

▼ **Browse Spaces**

No items to display. Click the 'Create Space' action to create a space.

Page 1

▼ **Content Items**

My Movie.wmv (i)

37.44 MB

15 December 2010 00:39

Page 1

5. Open the details screen of this content and click on **Run Action**. In the **Run Action Wizard**, select **Execute script** as the action to be performed and click on **Set Values and Add**.

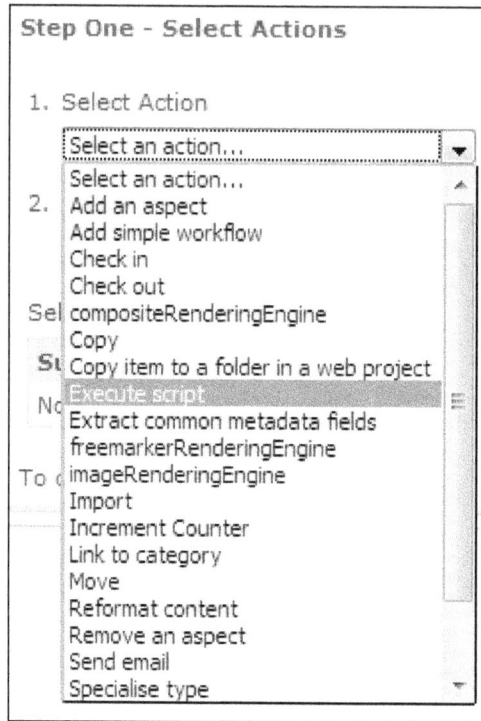

Step One - Select Actions

1. Select Action

```
Select an action...                    ▼
   Select an action...                 ▲
2. Add an aspect
   Add simple workflow
   Check in
   Check out
Sel compositeRenderingEngine
   Copy
Su Copy item to a folder in a web project
   Execute script                      ≡
No Extract common metadata fields
   freemarkerRenderingEngine
To imageRenderingEngine
   Import
   Increment Counter
   Link to category
   Move
   Reformat content
   Remove an aspect
   Send email
   Specialise type                     ▼
```

6. In the next screen, the list of available scripts is presented. You can select one of them and the script will be executed.

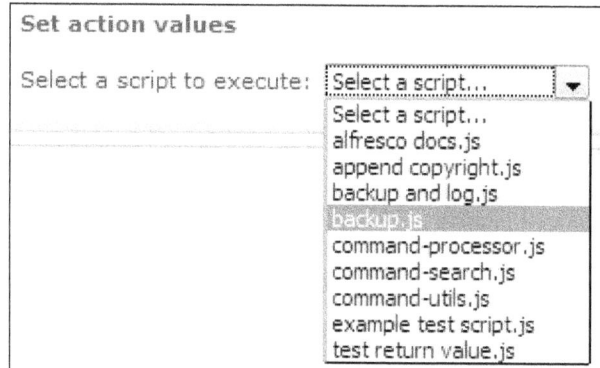

Set action values

Select a script to execute: Select a script...   ▼

```
Select a script...
alfresco docs.js
append copyright.js
backup and log.js
backup.js
command-processor.js
command-search.js
command-utils.js
example test script.js
test return value.js
```

7. As you can see, all the nine default scripts are available here – the same as the scripts present in the **Company Home > Data Dictionary > Scripts** space. However, since we are trying to execute the **backup.js**, we select the **backup.js** file and click **OK**. In the next screen, click **Finish** to complete the operation.

8. Now if you navigate to the original space (where the **My Movie.wmv** file was located), you will see that a new folder named **Backup** is created there.

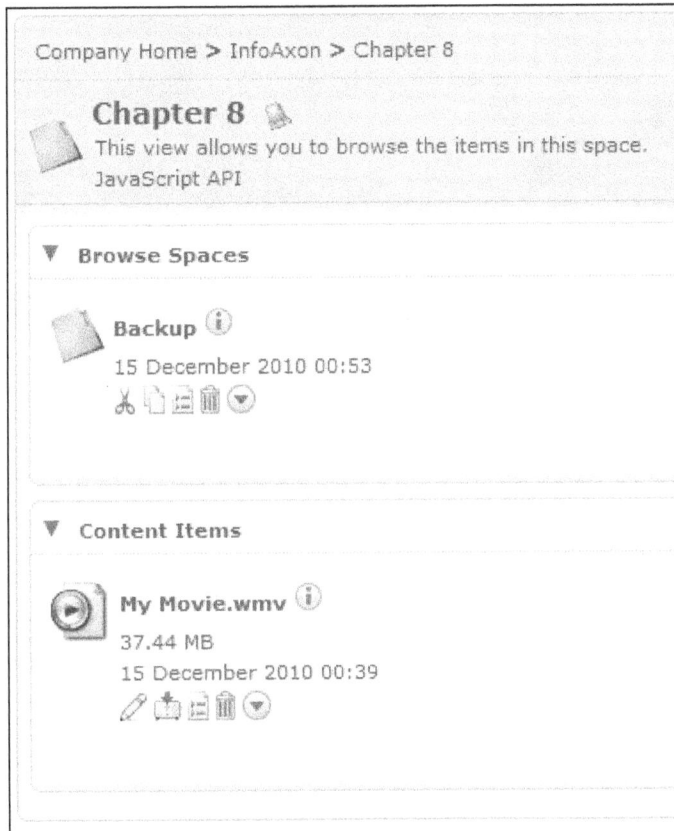

Company Home > InfoAxon > Chapter 8

Chapter 8
This view allows you to browse the items in this space.
JavaScript API

▼ **Browse Spaces**

Backup ⓘ
15 December 2010 00:53

▼ **Content Items**

My Movie.wmv ⓘ
37.44 MB
15 December 2010 00:39

9. A backup of the file **My Movie.wmv** has been generated in the `Backup` folder.

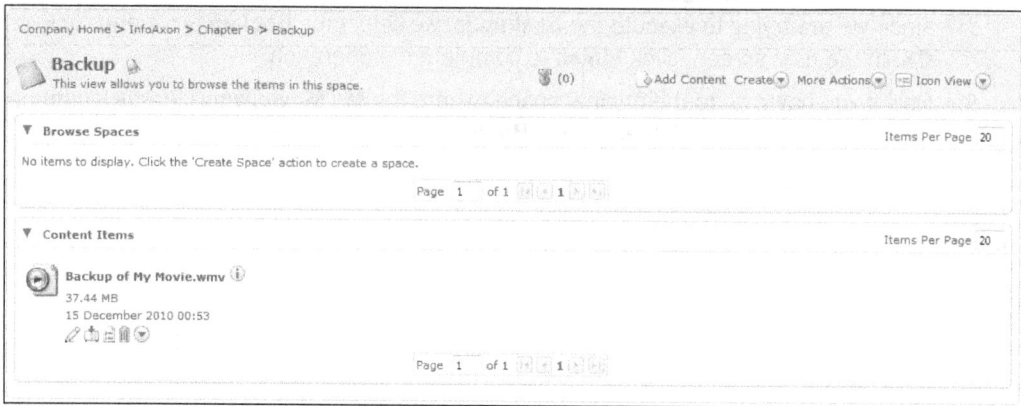

10. Thus the **backup.js** script has been executed and it has created a backup of the content item on which the script has been executed.

We now know how to execute a script file. We will now try to create a new script file and run it.

How to do it...

1. Open the Alfresco explorer and navigate to the **Company Home > Data Dictionary > Scripts** folder. Create a content item. Let's name it **transform.js**.

> Though the `.js` extension for the content name is optional here, it is a standard and good practice to name the JavaScript file `.js`

Step One - Specify name and select type
Specify the name and select the type of content you wish to create.

General Properties

Name: transform.js

Type: Content   ▼

Content Type: Plain Text ▼

Other Properties
Rules applied to this content may require you to enter additional information.

☑ Modify all properties when this wizard closes.

To continue click Next.

2. Let's say, we are writing the script for creating an Adobe PDF version for an MS Word file. Here is the code:

```
if (document.mimetype == "application/msword")
{
   var pdfDoc = document.transformDocument("application/pdf");
}
```

Step Two - Enter Content

Enter your document content into the repository.

```
if (document.mimetype == "application/msword")
{
    var pdfDoc = document.transformDocument("application/pdf");
}
```

3. Click on **Finish** to complete the creation of your script.

▼ Content Items   Items Per Page 20

alfresco docs.js ⓘ
Search and log all docs containing Alfresco text
0.52 KB
24 June 2010 23:20

append copyright.js ⓘ
Append Copyright line to text or HTML files
0.28 KB
24 June 2010 23:20

backup and log.js ⓘ
Backup files and log the date and time
1.04 KB
24 June 2010 23:20

backup.js ⓘ
Simple document backup script
0.58 KB
24 June 2010 23:20

command-processor.js ⓘ
Email Command Processor Script
1.7 KB
24 June 2010 23:20

command-search.js ⓘ
Email Search Command Script
7.06 KB
24 June 2010 23:20

command-utils.js ⓘ
Email Command Utils
2.21 KB
24 June 2010 23:20

example test script.js ⓘ
Example of various API calls
2.22 KB
24 June 2010 23:20

test return value.js ⓘ
Return a value from a script - for the command servlet
0.12 KB
24 June 2010 23:20

transform.js ⓘ
Script to transform MS Word documents into PDF.
0.11 KB
15 December 2010 12:41

Page 1   of 1

4. Now, as your script has been created, let's execute it.

5. Upload an MS Word document in a space. For example, we have uploaded a document named **Infoxon.doc**.

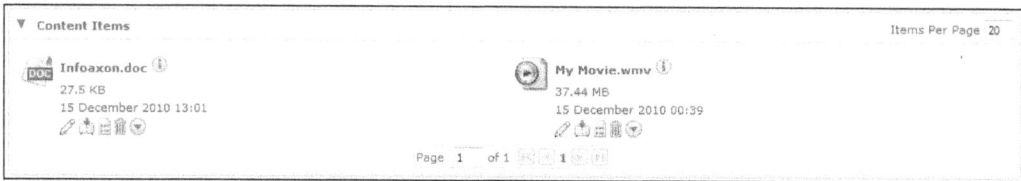

6. Open the details view of the document. Click on **Run Action** and select action as **Execute script**. You can see our new script **transform.js** is available in the list. Select this script and click **OK**.

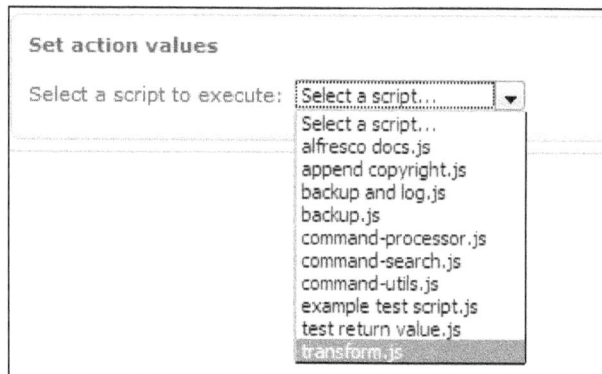

7. Click on **Finish** to execute the action. This will run the JavaScript we have written in the script file.

8. When you reopen the space contents, you can see a new PDF file has been created here. Since the original document name was **Infoaxon.doc**, the PDF is automatically named **Infoaxon.pdf**.

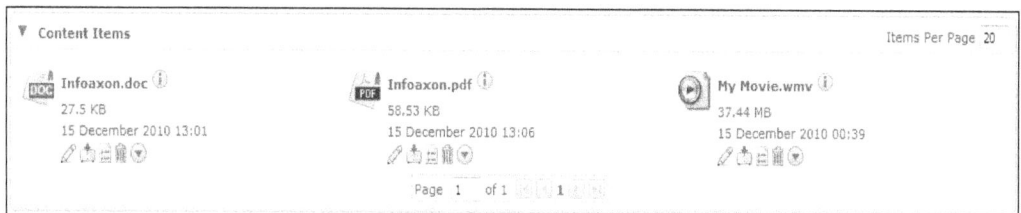

9. When you download the PDF file, you can see your Word file is transformed into a PDF document.

How it works...

There are a few interesting points to explore how this transformation happened.

There are simply two lines of code in your JS file.

```
if (document.mimetype == "application/msword")
```

The `document` object stands for the current document on which the script is being executed. In our case, it is the **Infoaxon.doc** document. Thus `document.mimetype` would return the mime type of the current document.

Since we want only to convert MS Word documents into PDF, we have added this condition. In case you run this script for a document which is not of type MS Word, the transformation won't take place.

```
var pdfDoc = document.transformDocument("application/pdf");
```

Again, the `document` object represents the current document. The `transformDocument` method is an API provided in a `ScriptNode` object where you need to supply the mimetype of the target document – in our case, it is a PDF document, hence the `application/pdf` mimetype.

The `transformDocument` method has another overloaded signature, where you can supply a second parameter – destination folder. Right now, the new PDF file is being created in the current folder. In case you want your transformed file to be created in another space, you must provide this parameter.

> In the background, Alfresco uses Open Office APIs to generate PDF documents from MS Office contents. For this, you must enable and establish Open Office in your Alfresco server.

> Running scripts via **Run Action** is one way of executing this. However, what if you want to generate PDF files whenever a new MS Word document is uploaded in a certain folder?
>
> For this, you use the Rule mechanism. You simply create a rule that will fire the execution of the `transform.js` script whenever a new document is placed in this folder.

There's more...

Now that we know how to write and execute scripts in the Alfresco explorer, let's dive deep into the important APIs supplied by Alfresco.

ScriptNode API

The following list is a subset of the available APIs and services of a `ScriptNode` object. More extensive properties, methods, and services are available in the JavaScript APIs.

- ▶ **properties**: Presents an array of the available properties of the current node object.

   For example, `var docname = document.properties["cm:name"];`

   In case of our custom model – `iabook:product` (defined in *Chapter 7*), if we want to extract the color of the product node, we will write:

   `var pcolor = document.properties["iabook:color"];`

- ▶ **children**: Supplies an array of `ScriptNode` objects of the child nodes of the current object.

- ▶ **isContainer**: This will return a boolean value denoting whether the current node object is a space or a document. This will return true if the node is a folder.

- ▶ **isDocument**: This will return a boolean value denoting whether the current node object is a space or a document. This will return true if the node is a content item.

- ▶ **downloadUrl**: Returns the content stream of the node as an HTTP1.1 attachment object. You should use this property if you want to provide the download URL of your document in the repository.

- ▶ **size**: Returns the size of the content item in bytes.

- ▶ **isLocked**: When a document is checked out, it is locked for other users. This property returns true if it is locked.

- ▶ **nodeRef**: Each object in the Alfresco repository has a unique ID – this is named as `NodeRef`. This property returns the `NodeRef` value as a string of the corresponding object.

- ▶ **childByNamePath**: This method returns the particular node specified in XPath. For example, `var mynode = companyhome.childByNamePath("InfoAxon/Chapter 8/Infoaxon.doc")` would return the particular referenced node in the specified path.

- ▶ **childrenByXPath**: This method searches for the matching nodes as per the specified XPath. Returns an array of nodes. For example, `var mynodes = companyhome.childrenByXPath("*[@cm:name='InfoAxon']/*")` returns all nodes with the name InfoAxon.

- ▶ **content**: Returns the text content for the node. This is a read/write property – meaning you can set or change the content using this property. For example, `mynode.content = "This is a sample content"`

▸ **createNode**: Method for creating a new node under a particular folder.

For example, `var newdoc = myspace.createNode("docname.txt")`. The method returns the `ScriptNode` object of the new content node created. The new node created will be of type `cm:content`. If you want to create a content node of your own type, you can use `var newdoc = myspace.createNode("docname.txt", "iabook:Product")`. You then use that object to set other properties and so on.

▸ **createFolder**: Method for creating a new space under a particular folder.

For example, `var newfolder = myspace.createFolder("foldername")`.

> You can see that the statement `var newfolder = myspace.createFolder("foldername")` and statement `var newfolder = myspace.createNode("foldername", "cm:folder")` will produce exactly the same result.

▸ **remove**: Removes the current node from the repository.

For example, `var success = mynode.remove()`. Upon successful operation, `mynode` will be deleted, and the variable `success` will have the value true or false, depending on the status of the operation.

▸ **copy**: Use this method to create a copy of the current node into another folder. More powerfully, you can copy the entire subfolder tree as well.

For example, `var newnode = mynode.copy(destinationfolder, true)`. This will copy the `mynode` space and all other subfolders and content items into the `destinationfolder` node. However, the second parameter is optional, with the default value `false`.

▸ **addAspect**: Adds a new aspect into the current node.

For example, `var success = mynode.addAspect("cm:versionable")`.

▸ **hasAspect**: If you want to check whether your content node has a certain aspect associated with it or not, you need to use this method.

For example, `mynode.hasAspect("iabook: relatedProducts")` would return `true` or `false`, depending on whether the `relatedProducts` aspect is associated with `mynode`.

▸ **write**: Copies the contents of the specified node into the current node.

For example, `mynode.write(sourcenode)` would copy the contents of `sourcenode` into `mynode`.

> There is a difference between the `copy` method defined above and the `write` method. The `copy` method copies the entire object and creates a new instance which is an exact replica of the source node; on the other hand, the `write` method only copies the contents of the node leaving the other properties unchanged.

- **hasPermission**: Returns true if the current user has the specified permission on the node.

  For example, `var permitted = mynode.hasPermission("Delete")`. The `permitted` value will be true if the current user can `Delete` the node or the sub-nodes. The commonly used permission checks are `Read`, `Write`, `Delete`, and `CreateChildren`. `CreateChildren` permission is especially interesting, as having this permission means you can create sub-nodes under the current node.

- **setPermission**: Applies the specified permission to the specified authority. An authority can be a user or a group.

  For example, `mynode.setPermission("Write")` would provide `Write` permission to all the users on `mynode`. The command `mynode.setPermission("Write", "snig.bhaumik")` would provide `Write` permission to the user `snig.bhaumik`.

- **removePermission**: Use this method to revoke some permission from an authority.

  For example, `mynode.removePermission("Write")` would retract `Write` permission from all users. Similarly, `mynode.removePermission("Write", "snig.bhaumik")` would retract `Write` permission from the user `snig.bhaumik`.

- **inheritsPermissions**, **setInheritsPermissions**: Just like your Windows® file system, where by default a subfolder inherits all permissions from its parent folder (unless explicitly overridden), a folder in the Alfresco repository also inherits the permission settings from the parent node.

  These methods are used to control this permission inheritance behavior.

Company Home > InfoAxon > Chapter 8

Manage Space Users 'Chapter 8'
User 'admin' is the current owner of this space.
Manage the permissions you have granted to users who access your space.

Invite   Local

Users and Groups   Close

Name   Username   Roles   Actions

Page 1   of 1   1

☑ Inherit Parent Space Permissions

Indicates whether current folder is
Inheriting Permission.

For example, `mynode.inheritsPermissions()` would return a Boolean value mentioning whether the `mynode` object is inheriting the permission settings from the parent folder. You can change this by using the `mynode.setInheritsPermissions(true)` (or `false`) method syntax.

- **checkout**: Method to checkout a node. After a successful execution of the statement, the corresponding node will be checked-out, it will be locked, and a new content item will be created and returned as the working copy of the content.

- **checkin**: After alteration on the working copy node, you must check in the working copy. After this, the original node will be updated and unlocked.

- **cancelCheckout**: Sometimes you may want to cancel the checkout operation. You do not want to continue the updating of the content. For that, you use this method `mynode. cancelCheckout()`.

- **isTagScope**: As part of the tagging API, this method returns whether the current node is the tag scope or not.

> A tag scope is a logical container for tagged content items. In the repository, you can have a number of such tag scopes which would define logical collections of tags.

- **tags**: Returns an array of tags of the current node. For example, `var mytags = mynode.tags` would set all the tags of the `mynode` object. You can also set the tags of the current node using this method.

- **addTag**: You can use this method to add a particular tag into the current node object. For example, `mynode.addTag("cookbook")` would add the tag `cookbook` with `mynode`.

- **removeTag**: Use this method in order to remove a tag from the current node. For example, `mynode.removeTag("cookbook")` would remove the tag cookbook from `mynode`.

> However, this method does not remove a particular tag from the tag scope.

- **specializeType**: Sometimes you want to change the content type of your content item. We have seen how to create and use custom content types in *Chapter 7*. If you want to change the content type of a content node, you use this method.

- **isSubType**: This is a useful method. With this, you can find out whether your content node is of a certain type or of any of the subtypes of the certain given content type.

  For example, `mynode.isSubType("iabook:product")` will return `true` if `mynode` is of `product` type.

People API

People API methods are used to perform several operations related to users and groups. These APIs offer access to Alfresco groups and people. The following list is a subset of the available APIs and services of a people object. More extensive properties, methods, and services are available in the JavaScript APIs.

- **createPerson**: Creates a new person or user, the new node created in the repository is of the type `cm:person`. You supply the username of the new person to be created.

- **deletePerson**: Deletes a user from the repository.

  For example, `people.deletePerson("snig.bhaumik")` would remove the user from the repository.

- **getPerson**: You use this method to retrieve the person object (object of type `cm:person`) having the given username.

  You can then use or change any property of this `ScriptNode` object. Some of the available properties of a person object are:

  - **cm:firstName**: Gets or sets the first name of the person.
  - **cm:lastName**: Gets or sets the last name of the person.
  - **cm:sizeQuota**: Gets or sets the quota size the person can use.
  - **cm:sizeCurrent**: Gets the current content size the person has already used. This is a read-only property.
  - **cm:username:** Gets the username of the person. This is a read-only property since you cannot change a person's username.
  - **cm:homeFolder**: Gets the Home Space `NodeRef` of the person.
  - **cm:jobtitle**: Gets or sets the job title of the person.
  - **cm:organizationId**: Gets or sets the organization of the person.
  - **cm:email**: Gets or sets the e-mail of the person.
  - **cm:mobile**: Gets or sets the mobile number of the person.

> As the person object returned here is a standard `ScriptNode` object, you can also use all advanced functionalities like `addAspect`, `createAssociation`, and so on to enhance the default behavior of the person object.

- **changePassword**: The `getPerson` object detailed above does not allow you to change a user's password. This method enables you to change the password of the current user. However, you must provide the old password as well in this method along with the new password, for example, `changePassword("oldpass", "newpass")`.

- **setPassword**: The **changePassword** method can only change the password of the current user. However, if you want to change the password of any user, then you need to use this method. For example, `people.setPassword("snig.bhaumik", "newpass")` would set the password as `newpass` for the user `snig.bhaumik`.

> However, quite understandably, for using this method, you must have admin rights in the repository.

- **isAdmin**: Use this method to determine whether the specified person is an administrator or not.
- **createGroup**: Creates a new group in the system. The new node created in the repository is of type `cm:authorityContainer`. You supply the user name of the new group to be created.

> Alfresco always prefixes the keyword GROUP_ with the name of the new group you have provided.

Child Name	Child Node	Primary	Association Type	Index
GROUP_ALFRESCO_ADMINISTRATORS	workspace://SpacesStore/GROUP_ALFRESCO_ADMINISTRATORS	true	children	0
GROUP_EMAIL_CONTRIBUTORS	workspace://SpacesStore/GROUP_EMAIL_CONTRIBUTORS	true	children	1
GROUP_Alfresco Cookbook Authors	workspace://SpacesStore/16a92c5a-9356-4624-afb0-bb250708ae76	true	children	2
GROUP_Chapter-5 Authors	workspace://SpacesStore/9641bb15-6579-4103-b697-488b06f41a63	true	children	3

- **getGroup**: Retrieves our group object from the repository. This method returns an object of type `cm:authorityContainer`.
- **getMembers**: Use this method to retrieve the list of member users of a certain group. You pass the group object as a parameter in this method. Returns an array of person object nodes. For example, `var userlist = people.getMembers(grpobj)`.

Search API

Search API is one of the important APIs you would use more frequently while developing custom solutions on Alfresco.

Alfresco uses Lucene to search content items for you. The properties and aspects you create and use in your content items are indexed in Lucene, and you can perform your searches using most of the standard Lucene search query syntaxes.

Apart from some XPath-based searches, searching in Alfresco mostly is done using Lucene. Alfresco supports very extensive Lucene-based search queries and functionalities. Most of the search API results return array `ScriptNode` objects.

Thus understanding search API in Alfresco mostly and essentially means understanding the Lucene syntaxes and usage in the APIs. However, there are a few other search APIs available in Alfresco which are worth investigating.

> Once you are familiar with the search APIs available, you need to get to the understanding of Lucene query syntaxes, since in most cases while searching for content items in the repository you will end up with writing some complex Lucene queries.

Here is a brief list of search APIs.

▸ **xpathSearch**: Returns an array of `ScriptNode` objects as per the XPath provided.

For example, `search.xpathSearch("*[@cm:name='InfoAxon']/*")`. This returns all nodes with the name `InfoAxon`.

▸ **findNode**: Searches for a node having the `nodeRef` passed.

For example, `search.findNode("workspace://SpacesStore/157d5f2d-579b-46dc-b1be-0242509367a7")` returns the node having this `noderef`. This method returns, at most, one object, or null in case no node exists by this `noderef`.

▸ **tagSearch**: Searches for nodes having the supplied tag associated.

For example, `search.tagSearch(null, "cookbook")` returns an array of ScriptNode objects which are tagged with `cookbook`. The first parameter null would have the search performed in the main store – **SpacesStore**. If you want to search other stores, you need to provide the store in the first parameter.

▸ **luceneSearch**: This is probably the mostly used search API. As the name suggests, you use this method for performing Lucene-based searches. There are a few overloaded `luceneSearch` methods available.

▸ **luceneSearch (query)**: Simplest version of the Lucene search method, in main store, **SpacesStore**.

▸ **luceneSearch (store, query)**: Simplest version of the Lucene search method, in the given store.

▸ **luceneSearch (query, sortcolumn, sortdirection)**: Performs search as per the query provided, sorts the result with the column provided as per the sort direction given, in the main store – **SpacesStore**.

▸ **luceneSearch (store, query, sortcolumn, sortdirection)**: Performs search as per the query provided, sorts the result with the column provided as per the sort direction given, in the given store.

In the query parameter, you put Lucene query statements.

For example, `search.luceneSearch("TEXT:InfoAxon")` will perform full text search in the repository and returns all nodes having the `InfoAxon` word in the content.

It is important to know that the PATH values, the property names, the type names, and so on are case sensitive in Lucene query.

See also

See the following recipes in *Chapter 10*, where the above JavaScript APIs are in action.

- ▶ *Display details of documents*
- ▶ *Send mail to user(s)*

Add/Change contents of a document

Now as we are aware of mostly used JavaScript APIs, Alfresco objects, and syntaxes, let's explore some example JavaScript. In the following example scripts, you will be able to witness the APIs and functionalities we discussed earlier in this chapter.

Getting ready

We will store the JavaScript files in the **Company Home>Data Dictionary>Scripts>Cookbook** folder (this folder does not exist in your repository and create this folder).

And will run the sample scripts against a document – **Test_JS_API.txt** in the folder **Company Home>InfoAxon>Chapter 8**. I have uploaded this text file with a simple line of text: A sample Document created to investigate in JavaScript API. and used our custom content type `iabook:Product`.

> We are running the sample scripts by this method, since this is one of the easiest ways to explore the scripts. However, you can also run your scripts via space rules. Later on, we will learn the most useful and prolific way of using JavaScripts – Alfresco Web Scripts.

```
if (document.hasPermission("Write"))
{
  if (document.mimetype == "text/plain")
  {
    if (!document.hasAspect("cm:versionable"))
      document.addAspect("cm:versionable");
```

```
    var wcopy = document.checkout();
    var cnt = wcopy.content;
    cnt += "\r\nThis line is added using the JavaScript.";
    wcopy.content = cnt;
    wcopy.checkin("Sample Line added via JS");
  }
}
```

How to do it...

1. Create a new script file in the **Company Home>Data Dictionary>Scripts>Cookbook** folder and save this code; let's say the file is named **changecontent.js**

2. Execute the script using **Run Action** on the document **Test_JS_API.txt** in the **Chapter 8** folder.

3. After running the script, a new version of the document will be created and a new line will be added in the document.

▼ Version History				
Version ●	**Notes ●**	**Author ●**	**Date ▼**	**Actions**
1.0	Sample Line added via JS	admin	23 December 2010 12:02	Properties View
		Page 1 of 1 ⃒ ◀ **1** ▶ ⃒		

4. Thus each time you run the script for this document, a line will be appended at the end of the content and a new version will be created.

How it works...

The document object here automatically refers to the current document, in our case, it is **Test_JS_API.txt**, since we have executed the script against this document.

First we have checked whether we have proper permission to perform the write operation on the document. If the permission is there, we check the mimetype of the document, since the textual content writing operation is possible only for a few mimetypes such as text, html, and so on.

After that, we check whether the document is versionable or not, by default, any content you upload in the repository is not versionable. So we add the cm:versionable aspect in case it is not there already.

Then we checkout the document and append the line of text we want in the working copy. After updating the content, we checking the working copy with a commit comment. This comment is visible in the **Version History** of the document.

Though it is not always mandatory to check for the required permissions, it is a good practice to confirm for the relevant permissions, otherwise Alfresco may throw runtime errors in case the required permissions are not available.

Creating a backup copy of a document

In this recipe, we will write a script to create a backup copy of a particular document.

How to do it...

1. Create a new script file in the **Company Home>Data Dictionary>Scripts>Cookbook** folder and add the following code. Let's say the file is named **createbackup.js**

```
var back = space.childByNamePath("Backup");
if (back == null && space.hasPermission("CreateChildren"))
{
  back = space.createFolder("Backup");
}

if (back != null && back.hasPermission("CreateChildren"))
{
  var copied = document.copy(back);
  if (copied != null)
  {
    var backName = "Backup of " + copied.name;
    copied.name = backName;
    copied.properties.description = "This is a Backup copy created
by JS";
    copied.save();
  }
}
```

2. Execute the script using **Run Action** on the document **Test_JS_API.txt** in the **Chapter 8** folder.

3. After executing the script, a new folder named **Backup** will be created (if it does not exist already) and a copy of this document (named **Backup of Test_JS_API.txt**) will be created in the backup folder.

Company Home > InfoAxon > Chapter 8 > Backup

Backup
This view allows you to browse the items in this space.   (0)   Add Content Create⊙ More Actions⊙ Details View⊙

▼ **Browse Spaces**   Items Per Page 20

No items to display. Click the 'Create Space' action to create a space.

Name ▲	Description ●	Created ●	Modified ●	Actions

Page 1   of 1

▼ **Content Items**   Items Per Page 20

Name ▲	Description ●	Size ●	Created ●	Modified ●	Actions
Backup of Test_JS_API.txt ⓘ	This is a Backup copy created by JS	0.1 KB	23 December 2010 14:05	23 December 2010 14:05	

Page 1   of 1

How it works...

The `space` object here automatically refers to the current space. In our case, it is **Chapter 8**, since we have executed the script against a document from this folder.

The `document` object here automatically refers to the current document. In our case, it is **Test_JS_API.txt**, since we have executed the script against this document.

First we have checked whether a space already exists there with the name **Backup** under **Chapter 8**. If not, we create the space. This is the space where we intend to create our backup copy.

After that, we check whether we have the proper permission to create a new document in the backup folder. We do this by checking the `CreateChildren` permission.

If we have the proper required permission, we create a copy of the document in the backup folder. Then we change a few properties of the copied document – we change the name and description, for instance. After changing the properties, we save the changes.

> Note that you do not need to save after changing the content of a document. However, you need to do this in case you change any property of the content item.

See also

▶ *Writing and executing scripts*

Adding a tag to a document

In this recipe, we will write a script that can be used to tag a document.

How to do it...

1. Create a new script file in the **Company Home>Data Dictionary>Scripts>Cookbook** folder and add the following code; let's say the file is named **addtag.js**

   ```
   if (!document.hasAspect("cm:taggable"))
     document.addAspect("cm:taggable");


   document.addTag("test");
   ```

2. Execute the script using **Run Action** on the document **Test_JS_API.txt** in the **Chapter 8** folder.

3. The document will not be taggable, and a new tag has been added with the document – test. This is reflected in the property sheet of the document.

▼ Properties

Name:	Test_JS_API.txt
Title:	Test_JS_API.txt
Description:	
Author:	
Version Label:	1.0
Auto Version:	Yes
Creator:	admin
Created Date:	23 December 2010 11:23
Modifier:	admin
Modified Date:	23 December 2010 14:25
Edit Inline:	Yes
Tags:	test
Content Type:	Plain Text
Encoding:	UTF-8
Size:	0.1 KB
Product SKU:	
Manufacturer:	
Product Color:	
Manufacturer Brand:	
Product Unit Price:	
Date until Product should be displayed:	
Competitor Products List:	
Details of Competitor Products:	

4. Now, you can also add more tags using the property editor dialog.

Properties

Name: Test_JS_API.txt

Title: Test_JS_API.txt

Description:

Author:

Auto Version: ☑

Edit Inline: ☑

Tags	Add a tag
cookbook	⊕
infoaxon	⊕
test	

OK   Cancel

Tags: test

Content Type: Plain Text

Encoding: UTF-8

Product SKU:

Manufacturer:

Product Color: Red

Manufacturer Brand:

Product Unit Price:

Date until Product should be displayed: None

Add to List

Competitor Products List: Selected Items

Name

No selected items.

How it works...

The code we presented is rather simple in this case. As usual, the `document` object here automatically refers to the current document. In our case, it is **Test_JS_API.txt**, since we have executed the script against this document.

First we have checked whether the document already has the `cm:taggable` aspect associated with it, if not we add this aspect.

Then it is just about adding a tag – we added a tag `test`.

> You can also add multiple tags at a time using the `addTags` method (we have used the `addTag` method to add a single tag in our example).

Assigning permissions to a user

We will see in this recipe how to assign various permissions to a particular user.

How to do it...

1. Create a new script file in the **Company Home>Data Dictionary>Scripts>Cookbook** folder and save this code. Let's say the file is named `assignpermission.js`.

```
var qry = "@cm\\:name:\"Test_JS_API.txt\"";
var docs = search.luceneSearch(qry);

if (docs.length > 0)
{
  var doc = docs[0];
  if (doc.hasPermission("ChangePermissions"))
  {
    var usr = people.getPerson("snig.bhaumik");
    if (usr != null)
    {
      doc.setPermission("Write", "snig.bhaumik");
      doc.setPermission("Delete", "snig.bhaumik");
      doc.setPermission("AddChildren", "snig.bhaumik");
      doc.setPermission("Execute", "snig.bhaumik");
    }
  }
}
```

2. Execute the script using **Run Action** on the document **Test_JS_API.txt** in the **Chapter 8** folder.

3. Upon executing the script, the user **snig.bhaumik** will have write, delete, and execute the permission of this document.

4. Let's examine what happened behind the scenes. This was the original permission set of this document.

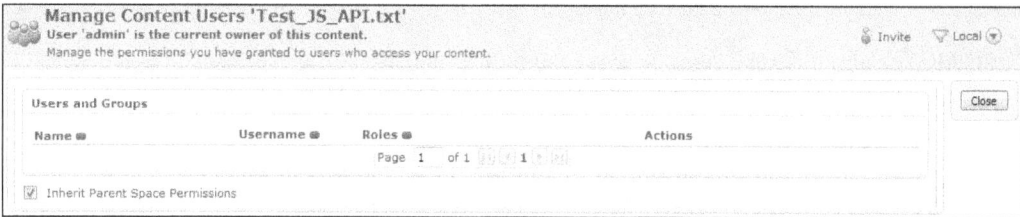

Manage Content Users 'Test_JS_API.txt'
User 'admin' is the current owner of this content.
Manage the permissions you have granted to users who access your content.

Invite   Local

Users and Groups   Close

Name   Username   Roles   Actions
                      Page 1   of 1   1

☑ Inherit Parent Space Permissions

As you can see, apart from the default privileges, no other permissions are set. When the user **snig.bhaumik** logs in, here is what he can do with this document.

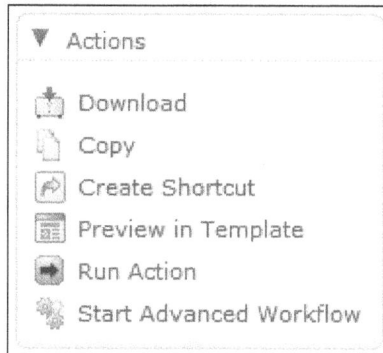

▼ Actions

Download

Copy

Create Shortcut

Preview in Template

Run Action

Start Advanced Workflow

5. However, after the execution of the script, this is the permission set of the document.

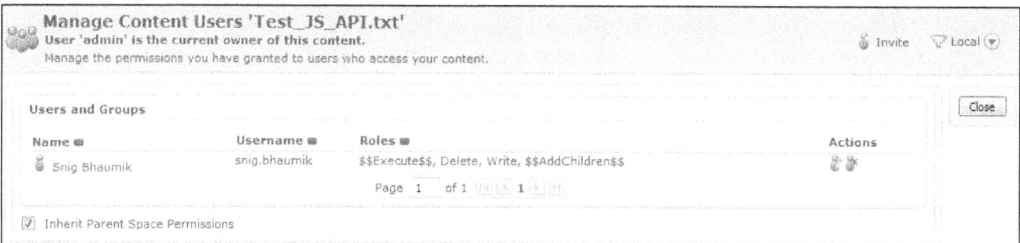

Manage Content Users 'Test_JS_API.txt'
User 'admin' is the current owner of this content.
Manage the permissions you have granted to users who access your content.

Invite   Local

Users and Groups   Close

Name   Username   Roles   Actions
Snig Bhaumik   snig.bhaumik $$Execute$$, Delete, Write, $$AddChildren$$
                          Page 1   of 1   1

☑ Inherit Parent Space Permissions

6. And, when the user **snig.bhaumik** logs in, here is what he can now do on this document.

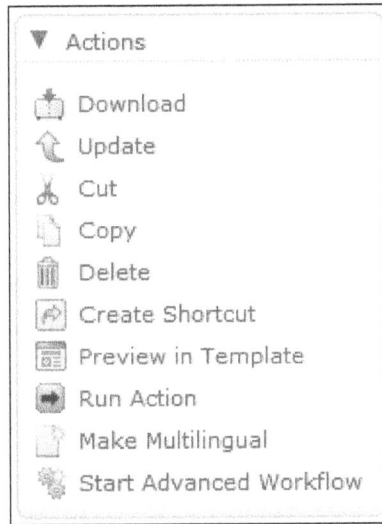

7. Thus you can see proper permissions have been assigned to the user **snig.bhaumik** on this document.

How it works...

There are a few things we have used in this script.

First of all, we have searched for the document named **Test_JS_API.txt** using Lucene. Although we could have done this using the document object, since we are executing the script on this document only, we have used Lucene search here, just to demonstrate the search operations.

As a result, we can now execute this script on any content item (not limited to only the **Test_JS_API.txt** document), and the permissions will affect this document only. Here, we have searched for documents in the repository with the name **Test_JS_API.txt**, the search results as JavaScript array in the docs variable. We have used only the first element of this array. Thus if there are multiple documents in the repository by this name, only the first element will be affected by this code.

However, if we want our code to affect only the current document, you use our good old document object, no need to search for documents. Here is the code for this:

```
if (document.hasPermission("ChangePermissions"))
{
  var usr = people.getPerson("snig.bhaumik");
  if (usr != null)
  {
    document.setPermission("Write", "snig.bhaumik");
```

```
      document.setPermission("Delete", "snig.bhaumik");
      document.setPermission("AddChildren", "snig.bhaumik");
      document.setPermission("Execute", "snig.bhaumik");
   }
}
```

After that, we find whether there is a user with the name **snig.bhaumik**. If the user exists, we assign the required permissions to this user.

Debugging Alfresco JavaScript

As you have seen, using Alfresco JavaScript you write scripts which execute in your server, not at your client browser end. You cannot write user interactive JavaScript code such as `alert`, `inputbox`, and so on. As a developer, this makes things a bit complex in terms of debugging and troubleshooting your code.

However, Alfresco comes to your rescue yet again.

There are two ways to debug your code.

1. **Using the Logging API:**

    Like other root level APIs, Alfresco provides a `logger` object which exposes two methods to log your debug code in your console logger.

    - **isLoggingEnabled**: This helps to identify whether console logging is enabled or not. By default, it is disabled.

    - **log**: You pass your log string value into this method. And if logging is enabled, you get your messages logged in console output.

2. **Using the JavaScript Debugger:**

This is another advanced user interface Alfresco offers for debugging, which allows step-by-step execution and debugging in the JS code.

> It must be executed on the same machine as the Alfresco Server — remote debugging is not yet supported.

How to do it...

Here, we will see how to debug the script using the JavaScript Debugger.

1. As an administrator, you can enable or disable the debugger by this URL (assuming localhost as the server and 8080 is the server port).

    ```
    http://localhost:8080/alfresco/service/api/javascript/debugger
    ```

2. The following web page will appear. You can use the button to enable the debugger.

3. A debugger window will appear and is ready to debug your scripts.

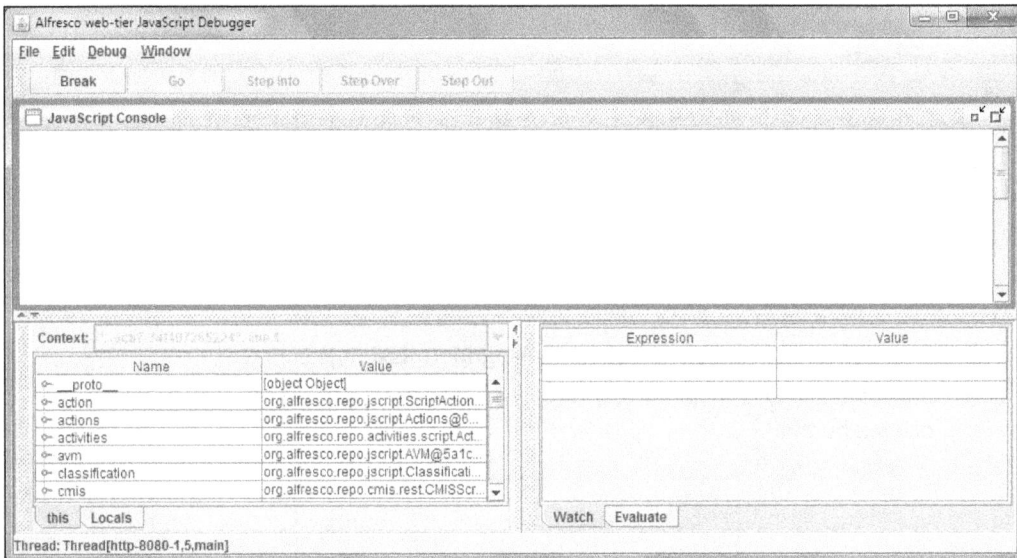

4. Now, try to again execute a script. The debugger will automatically catch up and you can debug your code line-by-line.

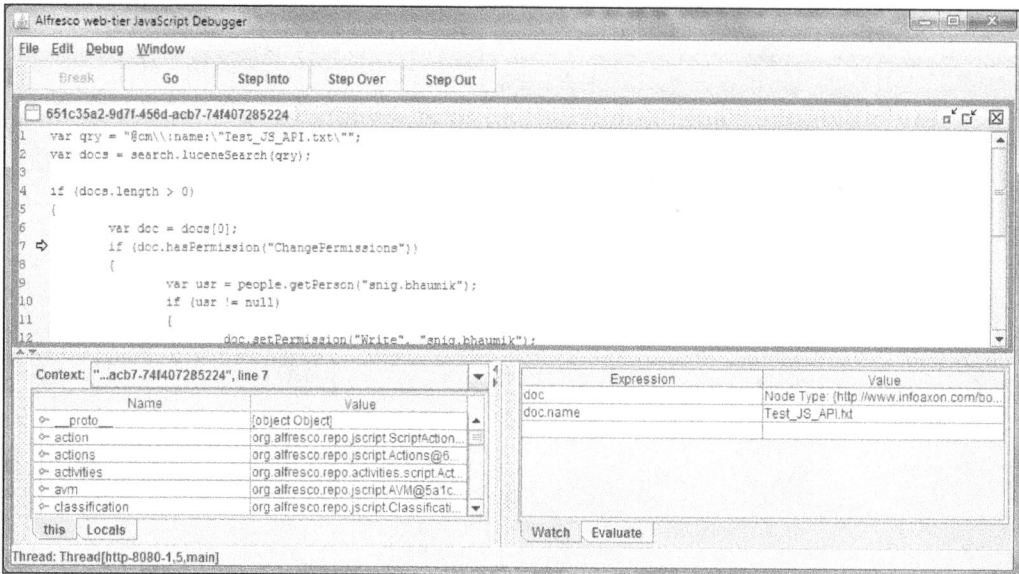

5. In this example, I have executed the **assignpermission.js** script.

6. After debugging completes, you should disable the debugger by clicking on the disable button.

How it works...

The debugger is a Swing client application which executes in the Java VM of the server where Alfresco is deployed.

Right now, it must be executed in the same machine as the Alfresco server, as remote debugging is not yet supported up to version 3.4.

9
FreeMarker Templates

In this chapter, we will cover:

- ▶ Creating and using a template
- ▶ Creating a template to display all documents in current space
- ▶ Displaying all versions of a particular document
- ▶ Displaying all assigned tasks of the current user
- ▶ Displaying all spaces and sub-spaces recursively

Introduction

A template is a document that can be applied on a data object to produce another document. Thus templates are used to present data or content in different styles and formats.

A typical template engine works in the following way:

The template engine accepts both data and the template, and a new document is generated and returned as per the template provided.

For example, an XML document can be used as data, and an XSLT document works as the template – this generates a new document that can be in HTML or Word format.

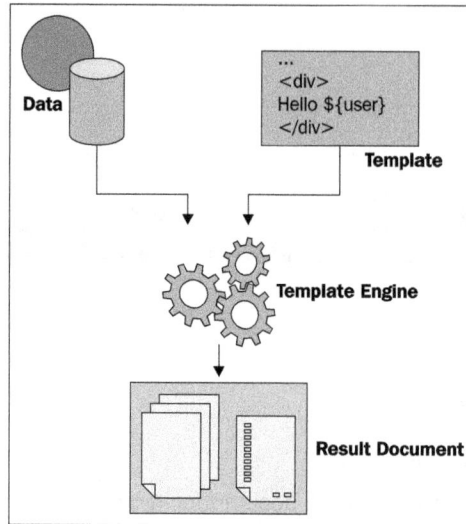

There are quite a few template engines available. XSLT is probably the most popularly used. Other engines are like FreeMarker templates, Velocity templates, and so on. Alfresco uses FreeMarker as the default template engine.

FreeMarker templates in Alfresco

Consider the following model:

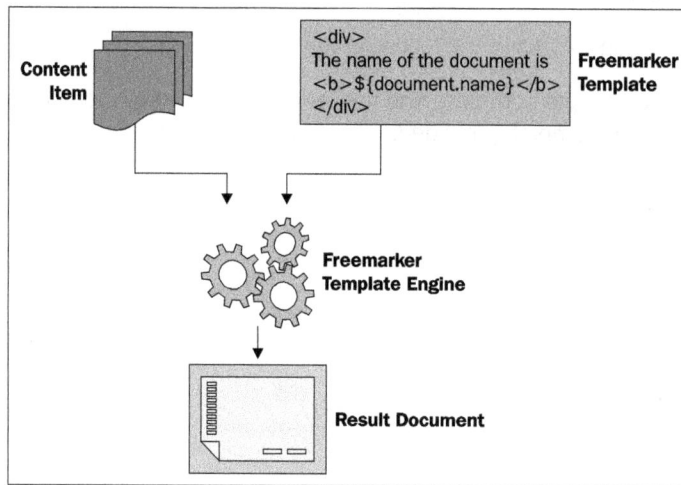

At first, a content item is passed as the data before a FreeMarker template is created and then finally a formatted document is produced. If the document passed is with the name `About Infoaxon.html` in this, the template (as per the template code in the diagram) will return the following:

```
<div>
The name of the document is <b>About Infoaxon.html</b>
</div>
```

Thus you can use FreeMarker templates in Alfresco to generate several different views and representations of a single content item. For example, you can create and use a template script that generates an HTML document on top of a content item or a space stored in the repository.

In Alfresco, we can use the FreeMarker templates for several different purposes:

- Custom views, presentations
- E-mail templates
- Web Scripts
- RSS templates
- Message templates

This is an example of a custom view of spaces. Later in this chapter, we will see how to create the custom view.

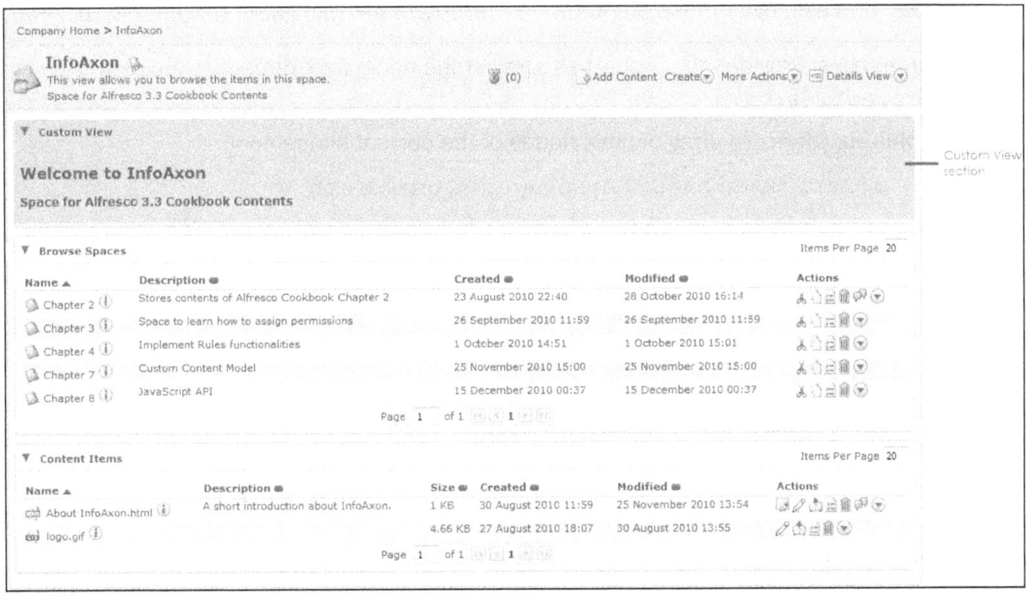

Template models

Alfresco has offered a default model that exposes a number of root objects that are available in a template file as source data. This works just like the root objects available in JavaScript files in Alfresco.

You can use these root level objects in your FreeMarker templates in Alfresco and implement various views or output files.

Some of these root-level objects are:

- **companyhome**: The Company Home template node
- **userhome**: The home space template node of the current user
- **person**: The current user template node
- **document**: The current document template node on which the template is running
- **space**: The current space template node on which the template is running
- **session**: Provides a current session ticket as the `session.ticket` value
- **url**: Renders the current Alfresco web server context path as `url.context`
- **workflow**: Offers various workflow-related functionalities

These objects come with all the properties that you can use in your template files.

Each of the template nodes exposes access to common Alfresco concepts such as properties, associations, and aspects – these are known as *Template API* (similar to the *JavaScript API*).

- **properties**: Provides the properties array of the node; for example, `document. properties.name`
- **children**: Offers an array of child nodes of the current space node
  - `url, downloadUrl,displayPath, qnamePath`
  - `isContainer, isDocument, isCategory, isLocked`
  - `mimetype, size, type, typeShort`
  - `permissions, inheritsPermissions, hasPermission`
  - `childByNamePath, childByXPath`
  - `versionHistory`

The template API offers version API as well which includes properties like:

- `id, nodeRef, name`
- `createdDate, creator, versionLabel, description, url`

The workflow API provides functionalities such as:

- assignedTasks, pooledTasks, completedTasks
- getTaskById

> You might have noticed a few similarities between API objects exposed in JavaScript API and in Template API. However, it is important to note that these two APIs are quite different. If a syntax or property works in one of these APIs, it does not guarantee that the same will work in the other API as well.
>
> For example, the qnamePath property is available in Template API, not in JavaScript API. Similarly, space.children.length can be used in JavaScript API, but not in Template API.

There's more...

Before jumping into writing your own FreeMarker templates, you need to understand the FreeMarker syntaxes. The FreeMarker manual has well-organized documentation to help you understand this. Please see http://FreeMarker.sourceforge.net/docs/index.html.

FreeMarker offers a rich set of built-in functions that you can use in your template – To see list of built-in functions of Freemarker, please see http://FreeMarker.sourceforge.net/docs/ref_builtins.html.

It is also important to be familiar with some standard programming directives such as – To see list of available directives of Freemarker, please see http://FreeMarker.sourceforge.net/docs/ref_directives.html.

Creating a FreeMarker template

Now that we understand the syntax and structure of a FreeMarker template, in this recipe, you will learn how to create a basic FreeMarker template.

How to do it...

1. Open the Alfresco web client and navigate to the **Company Home > Data Dictionary > Presentation Templates** space. Just like the **Company Home > Data Dictionary > Scripts** space contains all the executable scripts in the repository, similarly the **Presentation Templates** space holds all the FreeMarker templates that can be used in custom presentations of various contents in the repository.

2. You can see a number of sample FTL files (`ftl` is the standard extension of FreeMarker template files) are stored in this folder. Each of the FTL files are standard text files.

3. Thus you need to create FTL files in this space and Alfresco will use these templates in custom presentations.

4. In the **Company Home > Data Dictionary > Presentation Templates** space, create a new content. Let's name it **space_details.ftl**.

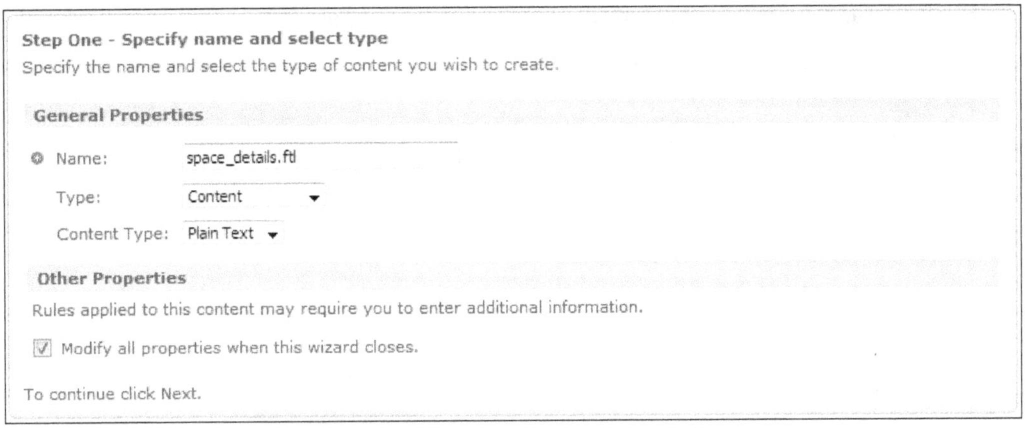

Step One - Specify name and select type

Specify the name and select the type of content you wish to create.

General Properties

Name: space_details.ftl

Type: Content ▾

Content Type: Plain Text ▾

Other Properties

Rules applied to this content may require you to enter additional information.

☑ Modify all properties when this wizard closes.

To continue click Next.

5. The content of the **space_details.ftl** is:

```
<#if space??>
  <h2>
    Welcome to ${space.name}
  </h2>
  <h3>
    ${space.properties["cm:description"]}
  </h3>
<#else>
  <h3>
    No current space!!!
  </h3>
</#if>
```

6. Save the template.

7. Now we want to use this template as a custom view of a space. Let's take the **InfoAxon** (**Company Home** > **InfoAxon**) space for this.

8. By default, there is no custom view available for the space.

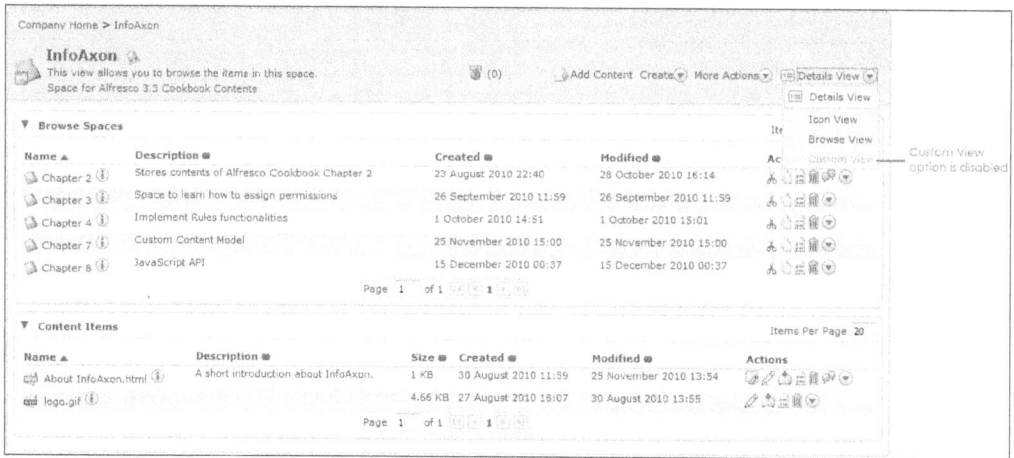

9. Now open the details of the space. In the **Custom View** section, click on the **Apply Template** or **Modify** link.

10. In the available list of templates, our new template `space_details.ftl` will be visible. Select this template and click **OK**.

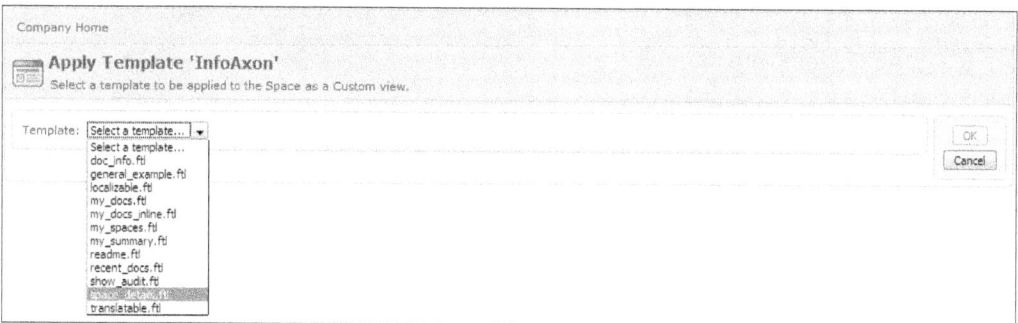

11. Now you can see that a custom view of the space is appearing in the page.

Company Home > InfoAxon

InfoAxon
This view allows you to browse the items in this space.
Space for Alfresco 3.3 Cookbook Contents

(0)   Add Content Create ▼ More Actions ▼ Details View ▼

▼ Custom View

Welcome to InfoAxon

Space for Alfresco 3.3 Cookbook Contents

▼ Browse Spaces   Items Per Page 20

Name ▲	Description	Created	Modified	Actions
Chapter 2	Stores contents of Alfresco Cookbook Chapter 2	23 August 2010 22:40	28 October 2010 16:14	
Chapter 3	Space to learn how to assign permissions	26 September 2010 11:59	26 September 2010 11:59	
Chapter 4	Implement Rules functionalities	1 October 2010 14:51	1 October 2010 15:01	
Chapter 7	Custom Content Model	25 November 2010 15:00	25 November 2010 15:00	
Chapter 8	JavaScript API	15 December 2010 00:37	15 December 2010 00:37	

Page 1 of 1 |◄ ◄ 1 ► ►|

▼ Content Items   Items Per Page 20

Name ▲	Description	Size	Created	Modified	Actions
About InfoAxon.html	A short introduction about InfoAxon.	1 KB	30 August 2010 11:59	25 November 2010 13:54	
logo.gif		4.66 KB	27 August 2010 18:07	30 August 2010 13:55	

Page 1 of 1 |◄ ◄ 1 ► ►|

12. You can also enable only the custom view of the space. For this, in the views drop-down, click on **Custom View**.

Company Home > InfoAxon

InfoAxon
This view allows you to browse the items in this space.
Space for Alfresco 3.3 Cookbook Contents

Custom View ▼

Custom View

Welcome to InfoAxon

Space for Alfresco 3.3 Cookbook Contents

13. In this way, you can create presentation templates and use them to produce different custom views for your spaces. The custom views are available for content items as well.

14. For this, click on **Preview in Template**, as shown in the following screenshot:

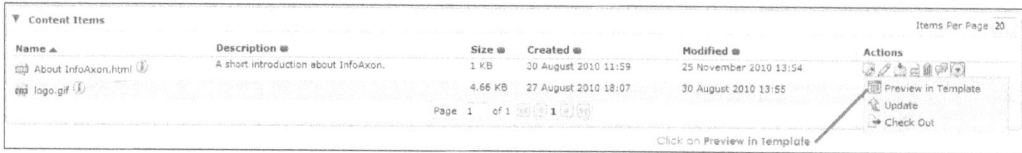

Click on Preview in Template

15. A list of the available templates will be presented. Choose one template, and a custom view of the content item will be produced.

How it works...

The `space` object referred to in the template assumes the value of the current space. Since we have associated the template with the **InfoAxon** folder, it rendered values as per this folder.

We have also used a syntax `<#if space??>` – this is similar to `<#if space?exists>`. This returns true if there is a space object available.

After this, we have just displayed the space name and description in HTML components.

In the next few recipes, we will explore some example templates.

Displaying all documents in current space

We have seen a simple template that displays current space's name and description. Now let's create a template that will list all the documents of the current space, along with the snapshot of the images.

How to do it...

1. In the **Company Home > Data Dictionary > Presentation Templates** space, create a new content. Let's name it **space_details.ftl**.

2. Put the following template code:

```
<#if space??>
  <h2>
    Documents in ${space.name}
  </h2>
  <table>
    <#assign cnt=0>
    <#list space.children as c>
      <#if c.isDocument>
        <#assign cnt=cnt+1>
```

```
        <tr><td>${cnt}. <a href="${url.context}${c.
downloadUrl}">${c.properties.name}</a></td></tr>
        <#if c.mimetype = "image/jpeg" || c.mimetype = "image/png"
|| c.mimetype = "image/gif">
          <tr><td style='padding-left:20px'><img width=100
height=65 src="${url.context}${c.url}"><td></tr>
        </#if>
      </#if>
    </#list>
  </table>
<#else>
  <h3>
    No current space!!!
  </h3>
</#if>
```

3. Apply this template as the custom view of the **Company Home > InfoAxon** space and you will see the custom view of the space is appearing on the page.

How it works...

The template iterates through all the child nodes under the current space. Each of the child nodes are denoted as c in this template. cnt is a variable we have created just to display the document index or counter. As we want to display only the documents under the current space, we have ensured this by using the c.isDocument clause. Thus all the sub-spaces have been excluded.

We have offered the download link on the document name using the c.downloadUrl property. In this template, image thumbnails are displayed – we have checked the mimetype of the document, if the mimetype is of image type then we have displayed a snapshot of the image.

Finally, the template renders the following view:

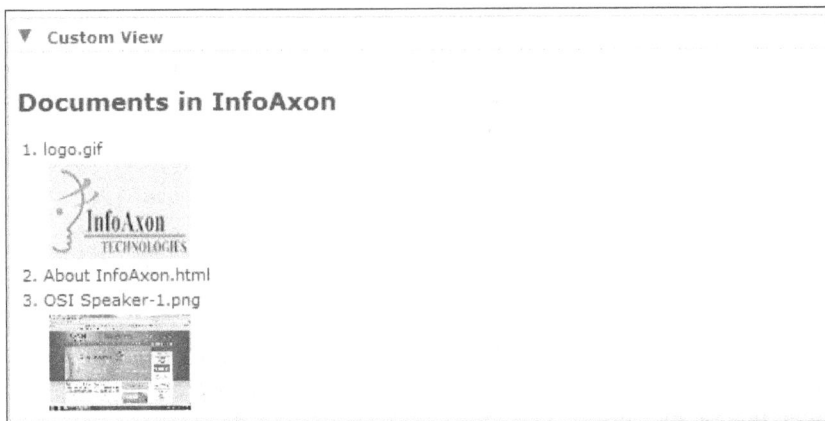

Displaying all versions of a particular document

In this recipe, we will see how to display all previous versions of the document.

How to do it...

1. In the **Company Home > Data Dictionary > Presentation Templates** space, create a new content. Let's name it **doc_versions.ftl**.

2. Put the following template code:

```
<#if document?exists>
  <h3>Version History of <u>${document.name}</u></h3>
  <table cellspacing=10>
    <tr align=left><th>Version</th><th>Name</th><th>Description</
th><th>Created Date</th><th>Creator</th></tr>
    <#list document.versionHistory as v>
      <tr>
        <td><a href="/alfresco${v.url}" target="new">${v.
versionLabel}</a></td>
        <td><a href="/alfresco${v.url}" target="new">${v.name}</
a></td>
        <td><#if v.description?exists>${v.description}</#if></td>
        <td>${v.createdDate?datetime}</td>
        <td>${v.creator}</td>
      </tr>
    </#list>
  </table>
<#else>
  No document found!
</#if>
```

3. Apply this template as the custom view of the **Company Home** > **InfoAxon** > **About InfoAxon.html** document and you will see the custom view of the space is appearing in the page.

How it works...

First we check whether the document object carries a valid document node. This is done by the `document?exists` condition.

As we know, the `document.versionHistory` property returns an array of all previous versions of the document. We thus iterate through this and display properties of each version in a structured tabular fashion.

For example, `v.url` returns the download URL of that particular version object. `v.createdDate` and `v.creator` return the date when the version was created and who created the version.

Similarly, `v.versionLabel` returns the label of the particular version, such as 1.0, 1.1, and so on.

Finally, the template renders the following:

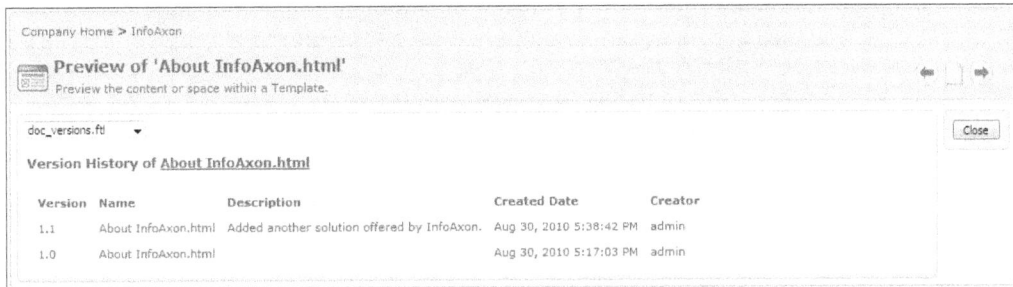

Displaying all assigned tasks of the current user

This template will display all the tasks assigned to the current user.

How to do it...

1. In the **Company Home > Data Dictionary > Presentation Templates** space, create a new content. Let's name it **task_list.ftl**.

2. Add the following template code:

```
<h3>Tasks of user <u>${person.properties.userName}</u></h3>

<table cellspacing=0 cellpadding=2>
  <tr>
    <th>Type</th>
    <th>Name</th>
    <th>Description</th>
    <th>Created Date</th>
    <th>Start Date</th>
    <th>Due Date</th>
    <th>Priority</th>
    <th>% Complete</th>
    <th>Status</th>
    <th>Completed</th>
```

```
        </tr>
        <#list workflow.assignedTasks as t>
          <tr>
            <td>${t.type}</td>
            <td>${t.name}</td>
            <td>${t.description}</td>
            <td>${t.properties["cm:created"]?datetime}</td>
            <td><#if t.properties["bpm:startDate"]?exists>${t.properties
["bpm:startDate"]?datetime}<#else><i>None</i></#if></td>
            <td><#if t.properties["bpm:dueDate"]?exists>${t.properties["
bpm:dueDate"]?datetime}<#else><i>None</i></#if></td>
            <td>${t.properties["bpm:priority"]}</td>
            <td>${t.properties["bpm:percentComplete"]}</td>
            <td>${t.properties["bpm:status"]}</td>
            <td>${t.isCompleted?string("Yes", "No")}</td>
          </tr>
        </#list>
      </table>
```

3. Apply this template as the custom view of the **Company Home** space (or any other space) and you will see that the custom view of the space is appearing in the page.

How it works...

The current username is displayed using the `person.properties.userName` property.

The current user's assigned tasks are returned by the `workflow.assignedTasks` object. Each element of this array is iterated using the variable `t`. This `t` stands for each task node.

Most of the important tasks' details are displayed wrapped in a table.

- ▸ `t.name` returns the name of the task
- ▸ `t.properties["cm:created"]` returns the date when the task was created, similarly `t.properties["bpm:dueDate"]` gives the due date of the task
- ▸ Task priority is returned by `t.properties["bpm:priority"]`. Status can be gotten from `t.properties["bpm:status"]`. `t.isCompleted` is a boolean value which returns whether the task is closed or opened.

The output would be as shown in the following screenshot:

| | ▼ Custom View | | | | | | | | | |

Tasks of user admin

Type	Name	Description	Created Date	Start Date	Due Date	Priority	% Complete	Status	Completed
Adhoc Task	Adhoc Task allocated by colleague	Get ticket of the World Cup match!	Jan 12, 2011 7:04:13 PM	None	Jan 3, 2011 7:03:00 PM	2	0	Not Yet Started	No
Review	Review Documents to Approve or Reject them	Please review this document.	Jan 12, 2011 7:05:38 PM	None	Jan 4, 2011 7:05:00 PM	2	0	Not Yet Started	No

See also

▶ *Creating and deploying custom Workflows, Chapter 11.*

Displaying all spaces and sub-spaces recursively

By now, you may have understood how to display the contents of a particular space.

But you know Alfresco spaces are hierarchical and these can be very complex – much like the MS Windows folder structure. So what if we want to display all the spaces and sub-spaces under the current space?

How to do it...

1. In the **Company Home** > **Data Dictionary** > **Presentation Templates** space, create a new content. Let's name it **all_spaces.ftl**.

2. Add the following template code:

```
<#macro return_spaces node depth>
  <#if node.isContainer>
    <tr>
      <td align='left'>(${depth})
        <#if (depth>0) >
          <#list 1..depth as i>.</#list>
        </#if>
        <img src="/alfresco${node.icon16}"> <a href="/
alfresco${node.url}">${node.properties.name}</a>
      </td>
    </tr>

    <#list node.children as child>
      <#if child.isContainer && node.children?size != 0 >
        <@return_spaces node=child depth=depth+1/>
      </#if>
    </#list>
```

```
    </#if>
  </#macro>

  <b>Full in-depth Listing of Spaces:</b>
  <table border="1" celpadding="1" cellspacing="1">
    <tr><th> Name Space </th></tr>
    <@return_spaces node=space depth=0/>
  </table>
```

3. Apply this template as the custom view of the **Company Home > InfoAxon** space and you will see that the custom view of the space is appearing on the page.

How it works...

Here we have introduced a new concept in FreeMarker template, namely, macro. Macros are predefined and reusable methods that you can define and call in a template.

Here, we have defined a macro named `return_spaces` – it takes two arguments – node and depth. The macro calls itself for all the sub-spaces under the current node, and it goes on until all the sub-spaces are completed.

Finally, we call the macro with the `space` object (with the line `<@return_spaces node=space depth=0/>`). Thus this template is capable of displaying a tree of sub-spaces of any folder where it is executed.

If we run this template for our **InfoAxon** space, it returns the following screenshot:

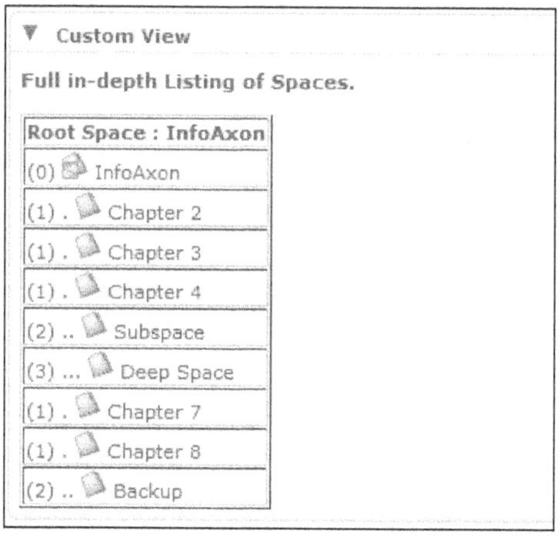

Be careful when running this template on Company Home – it can render a long list, depending on how much data you have in the repository.

10

Web Scripts

In this chapter, we will cover:

- ▶ Writing and deploying Web Scripts
- ▶ Displaying details of documents
- ▶ Sending e-mails using a Mail Template

Introduction

You all know about Web Services – which took the web development world by storm a few years ago. Web Services have been instrumental in constructing Web APIs (Application Programming Interface) and making the web applications work as Service-Oriented Architecture. In the new Web 2.0 world, however, many criticisms arose around traditional Web Services – thus RESTful services came into the picture. **REST** (**Representational State Transfer**) attempts to expose the APIs using HTTP or similar protocol and interfaces using well-known, light-weight and standard methods such as GET, POST, PUT, DELETE, and so on.

Alfresco Web Scripts provide RESTful APIs of the repository services and functions. Traditionally, ECM systems have been exposing the interfaces using **RPC** (**Remote Procedure Call**) – but gradually it turned out that RPC-based APIs are not particularly suitable in the wide Internet arena where multiple environments and technologies reside together and talk seamlessly. In the case of Web Scripts, the RESTful services overcome all these problems and integration with an ECM repository has never been so easy and secure. Alfresco Web Scripts were introduced in 2006 and since then it has been quite popular with the developer and system integrator community for implementing services on top of the Alfresco repository and to amalgamate Alfresco with any other system.

What is a Web Script?

A **Web Script** is simply a URI bound to a service using standard HTTP methods such as `GET`, `POST`, `PUT`, or `DELETE`. Web Scripts can be written using simply the Alfresco JavaScript APIs and Freemarker templates, and optionally Java API as well with or without any Freemarker template.

For example, the `http://localhost:8080/alfresco/service/api/search/person.html ?q=admin&p=1&c=10` URL will invoke the search service and return the output in HTML.

Internally, a script has been written using JavaScript API (or Java API) that performs the search and a FreeMarker template is written to render the search output in a structured HTML format.

> All the Web Scripts are exposed as services and are generally prefixed with `http://<<server-url>>/<<context-path>>/<<service-path>>`. In a standard scenario, this is `http://localhost:8080/alfresco/service`

Web Script architecture

Alfresco Web Scripts strictly follow the MVC architecture.

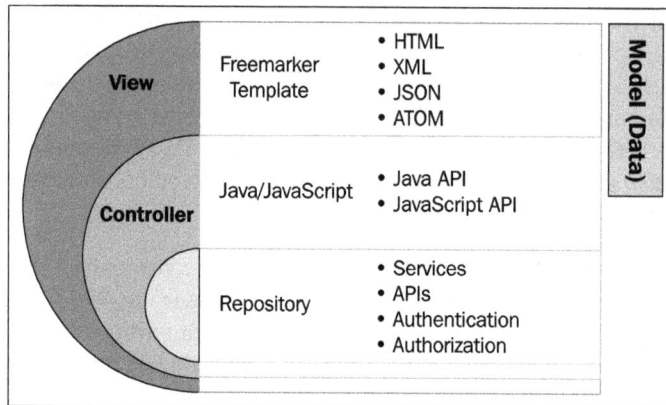

- ► **Controller**: Written using Alfresco Java or JavaScript API, you implement your business requirements for the Web Script in this layer. You also prepare your data model that is returned to the view layer. The controller code interacts with the repository via the APIs and other services and processes the business implementations.

- ▶ **View**: Written using Freemarker templates, you implement exactly what you want to return in your Web Script. For data Web Scripts you construct your JSON or XML data using the template; and for presentation Web Scripts you build your output HTML. The view can be implemented using Freemarker templates, or using Java-backed Web Script classes.

- ▶ **Model**: Normally constructed in the controller layer (in Java or JavaScript), these values are automatically available in the view layer.

Types of Web Scripts

Depending on the purpose and output, Web Scripts can be categorized in two types:

1. **Data Web Scripts**: These Web Scripts mostly return data in plenty after processing of business requirements. Such Web Scripts are mostly used to retrieve, update, and create content in the repository or query the repository.

2. **Presentation Web Scripts**: When you want to build a user interface using Web Scripts, you use these Web Scripts. They mostly return HTML output. Such Web Scripts are mostly used for creating dashlets in Alfresco Explorer or Alfresco Share or for creating JSR-168 portlets.

> Note that this categorization of Web Script is not technically different—it is just a logical separation. This means data Web Scripts and presentation Web Scripts are not technically dissimilar, only usage and purpose is different.

Web Script files

Defining and creating a Web Script in Alfresco requires creating certain files in particular folders. These files are:

1. Web Script Descriptor: The descriptor is an XML file used to define the Web Script – the name of the script, the URL(s) on which the script can be invoked, the authentication mechanism of the script and so on. The name of the descriptor file should be of the form: `<<service-id>>.<http-method>>. desc.xml`; for example, `helloworld.get.desc.xml`.

2. Freemarker Template Response file(s) optional: The Freemarker Template output file(s) is the FTL file which is returned as the result of the Web Script. The name of the template files should be of the form: `<<service-id>>.<<http-method>>.<<response-format >>.ftl`; for example, `helloworld.get.html.ftl` and `helloworld.get.json.ftl`.

3. Controller JavaScript file (optional): The Controller JavaScript file is the business layer of your Web Script. The name of the JavaScript file should be of the form: `<<service-id>>.<<http-method>>.js`; for example, `helloworld.get.js`.

4. Controller Java file (optional): You can write your business implementations in Java classes as well, instead of using JavaScript API.

5. Configuration file (optional): You can optionally include a configuration XML file. The name of the file should be of the form: `<<service-id>>.<<http-method>>. config.xml`; for example, `helloworld.get.config.js`.

6. Resource Bundle file (optional): These are standard message bundle files that can be used for making Web Script responses localized. The name of message files would be of the form: `<<service-id>>.<<http-method>>.properties`; for example, `helloworld.get.properties`.

The naming conventions of Web Script files are fixed – they follow particular semantics.

Alfresco, by default, has provided a quite rich list of built-in Web Scripts which can be found in the `\tomcat\webapps\alfresco\WEB-INF\classes\alfresco\templates \ webscripts\org\alfresco` folder. There are a few locations where you can store your Web Scripts.

1. Classpath folder: `\tomcat\webapps\alfresco\WEB-INF\classes\alfresco\ templates\webscripts\`

2. Classpath folder (extension): `\tomcat\webapps\alfresco\WEB-INF\classes\ alfresco\extension\templates\webscripts\`

3. Repository folder: `/Company Home/Data Dictionary/Web Scripts`

4. Repository folder (extension): `/Company Home/Data Dictionary/Web Scripts Extensions`

> It is not advised to keep your Web Scripts in the `org\alfresco` folder; this folder is reserved for Alfresco default Web Scripts. Create your own folders instead. Or better, you should create your Web Scripts in the extension folders.

Web Script parameters

You of course need to pass some parameters to your Web Script and execute your business implementations around that.

You can pass parameters by query string for the GET Web Scripts. For example:

```
http://localhost:8080/alfresco/service/api/search/person.
html?q=admin&p=1&c=10
```

In this script, we have passed three parameters – q (for the search query), p (for the page index), and c (for the number of items per page). You can also pass parameters bound in HTML form data in the case of POST Web Scripts. One example of such Web Script is to upload a file using Web Script, which is described later in this chapter.

Writing and deploying Web Scripts

As you know, writing a Web Script requires creating some files in certain locations. Here in this recipe we will see how this can be done. The best part is you do not require any Java development environment; no Eclipse is required for writing Web Scripts, no Java programming knowledge is essential. However, if you wish to create Java-backed Web Scripts, you may need these.

In the latter examples and illustrations, we will create our Web Scripts in the classpath folder in a new package, com\infoaxon. Let's say we will create a Web Script with the service-ID showhomedetails.

We expect the Web Script to return the contents of the current user's home space in a structured HTML format.

How to do it...

1. First we will create the folder where the Web Script files will be stored. Create a folder named com under \tomcat\webapps\alfresco\WEB-INF\classes\ alfresco\templates\webscripts\, create the folder infoaxon under this. Thus we will be creating our Web Script files under the folder \tomcat\webapps\ alfresco\WEB-INF\classes\alfresco\templates\webscripts\com\ infoaxon.

2. Next we need to write the Web Script descriptor. Open your favorite text editor (or you can use any XML editor such as **oXygen**).

3. Enter the following text:

```
<webscript>
    <shortname>Home Space Contents</shortname>
    <description>Retrieves and displays all contents under current
user's Home Space.</description>
    <url>/showhomedetails</url>
    <format default="html"/>
    <authentication>user</authentication>
    <transaction>required</transaction>
</webscript>
```

4. Save this file with the name showhomedetails.get.desc.xml.

5. Then we will create the response Freemarker template that will return the output HTML.

6. Open a new text file and enter the following text:

```
<html>
<body>
    <#if userhome?exists>
  <h2>Sub Folders</h2>
  <table cellpadding="5" cellspacing="5" border="1">
      <tr style="font-weight: bold"><td>Name</td><td>Create Date</
td><td>Creator</td><td>Offspring</td></tr>
      <#list userhome.children as c>
    <#if c.isContainer>
        <tr><td>${c.name}</td><td>${c.properties["cm:created"]
?datetime}</td><td>${c.properties["cm:creator"]}</td><td>${c.
children?size}</td></tr>
      </#if>
        </#list>
  </table>

  <h2>Content Items</h2>
  <table cellpadding="5" cellspacing="5" border="1">
      <tr style="font-weight: bold"><td>Name</td><td>Create Date</
td><td>Creator</td><td>Size (bytes)</td></tr>
      <#list userhome.children as c>
    <#if c.isDocument>
        <tr><td>${c.name}</td><td>${c.properties["cm:created"]?da
tetime}</td><td>${c.properties["cm:creator"]}</td><td>${c.size}</
td></tr>
      </#if>
        </#list>
  </table>
    <#else>
  <h3>User Home not Found!</h3>
      </#if>
</body>
</html>
```

7. That's all – you have created your first Web Script. Restart your server and navigate to `http://localhost:8080/alfresco/service/showhomedetails` (this is our Web Script URL). The system will ask for user credentials and you will be able to see some similar HTML output, as shown below (I am logged in as the **admin** user).

Sub Folders

Name	Create Date	Creator	Offspring
Data Dictionary	Jun 24, 2010 11:20:46 PM	System	16
Guest Home	Jun 24, 2010 11:20:46 PM	System	0
User Homes	Jun 24, 2010 11:20:46 PM	System	3
Sites	Jun 24, 2010 11:20:58 PM	System	0
InfoAxon	Jun 25, 2010 5:22:40 PM	admin	9

Content Items

Name	Create Date	Creator	Size (bytes)
InfoAxon_Data.acp	Oct 27, 2010 4:18:05 PM	admin	1,255,309
Filters in Query.doc	Dec 21, 2010 5:26:02 PM	admin	33,280

> It is not that you always have to restart your server after creating a new Web Script or updating an existing one. You can refresh the Web Script library as well – we will learn about that later in this chapter.

How it works...

We have assigned the URL of the service as `showhomedetails`. Thus, the full URL of the service becomes `http://localhost:8080/alfresco/service/showhomedetails`.

As the authentication option, we have given `<code>user</code>`. There are four authentication options available for Web Scripts to run. They are as follows:

1. `none`: Means no authentication required. Alfresco will not ask for any user credentials while running the script. However, most of the repository functionalities and services will be unavailable in this case.

2. `guest`: Means guest authentication required. Alfresco will not ask for any user credentials yet again, but will assume the guest permissions. Again, many of the repository functionalities and services will be unavailable in this case, since the guest user is not allowed to access most of the repository assets.

3. `user`: Means a valid user credential is required for running the script. Alfresco thus will ask for the username and password for running the script.

4. `admin`: Means only administrators can access the Web Script. You normally use this setting in case of any administrative jobs such as managing users, groups, and so on.

We want to return HTML output from the Web Script, thus we have created an HTML template file. The code of the template is pretty simple – just displaying the contents of the current user's home folder in two HTML tables.

You will notice that we have not created any controller script for this service. This is because for now we did not feel any need for that. However, we can restructure the code and make use of the controller script.

1. Create a new text file. Put the following code:

```
function main()
{
    var folders = new Array();
    var docs = new Array();

    if (userhome != null)
    {
    var children = userhome.children;
    for (i=0; i<children.length; i++)
    {
        var c = children[i];
        if (c.isContainer)      folders.push(c);
        else if (c.isDocuent)    docs.push(c);
    }
    }
    model.folders = folders;
    model.docs = docs;
}

main();
```

2. Save the file as `showhomedetails.get.js` in the same folder.

> You might recollect we had discussed about the available root-level objects in JavaScript API in *Chapter 8*. The `userhome` object we have used here in this script is one of these root-level objects.

3. The following is the updated template code. Put the following text in the `showhomedetails.get.html.ftl` file:

```
<html>
<body>
    <#if folders?exists>
    <h2>Sub Folders</h2>
    <table cellpadding="5" cellspacing="5" border="1">
        <tr style="font-weight: bold"><td>Name</td><td>Create Date</td><td>Creator</td><td>Offspring</td></tr>
```

```
    <#list folders as c>
    <tr><td>${c.name}</td><td>${c.properties["cm:created"]?d
atetime}</td><td>${c.properties["cm:creator"]}</td><td>${c.
children?size}</td></tr>
        </#list>
  </table>
    </#if>

    <#if docs?exists>
  <h2>Content Items</h2>
    <table cellpadding="5" cellspacing="5" border="1">
        <tr style="font-weight: bold"><td>Name</td><td>Create Date</
td><td>Creator</td><td>Size (bytes)</td></tr>
        <#list docs as c>
    <tr><td>${c.name}</td><td>${c.properties["cm:created"]?dateti
me}</td><td>${c.properties["cm:creator"]}</td><td>${c.size}</td></
tr>
        </#list>
  </table>
    </#if>
</body>
</html>
```

4. Run the Web Script and you will see the same HTML output.

> One important object here is the `model` object that is the bridge between the model and the view and it is available as a root object in the scope of the script. Thus whatever variables and values you assign into this object will be available in the template view.
>
> For example, we have assigned two variables, `folders` and `docs`, in the `model` object – these are available in the FreeMarker template. You can use these values in the view and display the values as per your requirement.

There's more...

We have used several FreeMarker syntaxes in this script.

1. You have already seen the use of the `<#if…>` tag in the *Displaying all documents in current space* recipe in the previous chapter.

2. The `<#list…>` tag is used to iterate through an array of objects – just like a `for each` loop in any other programming language.

3. For example, in `<#list folders as c>`, we have iterated through the `folders` array and each element of the array is represented by `c`.

4. The `ScriptNode` object we visited and used in various recipes in *Chapter 8* is available in the Web Script FreeMarker template as well. Thus you will be able to extract and use any of the properties of this object.

5. For example, by the statement `c.isContainer` – we have evaluated whether the current `ScriptNode` is a space or not. Similarly, `c.properties["cm:creator"]` returns the creator property value of the object. In this way, you can extract any available property of the current object.

Using the Alfresco Web Script browser

The Web Script browser is an interface provided by Alfresco explorer that helps you browse, view, manage, and run all the deployed Web Scripts.

This interface is available at `http://localhost:8080/alfresco/service/index`, assuming you are running Alfresco Tomcat at the localhost 8080 port.

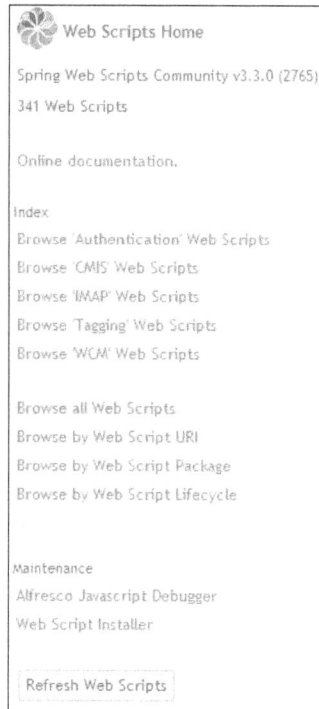

You can use this interface for quite a number of purposes.

- ▸ Browse and see all the Web Scripts deployed and configured
- ▸ Browse Web Scripts by URIs

▸ Browse Web Scripts by packages

Index of Web Scripts Package '/'

Spring Web Scripts Community v3.3.0 (2765)

0 Web Scripts

Back to Web Scripts Home

/com/infoaxon
/org/alfresco/avm
/org/alfresco/calendar
/org/alfresco/cmis
/org/alfresco/cmis/sample
/org/alfresco/collaboration
/org/alfresco/office
/org/alfresco/portlets
/org/alfresco/repository
/org/alfresco/repository/activities
/org/alfresco/repository/activities/feed
/org/alfresco/repository/activities/feed/control
/org/alfresco/repository/blogs/blog
/org/alfresco/repository/blogs/post
/org/alfresco/repository/blogs/posts
/org/alfresco/repository/comments
/org/alfresco/repository/dictionary
/org/alfresco/repository/discussions/forum
/org/alfresco/repository/discussions/posts

1. This is a partial output of the listing of Web Scripts by packages. You can notice that our new package /com/infoaxon is also registered there.

   You can see and validate all details of a particular Web Script by this interface. Let's see how we can view the details of our new script we have just created in the previous recipe.

   i. Click on **Browse by Web Script URI**.

   ii. Look for our new script with the URI **/showhomedetails**.

iii. Brief details of the Web Script will appear as follows:

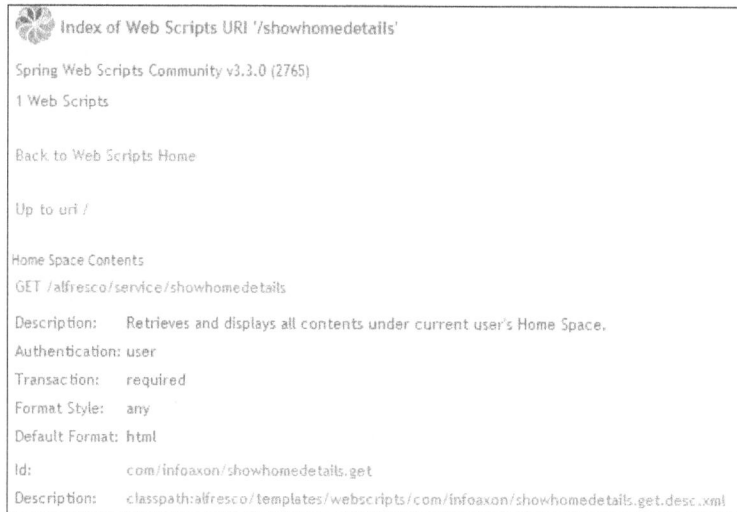

Index of Web Scripts URI '/showhomedetails'

Spring Web Scripts Community v3.3.0 (2765)

1 Web Scripts

Back to Web Scripts Home

Up to uri /

Home Space Contents

GET /alfresco/service/showhomedetails

Description: Retrieves and displays all contents under current user's Home Space.
Authentication: user
Transaction: required
Format Style: any
Default Format: html
Id: com/infoaxon/showhomedetails.get
Description: classpath:alfresco/templates/webscripts/com/infoaxon/showhomedetails.get.desc.xml

2. You can see that most of the details in this page are appearing from the descriptor XML file you can create for our script.

3. Click on the **GET /alfresco/service/showhomedetails** link to execute the script.

4. Click on the Id link (the **com/infoaxon/showhomedetails.get** link) to view the detailed information of the Web Script. This interface will render the full code and implementation set of the Web Script.

```
Web Script: com/infoaxon/showhomedetails.get

Generated from /alfresco/service/script/com/infoaxon/showhomedetails.get on Jan 17, 2011 12:53:38 AM


Script Properties

Id:                  com/infoaxon/showhomedetails.get

Short Name:          Home Space Contents

Description:         Retrieves and displays all contents under current user's Home Space.

Authentication:      user

Transaction:         required

Method:              GET

URL Template:        /showhomedetails

Format Style:        any

Default Format:      html

Negotiated Formats: [undefined]

Implementation:      class org.springframework.extensions.webscripts.DeclarativeWebScript

Extensions:          [undefined]


Store: workspace://SpacesStore/app:company_home/app:dictionary/cm:extensionwebscripts


[No implementation files]


Store: workspace://SpacesStore/app:company_home/app:dictionary/cm:webscripts


[No implementation files]


Store: classpath:alfresco/templates/webscripts


File: com/infoaxon/showhomedetails.get.desc.xml


<webscript>
        <shortname>Home Space Contents</shortname>
        <description>Retrieves and displays all contents under current user's Home Space.</description>
        <url>/showhomedetails</url>
        <format default="html"/>
        <authentication>user</authentication>
        <transaction>required</transaction>
</webscript>

File: com/infoaxon/showhomedetails.get.html.ftl


<html>
<body>
        <#if folders?exists>
                <h2>Sub Folders</h2>
```

- ❑ This is again a partial output of this page. You can see that almost all the information you need for a Web Script is presented in this page.

- ❑ The last link (description link) is to show the descriptor XML file.

5. Finally, using the **Refresh Web Scripts** button, you can reload the library of the Web Script.

Thus there is no need to restart the server each time you change a script or create a new one. Simply use this button and the Web Scripts will be refreshed.

> The refresh operation is required if you change in the controller scripts or in the descriptor file. Changes in the templates do not require refreshing the Web Scripts.

> If you feel your Web Script changes have not taken effect even after refreshing the scripts, check the Web Script detailed page to make sure that your code has been updated.

Now that we have understood the basics of Web Scripts and know how the Web Scripts can be created and deployed, let's begin creating some commonly used and example Web Scripts.

The next few recipes will demonstrate some sample Web Scripts.

Displaying details of documents

This Web Script will accept a string from a user, will search for documents with that name, and finally will display the details of all those documents.

How to do it...

1. We will have to create new files for the Web Script, let's name this script as `documentdetails`.

2. Open a text editor and create a new file with this code:

```xml
<webscript>
    <shortname>Document Details</shortname>
    <description>Searches document(s) and displays details of all
the documents.</description>
    <url>/com/infoaxon/docdetails</url>
    <format default="html"/>
    <authentication>user</authentication>
    <transaction>required</transaction>
</webscript>
```

3. Save the file with the name `docdetails.get.desc.xml` in the `\tomcat\webapps\alfresco\WEB-INF\classes\alfresco\templates\webscripts\com\infoaxon` folder. This is our Web Script descriptor file.

4. Now we create the JavaScript controller file. Here is the code:

```javascript
function main()
{
    var dname = args.dname;
```

```
    var qry = "@cm\\:name:*" + dname + "*";
    var docs = search.luceneSearch(qry);

    model.docs = docs;
    model.dname = dname;
}
main();
```

5. Save this file with the name `docdetails.get.js` in the same folder (all our Web Script files will be saved in this folder).

6. Finally we create the template file:

```
<html>
<body>
    <#if dname?exists>
    <h2>Found Documents with name: ${dname}</h2>
    <#if docs?exists>
        <table cellpadding="5" cellspacing="5" border="1">
        <tr style="font-weight: bold"><td>Name</td><td>Create Date</
td><td>Creator</td><td>Size (bytes)</td></tr>
        <#list docs as c>
            <tr><td>${c.name}</td><td>${c.properties["cm:created"]?da
tetime}</td><td>${c.properties["cm:creator"]}</td><td>${c.size}</
td></tr>
        </#list>
        </table>
    </#if>
        <#else>
    <h2>Search Parameter not provided.</h2>
        </#if>
</body>
</html>
```

7. Save this file with the name `docdetails.get.html.ftl`.

8. Refresh your Web Script list. The Web Script should now be deployed. Now let's run the script.

9. We have assigned the URL of the script as `/com/infoaxon/docdetails` – thus the full URL would be `http://localhost:8080/alfresco/service/com/infoaxon/docdetails`. If you access this URL, the output would be as shown in the following screenshot:

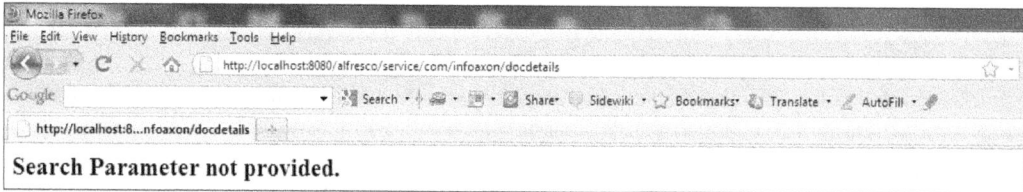

10. That means we have not provided the name of the document to search for. We provide this parameter in this way: `http://localhost:8080/alfresco/service/com/infoaxon/docdetails?dname=infoaxon` – just like a standard querystring in an HTTP GET call. Depending on the contents in your repository, now the output would be as shown in the following screenshot:

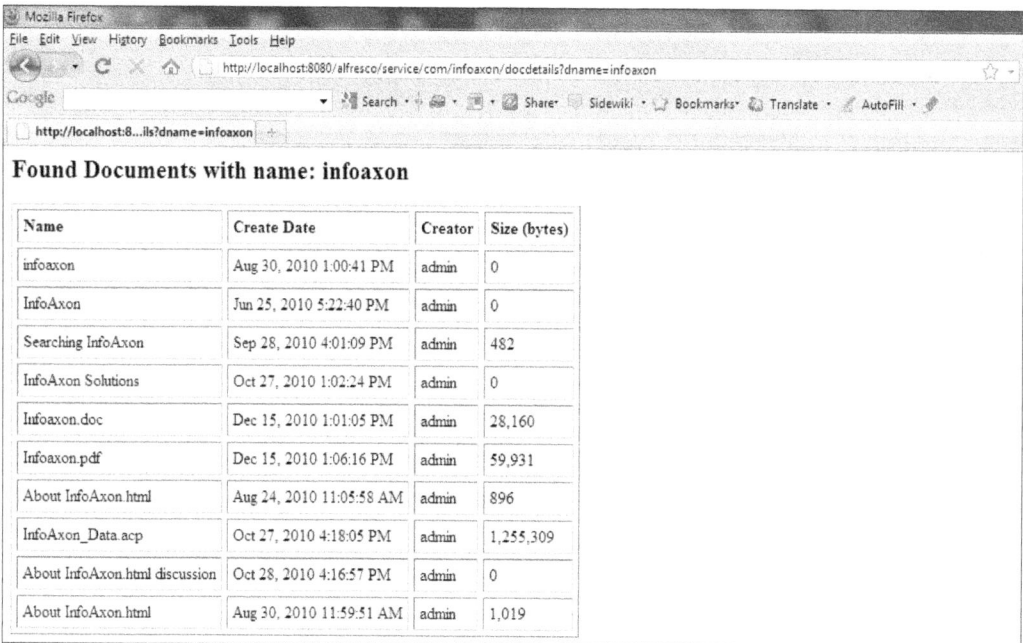

Found Documents with name: infoaxon

Name	Create Date	Creator	Size (bytes)
infoaxon	Aug 30, 2010 1:00:41 PM	admin	0
InfoAxon	Jun 25, 2010 5:22:40 PM	admin	0
Searching InfoAxon	Sep 28, 2010 4:01:09 PM	admin	482
InfoAxon Solutions	Oct 27, 2010 1:02:24 PM	admin	0
Infoaxon.doc	Dec 15, 2010 1:01:05 PM	admin	28,160
Infoaxon.pdf	Dec 15, 2010 1:06:16 PM	admin	59,931
About InfoAxon.html	Aug 24, 2010 11:05:58 AM	admin	896
InfoAxon_Data.acp	Oct 27, 2010 4:18:05 PM	admin	1,255,309
About InfoAxon.html discussion	Oct 28, 2010 4:16:57 PM	admin	0
About InfoAxon.html	Aug 30, 2010 11:59:51 AM	admin	1,019

11. You can change the querystring `dname` value to see the corresponding outputs.

How it works...

One of the most important things to be noticed here is how we retrieve the querystring arguments passed in the Web Script. For that, a root-level object `args` is provided that returns a JavaScript array of all parameters passed.

We have used the `dname` parameter here. In this way, you can pass any number of parameters and use them in the script or template.

We then search for documents which have the keyword anywhere in the name. We have used the Lucene query `"@cm\\:name:*" + dname + "*"`. When we pass `infoaxon` as the `dname` value, the Lucene query would be `"@cm\\:name:*infoaxon*"`.

So the search operation is looking for documents with `infoaxon` anywhere in the name. The search output is returned to the template and the template renders the HTML view of the documents. Now, suppose we want to return a JSON string instead of HTML of the same Web Script. For that, we create another template file named `docdetails.get.json.ftl` and put the following code:

```
<#if docs?exists>
[
    <#list docs as c>
    {
  "Name":"${c.name}",
  "Create Date":"${c.properties["cm:created"]?datetime}",
  "Creator":"${c.properties["cm:creator"]}",
  "Size":"${c.size}"
    }
    <#if c_has_next>,</#if>
    </#list>
]
<#else>
    "OutputMessage":"${outputmessage}"
</#if>
```

We invoke this via this URL `http://localhost:8080/alfresco/service/com/infoaxon/docdetails.json?dname=infoaxon` instead of `http://localhost:8080/alfresco/service/com/infoaxon/ docdetails?dname=infoaxon`.

As you can see, you can call different response templates by putting the extension in the Web Script URL itself.

In this example, the default response format is HTML (see the Web Script descriptor file). Thus, when no format is provided, by default, HTML is returned. However, for JSON output, we had to manually put the expected response format.

However, you can invoke this by the `http://localhost:8080/alfresco/service/com/infoaxon/docdetails?format=json&dname=cookbook` URL as well. This will also render the same output.

```json
[
    {
  "Name":"infoaxon",
  "Create Date":"Aug 30, 2010 1:00:41 PM",
  "Creator":"admin",
  "Size":"0"
    }
    ,
    {
  "Name":"InfoAxon",
  "Create Date":"Jun 25, 2010 5:22:40 PM",
  "Creator":"admin",
  "Size":"0"
    }
    ,
    {
  "Name":"Searching InfoAxon",
  "Create Date":"Sep 28, 2010 4:01:09 PM",
  "Creator":"admin",
  "Size":"482"
    }
    ,
    {
  "Name":"InfoAxon Solutions",
  "Create Date":"Oct 27, 2010 1:02:24 PM",
  "Creator":"admin",
  "Size":"0"
    }
    ,
    {
  "Name":"Infoaxon.doc",
  "Create Date":"Dec 15, 2010 1:01:05 PM",
  "Creator":"admin",
  "Size":"28,160"
    }
    ,
    {
  "Name":"Infoaxon.pdf",
  "Create Date":"Dec 15, 2010 1:06:16 PM",
  "Creator":"admin",
```

```
        "Size":"59,931"
        }
      ,
      {
"Name":"About InfoAxon.html",
"Create Date":"Aug 24, 2010 11:05:58 AM",
"Creator":"admin",
"Size":"896"
        }
      ,
      {
"Name":"InfoAxon_Data.acp",
"Create Date":"Oct 27, 2010 4:18:05 PM",
"Creator":"admin",
"Size":"1,255,309"
        }
      ,
      {
"Name":"About InfoAxon.html discussion",
"Create Date":"Oct 28, 2010 4:16:57 PM",
"Creator":"admin",
"Size":"0"
        }
      ,
      {
"Name":"About InfoAxon.html",
"Create Date":"Aug 30, 2010 11:59:51 AM",
"Creator":"admin",
"Size":"1,019"
        }
    ]
```

> It is good practice to validate the output JSON string from your Web Script by a JSON validator service. I normally use *JSONLint* - http://www.jsonlint.com/

There's more...

To search for contents, we have used the search root level object in the JavaScript here. You might recollect that this was discussed in *Search API* in *Chapter 8*.

Sending e-mails using a mail template

In this recipe, we will create a Web Script that will send a mail to a particular defined user. The content of the mail will be driven by a mail template. Finally, the mail content is returned as the Web Script response.

How to do it...

1. We will first create a Mail Template. Here is the template:

   ```
   Hello ${person.properties["cm:firstName"]},

   Welcome to Alfresco!
   Here are your registration details.

   First Name: ${person.properties["cm:firstName"]}
   Last Name: ${person.properties["cm:lastName"]}
   User Name: ${person.properties["cm:userName"]}

   Enjoy your Stay!

   Regards,
   the Alfresco Team.
   ```

2. Save this template in the **Company Home | Data Dictionary | EMail Templates** folder – with the name `userdetailsmail.ftl`

3. Now, we will create new files for the web script; let's name this script as `sendusermail`.

4. Open a text editor and create a new file with this code:

   ```
   <webscript>
       <shortname>Send Mail</shortname>
       <description>Searches for a user and sends mail to him about
   his details.</description>
       <url>/com/infoaxon/sendusermail</url>
       <format default="html"/>
       <authentication>admin</authentication>
       <transaction>required</transaction>
   </webscript>
   ```

5. This is the Web Script descriptor files, save this with the name `sendusermail.get.desc.xml` (in the same folder mentioned earlier).

6. We will now create the controller JS file. Here is the code:

   ```
   function main()
   {
       if (args.uname == null)
       {
       model.result = "No user";
       return;
   ```

```
        }
        var usr = people.getPerson(args.uname);
        if (usr == null)
        {
    model.result = "No user";
    return;
        }
        var mail = actions.create("mail");
        mail.parameters.to = usr.properties["cm:email"];
        mail.parameters.subject = "Welcome!";
        mail.parameters.from = "administrator@mydomain.com";
        mail.parameters.template = companyhome.childByNamePath("Data
Dictionary/EMail Templates/userdetailsmail.ftl");
        mail.parameters.text = "Welcome to Alfresco!";
        mail.execute(usr);

        var mailtemplate = companyhome.childByNamePath("Data
Dictionary/EMail Templates/userdetailsmail.ftl");
        var result = usr.processTemplate(mailtemplate);

        model.result = result;
}
main();
```

7. Save this file with the name `sendusermail.get.js`.

8. We create an HTML template file with the name `sendusermail.get.html.ftl` and put a very simple one liner code in this file:

    `${result}`

9. Run the script using the URL `http://localhost:8080/alfresco/service/com/infoaxon/sendusermail?uname=admin` (or put any other username).

10. If the mail property is properly configured for this user, a mail will be sent to the e-mail ID; and the mail content will be returned. It should be something like this:

```
Hello Administrator,

Welcome to Alfresco!
Here are your registration details.

First Name: Administrator
Last Name:
User Name: admin

Enjoy your Stay!

Regards,
the Alfresco Team.
```

How it works...

We first search for the username passed with the querystring. Once it is retrieved (using the `people.getPerson` method), we use the person's node reference for further processing.

Then we send the mail after preparing the mail object properly. The mail is sent using the `actions` provided by Alfresco. There are a number of such actions available to be performed in JavaScript API. One such action can be starting a workflow.

Finally, the Mail Template is processed against the user object, and finally the output is returned as the Web Script response.

There's more...

You have seen that you can configure the authentication mechanism of a Web Script in the descriptor XML file. This can be either of none, admin, user, or guest.

However, each time a user is authenticated, Alfresco opens a new session and generates a token for this session. This ticket can be retrieved by the `getTicket` method of the `session` global object.

For example,

```
var tkt = session.getTicket();
```

The variable `tkt` now has the authentication token of this session. You can use this ticket for calling of another Web Script like:

```
http://localhost:8080/alfresco/service/com/infoaxon/sendusermail?alf_
ticket=${tkt}&uname=admin
```

Thus, Alfresco won't ask for new user credentials if you pass a valid ticket in the `alf_ticket` querystring. However, if the session is expired, Alfresco will again pop up the user credential dialog.

The importance of this mechanism is often you would want to invoke another Web Script from one script in the client/browser side. There you would normally want to accept the user credentials once and use the session multiple times until the user actually leaves. Thus `alf_ticket` can help you – this name can pass the authentication token to another Web Script – thus sharing sessions.

You can invoke the Web Script through the Web Client authentication URL as well.

We have seen that the URL of a Web Script always starts with `http://localhost:8080/alfresco/service/`. However, you can also invoke a Web Script using `http://localhost:8080/alfresco/wcservice/`.

For example, `http://localhost:8080/alfresco/service/com/infoaxon/sendusermail` - this Web Script can be invoked using the `http://localhost:8080/alfresco/wcservice/com/infoaxon/sendusermail` URL as well.

The difference is, in the second case, Alfresco lets you use the user session of the Web Client application in the same browser session. This means if you are already logged on in the Web Client application, and you try to access a Web Script using the Web Client URL, Alfresco will not ask for user credentials. However, in the first case, where you use the `/service` URL instead of `/wcservice`, you will be prompted for user credentials again.

11
Working with Workflows

In this chapter, we will understand:

- ▶ Invoking a workflow
- ▶ Creating and deploying custom workflows
- ▶ Using the Alfresco Workflow Console

Introduction

A Workflow is a collection of task steps that are connected to be executed sequentially one after another or in parallel.

Let's assume that you have uploaded a document that needs to be reviewed and approved by your superior. Thus whenever you upload the document, your boss is assigned a task to review the document. The outcome of the task may be – he approves the document or rejects it. If he thinks the document is not up to the mark, he rejects it after putting some comments and you again receive a task to upload a new version of the document, thus you can improvise based on the feedback you receive. The same cycle repeats again until the document is approved and published to the wider audience.

Thus, a workflow depicts a business process definition that needs to be carried out to complete a certain operation. **Enterprise document management system** must have such workflow or business process management system by which any business process can be executed automatically within the system.

A workflow engine is required to perform these activities. Alfresco has jBPM integrated as the workflow engine in the repository, it uses jPDL 3.2 (`http://docs.jboss.com/jbpm/v3.2/userguide/html/`) as the process language for defining workflows.

A workflow process essentially consists of a few tasks connected to each other and to be performed by some actors or users. There are a number of events that take place while performing several actions during the life cycle of the workflow. Thus you can execute different operations in each of these events – for example, you might want to send a mail alert to the uploader of the document in case the document is rejected. The workflow process engine offers a number of such events that you can use to implement your extended business flow requirements.

Fortunately, Alfresco has integrated the JavaScript API engine into jBPM parsers, thus enabling you to write your business steps using the JavaScript API inside the jBPM process definition. In a more advanced and complex case (where the JavaScript API is not sufficient), you can write your Java classes and invoke them from the process definition file.

Also, you might want to create your own custom tasks, in addition to what Alfresco has by default provided. This works almost like creating custom content models.

Workflow components

A standard workflow deployed in Alfresco has the following components defined:

1. **Task Model (optional)**

   ❑ You define your custom tasks here. Alfresco has provided a number of default tasks (for example, review task), which you can use directly, or you can create your own task model.

   ❑ The default task models are defined in `tomcat\webapps\alfresco\WEB-INF\classes\alfresco\model\bpmModel.xml` file and in model files under `tomcat\webapps\alfresco\WEB-INF\classes\alfresco\workflow` folder.

   ❑ Creating a task model for your custom workflow is an optional step because you can use the default supplied tasks if that suits you. Otherwise, you will have to create your own task model.

   ❑ We will explore how to create a custom task model after a few recipes in this chapter.

2. **Resource Bundle (optional)**

   ❑ These are used to define the localized user interface messages and texts. This is an optional step, however, it is recommended help you create your resource bundle.

3. **Process Definition**

   ❑ This is of course the main process definition file using **jPDL** (**Java Process Definition Language**). The default supplied process definitions are in the `tomcat\webapps\alfresco\WEB-INF\classes\alfresco\workflow` folder.

    ❑   We will explore how to create our custom process definition later in this chapter.

4. **Web Client UI configurations**

    ❑   Now, once you have defined all components for your workflow, they need to be properly displayed in the Alfresco explorer interface.

    ❑   This is almost similar to the customizations you do for displaying your custom content model and aspects. We will set up these configurations in the `web-client-config-custom.xml` file later in this chapter.

5. **Share UI configurations**

    ❑   If you are using Alfresco share application. However, this discussion is out of the scope of this book.

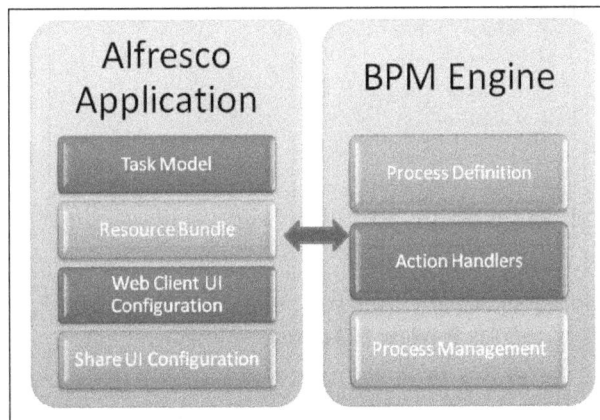

Invoking a workflow

As we now understand the background of Alfresco workflows, let us see how to invoke a workflow. This recipe will explore how a workflow is executed within Alfresco web client interface.

How to do it...

1. Start your server and open Alfresco web client, log in with user admin.

2. For properly demonstrating the workflow in action, we need to have at least two users, so that we can witness the tasks to flow from one user to another. So, we assume that there is another user named **snig.bhaumik** (we created this user in *Chapter 5*).

3. Upload a new document in a space. Say, we have uploaded a document named **recovery disc.pdf** in space **chapter 11**.

4. Open the details view of the document. In the **Actions** menu, you will see the last action is **Start Advanced Workflow** – click on this.

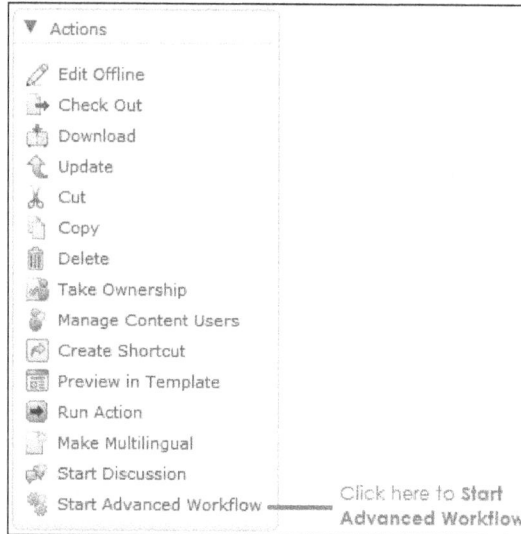

5. By default, two workflows are displayed here – **Adhoc Task** assignment and **Review & Approve**. We choose the **Review & Approve** workflow.

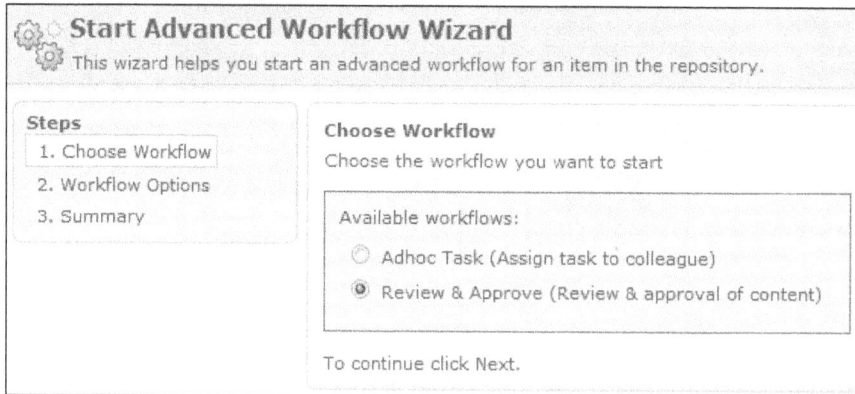

6. Clicking on **Next**, the **Workflow Options** form is presented, where you need to fill some mandatory information (or, properties) for the workflow and task to be started.

Start Review & Approve Workflow Wizard
This wizard helps you start an advanced workflow for an item in the repository.

Steps
1. Choose Workflow
2. Workflow Options
3. Summary

Workflow Options
Select options for the workflow

Properties

General

Description:

Review Priority: 2 ▾
Review Due Date: None

Users and their Roles

⊙ Reviewer: [Select...]

Property sheet, where you feed the workflow information, such as task due date, the user is assigned to perform the task, description of the workflow/task etc.

Resources

Name ▾	Description ● Path ●	Created ●	Modified ●	Actions
recovery disc.pdf	/Company Home/InfoAxon /Chapter 11	3 February 2011 13:15	3 February 2011 13:15	

Page 1 of 1 1

⤓ Add Resource

Resources (Documents) on which the workflow will be executed. You can add multiple documents also in the workflow.

To continue click Next.

7. We put the workflow property values as required. We want to assign the review job to the user **snig.bhaumik**, and put the other details like **Review Due Date**, and so on.

Workflow Options
Select options for the workflow

Properties

General

This is a Test Workflow.

Description:

Review Priority: 1 ▾
Review Due Date: 27 ▾   January ▾   2011 ▾   [Today] [None]

Users and their Roles

⊙ Reviewer: Snig Bhaumik [snig.bhaumik] 🗑 ✎

8. Click on **Next** and **Finish** to start the workflow.

Start Review & Approve Workflow Wizard
This wizard helps you start an advanced workflow for an item in the repository.

Steps	Summary	
1. Choose Workflow	The information you entered is shown below.	Next
2. Workflow Options		Back
3. Summary	**Start Advanced Workflow:** Review & Approve (Review & approval of content)	Finish
	To start the workflow press Finish. To review or change your selections click Back.	Cancel

9. The document details window appears back. In the **Workflows** section, you can see that the document is under a **Review & Approve** workflow.

▼ Workflows

Simple Workflow
This document is not part of a simple workflow.

Advanced Workflows
This document is part of the following advanced workflow(s):

- Review & Approve (This is a Test Workflow.) started on 3 February 2011 by Administrator.

10. Now, since we have assigned the task to user **snig.bhaumik**, let's log in by that user.

11. In the user's dashboard, we have one task for this workflow listed.

My Tasks To Do

Description ☰	Type ☰	Id ☰	Created ▼	Due Date ☰	Status ☰	Priority ☰	Actions
This is a Test Workflow.	Review	6	3 February 2011 13:52	27 January 2011	Not Yet Started	1	

Page 1 of 1 ◄ ◄ 1 ► ►

12. Click on the description link or **Manage Task** icon to invoke the task interface. This interface has a few sections, which are detailed as follows:

13. This section is used to put the task properties and information.

Task Properties

General

⊙ Identifier: `6`

Description: `This is a Test Workflow.`

Due Date: `27 ▾` `January ▾` `2011 ▾`

⊙ Priority: `1`

⊙ Status: `Not Yet Started ▾`

Comment:

14. The screenshot of the following section shows the Actions available in the particular task. You can see that **Approve** and **Reject** are two actions you can perform as the task owner. These actions are called as **Task Transitions** in jBPM world. The transitions define what the outcome of the current task would be and these trigger the startup of the next task in the full process flow.

[Save Changes]

[Approve]

[Reject]

[Cancel]

15. The lowermost section displays the **Workflow History** – what actions have been done until now in the current workflow.

Part of Workflow

Title: Review & Approve (Review & approval of content)
Initiated by: Administrator
Started on: 3 February 2011
Completed on: <In Progress>

▼ **Workflow History**

Description	Task Type	Id	Created	Assignee	Comment	Completed on	Outcome
This is a Test Workflow.	Start Review	5	3 February 2011 13:52	admin		3 February 2011 13:52	Task Done

16. Next, let's put some comments in task details and approve the document – click on **Approve**.

17. You can see the task is gone from your task list. Now, let's log in again as **admin** (remember admin was the user who had originally started the workflow – he is the initiator). The final task of the workflow is displayed to the admin user's dashboard. Click on **Manage Task** icon.

My Tasks To Do							
Description ⊟	Type ⊟	Id ⊟	Created ▼	Due Date ⊟	Status ⊟	Priority ⊟	Actions
⊛ This is a Test Workflow.	Approved	7	3 February 2011 17:34		Not Yet Started	3	⊛ ⊛
			Page 1 of 1 ⊟ ⊟ 1 ⊟ ⊟				

18. Notice the **Workflow History** section. All the steps executed until now are listed as workflow audit trail.

Part of Workflow	
Title:	Review & Approve (Review & approval of content)
Initiated by:	Administrator
Started on:	3 February 2011
Completed on:	<In Progress>

▼ **Workflow History**

Description	Task Type	Id	Created	Assignee	Comment	Completed on	Outcome
This is a Test Workflow.	Start Review	5	3 February 2011 13:52	admin		3 February 2011 13:52	Task Done
This is a Test Workflow.	Review	6	3 February 2011 13:52	snig.bhaumik	The document is great. Well done!	3 February 2011 17:34	Approve

19. The comments the reviewer had added are also displayed. In the **Outcome** column, you can see the reviewer has approved the document.

20. Click on **Task Done** to complete the workflow.

How it works...

The process definition which is controlling the flow in the background is the workflow defined in `tomcat\webapps\alfresco\WEB-INF\classes\alfresco\workflow\ review_ processdefinition.xml` file. It is the built-in **Review & Approve** process definition provided by Alfresco.

The definition is:

```
<?xml version="1.0" encoding="UTF-8"?>

<process-definition xmlns="urn:jbpm.org:jpdl-3.1" name="wf:review">

    <swimlane name="initiator" />
```

```
        <start-state name="start">
            <task name="wf:submitReviewTask" swimlane="initiator" />
            <transition name="" to="review" />
        </start-state>

        <swimlane name="reviewer">
            <assignment class="org.alfresco.repo.workflow.jbpm.
AlfrescoAssignment">
                <actor>#{bpm_assignee}</actor>
            </assignment>
        </swimlane>

        <task-node name="review">
            <task name="wf:reviewTask" swimlane="reviewer">
                <event type="task-create">
                    <script>
                        if (bpm_workflowDueDate != void) taskInstance.
dueDate = bpm_workflowDueDate;
                        if (bpm_workflowPriority != void) taskInstance.
priority = bpm_workflowPriority;
                    </script>
                </event>
            </task>
            <transition name="approve" to="approved" />
            <transition name="reject" to="rejected" />
        </task-node>

        <task-node name="rejected">
            <task name="wf:rejectedTask" swimlane="initiator" />
            <transition name="" to="end" />
        </task-node>

        <task-node name="approved">
            <task name="wf:approvedTask" swimlane="initiator" />
            <transition name="" to="end" />
        </task-node>

        <end-state name="end" />

    </process-definition>

    <process-definition xmlns="urn:jbpm.org:jpdl-3.1" name="wf:review">
```

xmlns is the jPDL version you are using, and name is the name of your workflow. wf is the workflow namespace defined for jBPM, thus it is pretty fixed, you would use wf namespace prefix in your process definitions.

```
<swimlane name="initiator" />
```

`swimlanes` are essentially the actors who will perform certain tasks. In this workflow, two swimlanes are defined – `initiator` and `reviewer`. In our execution example, `admin` was the `initiator` and `snig.bhaumik` was the `reviewer`. In your process definition, you will create a number of swimlanes, as per the number of actors involved in your process.

```
<start-state name="start">
```

A workflow would always start with a `start-state` tag. There you would mention the task name you would like to start your workflow with. Alfresco has used `wf:submitReviewTask` here, and `swimlane` assigned is the `initiator` for the task. One transition is defined that directs the flow to `task-node: review`. Thus, whenever the workflow is kicked off by the initiator, the reviewer receives the next task – `wf:reviewTask`.

```
<event type="task-create">
```

As the type suggests, this event is fired at the time of instantiation of the task. You can implement any business rule here using Alfresco JavaScript API.

Supported event types are `task-create`, `task-start`, `task-assign`, and `task-end`.

```
<transition name="approve" to="approved" />
<transition name="reject" to="rejected" />
```

There are two transitions defined in the review task – thus two actions were offered in the user interface we have seen earlier. The `name` attribute would be rendered as the caption of action button in the UI and `to` attribute is used to define as to which task should be invoked if the corresponding action is taken.

If we depict this process definition in a flow chart, it would be:

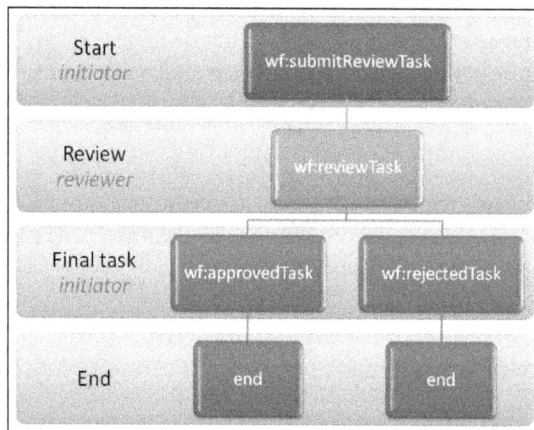

You can use your good old JavaScript to implement some business rules while a transition takes place, like:

```
<transition name="approve" to="approved">
  <action class="org.alfresco.repo.workflow.jbpm.AlfrescoJavaScript">
    <script>
    </script>
  </action>
</transition>
```

The resource bundle used by this workflow is tomcat\webapps\alfresco\WEB-INF\classes\alfresco\workflow\workflow-messages.properties. In this file, you can see the messages used for the Approve & Review workflow.

```
#
# Review & Approve Workflow
#

wf_review.workflow.title=Review & Approve
wf_review.workflow.description=Review & approval of content


# Review & Approve Task Definitions

wf_workflowmodel.type.wf_submitReviewTask.title=Start Review
wf_workflowmodel.type.wf_submitReviewTask.description=Submit documents
for review & approval
wf_workflowmodel.type.wf_reviewTask.title=Review
wf_workflowmodel.type.wf_reviewTask.description=Review Documents to
Approve or Reject them
wf_workflowmodel.type.wf_rejectedTask.title=Rejected
wf_workflowmodel.type.wf_rejectedTask.description=Rejected
wf_workflowmodel.type.wf_approvedTask.title=Approved
wf_workflowmodel.type.wf_approvedTask.description=Approved


# Review & Approve Process Definitions

wf_review.node.start.title=Start
wf_review.node.start.description=Start
wf_review.node.review.title=Review
wf_review.node.review.description=Review
wf_review.node.review.transition.reject.title=Reject
wf_review.node.review.transition.reject.description=Reject
wf_review.node.review.transition.approve.title=Approve
wf_review.node.review.transition.approve.description=Approve
wf_review.node.rejected.title=Rejected
wf_review.node.rejected.description=Rejected
wf_review.task.wf_rejectedTask.title=Rejected
wf_review.task.wf_rejectedTask.description=Rejected
wf_review.node.approved.title=Approved
```

```
wf_review.node.approved.description=Approved
wf_review.task.wf_approvedTask.title=Approved
wf_review.task.wf_approvedTask.description=Approved
wf_review.node.end.title=End
wf_review.node.end.description=End
```

Later in this chapter, we will explore how these workflow messages work.

Creating and deploying custom workflows

Now as we understand the components and basic concepts on workflow, let us try to create our own workflow definition. This recipe will help you to create a new workflow definition step by step:

1. Creating task model
2. Designing the process definition
3. Writing the resource bundle
4. Configuring web client to show the workflow and tasks properly
5. Deploying the process definition
6. Finally using the workflow

Before starting, let us say this is our process flow for which we want to create a workflow definition. We will take an example of a standard waterfall software development process only.

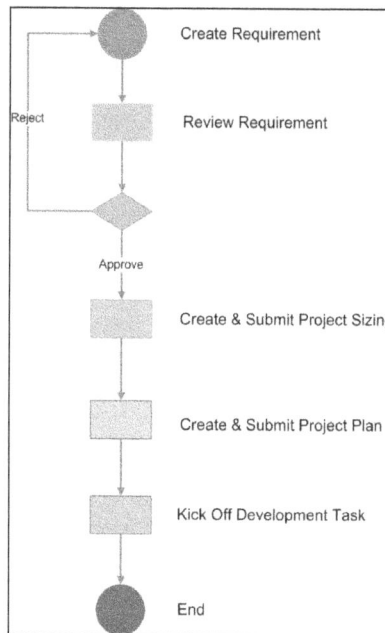

> It would be easier for you to write a BPM process definition if you first draw down the flow chart of your process model.

How to do it...

To carry out this recipe, we break it down into five different tasks:

Creating the Task Model:

1. For the task model, create all the components of our new custom workflow in the extension folder that is `tomcat\shared\classes\alfresco\extension` folder. You might recollect we had created our custom content model and so on in this folder only.

2. Create a new file named `pm_taskModel.xml` here. Paste the following code:

```xml
<?xml version="1.0" encoding="UTF-8"?>

<model name="iabookwf:BookWFModel" xmlns="http://www.alfresco.org/
model/dictionary/1.0">
  <imports>
    <import uri="http://www.alfresco.org/model/dictionary/1.0"
prefix="d"/>
    <import uri="http://www.alfresco.org/model/bpm/1.0"
prefix="bpm"/>
    <import uri="http://www.alfresco.org/model/content/1.0"
prefix="cm" />
  </imports>

  <namespaces>
    <namespace uri="http://www.infoaxon.com/book/models/
workflow/1.0" prefix="iabookwf"/>
  </namespaces>

  <types>
    <type name="iabookwf:startTask">
      <title>Project Start</title>
      <parent>bpm:startTask</parent>
    </type>

    <type name="iabookwf:createRequirementTask">
        <parent>bpm:workflowTask</parent>
      <properties>
        <property name="iabookwf:clientName">
```

```
            <title>Client Name</title>
            <type>d:text</type>
            <mandatory>true</mandatory>
          </property>
          <property name="iabookwf:projectName">
            <title>Project Name</title>
            <type>d:text</type>
            <mandatory>true</mandatory>
          </property>
          <property name="iabookwf:budget">
            <title>Project Estimated Budget</title>
            <type>d:double</type>
            <mandatory>true</mandatory>
          </property>
        </properties>

        <overrides>
            <property name="bpm:packageActionGroup">
               <default>add_package_item_actions</default>
            </property>
            <property name="bpm:packageItemActionGroup">
               <default>edit_package_item_actions</default>
            </property>
      </overrides>

          <mandatory-aspects>
            <aspect>bpm:assignee</aspect>
          </mandatory-aspects>
        </type>

        <type name="iabookwf:reviewRequirementTask">
            <parent>bpm:workflowTask</parent>

        <overrides>
            <property name="bpm:packageItemActionGroup">
               <default>edit_package_item_actions</default>
            </property>
      </overrides>

        <mandatory-aspects>
            <aspect>bpm:assignee</aspect>
          </mandatory-aspects>
        </type>
```

```xml
<type name="iabookwf:createProjectSizingTask">
   <parent>bpm:workflowTask</parent>
<properties>
 <property name="iabookwf:mandays">
   <title>Estimated Man Days</title>
   <type>d:int</type>
   <mandatory>true</mandatory>
 </property>
 <property name="iabookwf:totalCost">
   <title>Total Estimated Cost</title>
   <type>d:double</type>
   <mandatory>true</mandatory>
 </property>
</properties>

<overrides>
       <property name="bpm:packageItemActionGroup">
          <default>edit_package_item_actions</default>
       </property>
</overrides>

   <mandatory-aspects>
       <aspect>bpm:assignee</aspect>
   </mandatory-aspects>
</type>

  <type name="iabookwf:createProjectPlanTask">
   <parent>bpm:workflowTask</parent>
<properties>
 <property name="iabookwf:startDate">
   <title>Proposed Start Date</title>
   <type>d:date</type>
   <mandatory>true</mandatory>
 </property>
 <property name="iabookwf:endDate">
   <title>Proposed End Date</title>
   <type>d:date</type>
   <mandatory>true</mandatory>
 </property>
 <property name="iabookwf:releaseDate">
   <title>Proposed Final Release Date</title>
   <type>d:date</type>
   <mandatory>true</mandatory>
 </property>
```

```
        </properties>

        <overrides>
            <property name="bpm:packageItemActionGroup">
                <default>edit_package_item_actions</default>
            </property>
        </overrides>

        <mandatory-aspects>
            <aspect>bpm:assignee</aspect>
        </mandatory-aspects>
    </type>

      <type name="iabookwf:kickOffDevelopmentTask">
        <parent>bpm:workflowTask</parent>
    <properties>
     <property name="iabookwf:projectTeam">
       <title>Finalized Project Team</title>
       <type>d:text</type>
       <mandatory>false</mandatory>
       <multiple>true</multiple>
      </property>
      <property name="iabookwf:projectEnvDone">
       <title>Project Environment setup Done?</title>
       <type>d:boolean</type>
       <mandatory>true</mandatory>
      </property>
     </properties>

     <overrides>
            <property name="bpm:packageItemActionGroup">
                <default>edit_package_item_actions</default>
            </property>
     </overrides>

        <mandatory-aspects>
            <aspect>bpm:assignee</aspect>
        </mandatory-aspects>
     </type>

    </types>
  </model>
```

3. Now, we need to register this model into Alfresco bootstrap files. For this, open the `workflow-context.xml` file in the same extension folder, and put the following code:

```
<property name="models">
  <list>
    <value>alfresco/extension/pm_taskModel.xml</value>
  </list>
</property>
```

> By default you might not find this file, however, there would be a file named `workflow-context.xml.sample` – rename it to `workflow-context.xml`.

4. Our task model is created and ready to be deployed next time when you start your server.

Designing the Process definition:

1. To design the process definition, create a new file named `pm_processdefinition.xml` in the same extension folder that is `tomcat\shared\classes\alfresco\extension`. Paste the following code:

```xml
<?xml version="1.0" encoding="UTF-8"?>

<process-definition xmlns="urn:jbpm.org:jpdl-3.1"
name="iabookwf:pmprocess">

    <swimlane name="initiator" />

    <swimlane name="pmuser">
        <assignment class="org.alfresco.repo.workflow.jbpm.
AlfrescoAssignment">
            <actor>#{bpm_assignee}</actor>
        </assignment>
    </swimlane>


    <start-state name="start">
        <task name="iabookwf:startTask" swimlane="initiator" />
        <transition name="" to="submitRequirement" />
    </start-state>

    <task-node name="submitRequirement">
        <task name="iabookwf:createRequirementTask"
swimlane="initiator">
```

```
                    <event type="task-create">
                        <script>
                            if (bpm_workflowDueDate != void) taskInstance.
dueDate = bpm_workflowDueDate;
                            if (bpm_workflowPriority != void)
taskInstance.priority = bpm_workflowPriority;
                        </script>
                    </event>
                </task>
                <transition name="Submit Requirements"
to="reviewRequirement" />

        </task-node>


        <task-node name="reviewRequirement">
            <task name="iabookwf:reviewRequirementTask"
swimlane="pmuser">
                <event type="task-create">
                    <script>
                        if (bpm_workflowDueDate != void) taskInstance.
dueDate = bpm_workflowDueDate;
                        if (bpm_workflowPriority != void)
taskInstance.priority = bpm_workflowPriority;
                    </script>
                </event>
            </task>
            <transition name="Approve Requirements"
to="createProjectSizing" />
            <transition name="Reject Requirements"
to="submitRequirement" />

        </task-node>

        <task-node name="createProjectSizing">
            <task name="iabookwf:createProjectSizingTask"
swimlane="pmuser">
                <event type="task-create">
                    <script>
                        if (bpm_workflowDueDate != void) taskInstance.
dueDate = bpm_workflowDueDate;
                        if (bpm_workflowPriority != void)
taskInstance.priority = bpm_workflowPriority;
                    </script>
                </event>
            </task>
```

```
            <transition name="Submit Project Sizing"
to="createProjectPlan" />
    </task-node>


    <task-node name="createProjectPlan">
        <task name="iabookwf:createProjectPlanTask"
swimlane="pmuser">
            <event type="task-create">
                <script>
                    if (bpm_workflowDueDate != void) taskInstance.
dueDate = bpm_workflowDueDate;
                    if (bpm_workflowPriority != void)
taskInstance.priority = bpm_workflowPriority;
                </script>
            </event>
        </task>
        <transition name="Submit Project Plan"
to="kickOffDevelopment" />
    </task-node>


    <task-node name="kickOffDevelopment">
        <task name="iabookwf:kickOffDevelopmentTask"
swimlane="pmuser">
            <event type="task-create">
                <script>
                    if (bpm_workflowDueDate != void) taskInstance.
dueDate = bpm_workflowDueDate;
                    if (bpm_workflowPriority != void)
taskInstance.priority = bpm_workflowPriority;
                </script>
            </event>
        </task>
        <transition name="Kick Off Development" to="end" />
    </task-node>

    <end-state name="end" />


</process-definition>
```

2. Now, again we need to register this process definition into Alfresco bootstrap files. For this, open the `workflow-context.xml` file in the same extension folder, and put the following code:

```
<property name="workflowDefinitions">
  <list>
    <props>
```

```
        <prop key="engineId">jbpm</prop>
        <prop key="location">alfresco/extension/pm_
processdefinition.xml</prop>
        <prop key="mimetype">text/xml</prop>
        <prop key="redeploy">true</prop>
    </props>
  </list>
</property>
```

3. Our new process definition is ready and will be deployed when you restart your server. Next task is to create the Resource Bundle for your workflow.

Creating the Resource Bundle

1. Create a new file named `pm-workflow-messages.properties` in the same extension folder that is `tomcat\shared\classes\alfresco\extension`. Paste the following code:

```
# Workflow Definition
iabookwf_pmprocess.workflow.title=Project Management
iabookwf_pmprocess.workflow.description=Project Management sample
Flow for Cookbook


# Workflow Tasks
iabookwf_BookWFModel.type.iabookwf_startTask.title=Start new
Project
iabookwf_BookWFModel.type.iabookwf_startTask.description=Start new
Project

iabookwf_BookWFModel.type.iabookwf_createRequirementTask.
title=Create & Submit Requirement
iabookwf_BookWFModel.type.iabookwf_createRequirementTask.
description=Create & Submit Requirement

iabookwf_BookWFModel.type.iabookwf_reviewRequirementTask.
title=Review & Approve Requirements
iabookwf_BookWFModel.type.iabookwf_reviewRequirementTask.
description=Review & Approve Requirements

iabookwf_BookWFModel.type.iabookwf_createProjectSizingTask.
title=Submit Project Sizing
iabookwf_BookWFModel.type.iabookwf_createProjectSizingTask.
description=Submit Project Sizing

iabookwf_BookWFModel.type.iabookwf_createProjectPlanTask.
title=Prepare Project Plan
```

```
iabookwf_BookWFModel.type.iabookwf_createProjectPlanTask.
description=Prepare Project Plan

iabookwf_BookWFModel.type.iabookwf_kickOffDevelopmentTask.
title=Kick Off Development
iabookwf_BookWFModel.type.iabookwf_kickOffDevelopmentTask.
description=Kick Off Development
```

2. Register this into Alfresco bootstrap files. For this, open the `workflow-context.xml` file in the same extension folder, and put the following code:

```xml
<property name="labels">
  <list>
    <value>alfresco/extension/pm-workflow-messages</value>
  </list>
</property>
```

3. Open the `webclient.properties` file in `tomcat\webapps\alfresco\WEB-INF\classes\alfresco\messages` folder, and paste the following code at the end of the file:

```
iabookwf_pm=Project Manager
iabookwf_pm_header=Assign Project Manager
```

4. The resource bundle is also now ready to be deployed. Our final task is to provide the custom web client settings so that our new workflow and corresponding tasks are rendered properly.

   Finally, after registering the task model, process definition, and resource bundle, the `workflow-context.xml` file would look like this.

```xml
<?xml version='1.0' encoding='UTF-8'?>
<!DOCTYPE beans PUBLIC '-//SPRING//DTD BEAN//EN' 'http://www.
springframework.org/dtd/spring-beans.dtd'>

<beans>

    <bean id="parallel.workflowBootstrap"
parent="workflowDeployer">
    <property name="workflowDefinitions">
      <list>
        <props>
          <prop key="engineId">jbpm</prop>
          <prop key="location">alfresco/extension/pm_
processdefinition.xml</prop>
          <prop key="mimetype">text/xml</prop>
          <prop key="redeploy">true</prop>
        </props>
      </list>
```

```
        </property>
        <property name="models">
          <list>
                  <value>alfresco/extension/pm_taskModel.xml</value>
          </list>
        </property>
        <property name="labels">
          <list>
                  <value>alfresco/extension/pm-workflow-messages</
value>
          </list>
        </property>
      </bean>

    </beans>
```

Customizing the Web Client:

1. Open the `web-client-config-custom.xml` file in `tomcat\shared\classes\`
    `alfresco\extension` folder, and paste the following code at the end of the file
    (inside `alfresco-config` node of course):

    ```
    <config evaluator="node-type" condition="iabookwf:startTask"
    replace="true">
         <property-sheet>
             <separator name="sep1" display-label-id="general"
    component-generator="HeaderSeparatorGenerator" />
             <show-property name="bpm:workflowDescription" component-
    generator="TextAreaGenerator" />
             <show-property name="bpm:workflowPriority" />
             <show-property name="bpm:workflowDueDate" />
         </property-sheet>
      </config>


      <config evaluator="node-type" condition="iabookwf:createRequirem
    entTask" replace="true">
          <property-sheet>
          <separator name="sep1" display-label-id="general" component-
    generator="HeaderSeparatorGenerator" />
             <show-property name="iabookwf:clientName" />
             <show-property name="iabookwf:projectName" />
             <show-property name="iabookwf:budget" />
             <separator name="sep2" display-label-id="iabookwf_pm_
    header" component-generator="HeaderSeparatorGenerator" />
             <show-association name="bpm:assignee" display-label-
    id="iabookwf_pm" />
    ```

```
            </property-sheet>
        </config>


    <config evaluator="node-type" condition="iabookwf:createProjectS
izingTask" replace="true">
        <property-sheet>
         <separator name="sep1" display-label-id="general" component-
generator="HeaderSeparatorGenerator" />
            <show-property name="iabookwf:mandays" />
            <show-property name="iabookwf:totalCost" />
                <separator name="sep2" display-label-id="iabookwf_pm_
header" component-generator="HeaderSeparatorGenerator" />
                <show-association name="bpm:assignee" display-label-
id="iabookwf_pm" />
            </property-sheet>
        </config>


    <config evaluator="node-type" condition="iabookwf:createProjectP
lanTask" replace="true">
        <property-sheet>
         <separator name="sep1" display-label-id="general" component-
generator="HeaderSeparatorGenerator" />
            <show-property name="iabookwf:startDate" />
            <show-property name="iabookwf:endDate" />
            <show-property name="iabookwf:releaseDate" />
                <separator name="sep2" display-label-id="iabookwf_pm_
header" component-generator="HeaderSeparatorGenerator" />
                <show-association name="bpm:assignee" display-label-
id="iabookwf_pm" />
            </property-sheet>
        </config>


    <config evaluator="node-type" condition="iabookwf:kickOffDevelop
mentTask" replace="true">
        <property-sheet>
         <separator name="sep1" display-label-id="general" component-
generator="HeaderSeparatorGenerator" />
            <show-property name="iabookwf:projectTeam" />
            <show-property name="iabookwf:projectEnvDone" />
                <separator name="sep2" display-label-id="iabookwf_pm_
header" component-generator="HeaderSeparatorGenerator" />
                <show-association name="bpm:assignee" display-label-
id="iabookwf_pm" />
            </property-sheet>
        </config>
```

2. That's all. We have created all the components for our new workflow. Start your server, if everything goes fine, the workflow along with all the other components should be deployed.

Using our custom workflow:

Using the new workflow is pretty much same as in the case of the **Review & Approve** workflow.

1. Let's say we have a document for project initiation, we would start our workflow on this.

2. Open the details view of the document and click on **Start Advanced Workflow**.

Choose Workflow
Choose the workflow you want to start

Available workflows:

○ Adhoc Task (Assign task to colleague)

◉ Project Management (Project Management sample Flow for Cookbook)

○ Review & Approve (Review & approval of content)

To continue click Next.

---

3. You can see our new workflow has been listed here. Select this and click **Next**.

4. In the next screen, we set standard properties of the workflow such as **Due Date**, **Priority**, **Description** and so on, and click on **Next**. Click on **Finish** to start the workflow.

Start Project Management Workflow Wizard
This wizard helps you start an advanced workflow for an item in the repository.

Steps	Summary	
1. Choose Workflow	The information you entered is shown below.	Next
2. Workflow Options		Back
3. Summary	**Start Advanced Workflow:** Project Management (Project Management sample Flow for Cookbook)	Finish
	To start the workflow press Finish. To review or change your selections click Back.	Cancel

---

5. Go to user's dashboard and click on **My Alfresco** link at the top bar. You can see a new task has been assigned to you. The task is **Create & Submit Requirement** – you may remember this is the first task of our workflow.

My Tasks To Do

Description	Type	Id	Created ▾	Due Date	Status	Priority	Actions
New Project about to start on Enterprise Content Management for InfoAxon.	Create & Submit Requirement	32	4 February 2011 21:07	4 February 2011	Not Yet Started	1	

Page 1 of 1 1

---

6. Click on **Manage Task** to open the task window. Populate the project information in the task properties and click on **Submit Requirements**. You can also add another document in this workflow by clicking on **Add Resource**, I have added the project requirement document here.

Manage Task: Create & Submit Requirement
Create & Submit Requirement

Task Properties

General

- Client Name: InfoAxon
- Project Name: ECM Implementation
- Project Estimated Budget: 567.89

Assign Project Manager

- Project Manager:

  1. Search for and select an item.

  sn   Search

  Snig Bhaumik [snig.bhaumik]

  OK   Cancel

Resources

Name ▼	Description ● Path ●	Created ●	Modified ●	Actions
📄 Requirement Specification Document.docx	/Company Home/InfoAxon /Chapter 11	5 February 2011 09:41	5 February 2011 09:41	
📄 Project Initiation Document.docx	/Company Home/InfoAxon /Chapter 11	4 February 2011 20:54	4 February 2011 21:07	

Page 1 of 1 |◄ ◄ 1 ► ►|

📄 Add Resource

7. As I have assigned **snig.bhaumik** as the PM role, the next task will be assigned to user **snig.bhaumik**. Log in as **snig.bhaumik** and open the dashboard. **Review & Approve Requirements** task is assigned in the task list. Open the task window.

8. There you can download and review the documents – two actions are offered: you can either **Approve** or **Reject** the Requirement document.

> Save Changes
>
> Approve Requirements
>
> Reject Requirements
>
> Cancel

9. If you click **Reject**, the flow will get back to the original user who started it and uploaded the initial document, expecting to upload a newer version of the documents. However, we click **Approve** here.

10. Upon approval, the flow proceeds and **Submit Project Sizing** task is assigned to the user. There you can see, you cannot add new documents; however, you feed the estimated man days and an estimated cost of the project. Click on **Submit** button after doing so. You can also change the user for **Project Manager** role, if you want. If you change the user, the next task will be assigned to a new user.

Manage Task: Submit Project Sizing
Submit Project Sizing

Task Properties

General

- Estimated Man Days: _____
- Total Estimated Cost: _____

Assign Project Manager

- Project Manager: Snig Bhaumik [snig.bhaumik]

11. The next task assigned is **Prepare Project Plan**, where you are required to enter probable dates of the project. Click **Submit Project Plan** after entering the dates.

Manage Task: Prepare Project Plan
Prepare Project Plan

Task Properties

General

- Proposed Start Date: 1 ▾ February ▾ 2011 ▾   [Today] [None]
- Proposed End Date: 15 ▾ February ▾ 2011 ▾   [Today] [None]
- Proposed Final Release Date: 25 ▾ February ▾ 2011 ▾   [Today] [None]

Assign Project Manager

- Project Manager: Snig Bhaumik [snig.bhaumik]

12. You will receive the **Kick Off Development** task next. You can declare the project team members here, ensure the environment to carry out the project is done, and finally click **Kick Off Development**.

Manage Task: Kick Off Development
Kick Off Development

Task Properties

General

		Add to List

Selected Items

Name

Finalized Project Team:

Matt Holton

Brian Casters

Rahul Joshi

Ravi Kumar

⊕ Project Environment setup Done?: ☐

Assign Project Manager

⊕ Project Manager: Snig Bhaumik [snig.bhaumik]

13. At the bottom of the screen, you can see the **Workflow History** is displayed – all the activities that had been performed in this process are listed.

Title:	Project Management (Project Management sample Flow for Cookbook)						
Initiated by:	Administrator						
Started on:	4 February 2011						
Completed on:	<In Progress>						

▼ **Workflow History**

Description	Task Type	Id	Created	Assignee	Comment	Completed on	Outcome
New Project about to start on Enterprise Content Management for InfoAxon.	Prepare Project Plan	35	5 February 2011 09:55	snig.bhaumik		5 February 2011 09:57	Submit Project Plan
New Project about to start on Enterprise Content Management for InfoAxon.	Submit Project Sizing	34	5 February 2011 09:50	snig.bhaumik		5 February 2011 09:55	Submit Project Sizing
New Project about to start on Enterprise Content Management for InfoAxon.	Review & Approve Requirements	33	5 February 2011 09:43	snig.bhaumik		5 February 2011 09:50	Approve Requirements
New Project about to start on Enterprise Content Management for InfoAxon.	Start new Project	31	4 February 2011 21:07	admin		4 February 2011 21:07	Task Done
New Project about to start on Enterprise Content Management for InfoAxon.	Create & Submit Requirement	32	4 February 2011 21:07	admin		5 February 2011 09:43	Submit Requirements

14. Click on **Kick Off Development** to complete the task and eventually finish the workflow process.

How it works...

We have just seen how to create a new process definition and all the other essential components from scratch, how to deploy the workflow, and finally how to use the workflow. Let's now understand what is happening in the background to make these run properly.

The task definitions

If you have custom tasks in your process (custom means not supplied by Alfresco), designing the Task Model is as important as designing the process definition.

The namespace we have used for our workflow is `http://www.infoaxon.com/book/models/workflow/1.0` with a prefix as `iabookwf`.

We have created six tasks here:

1. `iabookwf:startTask`
2. `iabookwf:createRequirementTask`
3. `iabookwf:reviewRequirementTask`
4. `iabookwf:createProjectSizingTask`
5. `iabookwf:createProjectPlanTask`
6. `iabookwf:kickOffDevelopmentTask`

Defining the properties of each of these tasks is very similar to defining the content properties (you have seen that in *Chapter 7* while creating custom content model). However, there are a couple of points that demand attention.

- The documents you attach with a task constitute the workflow package. By the `overrides` node in the task model, you define the behavior of these package documents.

  ```
  <property name="bpm:packageActionGroup">
      <default>add_package_item_actions</default>
  </property>
  ```

- This activates the **Add Resource** link in the task interface – so that you can attach multiple documents in your workflow.

- Also, if you want the task owner to be able to check-out, remove an associated document in the task interface, and instead add this in the task model.

  ```
  <property name="bpm:packageItemActionGroup">
      <default>add_edit_package_item_actions</default>
  </property>
  ```

- By default, Alfresco displays the documents associated with the workflow in a read-only mode.

- `bpm:assignee` is one of the important workflow variable that defines the actor of the workflow or of the forthcoming next task. If you want the task owner to be able to change this, add the following in your task model and in the web client configuration, display this property.

  ```
  <mandatory-aspects>
      <aspect>bpm:assignee</aspect>
  </mandatory-aspects>
  ```

- The corresponding web client configuration is as follows:

  ```
  <show-association name="bpm:assignee" display-label-id="iabookwf_pm" />
  ```

- The `display-label-id` is the label name from `webclient.properties` file. If you do not use this, Alfresco will by default render the label as **Workflow Assignee**.

- A standard workflow task should be inherited from the `bpm:workflowTask` class, which is defined in the `bpmModel.xml` in the `tomcat\webapps\alfresco\WEB-INF\classes\alfresco\model` folder.

- Similarly, the start task of your workflow must be inherited from `bpm:startTask` class.

The process model:

Once you have designed all of your tasks individually, it is now time to bind all these tasks in the process definition file, define the actors of each task, and define the transitions from one task to another, thus producing the business process flow.

- You first set the name of your process definition – we have put this as `iabookwf:pmprocess` here.

  ```
  <process-definition xmlns="urn:jbpm.org:jpdl-3.1"
  name="iabookwf:pmprocess">
  ```

- Next, you define all the swimlanes of your workflow. Swimlane is a process role. It is the mechanism by which you specify that multiple tasks within the process should be done by the same actor.

- By default, usually one `swimlane` is defined – `initiator`. He is the actor who has started or initiated the workflow.

  ```
  <swimlane name="initiator" />
  ```

- We have created another swimlane named `pmuser` and assigned the `bpm:assignee` process variable into it. Thus, whenever a user changes `bpm:assignee` in the UI, the actor of `pmuser` gets updated, and the next task allocated to this swimlane is assigned to him.

> You can see we have used `bpm_assignee` in the assignment instead of `bpm:assignee`. This is because all the task and workflow properties are exposed in the jPDL context in this format.
>
> Thus, we have used `bpm_workflowDueDate` for `bpm:workflowDueDate`, `bpm_workflowPriority` for `bpm:workflowPriority`, and `bpm_assignee` for `bpm:assignee`.

- The initiation of the workflow should be with node `start-state` and we need to use a task inherited from `bpm:startTask` in this node, thus we have used `iabookwf:startTask` here in our process. The swimlane is the `initiator` and only one transition is defined `submitRequirement` – thus after start of the process the flow proceeds to `submitRequirement` node.

```
<start-state name="start">
    <task name="iabookwf:startTask" swimlane="initiator" />
    <transition name="" to="submitRequirement" />
</start-state>
```

- The `submitRequirement` task node invokes task `iabookwf:createRequirementTask` and flows to `reviewRequirement` once complete.

- The `reviewRequirement` node executes task `iabookwf:reviewRequirementTask` by swimlane `pmuser`. We have two transitions defined here – one for Approval, another for Rejection. In case of approval, the process flows ahead to the next step – `createProjectSizing`, and in case of rejection, it goes back to the `submitRequirement` step asking the initiator to probably upload the requirement document again.

```
<task-node name="reviewRequirement">
    <task name="iabookwf:reviewRequirementTask"
swimlane="pmuser">
        <event type="task-create">
            <script>
                if (bpm_workflowDueDate != void) taskInstance.
dueDate = bpm_workflowDueDate;
                if (bpm_workflowPriority != void)
taskInstance.priority = bpm_workflowPriority;
            </script>
        </event>
    </task>
    <transition name="Approve Requirements"
to="createProjectSizing" />
    <transition name="Reject Requirements"
to="submitRequirement" />

</task-node>
```

▶ The rest of the process steps work pretty much in a similar fashion. However, the workflow should be ended with an `end-state` node. Hence, after `kickOffDevelopment` (the last task) the process completes by calling `end` (name of the `end-state`)

```
<end-state name="end" />
```

> Here we have seen how to invoke JavaScript from workflow process events. You can also invoke Java classes and methods from such process events. For example,
> ```
> <event type="task-end">
>     <action class="com.infoaxon.workflow.handler.
> TaskEndHandler" />
> </event>
> ```
> This class must be deployed in the Alfresco classpath library.

The resource bundle:

Defining the labels and texts to be rendered in the web client for the workflow and task interfaces is done in the resource files. We had created the `pm-workflow-messages. properties` file for this. It is due to this file that proper labels are appearing in the interface.

You can remove the entry of this file from the `workflow-context.xml` file, restart the server, and see how the labels are appearing in various windows.

You need to understand the semantics of putting these labels (`title` and `description`).

```
iabookwf_pmprocess.workflow.title=Project Management
iabookwf_pmprocess.workflow.description=Project Management sample Flow
for Cookbook
```

Here we have defined the title and description of the workflow process.

▶ You can remember the name of the process is `iabookwf:pmprocess` – thus we need to put `iabookwf_pmprocess` for the process definition.

▶ The syntax is:
```
<<process-name>>.workflow.title = <<put the title here>>
<<process-name>>.workflow.description = <<put the description
here>>
```

For example:
```
iabookwf_BookWFModel.type.iabookwf_startTask.title=Start new
Project
iabookwf_BookWFModel.type.iabookwf_startTask.description=Start new
Project
```

▶ Here we defined the title and description of the `iabookwf:startTask` task.

- The syntax is:

  ```
  <<model-name>>.type.<<task-type-name>>.title = <<put the title
  here>>
  <<model-name>>.type.<<task-type-name>>.description = <<put the
  description here>>
  ```

- The model name defined in `pm_taskModel.xml` is `iabookwf:BookWFModel`

  **`<model name="iabookwf:BookWFModel" xmlns="http://www.alfresco.org/
  model/dictionary/1.0">`**

- Again, as earlier we replace the : with _ in the model and type the name.

  - Thus `iabookwf:BookWFModel` becomes `iabookwf_BookWFModel`

  - And `iabookwf:startTask` becomes `iabookwf_startTask`

- Defining the titles and descriptions of the rest of the tasks are pretty much the same.

> You can design and create jBPM process definition files using jBPM Eclipse plug-in. To find more about how to install and use the plug-in, please see `http://docs.jboss.org/jbpm/v3/gpd/installation.html` and `http://www.jboss.org/jbpm/components/eclipse-plugin`.

Using the Alfresco Workflow Console

Once started, the workflows execute in the background in the jBPM context. There is a little way to debug and see what is going on around the workflows.

Alfresco has provided a wonderful tool to investigate inside the workflow engine.

You can perform various common tasks using this console window

- Deploy, undeploy process definitions
- See all the deployed process definitions
- See all currently running workflows
- Start, stop, cancel a workflow
- See details of a workflow
- See paths of a workflow
- See any running task details along with task properties
- Create, assign process variable values
- See pending tasks, pooled tasks

In this recipe, we will see how to do some of these actions.

How to do it...

Open the URL `http://localhost:8080/alfresco/faces/jsp/admin/workflow-console.jsp`, admin access is required for some of the tasks we want to perform here.

The workflow console will appear, waiting to execute your commands.

```
      Workflow Console

Context
User:                admin
Workflow Definition: None

Command (type help for help)
_____     [ Submit ]

Last command: none
Duration: 0ms
-----

    ##
    ##  Meta commands
    ##

    ok> help

        List this help.

    ok> r

        Repeat last command.
```

The default screen renders the help output on how to use this interface, and lists the possible commands that can be executed in this console.

▶ **See the deployed process definitions**

Command:

show definitions all

Click on **Submit**. This is what I get in my installation. However, depending on what definitions you have created and deployed, the listing might change.

```
Command (type help for help)

                                                                    Submit

Last command: show definitions all
Duration: 57ms
-----

id: jbpm$17 , name: jbpm$iabookwf:pmprocess , title: Project Management , version: 2
id: jbpm$16 , name: jbpm$iabookwf:pmprocess , title: Project Management , version: 1
id: jbpm$7 , name: jbpm$imwf:invitation-moderated , title: Invitation - Moderated , version: 1
id: jbpm$6 , name: jbpm$inwf:invitation-nominated , title: Invitation - Nominated , version: 1
id: jbpm$4 , name: jbpm$wcmwf:changerequest , title: Change Request , version: 1
id: jbpm$3 , name: jbpm$wcmwf:submit , title: Web Site Submission , version: 1
id: jbpm$5 , name: jbpm$wcmwf:submitdirect , title: Web Site Submission (Direct) , version: 1
id: jbpm$2 , name: jbpm$wf:adhoc , title: Adhoc Task , version: 1
id: jbpm$1 , name: jbpm$wf:review , title: Review & Approve , version: 1
```

► **See currently running workflows**

Command:

```
show workflows all
```

In case no workflows are running, no outputs will be generated. This is what I get when our workflow is in action.

```
Command (type help for help)

                                                              Submit

Last command: show workflows all
Duration: 56ms
-----

id: jbpm$11 , desc: Another project to Start!!! , start date: 2011-02-05 12:37:14.0 , def: jbpm$iabookwf:pmprocess
```

► **See details of a workflow**

Command:

```
desc workflow jbpm$11
```

The syntax is desc workflow <<workflow-id>>. In our case, in the previous screenshot we have seen the current workflow ID is jbpm$11. The output is as follows:

```
Command (type help for help)
                                                                    Submit

Last command: desc workflow jbpm$11
Duration: 52ms
-----


definition: jbpm$iabookwf:pmprocess
id: jbpm$11
description: Another project to Start!!!
active: true
start date: 2011-02-05 12:37:14.0
end date: null
initiator: workspace://SpacesStore/9b4c8c83-ff81-47a4-8272-e651a8f1b590
context: workspace://SpacesStore/4a8e08a5-9040-4890-b493-7453d7678c70
package: workspace://SpacesStore/a6250fa1-5c06-4a6f-a462-8115215fc699
```

▶ **See details of a Task**

Command:

desc task jbpm$38

The syntax is desc task <<task-id>>. This is the output:

```
Command (type help for help)
                                                                    Submit

Last command: desc task jbpm$38
Duration: 12ms
-----

id: jbpm$38
name: iabookwf:createRequirementTask
title: Create & Submit Requirement
description: Create & Submit Requirement
state: IN_PROGRESS
path: jbpm$11-@
transitions: 1
 transition: Submit Requirements , title: Submit Requirements , desc: Submit Requirements
properties: 21
 {http://www.infoaxon.com/book/models/workflow/1.0}projectName = Another ECM Project
 {http://www.alfresco.org/model/bpm/1.0}description = Another project to Start!!!
 {http://www.alfresco.org/model/bpm/1.0}percentComplete = 0
 {http://www.alfresco.org/model/bpm/1.0}assignee = workspace://SpacesStore/2f326392-bfa1-46a4-8959-977b050fe800
 {http://www.alfresco.org/model/bpm/1.0}completionDate = null
 {http://www.alfresco.org/model/bpm/1.0}context = workspace://SpacesStore/4a8e08a5-9040-4890-b493-7453d7678c70
 {http://www.alfresco.org/model/bpm/1.0}outcome =
 {http://www.alfresco.org/model/bpm/1.0}pooledActors = []
 {http://www.alfresco.org/model/bpm/1.0}taskId = 38
 {http://www.alfresco.org/model/bpm/1.0}priority = 3
 {http://www.alfresco.org/model/content/1.0}owner = admin
 {http://www.alfresco.org/model/bpm/1.0}status = Not Yet Started
 {http://www.alfresco.org/model/bpm/1.0}dueDate = 2011-02-02 12:36:00.0
 {http://www.infoaxon.com/book/models/workflow/1.0}budget = 8679.46
 {http://www.alfresco.org/model/bpm/1.0}startDate = null
 {http://www.infoaxon.com/book/models/workflow/1.0}clientName = InfoAxon
 {http://www.alfresco.org/model/bpm/1.0}hiddenTransitions =
 {http://www.alfresco.org/model/bpm/1.0}package = workspace://SpacesStore/a6250fa1-5c06-4a6f-a462-8115215fc699
 {http://www.alfresco.org/model/content/1.0}created = 2011-02-05 12:37:14.0
 {http://www.alfresco.org/model/bpm/1.0}packageActionGroup = add_package_item_actions
 {http://www.alfresco.org/model/bpm/1.0}packageItemActionGroup = add_edit_package_item_actions
```

As you can see, all the task properties have been displayed, along with our custom properties.

▶ **Cancelling a workflow**

Command:

`end workflow jbpm$11`

The syntax is end workflow <<workflow-id>>. The following is the output:

```
Command (type help for help)
                                                            Submit
Last command: end workflow jbpm$11
Duration: 318ms
-----

workflow jbpm$11 cancelled.
```

▶ **Undeploying a process definition**

Command:

`undeploy definition name jbpm$iabookwf:pmprocess`

The syntax is undeploy definition name <<definition-name>>. The output would be as follows:

```
Command (type help for help)
                                                           Submit
Last command: undeploy definition name jbpm$iabookwf:pmprocess
Duration: 525ms
-----

undeploying... v2 v1
id: jbpm$7 , name: jbpm$imwf:invitation-moderated , title: Invitation - Moderated , version: 1
id: jbpm$6 , name: jbpm$inwf:invitation-nominated , title: Invitation - Nominated , version: 1
id: jbpm$4 , name: jbpm$wcmwf:changerequest , title: Change Request , version: 1
id: jbpm$3 , name: jbpm$wcmwf:submit , title: Web Site Submission , version: 1
id: jbpm$5 , name: jbpm$wcmwf:submitdirect , title: Web Site Submission (Direct) , version: 1
id: jbpm$2 , name: jbpm$wf:adhoc , title: Adhoc Task , version: 1
id: jbpm$1 , name: jbpm$wf:review , title: Review & Approve , version: 1
```

Thus, you have seen that Alfresco offers a great deal of functionality not only in terms of integration of JBPM workflow engine with the repository, but you can also use the JavaScript APIs in the jPDL process definition. Also, Alfresco has offered Workflow JavaScript Services APIs to manage workflows within your Web Scripts, and so on.

The workflow console is quite a helpful tool to debug your process definition, workflow execution, task behaviors.

12

Integrating with MS Outlook and MS Office

In this chapter, we will cover:

- ▶ Integrating Alfresco with Microsoft Outlook
- ▶ Integrating Alfresco with Microsoft Office

Introduction

Until now, you have learnt how to use Alfresco as a content management system in several common use cases such as:

- ▶ Creating a document folder, uploading, and organizing documents and contents
- ▶ Applying permissions to your contents and folders
- ▶ Searching contents and extending the default search mechanism
- ▶ Writing custom interfaces for the content display
- ▶ Implementing specific business rules in the system
- ▶ Developing services on top of the repository
- ▶ Creating and executing business processes around your documents and contents
- ▶ Building your custom content models and designs

Alfresco, however, offers integration mechanism with a number of external systems thus providing you enough flexibility to use Alfresco in your enterprise environment. This enables you to use Alfresco not only as a simple document management system, but also to deploy a full content management solution in your organization having touch-points with most of the commonly used tools, applications, and systems.

Why integration is required

First of all, let's understand why we should integrate Alfresco with other external systems, what are the merits of doing this, and in which situations should we implement and use such integrated environments.

Alfresco, as a family of products, offers web interfaces to work on the repository – Alfresco Explorer (Web Client), Alfresco Share, and Web Content Management. However, we have discussed the Explorer application in this book. All these applications are web-based, serving different purposes and different requirements. You have to invoke the web applications in your browser and complete your work.

What happens if you want to access the repository and save your files directly from within your Microsoft Office applications? Or, what if you can see the repository from your e-mail client like Microsoft Outlook or Mozilla Thunderbird?

In a normal scenario, if you want to upload a MS-Word file in the Alfresco repository, you have to save the file in your local machine, open the Alfresco web interface, log into the system, and upload the file from there. It is easier and more usable if you could save the file directly from the Word interface and also at the time of editing the file, you can open the file from the repository directly, no need to download before opening the file.

Similar to the Office documents and files, the mails and corresponding attachments are also important pieces of information that you might sometimes want to store in your repository. Consider a situation where you want to put one of your mails into the repository. The steps you might need to follow are (with MS Outlook as the e-mail client application):

1. Open MS Outlook to receive the mail from the POP3 server
2. Save the e-mail as HTML, MSG, or any other format
3. Open your web browser and open the Alfresco application
4. Log into the application and upload the saved e-mail file into the repository. The file will be uploaded into the repository as a standard document or any other file.

As an alternative system, imagine if the repository and the folders are available in the Outlook interface and for uploading the e-mail you need to copy and drag the e-mail item in the proper folder of the repository.

This saves a lot of time, improves productivity, and improves usability experiences for the end users who are accessing the repository for storing content documents.

There are several integration points that have been offered by Alfresco, we will discuss integration of MS Office and Outlook in this chapter.

Integrating Alfresco with Microsoft Outlook

Alfresco has offered a fully functional and feature-rich add-in for Microsoft Office, especially for MS-Word, Excel, and PowerPoint.

In this recipe, we will see how to download, install, and use this add-in from MS-Office 2003 applications.

Getting ready...

First you must check whether your MS-Office installation is fulfilling the pre-requisites for this Add-in.

You need .NET Framework 2.0 (or a higher version) for this Add-in to run.

You must ensure the *.NET Programmability Support* option has been installed for each of the Office applications you are installing the add-ins for. This option can be found by running the Office installation program within the list of available options for each application.

1. Open your web browser and navigate to the Alfresco community download page. For the 3.3 version of Alfresco, you open `http://wiki.alfresco.com/wiki/ Community_Edition_file_list_3.3`. In the last section of the download page, available **Microsoft Office add-ins** are listed. If you want to have the full MS-Office add-in installation, download the **alfresco-community-office2003-addins-3.3.zip** file. You can download this directly from the URL (this is basically a 3-in-1 installer) `http://process.alfresco.com/ccdl/?file=release/community/ build-2765/alfresco-community-office2003-addins-3.3.zip`.

2. However, if you want only specific add-ins for Word, Excel, or PowerPoint, you can download the corresponding add-in.

3. Let's say, we have downloaded the add-in for full MS-Office 2003. You will receive a file named **alfresco-community-office2003-addins-3.3.zip**. Unzip the file in a folder, and run the **AlfrescoOffice2003Setup.msi** installer.

> Make sure no Office applications are running in your machine while you install the add-in.

4. You will be greeted with a welcome screen. Click **Next>**.

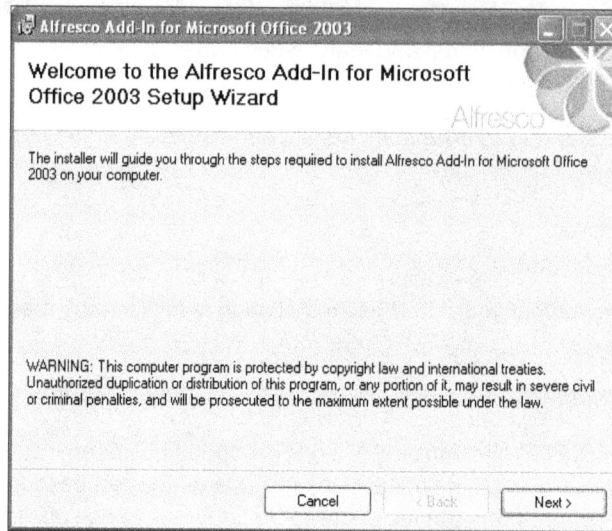

5. In the next screen, information and instructions about this add-in are presented. Click **Next>**.

6. Choose your installation folder in the next screen and click **Next>**.

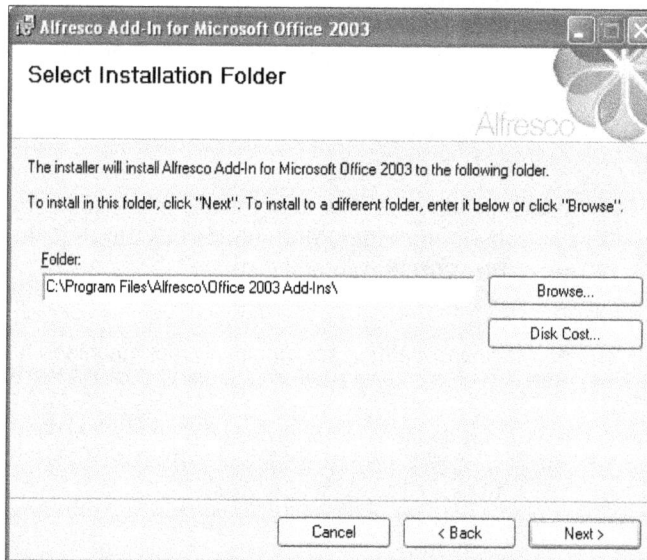

7. The setup is now ready to install the add-in. Clicking **Next >** would install the add-in on your computer.

8. A confirmation window should appear when the add-in is successfully installed. Click **Close** to finish the installation.

How to do it...

1. Start the MS-Office application, say MS-Word. Go to the **Add-ins** section, you will find a new add-in is available named Alfresco. Click on that and the configuration and login window will appear.

2. Set the Web Client URL and user credentials appropriately. In our example, suppose the Alfresco Tomcat server is running in your **localhost** and the username is default admin. If you want the Add-in to remember your user credentials, select **Remember authentication details**.

3. Click on **Save Settings** and the add-in will connect to Alfresco and will present different tabs exposing several functionalities.

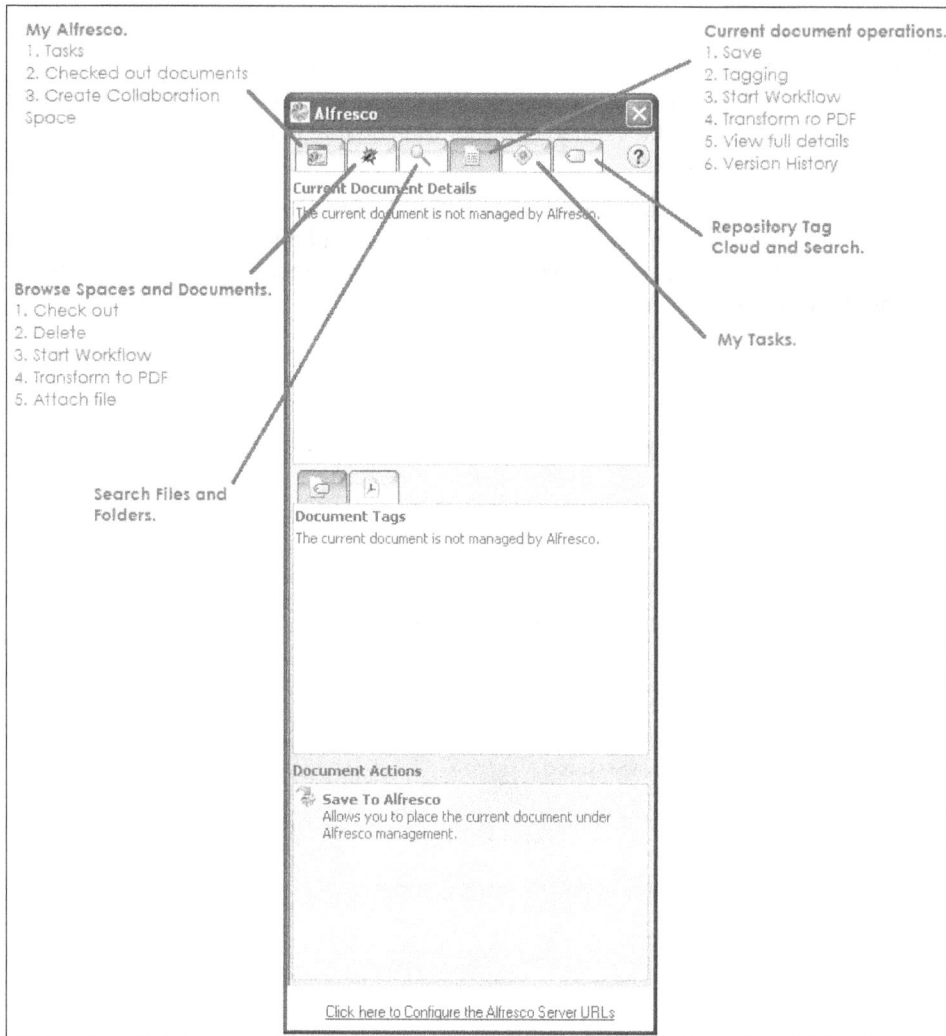

My Alfresco.
1. Tasks
2. Checked out documents
3. Create Collaboration Space

Current document operations.
1. Save
2. Tagging
3. Start Workflow
4. Transform ro PDF
5. View full details
6. Version History

Repository Tag Cloud and Search.

Browse Spaces and Documents.
1. Check out
2. Delete
3. Start Workflow
4. Transform to PDF
5. Attach file

My Tasks.

Search Files and Folders.

Alfresco

Current Document Details
The current document is not managed by Alfresco.

Document Tags
The current document is not managed by Alfresco.

Document Actions

Save To Alfresco
Allows you to place the current document under Alfresco management.

Click here to Configure the Alfresco Server URLs

4. Now as we are connected to the Alfresco server setting in MS Word, let's try to do some operations. First of all, let's save the document in the repository.

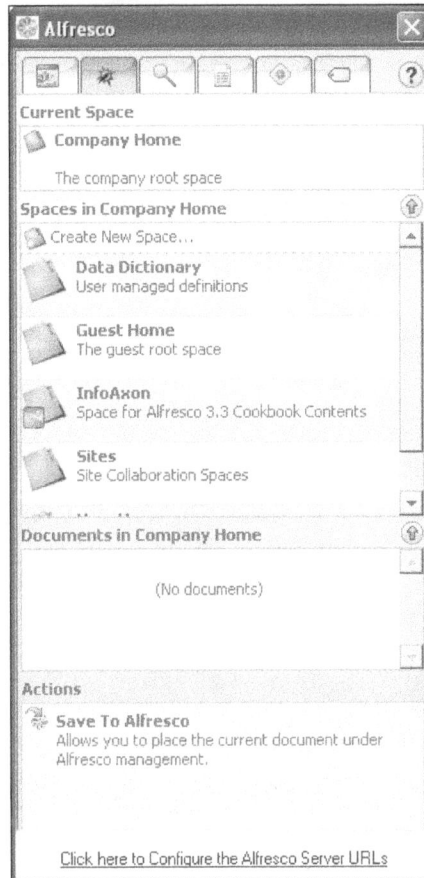

5. To save this document in a folder named **Chapter 12** in the **InfoAxon** space, click on **InfoAxon**. This makes it show all the folders and documents in the **InfoAxon** space.

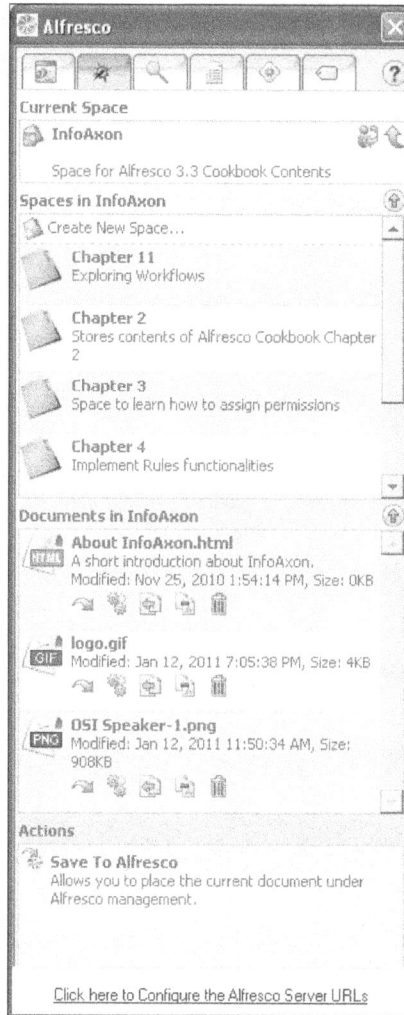

6. Click on **Create New Space**. Provide the details of the new space in the panel, click on **Submit** – the new space will be created. In our example, we have created a space named **Chapter 12** here.

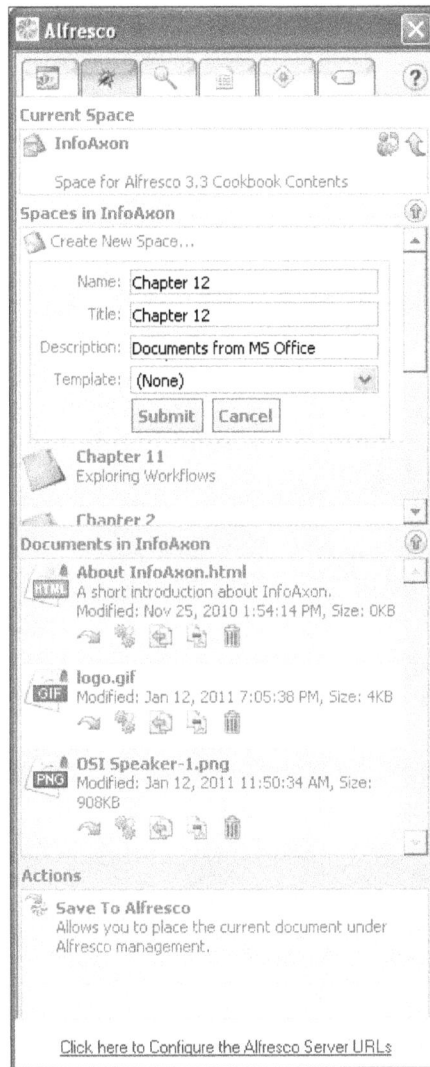

7. Click on the new space – **Chapter 12**. No documents should be displayed here. Click on **Save to Alfresco** since we want to save our document in this folder. Provide a name for your document and click **OK**.

8. You can see the details of the current document are displayed. You can now perform several operations on the document such as adding tags, starting workflows, transforming the document, see versions of the document, and so on.

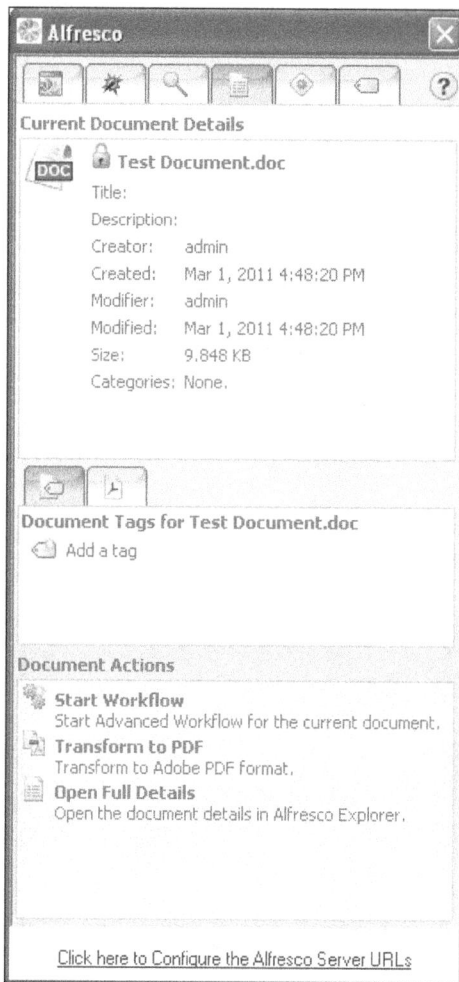

9. Let us now see how to open, edit, and save a document in the repository. Re-open MS-Word and open Alfresco Add-in. It might ask for user credentials in case you haven't saved the user details. There will be no current document opened.

10. Navigate to the **Chapter 12** space, one document should be displayed. Check out the document.

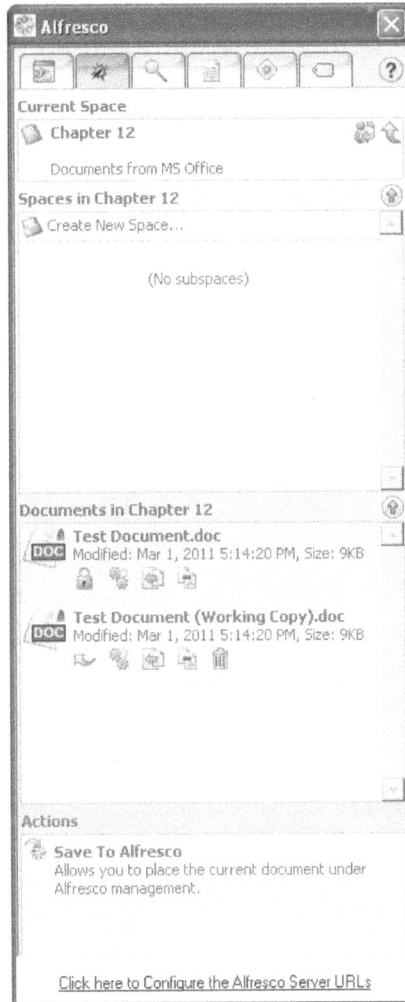

11. Click on the working copy version – **Test Document (Working Copy).doc** in our case. Update the document and save the document normally in MS-Word – the document will get saved into the repository.

12. Go to the first tab, namely, **My Checked Out Documents**. Our checked out documents will be listed there. **Check In** the working copy of the document.

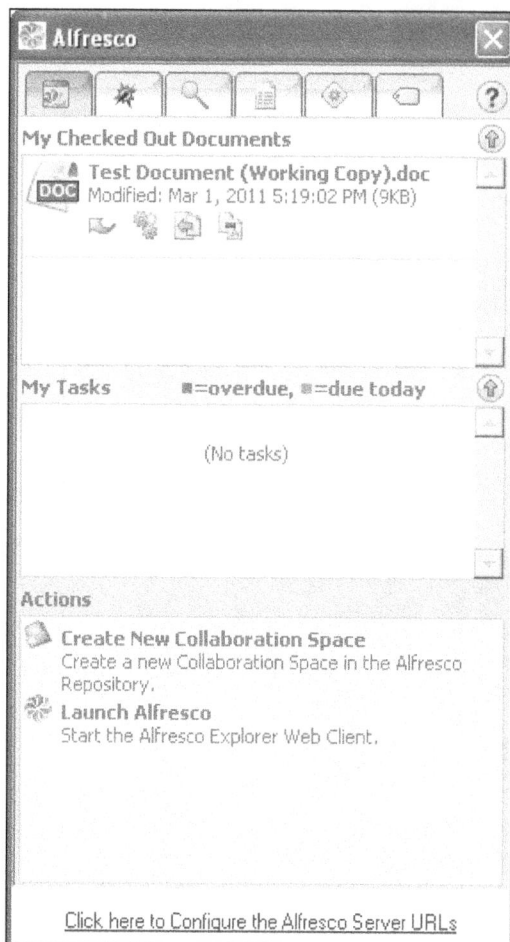

13. Your document will be saved and checked-in to the repository.

My Alfresco > InfoAxon > Chapter 12

Chapter 12
This view allows you to browse the items in this space.
Documents from MS Office

▼ **Browse Spaces**

No items to display. Click the 'Create Space' action to create a space.

Name ▲	Description ●	Create
	Page 1	

▼ **Content Items**

Name ▲	Description ●	Size ●
Test Document.doc ⓘ		9.91 KB
	Page 1	

There's more...

We just saw how to manage documents in the Alfresco repository without leaving the good old MS-Office applications. There is no need to open the Alfresco web application in a browser, and upload and work on documents there. Moreover, your documents are now not stored in the local drive, you work entirely in the repository.

The add-in is developed using *Microsoft .NET Framework* (version 2.0 onwards is supported) and *Microsoft Visual Studio Tools for Office* (VSTO).

Both these frameworks will be downloaded and installed automatically in case they are not there on your machine already.

For more information on VSTO, see web resources such as `http://en.wikipedia.org/wiki/Visual_Studio_Tools_for_Office` and `http://msdn.microsoft.com/en-us/vsto/default`.

> Though this add-in works with MS-Office 2007 as well it is built primarily for MS-Office 2003.

Integrating Alfresco with MS Outlook

Alfresco supports accessing the server and repository via IMAP (*Internet Message Access Protocol*) protocol. This allows e-mail client applications like Microsoft Outlook, Mozilla Thunderbird, Lotus Notes, and so on to connect and interact with the repository.

In the previous recipe, we saw how to integrate Alfresco with MS-Office applications such as MS-Word. We have learnt how to interact with the repository directly from the Office applications. In this recipe, we will see how the repository is accessible from e-mail clients as well; and we can push content items (e-mail items) into the repository from MS Outlook.

Getting ready...

First we need to configure and mount the Alfresco IMAP server. By default, in the community edition, IMAP service is disabled. Thus we need to enable the service, so that the e-mail client applications like Outlook can talk to Alfresco via IMAP protocol.

1. Open the `alfresco-global.properties` file from the `\tomcat\shared\ classes` folder. This is the file where global properties and settings of Alfresco are stored and managed.

> By default, the file is provided as `alfresco-global.properties. sample`. You may need to rename this as `alfresco-global. properties`.

2. Add the following code at the end of this file:

```
imap.server.enabled=true
imap.server.port=143
imap.server.attachments.extraction.enabled=true

imap.mail.from.default=alfresco@demo.alfresco.org

# Default IMAP mount points
imap.config.home.store=${spaces.store}
imap.config.home.rootPath=/${spaces.company_home.childname}
imap.config.home.folderPath=Imap Home
imap.config.server.mountPoints=AlfrescoIMAP
imap.config.server.mountPoints.default.mountPointName=IMAP
imap.config.server.mountPoints.default.modeName=ARCHIVE
imap.config.server.mountPoints.default.store=${spaces.store}
imap.config.server.mountPoints.default.rootPath=/${spaces.company_
home.childname}
imap.config.server.mountPoints.value.AlfrescoIMAP.
mountPointName=Alfresco IMAP
imap.config.server.mountPoints.value.AlfrescoIMAP.modeName=MIXED
```

3. Restart your Tomcat server. If you take a look at the Tomcat server log, messages

similar to this should appear. This means your Alfresco IMAP server is properly initiated and started.

```
    INFO   [management.subsystems.ChildApplicationContextFactory]
Starting 'imap' subsystem, ID: [imap, default]
    INFO   [alfresco.config.JndiPropertyPlaceholderConfigurer]
Loading properties file from class path resource [alfresco/
alfresco-shared.properties]
    INFO   [repo.imap.AlfrescoImapServer] IMAP service started on
host:port snigbhaumik:143.
    INFO   [management.subsystems.ChildApplicationContextFactory]
Startup of <imap> subsystem, ID: [imap, default] complete
```

How to do it...

Now as the Alfresco server is ready with the IMAP service started, we need to connect our Outlook with Alfresco. For that, we will create a new e-mail account in Outlook.

1. Open MS Outlook and go to **Tools | Account Settings**. Click **New** to create a new e-mail account.

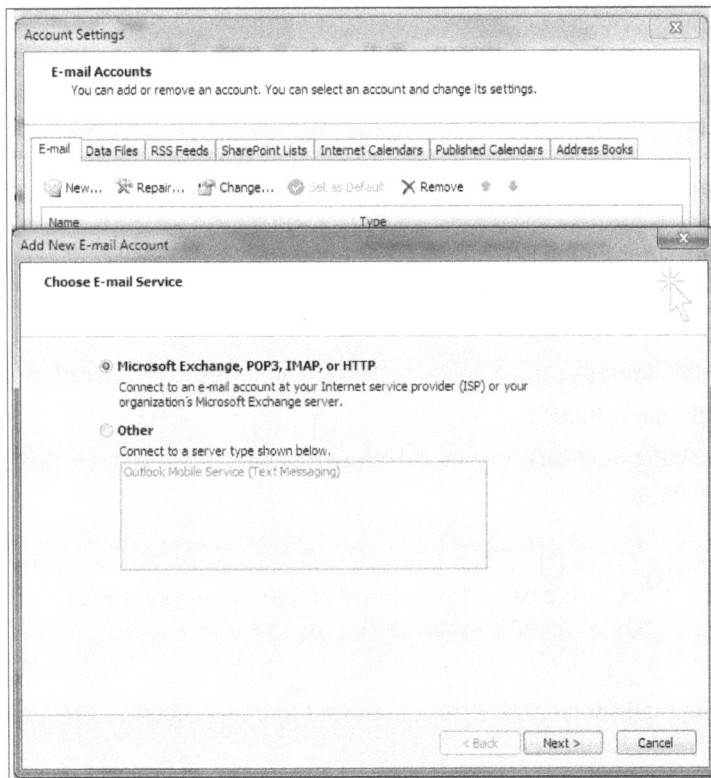

2. Click **Next** and select **Manually Configure server settings or additional server types**. Click **Next**.

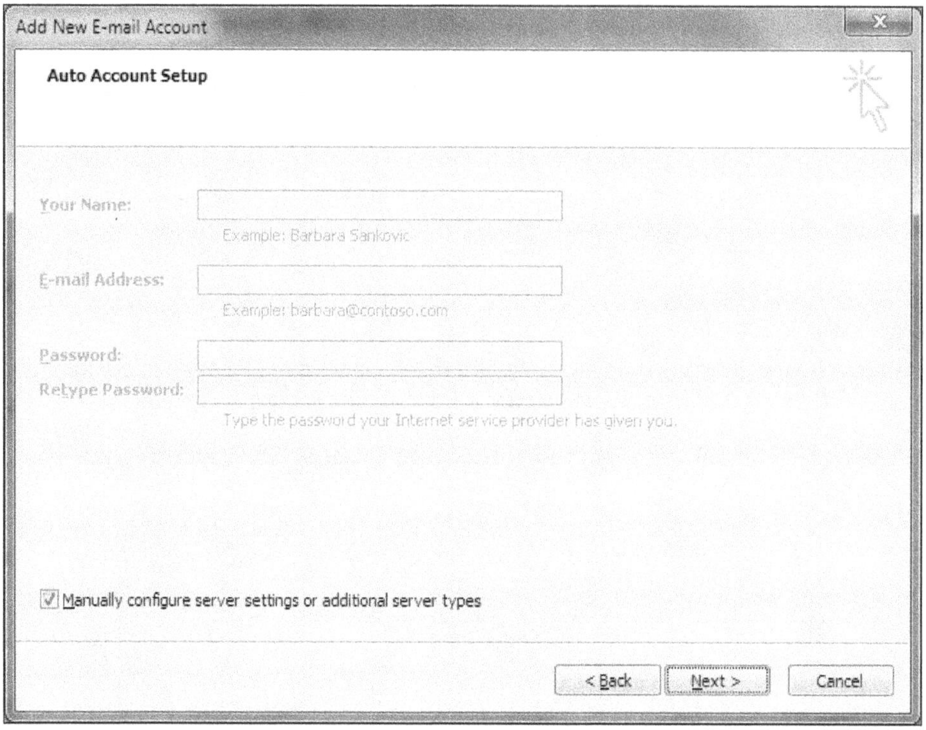

3. Select **Internet E-mail** in the next screen and click **Next>**.

4. Populate your account information in the next screen. This should match with your Alfresco user credentials.

5. The **E-mail address** should be the same as your Alfresco registered user's e-mail ID.

6. **Account Type** is **IMAP**.

7. The **Incoming mail server** is the IP of your machine – in this case, 192.168.1.216 is the IP of my machine.

> It is better to use the IP of the machine instead of `localhost` or `127.0.0.1` here.

8. **Outgoing mail server** (**SMTP**) is not relevant for this account, as we are supposed to send any mail for now.

9. In the **Logon Information**, put your Alfresco username and password.

10. Click on **Next>** and then **Finish** completing the account creation.

11. Outlook will pull the folders and other information from the Alfresco repository and will present the IMAP folders.

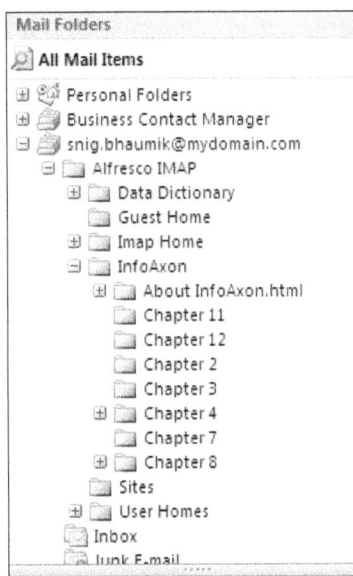

12. Click on **Chapter 12** in the folder list. Content items from this folder will be displayed. We had created one document (**Test Document.doc**) in this folder in the previous recipe.

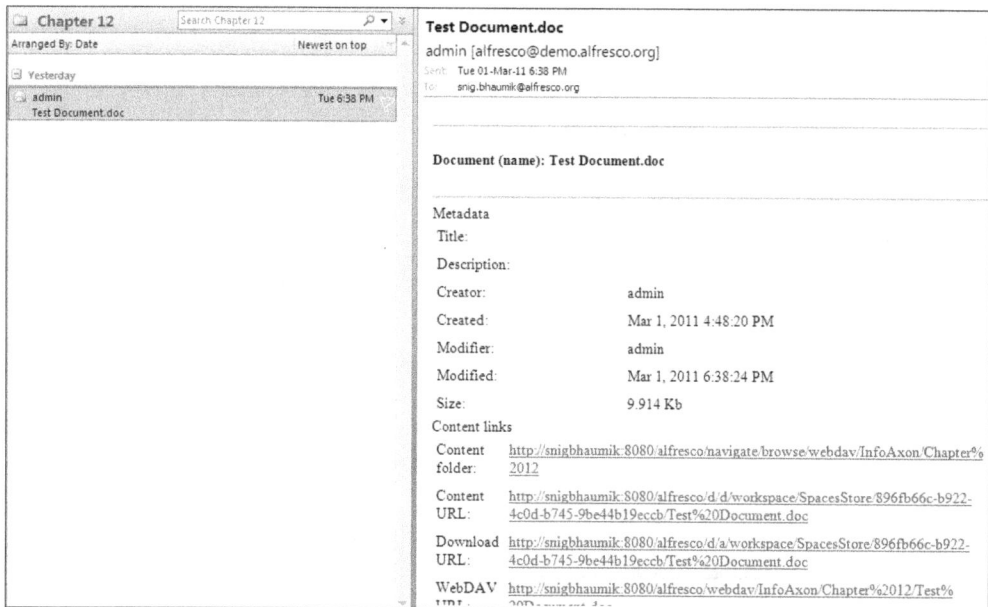

13. We can upload mails directly to the repository via the IMAP interface. Just drag a particular mail from any other regular e-mail folder (such as POP3) into the IMAP folder. The mail will be uploaded to Alfresco.

14. For example, I just dragged an e-mail from my inbox into the **Chapter 12** folder. If you have a look at the Alfresco web client, you will see that a new content item is created.

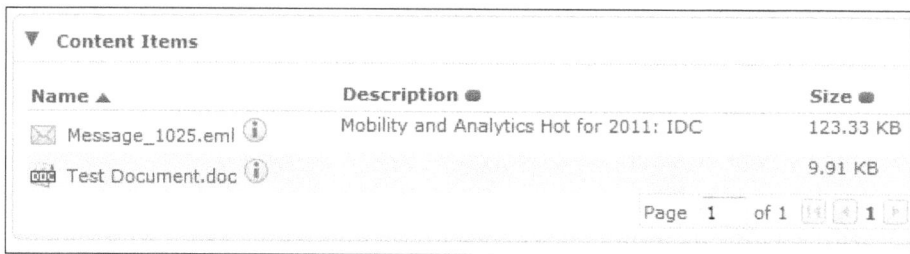

15. Thus you can easily copy your e-mails, or drag your important e-mails into the repository directly, without leaving your e-mail client like Outlook or Thunderbird. In fact, this method will work in any e-mail client application that supports IMAP.

16. You can also create some rules in Outlook that would copy some particular e-mails automatically into the repository folders. This would enable you to push important e-mails into the repository, thus efficiently securing, storing, and sharing e-mails.

How it works...

The configuration and behavior of the IMAP server is mostly governed by the settings provided in the `alfresco-global.properties` file, in our case.

```
imap.server.enabled=true
imap.server.port=143
imap.server.attachments.extraction.enabled=true
```

This setting enables the Alfresco IMAP server at the default port `143`. When the attachment extraction is set to true, Alfresco will automatically find out the e-mail attachments and will index and store them separately.

```
imap.config.home.store=${spaces.store}
imap.config.home.rootPath=/${spaces.company_home.childname}
```

This defines the home store and home folder path of the IMAP folders shown in the e-mail client. Here we have used **Company Home** as the `rootPath`. Thus all folders are displayed.

13
Configuring Alfresco E-Mail and File Servers

In this chapter, we will cover:

- ▶ Configuring Alfresco to send e-mails
- ▶ Sending e-mails by JavaScript API
- ▶ Configuring Alfresco for inbound e-mails
- ▶ Using and use CIFS server in Alfresco

Introduction

Sending e-mails is one of the basic features and feature you expect from a CMS system. For example, you would like to send some e-mail notification to certain users when a new document is uploaded, or when a new version of an important document is created in the system. E-mail notification is more essential when a new task is assigned to a particular user. You would for instance, also like to send e-mail alerts to users in case any of their allotted tasks become overdue.

Pulling e-mails is one unique feature of Alfresco, which can be utilized effectively under certain conditions. This feature enables Alfresco to act like a POP3 e-mail server and pull e-mails from certain e-mail accounts. For example, if you have an e-mail ID configured in Alfresco, the mails sent to this e-mail ID will be automatically pulled into the repository folders. This feature is particularly useful when you want mails, documents, and other contents to be stored automatically in the repository.

In this chapter, we will see how to configure Alfresco to send and receive e-mail messages.

We have seen different ways to access Alfresco – for example, from MS-Office applications and MS Outlook. These integrations work using MS SharePoint protocol and IMAP protocol respectively. However, the repository can also be exposed via some other standard protocols as well, such as FTP, CIFS, and so on.

Activating the FTP protocol would enable any FTP client software to access the repository – thus you can offer your users the use of Alfresco repository by a FTP client system.

The CIFS protocol on the other hand exposes the repository as a standard network shared drive. In this chapter, we will explore how to configure Alfresco to expose the repository via FTP or CIFS.

Configuring Alfresco to send e-mails

In this recipe, we first see how to configure Alfresco to send e-mails before sending e-mails from Alfresco web client.

Getting started

1. Open the `alfresco-global.properties` file from `\tomcat\shared\classes` folder. As you know, this is the file where global properties and settings of Alfresco are stored and managed.

2. Add the following lines of code at the end of the file:

```
# Outbound Mail Configurations.
mail.host=smtp.mydomain.com
mail.port=25
mail.username=myname@mydomain.com
mail.password=mypass
mail.encoding=UTF-8
mail.from.default=myname@mydomain.com
mail.smtp.auth=true
mail.protocol=smtp
# Outbound Mail Configurations End.
```

> These are sample values. You must replace these with actual values as per your SMTP server settings. Details of each of these parameters are described later in this recipe.

3. That's it. No more configurations required. Restart your Tomcat server, Alfresco is now ready to send e-mails.

How to do it...

We will see how we can send e-mails using Alfresco explorer:

1. Open Alfresco web client, and navigate to a space.

2. Let's say we have opened the **InfoAxon** space. Open the **details view** of any of the content items or documents inside this space. For example, consider we opened the details view of **About InfoAxon.html** content item.

3. We will send e-mail via **Run Action** wizard, as Alfresco has provided a packaged action for sending e-mails, Click on **Run Action**.

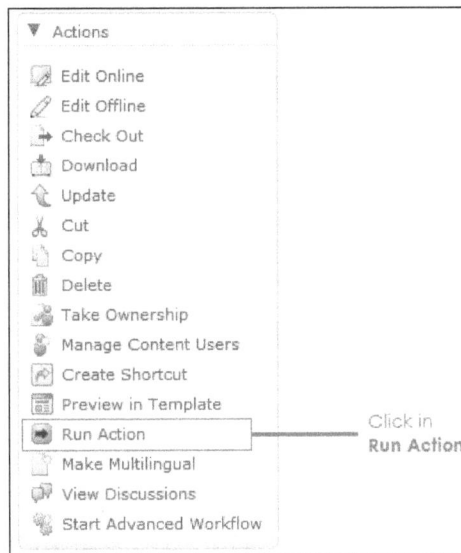

4. In the available list of actions, select **Send e-mail** and click **Send Values and Add**.

5. In the next screen, select the user who you want to send your mail to and of course, add your message which should include:

   ❑ Message subject

Message body (the template feature provided here will be explained in the *Sending e-mails via JavaScript API* recipe).

```
Set action values

Message Recipients
  1. Search for email recipients by Name or Group

    Users  ▼   sni                    [ Search ]
    Results for 'sni' in 'Users'. Clear Results

    ┌────────────────────────────────────────┐
    │ Snig Bhaumik [snig.bhaumik]          ▲ │
    │                                        │
    │                                        │
    │                                        │
    │                                        │
    │                                      ▼ │
    └────────────────────────────────────────┘

    [ Add ]

  2. Selected email recipients

    Name

    Snig Bhaumik  🗑

Email message
  Subject:        Welcome to Alfresco!                                    *

                  Use Template:  Select a template...  ▼  [ Insert Template ]  [ Discard Template ]

                  ┌──────────────────────────────────────────────────────────┐
                  │ Hi there                                               ▲  │
  Message:        │ Welcome to Alfresco - the leading Open Source Enterprise Content Management │
                  │ System.                                                    │
                  │  _   __                                                ▼  │
                  └──────────────────────────────────────────────────────────┘
```

6. After populating all values, click **OK**. If the e-mail address of the user is correct, and all settings are accurate as per your SMTP server settings, the mail will be forwarded.

How it works...

As you know, if you receive e-mails from POP3 or IMAP server, messages are sent using SMTP protocol. Thus in this recipe, while putting up the outbound e-mail setup for Alfresco, we enter the SMTP server configuration that will be used for e-mail forwarding.

- ▶ `mail.host`: Enter your SMTP server's address. For example, if you wish to use gmail server, the address is `smtp.gmail.com`.

- ▶ `mail.port`: This is usually `25` for SMTP server. For gmail server, the port is `465`.

- ▶ `mail.username`: Put the username by which you want to log on to the SMTP server.

- ▶ `mail.password`: It represents the corresponding password to the server.

> ▸ `mail.from.default`: Default "from" address used by Alfresco while sending mails.

> ▸ `mail.smtp.auth`: Enter `true` if your SMTP server requires authentication, otherwise `false`.

See also

> ▸ *Sending e-mails via JavaScript API*

Sending e-mails via JavaScript API

We have seen how easily we can send e-mails from the Alfresco web client interface. However, it is often necessary to send e-mails from your scripts and applications as well. Alfresco JavaScript API is fully capable of sending e-mails.

From the web client, we have sent e-mails using the **Run Action** method. In the JavaScript API also, e-mails can be sent by the actions execution only.

In this recipe, we will create a script that would send mail to a particular user, use a template to construct the e-mail message body, and finally invoke the script through a rule.

How to do it...

1. Open Alfresco web client and navigate to **Data Dictionary | E-mail Templates** space. This is the space where, by default all templates related to e-mails are stored.

    > Though it is not mandatory to have your e-mail templates in this space, conventionally the templates for e-mails are stored here.

2. Create a new template with a name **send-e-mail.ftl**, using the following code:

    ```
    Dear ${args["username"]}

    This is to inform you that a new document named ${args["docname"]}
    has been uploaded in space ${args["spacename"]}.

    Thanks
    The CMS Team.
    ```

3. Next we will create the script that will send the mail. Navigate to the **Data Dictionary | Scripts** space. Create a new script item named **send-mail.js**, use the following code:

```
varuserinfo = people.getPerson("snig.bhaumik");

varparams = new Array();
params["username"] = userinfo.properties["firstName"];
params["docname"] = document.name;
params["spacename"] = space.name;

var mail = actions.create("mail");
mail.parameters.subject = "Document Upload Alert!";
mail.parameters.from = person.properties.e-mail;
var template = companyhome.childByNamePath("Data Dictionary/E-mail
Templates/send-e-mail.ftl");
mail.parameters.text = document.processTemplate(template, params);
mail.parameters.to = userinfo.properties.e-mail;

mail.execute(document);
```

4. We now have a template and a JavaScript code to send e-mail. Now, let's see how to send the e-mail.

5. Sending e-mail is now all about executing the JS code – you can do this manually by **Run Action** and **Execute Script** or using a rule. Let's say we want to do this by a rule – whenever a new document is uploaded to a space this mail will be fired.

6. Create a new space under **InfoAxon** (say named **Chapter 13**) and create a new rule in this space.

7. In the rule condition, we will select **All Items**, in action we will select **Execute script**, and choose the script **send-e-mail.js** to execute. Let's name the rule as **E-mail Alert**; if you want you can apply the rule to subspaces as well.

8. Now after creating this rule, an e-mail will be fired to the specified user's e-mail ID.

How it works...

For sending e-mails, you need to use the action root-level object provided by Alfresco JS API, such as:

```
var mail = actions.create("mail");
```

The object accepts various parameters using which you are supposed to set the mail configurations. For example:

```
mail.parameters.subject = "Document Upload Alert!";
mail.parameters.from = person.properties.e-mail;
mail.parameters.to = userinfo.properties.e-mail;
```

And for the mail message body, we have used a template. In the e-mail template, you can see three parameters to be passed for constructing the e-mail message body. We have created these values in the JS script as:

```
varparams = new Array();
params["username"] = userinfo.properties["firstName"];
params["docname"] = document.name;
params["spacename"] = space.name;
```

We have used the template object created in the Data Dictionary space and have set the message body from the template.

```
var template = companyhome.childByNamePath("Data Dictionary/E-mail
Templates/send-e-mail.ftl");
mail.parameters.text = document.processTemplate(template, params);
```

Finally, when all the properties and values are set for e-mail action, just execute the action.

```
mail.execute(document);
```

Now since we have associated this script with a rule in space **Chapter 13**, anytime a document or content is created or uploaded in this space, the rule will get fired and an e-mail alert will be thrown to the specified user.

Configuring Alfresco to receive e-mails

We have seen how to send e-mails from different events from Alfresco. Another quite useful feature of Alfresco is that, the system can automatically pull e-mails, just like a standard SMTP server does, and store the e-mail messages in the repository along with all the attachments.

This is known as the inbound e-mail service of Alfresco. For example, you can configure a particular e-mail ID in Alfresco and whenever any e-mail is sent to this ID, the e-mail content is saved into the repository automatically. This can be used as a very efficient and useful way to store important information in the repository. No more manual copy, uploaded via the web application or any other systems.

Getting ready

First we will configure Alfresco for the inbound e-mail services.

1. Open the `alfresco-global.propertiesalfresco` file from `\tomcat\shared\classes` folder. As you know, this is the file where global properties and settings of Alfresco is stored and managed.

2. Add the following lines of code at the end of the file:

```
# Inbound Mail Configurations.
e-mail.inbound.unknownUser=anonymous
e-mail.inbound.enabled=true

e-mail.server.enabled=true
e-mail.server.port=25
e-mail.server.domain=alfresco.local
e-mail.server.allowed.senders=.*
#e-mail.server.blocked.senders=
# Inbound Mail Configurations End.
```

3. No more configurations required. Restart your server. Log in as `admin`.

4. We will now create a user – this account will be used to send e-mails. For that, go to **Administration Console | Manage System Users**. Create new user with first name **mail**, last name as **sender** and e-mail ID as **alfresco@alfresco.local**

Step One - Person Properties	
Enter information about this person.	
Person Properties	
⊙ First Name:	Mail
⊙ Last Name:	Sender
⊙ Email	alfresco@alfresco.local

> This e-mail ID is important here (name of the user can be anything), we use this ID while creating accounts for sending e-mails, which means this user account will be used for sending e-mails to the Alfresco repository.

5. Alfresco inbound e-mail server requires this user to be a member of the E-MAIL_ CONTRIBUTORS group. For that go to **Administration Console | Manage User Groups**. Click on **E-MAIL_CONTRIBUTORS** group.

6. Add the new user **mail.sender** in this group as a member. By default, Administrator is a member of this group.

Root Groups > EMAIL_CONTRIBUTORS

Groups

Page 1 of 1 1

Users

mail sender
mail.sender

Administrator
admin

Page 1 of 1 1

---

7. Now, we need to create/use a space where all the e-mails sent will be stored. Suppose we use the **Chapter 13** space we created a while ago.

> Each folder in Alfresco should be associated with an e-mail ID; e-mails sent to this ID will be automatically stored into the folder. However, for that you need to add E-mail Alias aspect to the space. This enables you to add the e-mail ID with the space.

8. Open the **Details View** of the space. Click on **Run Action**. In the **Action list**, select **Add an aspect**. Click on **Set Values and Add**.

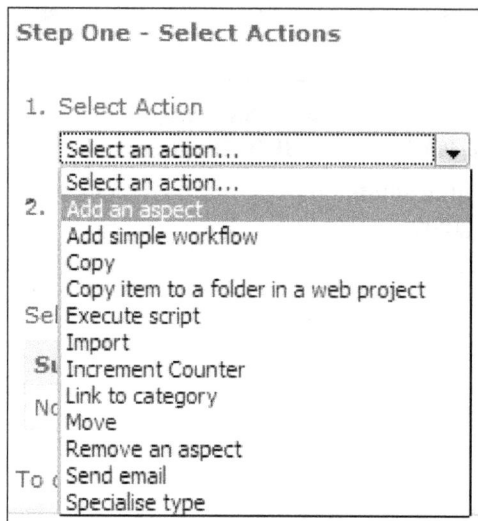

Step One - Select Actions

1. Select Action

Select an action...

Select an action...
2. Add an aspect
   Add simple workflow
   Copy
   Copy item to a folder in a web project
Sel Execute script
   Import
Su Increment Counter
Nc Link to category
   Move
   Remove an aspect
To Send email
   Specialise type

9. In the available list of aspects, select **E-mail Alias**, and click **OK**.

10. Click **Finish** to complete the operation.

11. You can see new property E-mail Alias has been added to the space. Click to edit properties, and add a suitable e-mail ID.

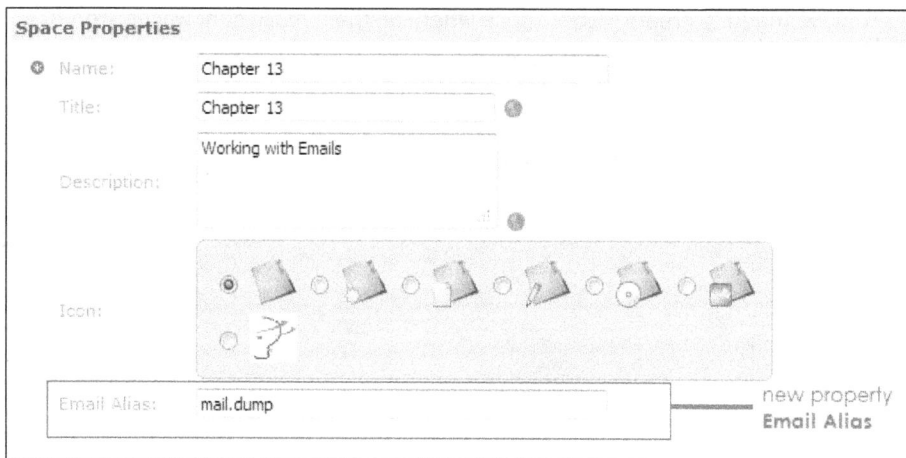

Space Properties

Name:	Chapter 13
Title:	Chapter 13
Description:	Working with Emails
Icon:	
Email Alias:	mail.dump

new property
Email Alias

Here we have used **mail.dump** e-mail alias, thus when we send an e-mail to `mail.dump@alfresco.local`, the mail content will be stored in this space.

The `@alfresco.local` e-mail domain has come from the `e-mail.server.domain` property we had added in `alfresco-global.properties` file in step 1 in this recipe.

In this way, you can use a number of different spaces and associate different e-mail IDs with each of them.

12. Finally, we need to provide write permission to the e-mail sender user into this space. Click on **Manage Space Users**, and click **Invite**.

Step One - Invite Users
Select the users and roles they will play in this space.

Specify Users/Groups
1. Select user/group and their role(s)

| Users ▼ | mail | Search |

Results for 'mail' in 'Users'. Clear Results

mail sender [mail.sender]

Role

Coordinator
Collaborator
Contributor
Editor
Consumer

2. Add to List

Selected users/groups and their role(s)

Name

mail sender (Coordinator) 🗑

13. Click on **Next** and **Finish** to complete the operation. All settings are in place and our environment is ready now, let's send e-mails and see how they are stored in the repository.

How to do it...

We will now create a new account in the e-mail client application from where we intend to send mails. In this example, we will use MS Outlook as the e-mail client.

1. Open MS Outlook, open **Tools | Account Settings**. You might recollect this is the same interface where we had created the IMAP account settings. We will now create a new account that will be used to send emails to Alfresco server.

2. Click **New** to create a new e-mail account. Click **Next>** and select **Manually Configure server settings or additional server types**. Click **Next>**.

3. Select **Internet E-mail** in the next screen and click **Next>**.

4. Populate your account information in the next screen. This should match with your Alfresco user credentials.

   ❑ The e-mail address should be same as the user we have created for sending e-mails in Alfresco – that is **alfresco@alfresco.local** (see step 4 in the *Getting ready* section in this recipe).

   ❑ **Account Type** is **POP3**.

   ❑ The **Incoming mail server** is the IP of the server where Alfresco is running – in this case, I have used **localhost**.

   ❑ Incoming mail server is not relevant for this account, since we will be using this account only to send mails for now.

   ❑ The logon credential is also not important here, only the **E-mail Address** should be validID. Similarly, in the **User Information**, the **Name** is not very significant here.

5. Click on **Next>** and then **Finish** to complete the account creation process.

6. All ready? Now let's try and send a simple e-mail using this new account. We will send the mail to the configured e-mail ID `mail.dump@alfresco.local`

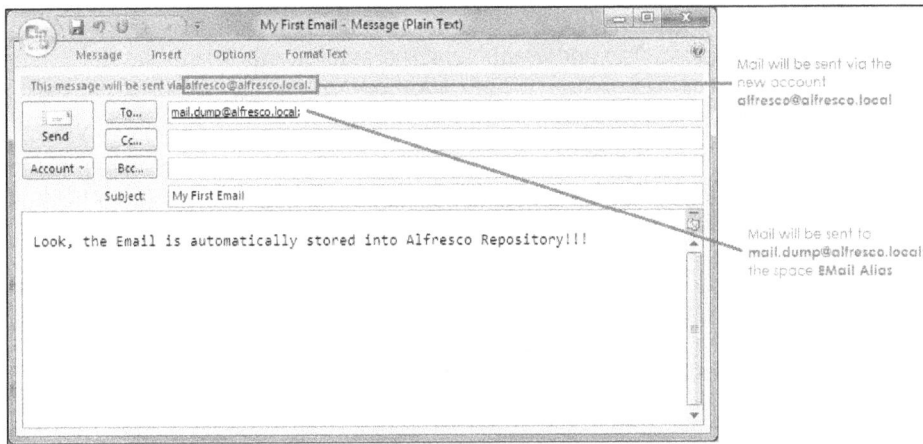

7. Check your Outlook's response, when the send/receive operation completes, see the contents of **Chapter 13** in Alfresco web client. A new content item is available.

8. See the properties of this new content item, details of the e-mail message are displayed, as shown in the following screenshot:

9. Thus we have sent a mail to a standard e-mail ID, and Alfresco has pulled the mail message and has stored it automatically into the repository.

How it works...

A couple of things are important to understand and remember here.

The e-mail sender user:

Alfresco is using this user's e-mail ID, account and credentials to store the mail message into the repository. In other words, Alfresco is using this user as the proxy account for storing e-mails.

That's why we have created an account with e-mail ID `alfresco@alfresco.local`, which is the same as the **Mail Sender** user account registered in Alfresco.

This user account in Alfresco must be a member of the **E-MAIL_CONTRIBUTORS** group, otherwise he is not allowed to send e-mails.

In addition, this user has to have proper write permission into the folders where the e-mail messages are expected to be stored.

You can create many such user accounts and use them as e-mail accounts; however, each of these accounts must fulfill the above criteria.

The E-mail Alias:

This is the e-mail ID to which you will be sending e-mails. One space in Alfresco repository is mapped to one unique e-mail alias; this tells Alfresco where and in which space incoming e-mails are to be stored.

If you have two separate spaces and each one of them is mapped with separate e-mail IDs, then e-mails will be dropped and organized easily.

That's why, in our example, e-mails sent to `mail.dump@alfresco.local` automatically get accumulated into **Chapter 13** space – as this space is configured with E-mail alias as **mail.dump**.

Configure and use Alfresco file servers

We have experienced a wide variety of ways and methods to interact with Alfresco. But, that is not all. The Alfresco repository can be exposed via several other filesystem protocols such as CIFS, FTP, WebDAV, and so on.

In this recipe, we will see how to configure and use the CIFS and FTP server. CIFS—stands for *Common Internet File System*—a protocol for file transfer that lets you get access to files that are local to the server from remote locations and read and write to them.

We will see that CIFS-enabled Alfresco repository can be used in Windows as a normal shared drive. We will also explore how we can use the Alfresco repository using standard FTP protocol.

How to do it...

In Alfresco 3.3 Tomcat distribution, CIFS and FTP file server are enabled by default. However, we will see what settings are required to enable the file servers.

1. Open the `file-servers.properties` file from the `\tomcat\webapps\alfresco\WEB-INF\classes\alfresco` folder.

2. Paste the following code in this file:

   ```
   filesystem.name=Alfresco

   cifs.enabled=true
   cifs.localname=${localname}
   cifs.domain=
   cifs.broadcast=255.255.255.255
   cifs.bindto=0.0.0.0
   cifs.ipv6=disabled
   cifs.hostannounce=true

   ftp.enabled=true
   ftp.ipv6=disabled

   nfs.enabled=false
   ```

   > You can also add these properties in `alfresco-global.properties` file. I have used the `file-servers.properties` file to show the original location of these settings.

3. Open the `file-servers.xml` file from the same folder (`\tomcat\webapps\alfresco\WEB-INF\classes\alfresco`). Note the first few lines there.

   ```
   <alfresco-config area="file-servers">

   <config evaluator="string-compare" condition="CIFS Server">
   <serverEnable enabled="${cifs.enabled}"/>

   <host name="${cifs.localname}A" domain="${cifs.domain}"/>
   <comment>Alfresco CIFS Server</comment>
   ```

4. The highlighted code line is the setting by which the CIFS share is exposed. For example, if your server machine hostname is `pluto`, the share name exposed would be `plutoA`.

5. Now let's try to access the CIFS share. In Windows, click **Start**, **Run**, type `\\plutoa`, press *Enter*.

> Thus you can access the repository as a standard Windows shared folder by `\\plutoA` or `\\plutoa` (this is because Windows folder names are not case sensitive. In case of Linux, obviously this will be case sensitive).
>
> You can change the `host name` in the `file-servers.xml` file to change this.

6. You will be asked for user credentials, enter Alfresco username and password (for example, admin/admin). The share windows will be opened.

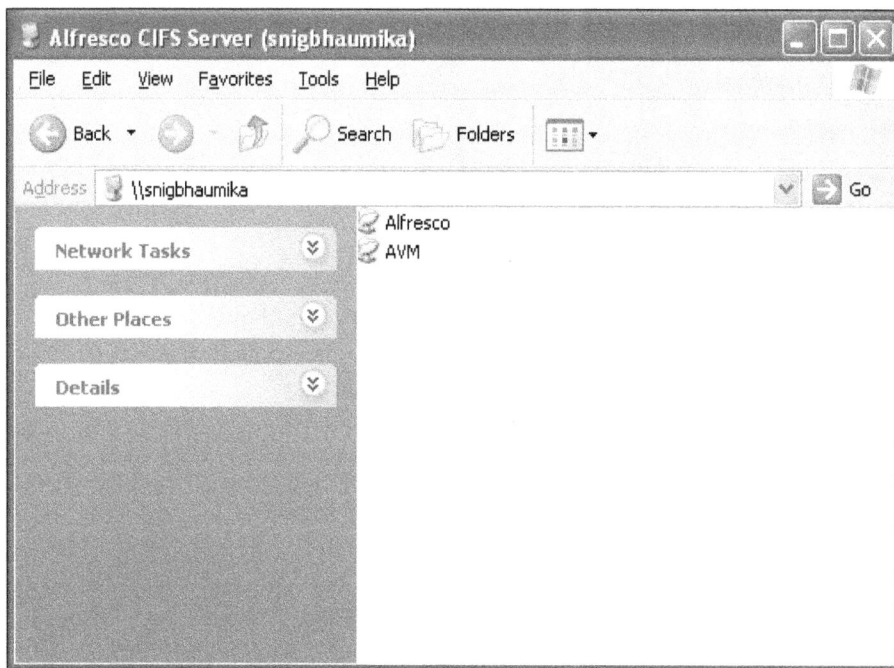

> My Alfresco server machine name is **snigbhaumik**, thus the share name is **snigbhaumika**.

7. Double-click on `Alfresco` folder; all Alfresco spaces will be displayed.

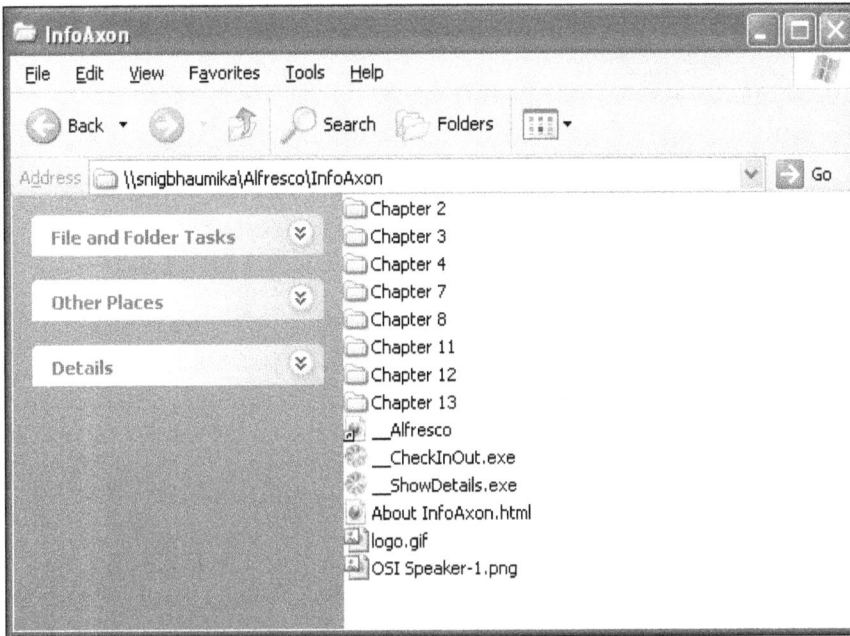

8. You can create files in these folders, just like a standard Windows folder. The files will be created in the Alfresco repository.

9. Similarly, we can access the repository via FTP as well.

10. Open your internet browser, type the URL as `ftp://localhost/alfresco` (assuming your server is running at localhost). Enter Alfresco user credential.

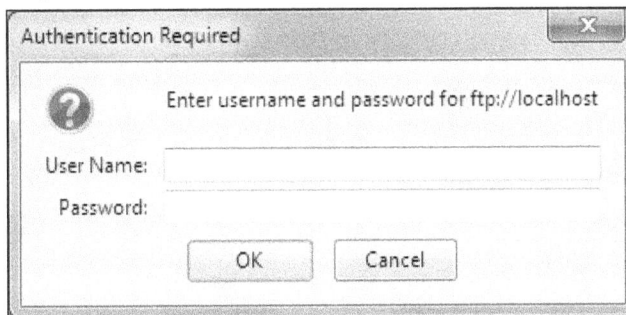

11. The Alfresco repository is displayed in the browser via FTP. You can upload/download files here via FTP.

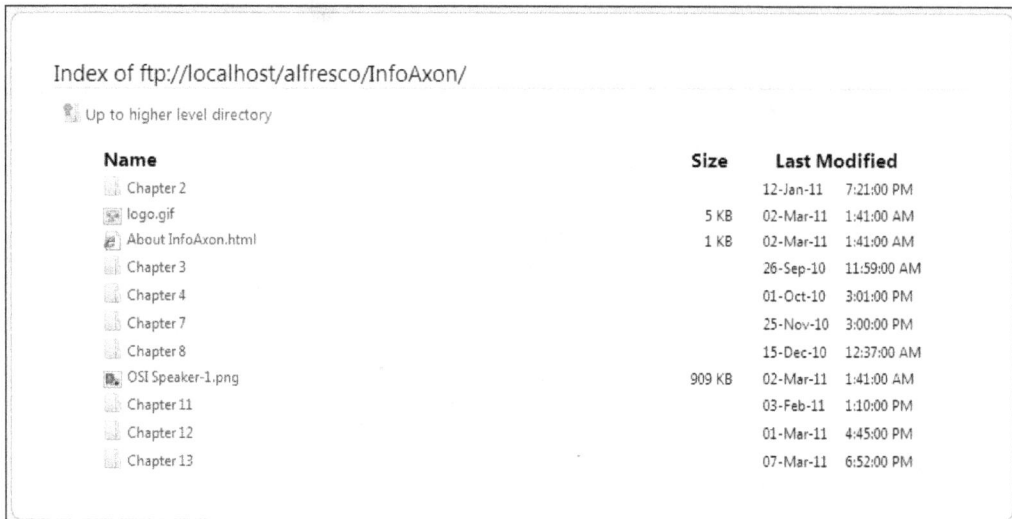

Index of ftp://localhost/alfresco/InfoAxon/

🐾 Up to higher level directory

Name	Size	Last Modified	
Chapter 2		12-Jan-11	7:21:00 PM
logo.gif	5 KB	02-Mar-11	1:41:00 AM
About InfoAxon.html	1 KB	02-Mar-11	1:41:00 AM
Chapter 3		26-Sep-10	11:59:00 AM
Chapter 4		01-Oct-10	3:01:00 PM
Chapter 7		25-Nov-10	3:00:00 PM
Chapter 8		15-Dec-10	12:37:00 AM
OSI Speaker-1.png	909 KB	02-Mar-11	1:41:00 AM
Chapter 11		03-Feb-11	1:10:00 PM
Chapter 12		01-Mar-11	4:45:00 PM
Chapter 13		07-Mar-11	6:52:00 PM

How it works...

The **Common Internet File System** (**CIFS**) also known as **Server Message Block** (**SMB**) is a network protocol, most commonly used for sharing files over a LAN or over a WAN via VPN. The protocol allows a client to access servers or files on the LAN from the local machine. CIFS is a fairly platform-independent protocol that can be used in Windows, Linux, or Apple.

Similarly, FTP is another widely used and accepted protocol for file sharing.

The Alfresco repository can be exposed via CIFS and FTP. The `file-servers.properties` and `file-servers.xml` files can be used to configure and expose the repository.

14
Building Alfresco

In this chapter, we will cover:

- ▸ Installing Subversion client - TortoiseSVN
- ▸ Downloading Alfresco's source code
- ▸ Compiling and building Alfresco
- ▸ Running Alfresco on your machine

Introduction

Alfresco, as you know, is an **Open Source Enterprise Content Management system**, distributed under **GPL** (**GNU General Public License**) license.

> To know more on GPL model, read on
> http://www.gnu.org/licenses/gpl.html

The community version of Alfresco's source code is freely available to download and it allows you to configure your environment, change and build the code, include enhancements, and finally contribute back to the community so that the Alfresco source code gets bigger, richer, and more enduring.

The Alfresco community source code uses **Subversion** as the source code control system. You need to download the source code from the Alfresco subversion server. Then build and deploy in your own application server (Tomcat, JBoss, Geronimo, and so on).

In this chapter, we will explore how to set up the Alfresco development environment, configuring your system with all the dependencies installed, compiling and building Alfresco's source code and finally deploying the Alfresco application in your application server, for the Windows operating system.

Installing Subversion client - TortoiseSVN

As we know, Alfresco community source code is available at Alfresco Subversion server. For connecting to the server and downloading the source code, we need to have a client subversion program.

Many client applications are available for subversion; however, in this chapter we will use one of the most popular client applications – **TortoiseSVN.**

In this recipe, we will see how to download and install **TortoiseSVN** in a 32-bit Windows machine.

Before installing TortoiseSVN, you should ensure the following prerequisites are installed and configured in the machine where you are establishing the Alfresco development environment.

Getting ready

Here is some of the software and applications you need to install and configure on the machine where you are planning to build the Alfresco environment.

1. JDK 1.5.x or higher.

> You can download and install JDK from `http://java.sun.com/javase/downloads/index_jdk5.jsp`.

> Ensure that your `JAVA_HOME` environment variable is properly pointing to the valid Java installation folder.

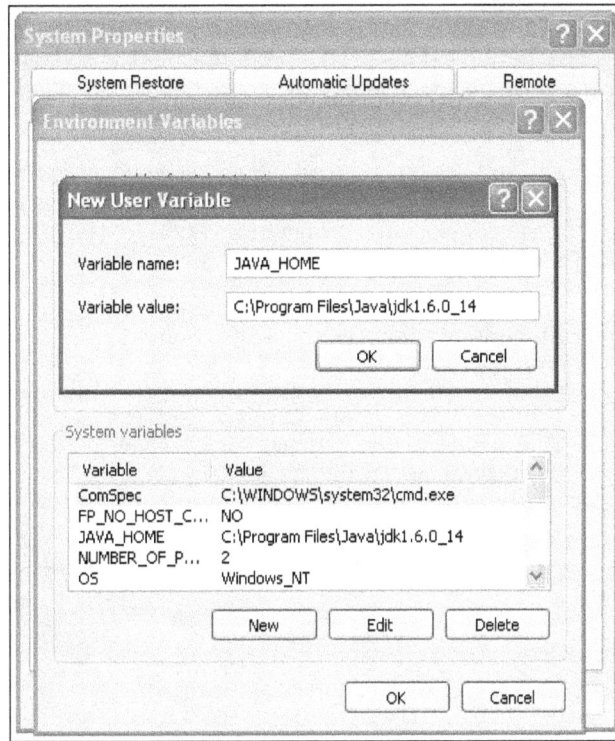

2. Apache Ant 1.6.5 or higher.

> All Apache Ant packages are available at `http://archive.apache.org/dist/ant/binaries/`. Or you can download Ant 1.7.1 directly from `http://archive.apache.org/dist/ant/binaries/apache-ant-1.7.1-bin.zip`.

> For installing Ant, you just have to unzip the package in a particular folder, and append the Ant bin folder path in your Windows `PATH` environment variable.

3. Subversion client:

   We will go through the step-by-step process for installing this in our next recipe.

4. Apache Tomcat 6.x:

You can have Apache Tomcat installed on your machine, or you can download the Tomcat server archive unzipped in a particular folder on your machine.

> If you have decided to go with JBoss server instead of Tomcat, the recommended version is JBoss 2.0 or higher. You can download JBoss from `http://www.jboss.org/jbossas/downloads.html`.

You can download the Tomcat installer packages from `http://tomcat.apache.org/download-60.cgi`.

> After installing Tomcat, make sure you have TOMCAT_HOME environment variable properly set to the Tomcat folder.

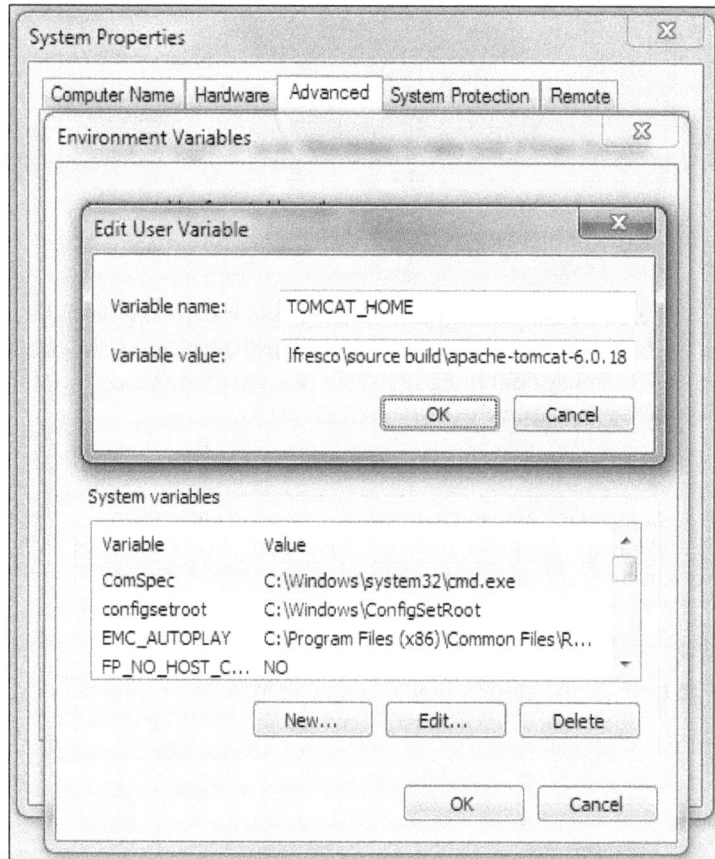

Similarly, you need to have APP_TOMCAT_HOME and VIRTUAL_TOMCAT_HOME environment variables configured and pointing to corresponding Tomcat servers.

5. MySQL database server 4.1.x or higher

   Although it is published MySQL server 4.1.x and higher is supported, it is good to have MySQL 5 or higher. As you will remember, we have discussed how to install MySQL server as well as client in *Chapter 1*.

6. SWF Tools, Image Magick, Open Office

   These are optional applications used by Alfresco in order to prepare the thumbnails and web previewer.

> You can download and install SWF Tools from http://www.swftools.org/download.html.
>
> Binary downloads of Image Magick for Windows are available at http://www.imagemagick.org/script/binary-releases.php#windows.
>
> You can download and install Open Office from
>
> http://download.openoffice.org/.

> The installation path of these applications needs to be added in your windows PATH environment variable.

How to do it...

1. Open your browser and navigate to http://tortoisesvn.net/downloads.html, or you can directly download the Windows installer from http://downloads.sourceforge.net/tortoisesvn/TortoiseSVN-1.6.14.21012-win32-svn-1.6.16.msi?download.

2. Download the Windows installer and install TortoiseSVN in a folder. If after installation, it asks for a Windows restart, please do so.

3. TortoiseSVN has been implemented as a Windows shell extension, thus it seamlessly integrates with Windows Explorer.

> One of the main advantages of TortoiseSVN is that it does not come with any specific integration with any IDE like Eclipse, so you can use it along with any development environment or tools.

4. Once you have properly installed TortoiseSVN, you will have some more options available in your Windows explorer menu.

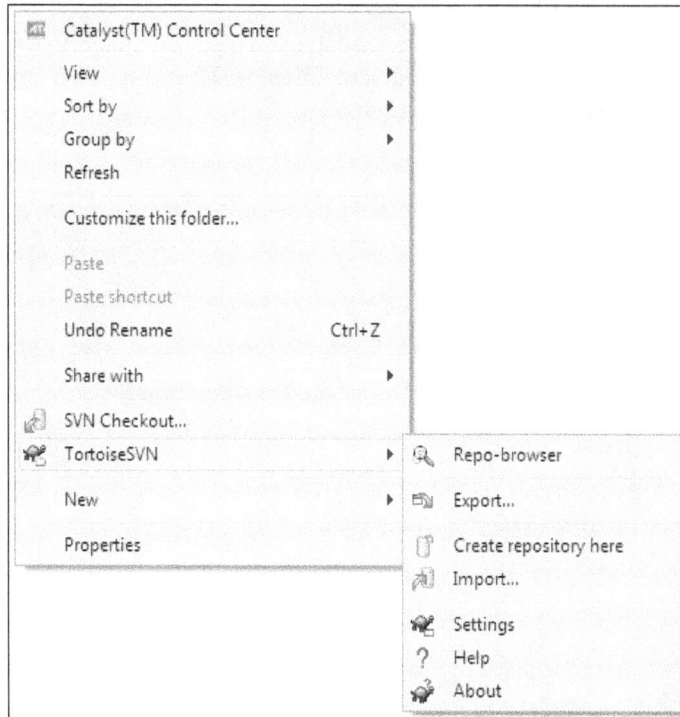

Downloading Alfresco's source code

Now that we have installed Subversion client application, we can connect with the Alfresco source repository and download the source code.

How to do it...

1. Create a new folder on your machine. In this recipe, let's create a folder named `Alfresco Source` in the `E:\`.

2. Open the folder in Windows Explorer, right-click on it. Select the **SVN Checkout** menu option.

3. The TortoiseSVN checkout window will be displayed. Put the **URL of repository** as `svn://svn.alfresco.com/alfresco/HEAD/root`. Leave the rest of the options as it is, Click **OK**.

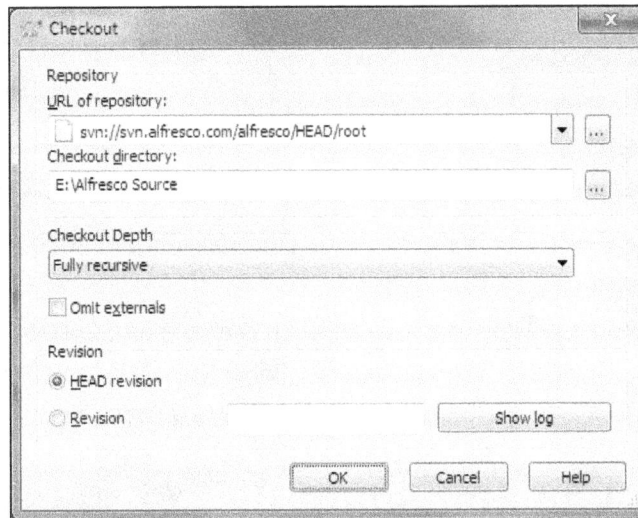

> svn://svn.alfresco.com/alfresco/HEAD/root is the Alfresco
> Subversion repository source code URL. This will check out the current
> revision from the SVN code repository.

4. **TortoiseSVN** will now check out Alfresco source code on your machine. Be patient, this may take some time depending on the internet speed you have, over 500 MB of data will be downloaded.

5. Click **OK** after the full source code checkout is complete.

6. The following screenshot shows source code folders downloaded:

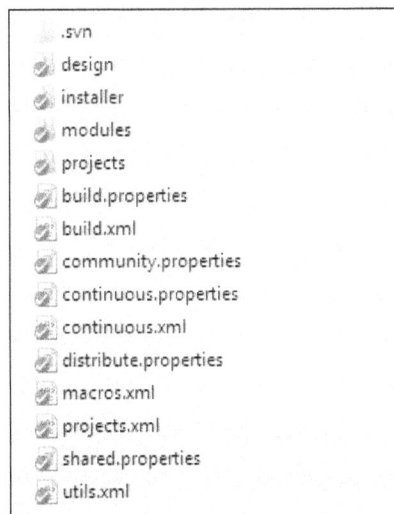

7. We have downloaded Alfresco source code from the SVN location. We are now ready to build Alfresco.

How it works...

Alfresco has exposed the source code repository as a public read-only access by two methods.

`svn://svn.alfresco.com/alfresco/HEAD` – this requires port 3690 to be accessible from your machine.

However, in case your firewall does not allow this, you can use port 80 HTTP URL as follows – `http://svn.alfresco.com/repos/alfresco-open-mirror/alfresco/HEAD`.

In our example, we have used the earlier one; you can use the HTTP URL in a similar fashion.

Compiling and building Alfresco

Building Alfresco in the default source code necessarily means just running an **Ant** build script; given that we have prepared our environment properly and met all the prerequisites as desired, it is quite easy to build Alfresco.

Getting ready

Make sure you have properly installed all the prerequisites mentioned in the first recipe. Apart from the optional last step, you must install and configure the rest.

How to do it...

1. Let's check the deployed application in our Tomcat server. Assuming we have Tomcat installed in the `E:\Alfresco Tomcat\apache-tomcat-6.0.18\` folder, the following screenshot shows the default `webapps` content:

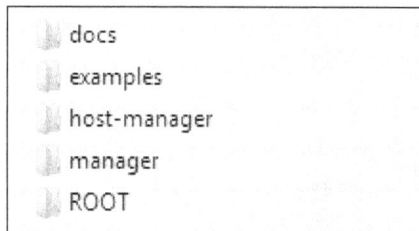

```
docs
examples
host-manager
manager
ROOT
```

2. Thus, you can see we have no web applications in the Tomcat server.

3. Now to build Alfresco open the Windows command prompt.

4. Move to the folder where the Alfresco source code is downloaded. In my case, I have downloaded the code in the `E:\Alfresco Source` folder.

5. Type command `ant build-tomcat` and press *Enter*.

6. Be patient now. If you have configured your system properly, and everything works well, you should receive a **BUILD SUCCESSFUL** message from the Alfresco build scripts.

7. This means you have successfully compiled and deployed Alfresco in your Tomcat server.

8. Let's now see the outcome. Open the `E:\Alfresco Tomcat\apache-tomcat-6.0.18\webapps` (remember, this is where we have configured our Tomcat server) folder again, you can see that two new web application archives have been included here.

So we have built and deployed the Alfresco application in Tomcat. In the next recipe, we will see how we can run this.

How it works...

There are a few Ant targets defined in the Alfresco build script. You should use one of them as per your requirement.

1. `ant build-tomcat`: Builds and deploys Alfresco for Tomcat.
2. `ant incremental-tomcat`: Incrementally builds and deploys Alfresco for Tomcat.
3. `ant start-tomcat-application`: Executes the Tomcat start up script.
4. `ant build-jboss`: Builds and deploys Alfresco for JBoss.
5. `ant incremental-jboss`: Incrementally builds and deploys Alfresco for JBoss.
6. `ant start-jboss`: Executes the JBoss start up script.
7. `ant test`: Runs unit tests for the entire project.

We had used the build-tomcat target since we wanted to build Alfresco and create or deploy web application archive for the Tomcat server.

Running Alfresco on your machine

Until now, we have compiled, built, and deployed Alfresco in a Tomcat server. In this recipe, we will configure the rest of the necessary settings and run Alfresco.

At the end of this recipe, you will have Alfresco running in your machine compiled, built, deployed, and executed entirely by yourself; and in your own stack.

How to do it...

There are a few settings and steps left to make sure Alfresco is running properly in the compiled stack you have just built.

1. The build script has created the `E:\Alfresco Tomcat\apache-tomcat-6.0.18\shared\classes\` folder for you. Here you can add your `alfresco-global.properties` file where you can add your custom settings.

2. Create a new file in this folder named `alfresco-global.properties`, and add the following contents into it:

```
###############################
## Common Alfresco Properties #
###############################


#
# Sample custom content and index data location
#-------------
dir.root=./alf_data
```

```
#
# Sample database connection properties
#-------------
db.name=alfresco
db.username=alfresco
db.password=alfresco
db.host=localhost
db.port=3306


#
# External locations
#-------------
#ooo.exe=soffice
#ooo.enabled=false
#img.root=./ImageMagick
#swf.exe=./bin/pdf2swf


#
# MySQL connection
#-------------
db.driver=org.gjt.mm.mysql.Driver
db.url=jdbc:mysql://${db.host}:${db.port}/${db.name}


#

# PostgreSQL connection (requires postgresql-8.2-504.jdbc3.jar or
equivalent)

#

#db.driver=org.postgresql.Driver

#db.url=jdbc:postgresql://${db.host}:${db.port}/${db.name}


#

# Index Recovery Mode

#-------------

#index.recovery.mode=AUTO


#

# Outbound Email Configuration
```

```
#-------------

#mail.host=

#mail.port=25

#mail.username=anonymous

#mail.password=

#mail.encoding=UTF-8

#mail.from.default=alfresco@alfresco.org

#mail.smtp.auth=false


#

# Alfresco Email Service and Email Server

#-------------


# Enable/Disable the inbound email service.  The service could be
used by processes other than

# the Email Server (e.g. direct RMI access) so this flag is
independent of the Email Service.

#-------------

#email.inbound.enabled=true


# Email Server properties

#-------------

#email.server.enabled=true

#email.server.port=25

#email.server.domain=alfresco.com

#email.inbound.unknownUser=anonymous


# A comma separated list of email REGEX patterns of allowed
senders.
```

```
# If there are any values in the list then all sender email
addresses

# must match. For example:

#    .*\@alfresco\.com, .*\@alfresco\.org

# Allow anyone:

#-------------

#email.server.allowed.senders=.*


#

# The default authentication chain

# To configure external authentication subsystems see:

# http://wiki.alfresco.com/wiki/Alfresco_Authentication_Subsystems

#-------------

#authentication.chain=alfrescoNtlm1:alfrescoNtlm


#

# URL Generation Parameters (The ${localname} token is replaced by
the local server name)

#-------------

#alfresco.context=alfresco

#alfresco.host=${localname}

#alfresco.port=8080

#alfresco.protocol=http

#

#share.context=share

#share.host=${localname}

#share.port=8080

#share.protocol=http
```

3. Put your MySQL database information in this file.

   ❑ Database name

   ❑ User Name

   ❑ Password

   ❑ Database host name and port at which MySQL is running

> In the example code, the default setting is provided. If you wish to retain this setting, you need to create a database with the name `alfresco`, create a user named `alfresco` in your local machine. Otherwise, change the settings as per your database information. Remember to grant permission of the database to the mentioned user here.

4. You can also change the other parameters if you like. For example, for enabling the e-mail services, setting up the *Image Magick*, *SWFTools*, and so on.

5. Once we have created the `alfresco-global.properties` file, we need to configure Tomcat server to read the file.

6. For that, open the `catalina.properties` file from the `E:\Alfresco Tomcat\apache-tomcat-6.0.18\conf` folder.

7. Add the `shared.loader` settings (should be around line 74) as:

8. `shared.loader=${catalina.base}/shared/classes,${catalina.base}/shared/lib/*.jar`

9. Finally, the file would be similar to the following block of code:

```
# Licensed to the Apache Software Foundation (ASF) under one or
more
# contributor license agreements.  See the NOTICE file distributed
with
# this work for additional information regarding copyright
ownership.
# The ASF licenses this file to You under the Apache License,
Version 2.0
# (the "License"); you may not use this file except in compliance
with
# the License.  You may obtain a copy of the License at
#
#      http://www.apache.org/licenses/LICENSE-2.0
#
# Unless required by applicable law or agreed to in writing,
software
# distributed under the License is distributed on an "AS IS"
BASIS,
```

```
# WITHOUT WARRANTIES OR CONDITIONS OF ANY KIND, either express or
implied.
# See the License for the specific language governing permissions
and
# limitations under the License.

#
# List of comma-separated packages that start with or equal this
string
# will cause a security exception to be thrown when
# passed to checkPackageAccess unless the
# corresponding RuntimePermission ("accessClassInPackage."+packa
ge) has
# been granted.
package.access=sun.,org.apache.catalina.,org.apache.coyote.,org.
apache.tomcat.,org.apache.jasper.,sun.beans.
#
# List of comma-separated packages that start with or equal this
string
# will cause a security exception to be thrown when
# passed to checkPackageDefinition unless the
# corresponding RuntimePermission ("defineClassInPackage."+packa
ge) has
# been granted.
#
# by default, no packages are restricted for definition, and none
of
# the class loaders supplied with the JDK call
checkPackageDefinition.
#
package.definition=sun.,java.,org.apache.catalina.,org.apache.
coyote.,org.apache.tomcat.,org.apache.jasper.

#
#
# List of comma-separated paths defining the contents of the
"common"
# classloader. Prefixes should be used to define what is the
repository type.
# Path may be relative to the CATALINA_HOME or CATALINA_BASE path
or absolute.
# If left as blank,the JVM system loader will be used as
Catalina's "common"
# loader.
# Examples:
#     "foo": Add this folder as a class repository
```

```
#       "foo/*.jar": Add all the JARs of the specified folder as
class
#                   repositories
#       "foo/bar.jar": Add bar.jar as a class repository
common.loader=${catalina.home}/lib,${catalina.home}/lib/*.jar


#
# List of comma-separated paths defining the contents of the
"server"
# classloader. Prefixes should be used to define what is the
repository type.
# Path may be relative to the CATALINA_HOME or CATALINA_BASE path
or absolute.
# If left as blank, the "common" loader will be used as Catalina's
"server"
# loader.
# Examples:
#       "foo": Add this folder as a class repository
#       "foo/*.jar": Add all the JARs of the specified folder as
class
#                   repositories
#       "foo/bar.jar": Add bar.jar as a class repository
server.loader=


#
# List of comma-separated paths defining the contents of the
"shared"
# classloader. Prefixes should be used to define what is the
repository type.
# Path may be relative to the CATALINA_BASE path or absolute. If
left as blank,
# the "common" loader will be used as Catalina's "shared" loader.
# Examples:
#       "foo": Add this folder as a class repository
#       "foo/*.jar": Add all the JARs of the specified folder as
class
#                   repositories
#       "foo/bar.jar": Add bar.jar as a class repository
# Please note that for single jars, e.g. bar.jar, you need the URL
form
# starting with file:.
shared.loader=${catalina.base}/shared/classes,${catalina.base}/shared/
lib/*.jar


#
# String cache configuration.
```

```
tomcat.util.buf.StringCache.byte.enabled=true
#tomcat.util.buf.StringCache.char.enabled=true
#tomcat.util.buf.StringCache.trainThreshold=500000
#tomcat.util.buf.StringCache.cacheSize=5000
```

10. We are almost done. The third and final step is to create a new environment variable named JAVA_OPTS with the value.

```
-Xms512m -Xmx1024m -Xss1024k -XX:MaxPermSize=256m
-XX:NewSize=256m
```

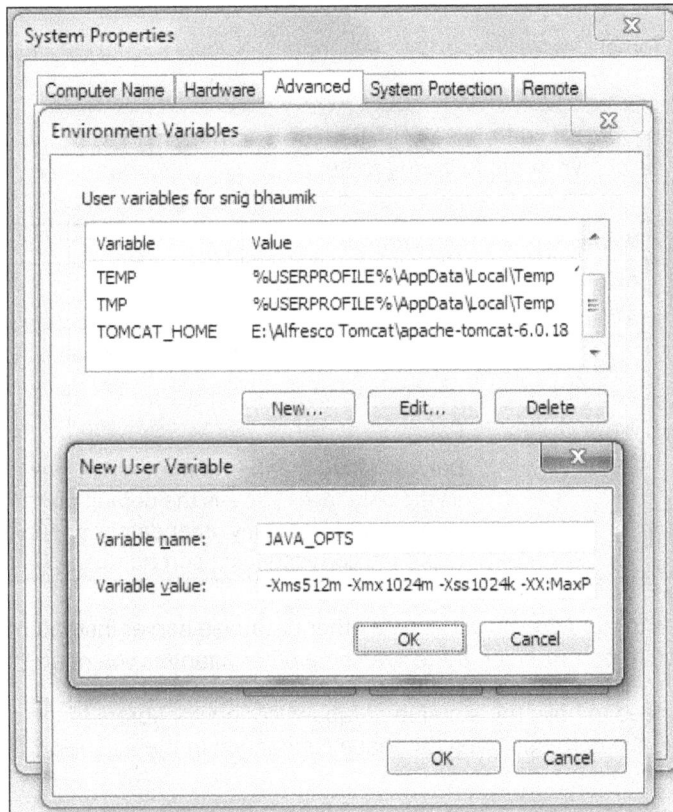

11. The settings are ready. Open E:\Alfresco Tomcat\apache-tomcat-6.0.18\ bin folder and execute startup.bat. Alfresco application should start up.

Image Magick and PDF2SWF executables are not mapped here. Thus, these functionalities may not work under the current setup. However, you can add path of these binaries to the correct path in the alfresco-global.properties file.

How it works...

In this final recipe, we have deployed and configured the `alfresco-global.properties` file in the Tomcat server.

Configuration of the Tomcat server includes enabling the shared folder into which the `alfresco-global.properties` file is created. For that, we have added `shared.loader=${catalina.base}/shared/classes,${catalina.base}/shared/lib/*.jar` in the `catalina.properties` file from the `E:\Alfresco Tomcat\apache-tomcat-6.0.18\conf` folder.

This ensures that Tomcat server reads the files under the `/shared/classes` and `/shared/lib` folder.

We have entered the Alfresco database configuration parameters in `alfresco-global.properties` file, as shown in the following table:

Parameter	Value	Description
db.name	alfresco	Name of the Alfresco database
db.username	alfresco	Database username – Alfresco application will interact with the database using this user credential
db.password	alfresco	User password
db.host	localhost	Database server
db.port	3306	Database port number, in our example we are using MySQL as the database. 3306 is the default port of MySQL. In case you are using any other database server, you will have to put the corresponding port number.

In case you choose to run Alfresco with some other database server instead of MySQL, apart from the difference in port number, there are some other changes you need to ensure.

For example, you need to have the suitable database connector library in the stack; and you need to enable the corresponding database connection in the `alfresco-global.properties` file.

In our case, we can uncomment the following lines:

`db.driver=org.postgresql.Driver`

`db.url=jdbc:postgresql://${db.host}:${db.port}/${db.name}`

In the `alfresco-global.properties` file as demonstrated previously, and comment the following lines of the MySQL connection:

`#db.driver=org.gjt.mm.mysql.Driver`

`#db.url=jdbc:mysql://${db.host}:${db.port}/${db.name}`

Index

Public Search 89
PUTmethod 9, 240

Q

qnamePath property 227

R

Rapid Application Development 9
RDBMS 8
read access, authorization aspect 66
refresh operation 252
Remote Procedure Call. *See* RPC
remove method 205
removePermission method 206
removeTag method 207
Representational State Transfer. *See* REST
resource bundle
   about 264, 293, 294
   creating 282, 283
Resource Bundle file 242
REST 9, 239
RESTful services 239
RESTful web service 9
reviewRequirement node 292
roles, Alfresco
   about 67
   collaborator 67
   consumer 67
   contributor 67
   coordinator 67
   editor 67
root scope objects 195
RPC 239
rule inheritance 108
rules
   about 91
   actions, offered by Alfresco 104-107
   applying 94-99
   asynchronous rule 108
   characteristics 92
   components 93
   conditions 99-104
   creating 94-99
   disabled rule 109
   editing 109

   example 91
   execution flow 93
   inheritance 108
rules, components
   action 93
   condition 93
   event 93
rules engine 91
Run Action method 196

S

saved search, Alfresco
   using 89, 90
ScriptNode API
   about 204
   addAspect method 205
   addTag method 207
   cancelCheckout method 207
   checkin method 207
   checkout method 207
   childByNamePath method 204
   childByXPath method 204
   children property 204
   content property 204
   copy method 205
   createFolder method 205
   createNode method 205
   downloadUrl property 204
   hasAspect method 205
   hasPermission method 206
   inheritsPermissions method 206
   isContainer property 204
   isDocument property 204
   isLocked property 204
   isSubType method 207
   isTagScope method 207
   nodeRef property 204
   remove method 205
   removePermission method 206
   removeTag method 207
   setInheritsPermissions method 206
   setPermission method 206
   size property 204
   specializeType method 207
   tags property 207
   write method 205

Thank you for buying
Alfresco 3 Cookbook

About Packt Publishing

Packt, pronounced 'packed', published its first book "*Mastering phpMyAdmin for Effective MySQL Management*" in April 2004 and subsequently continued to specialize in publishing highly focused books on specific technologies and solutions.

Our books and publications share the experiences of your fellow IT professionals in adapting and customizing today's systems, applications, and frameworks. Our solution based books give you the knowledge and power to customize the software and technologies you're using to get the job done. Packt books are more specific and less general than the IT books you have seen in the past. Our unique business model allows us to bring you more focused information, giving you more of what you need to know, and less of what you don't.

Packt is a modern, yet unique publishing company, which focuses on producing quality, cutting-edge books for communities of developers, administrators, and newbies alike. For more information, please visit our website: www.packtpub.com.

About Packt Open Source

In 2010, Packt launched two new brands, Packt Open Source and Packt Enterprise, in order to continue its focus on specialization. This book is part of the Packt Open Source brand, home to books published on software built around Open Source licences, and offering information to anybody from advanced developers to budding web designers. The Open Source brand also runs Packt's Open Source Royalty Scheme, by which Packt gives a royalty to each Open Source project about whose software a book is sold.

Writing for Packt

We welcome all inquiries from people who are interested in authoring. Book proposals should be sent to author@packtpub.com. If your book idea is still at an early stage and you would like to discuss it first before writing a formal book proposal, contact us; one of our commissioning editors will get in touch with you.

We're not just looking for published authors; if you have strong technical skills but no writing experience, our experienced editors can help you develop a writing career, or simply get some additional reward for your expertise.

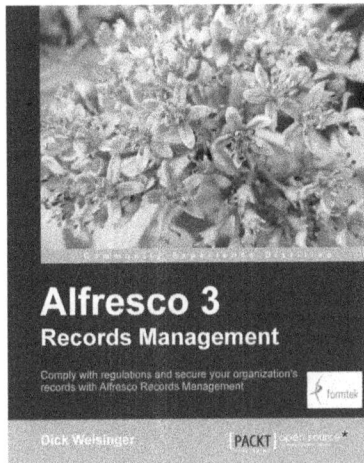

Alfresco 3 Records Management

ISBN: 978-1-849514-36-1   Paperback: 488 pages

Comply with regulations and secure your organization's records with Alfresco Records Management

1. Successfully implement your records program using Alfresco Records Management, fully certified for DoD-5015.2 compliance

2. The first and only book to focus exclusively on Alfresco Records Management

3. Step-by-step instructions describe how to identify records, organize records, and manage records to comply with regulatory requirements

4. Learn in detail about the software internals to get a jump-start on performing customizations

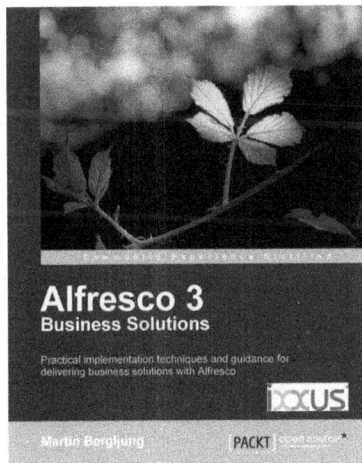

Alfresco 3 Business Solutions

ISBN: 978-1-849513-34-0   Paperback: 608 pages

Practical implementation techniques and guidance for delivering business solutions with Alfresco

1. Deep practical insights into the vast possibilities that exist with the Alfresco platform for designing business solutions.

2. Each and every type of business solution is implemented through the eyes of a fictitious financial organization - giving you the right amount of practical exposure you need.

3. Packed with numerous case studies which will enable you to learn in various real world scenarios.

Please check **www.PacktPub.com** for information on our titles